The Student Writer
Editor and Critic

FOURTH
EDITION

The Student Writer
Editor and Critic

BARBARA FINE CLOUSE

With a Contribution by
Joy Johnson DeSalvo

McGRAW-HILL, INC.

New York St. Louis San Francisco Auckland Bogotá Caracas Lisbon
London Madrid Mexico City Milan Montreal New Delhi
San Juan Singapore Sydney Tokyo Toronto

The Student Writer: Editor and Critic

Acknowledgments appear on pages 489–491, and on this page by reference.

This book is printed on acid-free paper.

1 2 3 4 5 6 7 8 9 0 DOC DOC 9 0 9 8 7 6 5

ISBN 0-07-011448-X

This book was set in Plantin Light by ComCom, Inc.
The editors were Tim Julet, Laura Lynch, and Jean Akers;
the designer was Joan Greenfield;
the production supervisor was Denise L. Puryear.
R. R. Donnelley & Sons Company was printer and binder.

Library of Congress Cataloging-in-Publication Data

Clouse, Barbara Fine.
The student writer: editor and critic / Barbara Fine Clouse.—4th ed.
p. cm.
Includes index.
ISBN 0-07-011448-X
1. English language—Rhetoric. 2. Criticism. 3. Editing.
I. Title.
PE1408.C537 1996
808'.042—dc20 95-14357

About the Author

BARBARA FINE CLOUSE is a seasoned writing instructor who has taught all levels of college composition, first at Youngstown State University in northeastern Ohio and then at Slippery Rock University in western Pennsylvania. She has written a number of composition texts for McGraw-Hill including *Writing: From Inner World to Outer World; Working It Out: A Trouble-Shooting Guide for Writers; Transitions: From Reading to Writing;* and *Patterns for a Purpose.* Another of her most recent McGraw-Hill publications is *Jumpstart! A Workbook for Writers.* In addition, she has developed *Cornerstones: Readings for Writers,* a short prose reader for developmental students, which is the newest addition to Primis, McGraw-Hill's electronic database. Barbara's publications also include *Process and Structure in Composition* and the third edition of *Progressions* for Allyn and Bacon.

Barbara appreciates getting comments and suggestions from instructors and students who use her texts, so feel free to write to her:

Barbara Clouse
c/o College English Editor
McGraw-Hill, Inc.
1221 Avenue of the Americas
New York, NY 10020

In loving memory of
Rose Lewin and
Chance Crago Tatman

Contents

APPENDIXES

Preface

A primary focus of *The Student Writer: Editor and Critic* is to help students develop their own successful writing processes. To this end, the text describes a wide range of procedures for handling idea generation, drafting, organizing, revising, editing, and proofreading, and it helps students sample these procedures to discover techniques that work well for them. Throughout the text, students consider what they do when they write, evaluate the effectiveness of their procedures, and try alternative techniques in an ongoing effort to improve their processes.

A second focus of *The Student Writer* is to help students become skilled at revision. To do so, the text targets two concerns: accurately judging the strengths and weaknesses of a draft and successfully effecting the necessary changes. To help students judge writing reliably so they can make accurate revision decisions, the text includes a large number of student essays with both strengths and weaknesses. Students study these essays and assess those strengths and weaknesses to hone their critical abilities and thereby become better judges of their own drafts. To help students learn how to effect necessary changes, many revision strategies are described for students to sample until they discover their own effective, efficient revision procedures.

The focus on revision gives the text its subtitle: *editor* is used in its broadest sense to refer to one who makes changes to improve writing; *critic* refers to one who evaluates writing to determine what changes need to be made.

In addition to focusing on process, *The Student Writer* also treats essay structure and the qualities of an effective essay: Chapter 2 discusses essay structure and characteristics; Chapter 4 treats sentence effectiveness; the chapters in Part 2 deal with the structure of different rhetorical patterns; and the questions after the professional essays speak to essay structure. In fact, throughout the text, the dual concern for process and product is apparent.

FEATURES OF THE TEXT

Part 1, The Writer's Process and the Essay's Structure, has the following features:

- Procedures for helping students identify their own processes and ways to improve them
- Descriptions of a wide range of techniques for shaping topics, generating ideas, determining purpose, establishing audience, drafting, revising, editing, and proofreading
- Charts headed "How the Process Works" that highlight important aspects of the writing process
- A detailed treatment of essay structure
- Explanations and illustrations of the qualities of effective writing, including logical organization; adequate, relevant detail; and sentence effectiveness
- Charts headed "How the Structure Works" that highlight important aspects of essay structure
- An annotated essay to illustrate essay structure
- Activities called "Essay in Progress" that help students write their first essay of the term and experiment with procedures
- Collaborative and individual exercises

Part 2, Patterns of Development, has a chapter each on description, narration, illustration, comparison-contrast, process analysis, cause-and-effect analysis, definition, classification, and argumentation-persuasion. Each of these chapters has the following features:

- A discussion of detail, structure, audience, and purpose
- Professional and student essays
- Writing topics, both rhetorical and thematic
- Writing procedures to sample
- Revision checklists for each pattern of development
- Prompts for securing reader response to drafts
- Activities called "Tryouts" to give students an opportunity to practice a skill or technique associated with the pattern under discussion
- Collaborative activities for evaluating the student essays
- Topics for group discussion or journal writing after each professional essay
- Sections on becoming a reliable critic that help students improve their abilities to assess the strengths and weaknesses of writing

Part 2 also includes a chapter on research writing that focuses both on the traditional research paper and on using research material to supplement the student's own supporting details. In addition, Part 2 includes a chapter on writing in response to reading that explains how to handle some of the more frequently occurring writing tasks students will face in college. Six previously published essays appear in this chapter, accompanied by a range of writing assignments that call upon students to write in response to those readings.

Part 3, An Editing Guide to Frequently Occurring Errors, treats word choice, sentence fragments, run-on sentences and comma splices, subject-verb agreement, tense shifts, pronoun problems, problems with modifiers, punctuation, and mechanics. Each chapter also includes exercise material.

Two appendixes provide students with helpful resources:

- Appendix 1 is a quick guide to procedures for solving writing problems.
- Appendix 2 shows a student essay in progress.

CHANGES FOR THE FOURTH EDITION

In response to suggestions made by those who used and reviewed the third edition, the following changes have been made:

- The text is now sharper, thanks to tighter prose and a new design.
- "Methods of development" are now called "patterns of development."
- Material has been added on unfocused freewriting; freewriting for finding a topic; journal writing; and objective and subjective description.
- Sections called "Composing at the Computer" describe strategies for those who use computers and word processors.
- The discussions of the thesis, introduction, specific diction and wordiness have been expanded.
- The discussions of outlining, revising, and editing have been improved.
- A number of collaborative exercises have been added.
- The discussions of concrete sensory detail have been consolidated in Chapter 5.
- The discussions of troublesome words and phrases and parallelism have been moved to Chapter 4; the discussion of frequently confused words has been moved to Part 3. The order of Chapters 14 and 15 has been reversed.
- In the chapters on patterns of development, headnotes have been added before the professional essays. Topics for journal writing and collaborative discussion and thematic writing topics (including one topic dealing with multiple essays) have been added after the essays.

- The "Points to Remember" charts have been replaced by charts called "How the Process Works," "How the Structure Works," and revision checklists.
- Reader-response prompts have been added.
- Approximately one-third of the student and professional essays have been replaced, and the "Postwriting Evaluation of Your Process" sections have been omitted.
- Several of the exercises have been replaced by "Tryout" activities that allow students to practice an important skill.
- The "Evaluating Student Writing" sections have been streamlined, reconfigured as collaborative activities, and renamed "Becoming a Reliable Critic."
- To make discussion easier, the paragraphs are numbered in the student essays.
- The chapter on persuasion now covers argumentation-persuasion. It includes an improved discussion of both raising and countering objections; a new discussion of induction and deduction; and an expanded discussion of logic.
- The chapter on research writing now includes the traditional research paper. It also has expanded coverage of the research process, works-cited forms, and the APA stylesheet.
- Coverage in Part 3 has been expanded to include more on fragments and run-ons; information on comma splices; more on pronouns and modifiers; and information on quotation marks, the hyphen, and mechanics.

ACKNOWLEDGMENTS

I am deeply indebted to the following reviewers, whose sound counsel informs this book: Richard Betting, Valley City State University; Mary Alice Dyer, Schoolcraft College; Robert McIlvaine, Slippery Rock University; John Reid, Rowan Cabarrus Community College; Linda Rollins, Motlow State Community College; and Paulette Vrett, McHenry Community College.

As always, I owe profound gratitude to my husband, Dennis, and to my sons Gregory and Jeffrey for their patience, understanding, and indulgence. For her contribution to the first edition, I thank Joy Johnson DeSalvo. She is a respected colleague, a superior teacher and administrator, and a cherished friend. At McGraw-Hill, I thank Tim Julet, Laura Lynch, and Jean Akers for their continued support and comfort.

Barbara Fine Clouse

The Student Writer
Editor and Critic

PART I

The Writer's Process and the Essay's Structure

CHAPTER 1

Shaping Topics and Discovering Ideas

Many people believe that a writer's ideas come in a blinding flash of inspiration—in some magic moment of discovery that propels the writer forward and causes word upon wonderful word to spill onto the page. Yes, such moments do occur from time to time, but they are the exception rather than the rule. More typically, writers cannot depend on inspiration, because it does not make scheduled appearances. Often it does not arrive at all.

So what is a writer to do in the absence of inspiration? Fortunately, when ideas do not come to the writer, there are ways the writer can go after ideas. That is what this chapter is about—ways you can discover ideas when inspiration does not strike at the moment you need it.

THE WRITING SUBJECT AND THE WRITING TOPIC

Sometimes your writing topic is determined for you by an instructor, boss, or situation (such as when you write a letter to a company protesting an incorrect bill). When your topic is not predetermined, however, your first step is topic selection.

If you need a writing topic and you are not inspired, you can take steps to discover one. However, before discussing those steps, let's consider the difference between a writing subject and a writing topic.

A **subject** is a broad area you want to write about. A **topic** is the narrow territory within that subject area that you stake out as the specific focus for your writing. For example, say you want to write about presidential elections. That's a subject area because "presidential elections" takes in a great deal. If you settle on arguing that electing the president by popular vote is better than by electoral vote, then you have a topic—a narrow focus for your essay. In the most general sense, **topic selection** involves choosing a broad subject area and paring it down until you have a narrow topic.

Anything Can Be a Subject

Anything, and I mean *anything,* can be a writing subject. As proof of this, consider the variety of subjects that appear in syndicated columns in newspapers. For example, Andy Rooney writes a syndicated column that appears in over 150 newspapers, and he also appears regularly on *60 Minutes.* Among his honors are Emmys, Writers Guild Awards, and the Peabody Award. Mr. Rooney has written about chairs, soap, warranties, directions, sizes, catalogs, mail, fences, street names, bank names, signs, hair, eyeglasses, gender, telephones, dirty words, calendars, and ugliness. You may think that these are unlikely writing subjects, but remember—there is nothing that cannot be shaped and narrowed into a workable topic.

Finding a Subject

Anything can serve as the subject for an essay. However, when you are seeking your own subjects, there may be little comfort in knowing that you can write about anything. You need to discover which of the many "anythings" you want to write about. Fortunately, writers can do several things to find subjects, and some of these techniques are described here.

1. TRY FREEWRITING

Freewriting shakes loose ideas by freeing writers of worry about correctness, organization, and even logic. To freewrite for a writing subject, write nonstop for 5 or 10 minutes. Record *everything* that comes to mind, even if it seems silly or irrelevant. DO NOT STOP WRITING FOR ANY REASON. If you run out of ideas, then write names of your family members; or write, "I don't know what to say," or write the alphabet—anything. You won't be sharing your freewriting with a reader, so you can say what you want and you can forget spelling, grammar, neatness, and form. Just get your ideas down any way you can. After 5 or 10 minutes, read over your freewriting and you are likely to find at least one idea for a writing subject. Here is an example that yields several possible subjects.

> *I have to find a writing subject. Let's see, there's politics and school, but politics is boring and school is done to death (and it's going to kill me, hah). What else? Television, there ought to be a lot there. The shows, the commercials, the sex and violence. I could do something with arguing about the violence. Pop culture is possible too, especially MTV. I haven't watched it for awhile but it used to be really racy. What about soaps? Let's see, what else? A B C D E F G H What else? My friends, my family. I could write about Dad—he'd be a book, not an essay. Especially if I write about his drinking—no, better not. I could write about Janet's accident and the courage she showed*

or I could write about courage in general. That could be hard. I don't know, what else? Teachers roommates studying grades? Stress? I should have enough now.

2. BROWSE THROUGH A DICTIONARY

You may not want to write about aardvarks or Zyrian, but there are many entries in between that you may wish to discuss. Perhaps an entry will trigger your thinking because it is associated with something. Who knows? The entry for *balloon* might remind you of that summer day at the fair when you were 6 and your first helium balloon escaped your grasp, an episode that could make a fine narrative essay.

3. READ YOUR LOCAL AND CAMPUS NEWSPAPERS

The events, issues, controversies, and concerns reported in newspapers can be essay subjects. Tax hikes, building projects, curriculum changes, pending legislation, demonstrations, actions of officials or citizens or students—all of these and more are reported in the papers and can suggest interesting, worthwhile subjects.

4. KEEP AN ESSAY-SUBJECT NOTEBOOK

Get a small spiral notebook to keep in your backpack, pocket, or purse. During the day you will have thoughts and experiences that could serve as future essay subjects. If you write these down, you can refer to them later when you are searching for things to write about.

5. FILL IN THE BLANKS

You can discover a subject by filling in the blanks in key sentences like these.

```
I'll never forget the time I ______________________________.
____________________ is the most ____________________ I know.
After ___________________________ I was never the same again.
College can best be described as ___________________________.
Is there anything more frustrating (interesting/exciting) than
____________________________________________________________?
This world can certainly do without ________________________.
What this world needs is ___________________________________.
____________________________ made a lasting impression on me.
After _______________ I changed my mind about ______________.
My biggest success (failure) was ___________________________.
Life with ___________________ is ___________________________.
Life would be easier if only _______________________________.
I get so angry (annoyed/frightened) when ___________________.
```

```
________________ is better (or worse) than ________________.
The main cause of __________________ is __________________.
The main effect of __________________ is __________________.
Most people do not understand the real meaning of ___________.
The best way to do __________________ is __________________.
```

6. GIVE YOURSELF ENOUGH TIME

Deciding on a writing subject can take time, so be fair to yourself. Allow yourself a day or two for ideas to surface. Go about your business for a while with a portion of your brain considering what you experience and observe. You may be inspired. For example, a routine walk across campus may not ordinarily prompt an essay subject. But if you take that walk aware that you need a subject, you might see the library you pass every day in a new light—as the subject for an essay, perhaps one about the different ways people study in the library.

Shaping the Topic

When you shape a topic from a subject, keep the following points in mind.

1. SHAPE A TOPIC THAT WILL HAVE AN IMPACT ON YOUR READER

A topic should interest you as the writer, but it should also have some significance for the reader. After all, you are writing something that will be read by someone else, and you do not want to bore your reader.

To determine whether your topic can have an impact on a reader, ask yourself the following questions:

1. In what ways can the topic inform a reader?
2. In what ways can the topic entertain a reader?
3. In what ways can the topic influence a reader to think or act differently?
4. In what ways can the topic arouse a reader's emotions?
5. Why would the topic interest a reader?
6. How can I make my topic interesting to a reader?

If your topic will not affect a reader in at least one of the ways suggested by the above questions, then it is not a suitable topic, and you should reshape it or find another one.

2. SHAPE A TOPIC YOU KNOW ENOUGH ABOUT

Shape a topic you have some firsthand experience with or one you know through observation, reading, classwork, or watching television. It makes little sense, for example, to write about saving the whales if you did not know they were in trouble until you saw that bumper sticker yesterday.

If you are not sure whether you know enough about a topic to develop an essay, answer the questions below. They can serve both as a way to generate ideas to include in your writing and as a way to discover whether your knowledge is sufficient.

1. What have I experienced that relates to my topic?
2. What have I observed that relates to my topic?
3. What have I read that relates to my topic?
4. What have I heard that relates to my topic?
5. What have I learned in school that relates to my topic?
6. What have I seen on television that relates to my topic?

If you come up with little after answering the above questions, you probably should reshape your topic or find another.

3. SHAPE A TOPIC THAT CAN BE HANDLED IN AN APPROPRIATE LENGTH

It is better to treat a narrow topic in depth than a broad topic superficially. A superficial treatment will never satisfy a reader because the essay will be vague and general, and your reader will be left feeling that you did not come to terms with the topic.

If your topic takes in too much territory, then to develop it appropriately you would be forced to write a very long piece. For example, how would you like to be stuck writing an essay about why *Major League, Bull Durham,* and *Field of Dreams* are better sports movies than *Eight Men Out, North Dallas Forty,* and *Everybody's All American?* If you did that in 500 words, you would not treat any of these movies adequately. If you gave each movie adequate development, your essay would be so long that three friends would have to help you deliver it to your instructor. However, if you narrowed your topic to showing that *North Dallas Forty* is a more realistic portrayal of professional sports than *Bull Durham,* you could treat a topic in depth in a comfortable length.

How to Narrow

Shaping a topic can involve a series of narrowings. Let's say, for example, that you have decided to write about unemployment. Much can be said on that subject, and you cannot say it all in one essay. But unemployment does give you a subject area. Now you must narrow this subject to something that can be managed in a reasonable length. You could narrow first by deciding to write about the causes and effects of the high unemployment rate in our country. Yet it is unlikely one essay could say everything about the causes and effects of unemployment in this country, so yet another restriction is necessary. You may settle on a discussion of the causes *or* of the effects. These are narrower, but they still take in quite a bit, so another narrowing is in order. Perhaps you could narrow to discuss the effects of your father's unemployment on your family. If you feel there is too much to say about that topic, you could narrow once more to discuss the effects of your father's unemployment on you. Such a topic would be narrow enough for treatment in a single essay.

Here is a graphic representation of the process of shaping a topic from a subject.

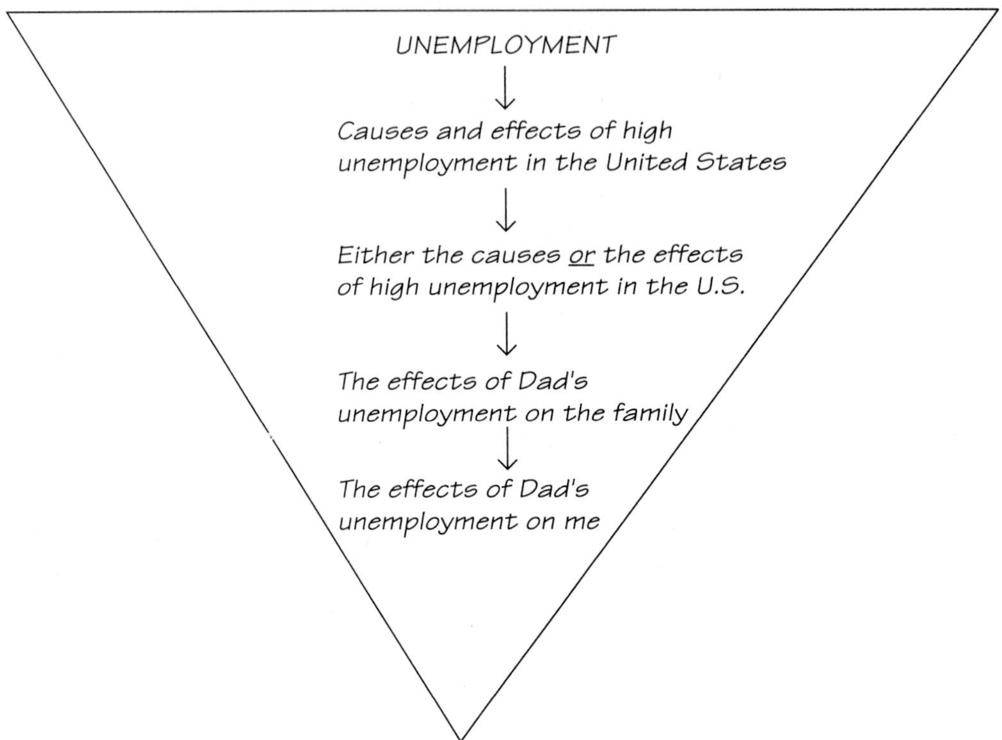

If you need help narrowing a subject to a topic, try one of the following procedures.

1. FREEWRITE

To find a topic, try 10 to 15 minutes of freewriting on your general subject. (See page 4 on how to freewrite.) Here is a sample freewriting on soap operas, one of the subjects that surfaced as a result of the freewriting on page 4.

> *Soap operas have been around a long time. They are hugely popular. They're on day and night. Lots of different kinds of people watch them. Even very bright, professional people who you would think have better things to do. What now? ABCDE. Let's see. Soaps are interesting to some people and entertaining to others, but why I don't know because I think they are pretty stupid. Have you ever really listened to these things? Must be a reason people like them. Maybe several reasons. Entertainment? People are bored? Lots of*

famous actors started on soaps. I can't think of who, though. At 1:00 half my residence hall meets to watch All My Children. Some people even schedule their classes around their favorite soaps. Good grief. My mother used to call them her "stories."

This freewriting suggests several possible topics, including: what people watch soaps, why people watch soaps, what soaps are like, and how the author's mother felt about her soaps.

2. MAKE A LIST

Write your subject at the top of a page and below it list every aspect of the subject you can think of. Do not evaluate the worth of the items; just list everything that occurs to you. A list for the subject "stress" might look like this.

Stress

effects on health
stress management
fear of failure
exam anxiety
school stress
job stress
stress in children
stress in athletes
peer pressure

Sometimes this list is enough to prompt a suitable topic. For example, you might look at it and decide to write about "exam anxiety," perhaps focusing on ways students can cope with this anxiety. At other times, you may need a second list to narrow a subject in the first list. For example, you could look at the first list and narrow to "school stress." That's a step in the right direction, but "school stress" is still broad and without a specific focus. You could try a second list, which might look something like this.

School Stress

exam anxiety
coping with a roommate
picking a major
dealing with stress
effects on studies
fear of flunking out
trying to fit in

Your second list could lead you to one of several topics. For example, studying this list could lead you to write about ways a college student can deal with stress.

3. EXAMINE YOUR SUBJECT FROM DIFFERENT ANGLES

Another way to move from subject to topic is to ask these key questions about your subject, so that you can view it from different angles.

> Can I describe my subject?
> Can I compare my subject with something?
> Can I contrast my subject with something?
> What is my subject related to?
> Can my subject be broken down into parts?
> Can I explain how my subject works?
> Is my subject good for something?
> Would anyone find my subject useful?
> What arguments or controversies surround my subject?

Answers to these questions can reveal aspects of your subject to help you discover ways to narrow to a topic.

4. TRY CLUSTERING

To cluster, write your general subject in the center of a page and circle it, like this:

drinking

Next, let your thoughts flow freely and record all the associations that occur to you; circle and connect these associations to the core circle, like this.

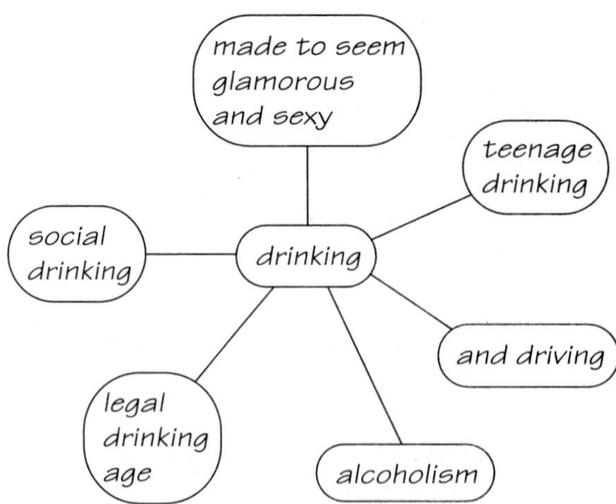

As ideas continue to strike you, write them and connect them to the appropriate circles.

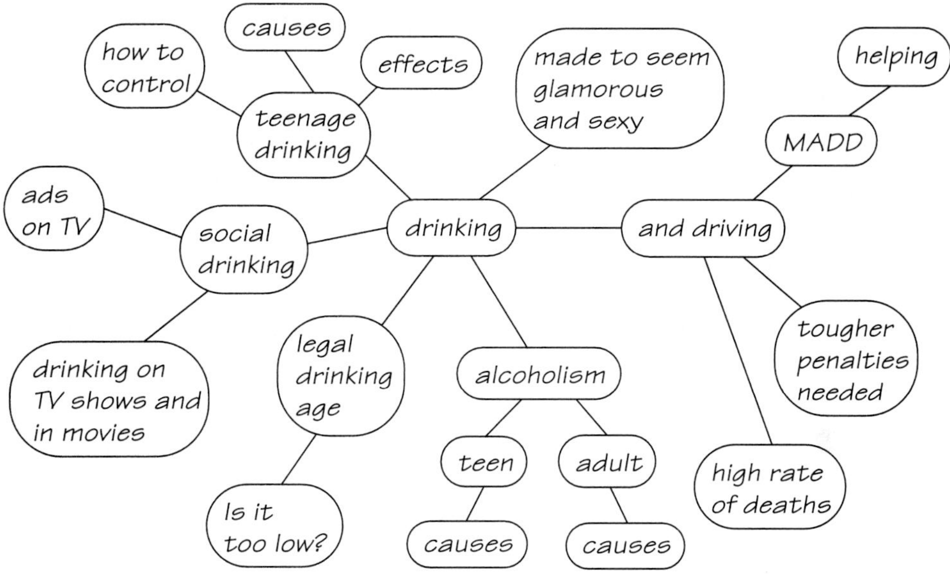

The previous clustering reveals several areas to explore for topics based on the subject "drinking."

1. *The causes of teenage drinking*
2. *The effects of teenage drinking*
3. *How to control teenage drinking*
4. *How MADD (Mothers Against Drunk Driving) is working to end drunk driving*
5. *The need for tougher penalties for drunk driving*
6. *The causes of teenage alcoholism*
7. *The causes of adult alcoholism*
8. *What the legal drinking age should be*
9. *How drinking is made to seem glamorous and sexy on television and in the movies*

When clustering, do not censor yourself; instead, allow a free flow of ideas without evaluating the worth of these ideas. If you get stuck, doodle a while or trace over what you have already written until new ideas surface.

Composing at the Computer

You can use your computer or word processor very successfully to freewrite for general subjects and writing topics. (See pages 4 and 8 on freewriting.) Simply sit at the keyboard with a blank screen in front of you. Then write whatever occurs to you without deleting anything, hitting the backspace key, or moving the cursor in any way. Fill the screen with whatever comes into your mind. Depending on your keyboard skills, that should take about 5 minutes. If your word processor has a small display, write for 5 minutes or so and fill several screens. Save and print your freewriting. Then read it over and underline usable ideas. If necessary, do a second freewriting.

HOW THE PROCESS WORKS

Shaping Topics

1. Sometimes writers identify a broad subject they are interested in and then carve a narrow topic from that broad area.
2. Techniques to help the writer find subjects and topics include:
   a. Freewriting (on paper or at the computer)
   b. Browsing through a dictionary
   c. Reading newspapers
   d. Filling in the blanks in sentences
   e. Keeping an essay-subject notebook
   f. Thinking and observing
   g. Making lists
   h. Examining the subject from different angles
   i. Clustering
3. Remember, suitable essay topics should
   a. Have an impact on the reader
   b. Be narrow enough to be treated with penetration in a reasonable length
   c. Be something the writer knows enough about

EXERCISE | **Shaping Topics**

1. Identify five subjects you could write an essay about. If you cannot arrive at five after some thought, try one or more of the techniques for finding subjects described in this chapter.
2. For each topic below, write a *B* if the topic is too broad to be handled with penetration in a 500- to 700-word essay. Write an *N* if the topic is narrow enough to be handled in a 500- to 700-word essay.
   a. The day I learned a lie can be less harmful than the truth
   b. My favorite people

c. Being the oldest of six children has dozens of disadvantages
d. Being the oldest of six children has two chief disadvantages
e. It's a mistake to teach children to read in kindergarten
f. Cigarette smokers have their rights too
g. Our public schools are deteriorating in every way
h. How to teach a 6-year-old to ride a bike
i. There are more similarities than differences among modern religions
j. Computer science should be taught in elementary school
k. Television soap operas present an unrealistic and potentially dangerous view of the ways people relate to each other
l. For pure fun, nothing is better than watching an old monster movie

3. Using three of the five subjects you gave as your response to number 1 above, shape three suitable essay topics. If necessary, use one or more of the techniques described in this chapter.

4. Below are five broad writing subjects. Select two of them and write one narrow topic for each. Use any of the techniques described in this chapter.

   a. Studying for exams
   b. Team sports
   c. The changing role of women (or men)
   d. Difficult decisions
   e. Interesting (or unusual) people

DISCOVERING IDEAS TO DEVELOP TOPICS

After shaping a topic, you can begin writing your essay. So you pour yourself a cold drink, empty the last of the potato chips into a bowl, and push the clutter on your desk to one side. You get comfortable, reach for some fresh paper, and begin—and idea after idea tumbles forth as you write through your first draft, right? Yes, if you are lucky enough to be inspired. No, if inspiration is too busy helping the redhead in the third row to bother with you. So once again, if ideas do not come to you, you must go after the ideas.

All writers (not just students) experience writer's block. Sometimes we draw a blank—not a single idea comes to mind. Sometimes we have a hazy idea but it is too vague to get us anywhere, so we find ourselves saying something like, "I know what I want to say, but I can't explain it."

Fortunately, writer's block can be overcome with techniques that start the flow of ideas. These techniques come under the broad heading of prewriting. Although the term **prewriting** suggests that the techniques occur *before* writing, they are really writing procedures that stimulate thought. Actually, you already know something about prewriting because the techniques you learned for discovering subjects and shaping topics are forms of prewriting. The next pages, however, will offer ways to use prewriting to overcome writer's block.

Freewriting

You have learned that freewriting can help the writer find subjects and topics. However, it is also a useful technique for the first-draft writer who needs ideas to develop a topic. To freewrite for ideas to develop a topic, write down anything and everything that occurs to you about your topic without evaluating the worth of the ideas. You can shift direction abruptly to pursue a new idea that suddenly strikes you, or you can pursue a single idea as far as you can take it. You can make random, wild associations. You can be flip, serious, or angry. Just be relaxed, and go with your flow of thoughts. Do not stop writing. If you run out of ideas, write the alphabet or write about how you feel until new ideas strike you. Remember, freewriting is *free,* so do not be concerned with grammar, spelling, logic, or neatness.

After 10 minutes or so, read what you have (most likely you will have filled about two pages). It will be rough, but you will notice at least one or two ideas that can be polished and developed in an essay. Underline these ideas. Sometimes they will be enough to start you off on an outline or draft. At other times you may need a boost from a second freewriting. If this is the case, write for 5 to 10 more minutes, this time focusing on the ideas you underlined in the first freewriting. When you are done, read your material and again underline the good ideas. Between the two freewritings, you may generate what you need to get started.

A Sample Freewriting

Here is a sample freewriting written to discover ideas for an essay on why people watch soap operas. (This topic was discovered as a result of the freewriting on page 8.) Potentially usable ideas have been underlined.

Why do people watch soap operas? I guess <u>some people find them entertaining</u>, but they must like pretty mindless stuff. Probably <u>the sick and elderly get hooked on them. After awhile the people on soaps probably seem like family</u>. I don't know what to say now. cow how sow plow Let me think. Well, <u>sometimes people want entertainment that doesn't require them to think too much</u>. Also, <u>today's soaps can be very steamy</u>. <u>And people love to watch sex</u>. Anything else? <u>They deal with important social issues, like Aids</u>. Are people who watch lonely? Not always. Lots of people I know watch them and I'm sure they're not all lonely. <u>Soaps are campy and fun</u>. That may be why college students like them. ABCDEFGHIJKL I can't think of anything else right now. Maybe <u>the storylines are good</u>. I'll have to watch some more and see.

List Writing

You read about list writing as a technique for shaping topics from subjects (see page 9). This prewriting activity is also helpful for generating ideas to develop these topics. For this purpose, list writing works like this: in a column list every idea that occurs to you about your topic. Do not stop to decide whether you like these ideas or whether they will "work" in your essay.

When you run out of ideas, review your list. Now you can evaluate whether or not each idea is suitable for your essay. If you find ideas that do not seem relevant to your topic or do not seem worthy of inclusion for some other reason, simply cross these ideas out.

Next, study the first idea remaining on your list. Think about it a few moments. As you do, you may discover one or two related ideas that can be added to your list. Proceed this way down your list, studying each idea and adding thoughts.

Many writers find that this list writing meets their needs. Others like to go one step further by turning their list into a **scratch outline.** To turn a prewriting list into a scratch outline, group together related ideas. For example, say you have a list of ideas for an essay about the day you baby-sat for 2-year-old twin boys. You want the essay to explain that the experience was one of the most nerve-wracking of your life. When you look over your list, you discover that three of your ideas pertain to feeding the children lunch, four of them pertain to trying to bed them down for a nap, and five of them pertain to keeping them out of mischief. If this is the case, you make three lists—one of ideas about lunch, one of ideas about the nap, and one of ideas about mischief. When you group ideas in this way, you are doing more than listing your ideas; you are also organizing them.

A Sample List and Scratch Outline

Below is a list one student developed before writing an essay about the trauma he experienced when his family moved to a new town and he had to change schools.

loved old school
comfortable with friends—knew them 12 years
at new school I was outsider
everyone belonged to a clique
sleepless nights for weeks before the move
asked if I could live with my aunt so I wouldn't have to move
~~*my parents tried to reassure me*~~
I knew I would never see my old friends again
scared to leave familiar for unknown
new school was ugly
~~*I resented my parents for transplanting me*~~

~~*I became argumentative with my parents*~~
I was behind in my school work at new school
I didn't get on basketball team at new school

Some of the ideas in the list are crossed out because after reviewing the list the writer decided he did not wish to treat these ideas after all, probably because they focused on his relationship with adults, and he wanted to center on his adjustment to the school and his relationship with his classmates.

After the writer eliminated ideas he judged unsuited to his purpose, he reviewed his list and added ideas he thought of. After this step, the list looked like this:

loved old school
comfortable with friends—knew them 12 years
at new school I was an outsider
everyone belonged to a clique
sleepless nights for weeks before the move
asked if I could live with my aunt so I wouldn't have to move
~~*my parents tried to reassure me*~~
I knew I would never see my old friends again
scared to leave familiar for unknown
new school was ugly
~~*I resented my parents for transplanting me*~~
~~*I became argumentative with my parents*~~
I was behind in my school work at new school
I didn't get on basketball team at new school
~~*new math teacher tried to help me adjust*~~
at new school I was stared at like a freak
I would skip lunch because I didn't know anyone to sit with
I was popular & respected at old school—at new I was a nobody
new school was old, needed repair—describe ugly classrooms
math & science classes were way ahead of my old ones & my grades suffered
I was center on basketball team before—at new school I didn't make team
I couldn't go to games & cheer for a team I wasn't playing on & felt no loyalty toward

After adding new ideas to the list, the writer decided to form a scratch outline by grouping together related ideas. The result appears below.

Before Move

loved old school
comfortable with friends—
knew them 12 years
sleepless nights for weeks
before the move
I knew I would never
see my old friends
again
asked if I could live
with my aunt
scared to leave familiar
for unknown

After Move

Classmates
I was outsider
everyone belonged to clique
stared at like a freak
skipped lunch cause had no one to
sit with
I was a nobody instead of popular
& respected

Basketball
didn't make team—was center before
couldn't go to games & cheer for a
team I wasn't playing on & felt
no loyalty toward

Surroundings
new school was ugly
new school was old & needed repairs
describe classrooms

School work
I was behind
math & science classes way ahead of
me & my grades suffered

The ideas in your list will not necessarily cover every point, example, and piece of detail that you will include in your essay. Instead, the ideas in your list can serve as your starting point.

Answering Questions

Answering questions about your topic is a good way to generate ideas for developing that topic. Some of the most useful questions are the standard journalistic ones: Who? What? When? Where? Why? How? These questions can be shaped in a variety of ways, according to the nature of your topic. Here are some examples; you will develop your own to suit your topic.

Who is involved?
Who is affected?
Who is for (or against) it?
Who is interested in it?

When is it important?
Why does it happen?
Why is it important?
Why is it interesting?

What happened?
What does it mean?
What causes it?
What are its effects?
What is it like (or different from)?
What are its strengths (weaknesses)?
What are its parts?
When does it happen?
When will it end (or begin)?
Why is it true?
Where does it happen?
How does it happen?
How does it make people feel?
How does it change things?
How often does it happen?
How is it made?
How should people react to it?

Answering questions can be especially helpful with a partner. Simply ask each other questions about your topic.

Sample Questions and Answers

Below are the questions a student asked herself for an essay about what happened when her friend died of leukemia.

1. *What happened?*
   Judy died of leukemia.
2. *What was the effect?*
   I became depressed.
3. *What was the effect of the depression?*
   I wouldn't associate with people.
4. *Why wouldn't you associate with people?*
   I was afraid of getting close and then losing them.
5. *How long did that last?*
   a year
6. *What ended it?*
   my pastor
7. *How did your pastor end it?*
   He gave me a copy of the book When Bad Things Happen to Good People.
8. *How did the book help?*
   It made me realize I couldn't stop living.
9. *How is your experience significant to others?*
   We all lose loved ones and must find a way to keep going.
10. *How has Judy's death changed you?*
    I don't take anything or anyone for granted anymore.
11. *Why is this important?*
    My life is richer now because I appreciate the people around me more.

When the student wrote her essay, she did not use all the points that resulted from her questioning. Also, her essay included ideas she developed along the way, *after* her questioning. That's fine.

Clustering

On pages 10–11 you read that clustering can help a writer move from general subject to restricted topic. However, clustering can also help a writer discover ideas to develop a topic.

To discover ideas for developing a topic, write your topic in the center of a page and circle it. Below is one of the restricted topics discovered in the clustering illustrated on page 11.

how to control teenage drinking

Next, let your thoughts flow freely and record all the ideas that occur to you, circling and connecting the ideas as appropriate. Do not pause to evaluate ideas; just go with the flow of your thoughts. If you run out of ideas, study the branches of your clusters to see relationships among ideas. These relationships may suggest new ideas. Or try retracing what you have written until ideas strike you. Here is a clustering to generate ideas for an essay about how to control teenage drinking.

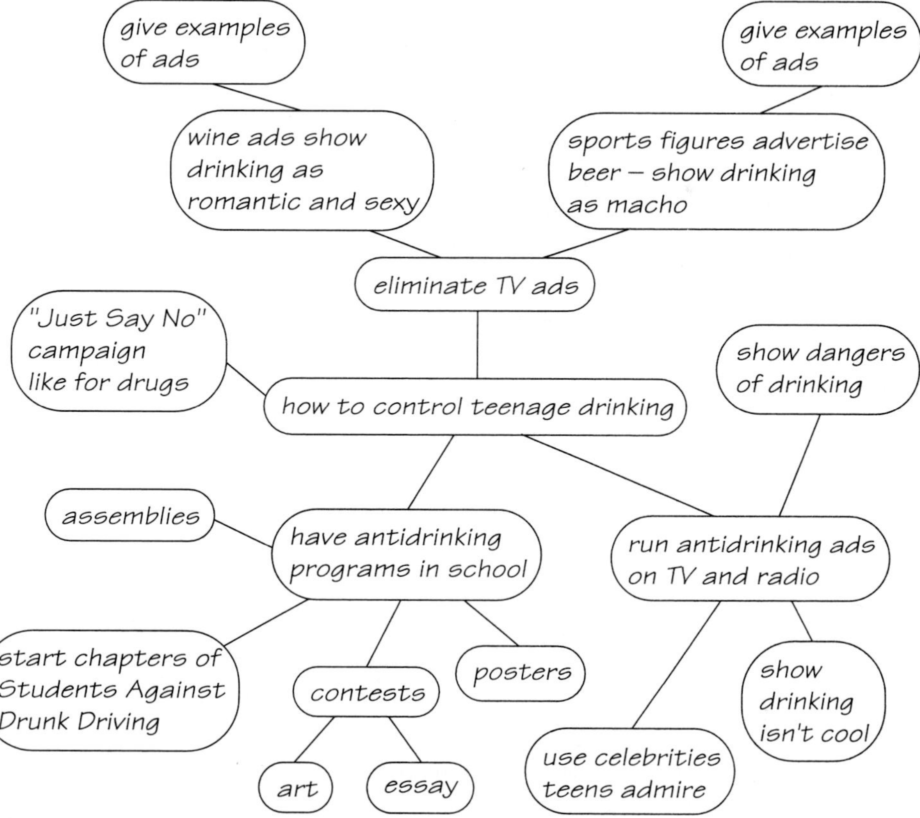

NOTE: Your clustering can include ideas that never make it into your first draft, and your draft can include ideas not in the clustering.

Letter Writing

Sometimes writers have trouble generating ideas because they do not relax enough to allow a free flow of thought. If this happens to you, try letter writing, a prewriting technique that relaxes the writer. Simply write a "letter" to someone you feel comfortable with and can open up to easily. The subject of your letter is your essay topic. Use this letter as an opportunity to express and explore ideas about your topic. Since you are writing to someone you are comfortable with, you will not hold anything back. Of course, this is all just a way to stimulate your thought, so you need not actually mail your letter.

Some people like to write letters to themselves rather than to others. If this appeals to you, give it a try. After all, when it comes to prewriting, anything that works is a good technique.

To discover ideas for developing her topic—the changing roles of women—a student wrote the letter that appears below. The letter explores some difficulties the writer faces meeting the demands of her various roles.

Dear Liz,

I guess I'm what you'd call a modern woman, but I'm not sure I like it very much. I know this is what I asked for, but it's a lot rougher than I expected and frankly less exciting.

The kids are 10 and 13 now, so they are fairly independent, but they still make a lot of demands on my time. Katie's adolescence has her turned inside out, and half the time she's crying and the other half she's mad at me for something. She's really on my mind a lot. Jenny is pretty together, but her gymnastics, Camp Fire activities, and swim meets really keep me on the fly. She makes a big demand on my time.

Then there's the job. I know it's only part-time, but those 20 hours really eat up my week. I can't keep up with the cleaning or the kids. And poor Jim really gets shortchanged. Actually, I feel pretty guilty that he works all day and then has to come home and help with laundry, dinner, and things. He doesn't mind, but I do. I feel like he's always picking up my slack and I'm not pulling my weight.

To top it off, now I'm in school. I must be crazy to make my work load even heavier than it already is. Still, I want my degree badly. I don't know, maybe I'm just in a slump, but I feel like I'm not doing anything well. Being liberated is not all I thought it would be. It's really very hard. I think I'm paying a big price for being a modern woman.

Love,
Marge

Thinking without Writing

Freewriting, listing, answering questions, clustering, letter writing—these prewriting techniques stimulate thought. Yet often our thinking does not need prodding, for if we just allow enough time, ideas surface on their own.

If your prewriting includes thinking without writing, remember these five hints.

1. Allow plenty of time to think. As soon as you discover you have a writing task, begin thinking about it. Don't wait until the last minute.
2. Think about your writing project while you are involved in your normal routine. As you are cooking, shopping, walking to class, showering, and so forth, turn a corner of your brain to the writing task.
3. Think about your writing before falling asleep at night. While you are sleeping, your mind will work on the task, and you may wake up with an idea or two.
4. Although this is thinking without writing, jot down ideas that occur to you in case you forget on Wednesday what you thought of on Tuesday.
5. Do not expect ideas to come to you in perfect form. Just as the written prewriting techniques yield rough ideas to be polished later, so will your thinking produce just the seeds of good ideas.

Keeping a Journal

Journal writing is more than a prewriting activity; it is a way to record thoughts, feelings, and responses to the events in your life. Because keeping a journal allows you to explore and examine what you think and feel, it can be a very satisfying experience. In fact, many people make journal writing a routine part of their lives because it can be so rewarding.

Sometimes instructors collect and respond to journals, but even so, they are considered private, rather than public writing, so you need not worry about grammar, spelling, and such. Also, some instructors give specific assignments for journal entries. At other times, students can write on whatever they want. (Keep in mind, though, that a journal is not a diary that merely records the events of your day.) If you need ideas for journal entries, try some of these.

1. Freewrite by beginning with the first thought that comes to mind.
2. Write about someone you admire.
3. Write about how your writing class is going.
4. Write about your feelings about college.
5. Explore your goals for the coming year.
6. Explain where you see yourself 5 years from now.
7. React to a book you recently read or to a movie you recently saw.
8. Write about a problem you have and explore possible solutions.
9. Write about your best attribute.
10. Record a vivid childhood memory.
11. Write about an event of the day that caused you to feel a strong emotion (anger, fear, frustration, happiness, relief, etc.).
12. Write about your family relationships.
13. Describe your writing process.
14. Tell about a change you would like to make.
15. Tell about a valued possession.

Journals can be handwritten in a special notebook reserved for the journal, or they can be a separate file on your word processor. Either way, date and begin each entry on a new page. Write each day or two religiously, and soon journal writing will become a habit. Then, when you need ideas for topics or details to develop a topic, scan your journal for ideas.

Composing at the Computer

Most of the techniques discussed for discovering ideas to develop topics can be very effective when done on a computer or word processor. However, you may find the following techniques particularly helpful.

Turn down the brightness dial on your screen until you can no longer see what you type in. Then write for 5 to 10 minutes on your topic. When you are finished, you are likely to have a great many typographical errors, but ignore them. You are also likely to have a number of ideas suitable for developing your topic. This technique works for people who find that when they cannot see and react to what they have written, their thoughts flow more freely.

Many people like to list and develop a scratch outline at the computer. To do so, type in the first idea that occurs to you and press the enter key. Then type the second idea and hit the enter key again. Continue in this fashion until you run out of ideas. Then you will have your list. Study this list and use your delete function to eliminate ideas you do not care to use and your insert key to add ideas that occur to you. Finally, use your copy-move functions to arrange the ideas in the order you want. Of course, with the computer, you can rearrange your ideas as many times as you need to in order to come up with a suitable sequence. Once you have that sequence, you have your scratch outline.

HOW THE PROCESS WORKS

Prewriting

Regardless of the prewriting techniques you favor, some generalizations can be made.

1. The writing process seldom progresses in a straight line from step 1 to step 2 to step 3 and so on. Often writers move forward and then step back to alter something done earlier. For example, while drafting, a writer may think of additional ideas—even though formal idea generation came earlier. While revising, a writer may decide to reshape the topic somewhat. Because writers can step back several times, the final paper can be very different from what the writer first had in mind.
2. Idea generation takes time.
3. You may find that a combination of prewriting activities yields more ideas than one technique by itself.
4. Experiment with all of the prewriting techniques. When you do, you may settle on two or three that work best for you.
5. If a technique that has been successful in the past does not work in a particular instance, switch to another technique and try the favored approach again next time.

EXERCISE

Discovering Ideas

1. How do you usually develop ideas for topics? Have your past procedures been successful? Explain.
2. When you responded to number 3 and number 4 of the exercise on page 13, you shaped a total of five essay topics. (If you did not complete this exercise, do so now). For each of these topics, discover at least four ideas worthy of inclusion in an essay. To generate these ideas, try each of the techniques described in this chapter (freewriting, listing, answering questions, letter writing, clustering, and thinking without writing) at least once.
3. For each idea you generated for number 2 above, note the technique that yielded the idea. Which technique(s) do you think worked best for you? Which are you likely to use in the future?

PURPOSE

Early on you should ask yourself why you are writing a particular piece. The answer to this question will form your **purpose**. In the most general sense, writers can establish one or a combination of these four purposes for their writing.

1. To share feelings, ideas, and/or experiences with the reader.
2. To inform the reader of something.
3. To persuade the reader to think or act a certain way.
4. To entertain the reader.

Writers must have a clear purpose in mind, because the reason for writing influences the nature of the piece. Let's say, for example, that your writing topic is the difficulties you encountered during your first term of college. If your purpose is to share your experiences with a reader, you might include accounts of what went wrong for you, along with descriptions of your emotional reactions to these happenings. If your purpose is to inform your reader that college life is not as easy as it seems, you might provide explanations of the problems you encountered, without a discussion of your reactions. If your purpose is to persuade your reader that a better orientation program is needed, you might offer only those unpleasant experiences that could have been avoided if a better orientation program existed. If your purpose is to entertain your reader, you would tell amusing stories of the difficulties you encountered.

Even this does not fully indicate how clearly your purpose should be established. You should be even more precise by asking yourself *why* you want to share or inform or persuade or entertain. Let's return to the purposes for writing about the difficulties encountered during the first term of college to see how asking "why" can sharpen your purpose. If you ask why you want to share your experiences of the first term, you might answer, "To vent frustration and earn some sympathy." If you ask why you want to inform your reader that college is not as easy as it seems, you might answer, "So my reader understands better what college life entails," or "So my reader knows what to expect when he or she begins college." If you ask yourself why you want to persuade your reader that a better orientation program is needed, you might respond, "So pressure is applied on the administration to institute the program." If you ask yourself why you want to entertain your reader, you might answer, "To help my reader appreciate the humor or absurdity of a situation."

To establish your purpose, you can answer the following questions.

1. Can I share my ideas, feelings, and/or experiences with my reader? If so, what do I want to share, and why?
2. Can I inform my reader? If so, what do I want to inform my reader of and why do I want to do so?
3. Can I persuade my reader to act or think a certain way? If so, what can I persuade my reader of and why do I want to do so?
4. Can I entertain my reader? If so, in what way, and why do I want to do so?

AUDIENCE

Like your purpose, your audience shapes your writing. An essay about freshman life may need a great deal of explanatory information if it is written for someone who knows little about college. However, such information would not be necessary for the reader who recently attended the same school you do. Similarly, if you wish to convince the administration to improve the orientation program and it claims there is no money to do so, then you would have to show that the program's cost is affordable. Such cost information might not be necessary if you were writing to persuade the student council to run the program and the council had the money. To convince the council, though, you might discuss how such a program could increase student support for council-sponsored activities. This latter fact, however, would not appear in writing aimed at the administration.

Audience and purpose must be compatible. For example, if your purpose for writing about your first-term difficulties is to vent frustration and earn sympathy, your audience could be your parents or your advisor. If your purpose is to inform readers about the nature of college life, your audience might be college-bound high school seniors. If your purpose is to convince the reader that a better orientation program is needed, your audience could be the dean of student services.

You might be thinking that because you are in a writing class, your audience is your instructor. And, of course, you are right. Yet writing teachers can assume the identities of different readers, so you are free to write for different audiences. You can also identify your audience as "the average, general reader"—someone who knows something about your subject but less than you do. You might think of the average, general reader as the typical reader of a large daily newspaper.

To decide on a suitable audience for your writing, you can answer the following questions.

1. Who could learn something from my writing?
2. Who would enjoy reading about my topic?
3. Who could be influenced to think or act a certain way?
4. Who shares an interest in my topic or would be sympathetic to my point of view?
5. Who would find my topic important?
6. Who needs to hear what I have to say?

Once you have identified your audience, you must assess that audience so you can provide the detail that will fill your reader's needs and help you achieve your purpose. These questions can help.

1. What does my reader already know about my topic?
2. What information will my reader need to appreciate my view?
3. Does my reader have any strong feelings about my topic?
4. Is my reader interested in my topic or will I have to arouse interest?
5. How receptive will my reader be to my view? Why?
6. Will my reader's age, sex, level of education, income, job, politics, or religion affect reaction to my topic?

EXERCISE

Determining Purpose, Establishing Audience, and Discovering Ideas

1. Develop an essay topic about campus life, using one or more of the techniques described in this chapter. Then establish a purpose for an essay on this topic by answering the questions on page 24.
2. Establish the audience for this essay by answering the questions on page 25.
3. Determine the nature of the audience by answering the questions above.
4. Use any two techniques described in this chapter and generate at least five ideas that could be included in an essay with the topic from number 1. After generating the ideas, determine whether they are compatible with the audience and purpose you have established.
5. If some of your ideas will not work with your audience and/or purpose, what options do you have?

WRITING ASSIGNMENT

When you completed the previous exercise, you shaped an essay topic about campus life. In addition, you determined a purpose for this essay, established and assessed audience, and discovered at least five ideas. Now you can develop this material into an essay. As you do so, keep the following points in mind.

1. Nothing is sacred about the material you have already developed. Any or all of it can be changed. You can even start over with a new topic if you like.
2. You may have to discover additional ideas to include in your essay.
3. To plan your essay, consider listing your ideas in the order you think they should appear.
4. Write a rough draft from this list of ideas. Do not be concerned about the quality of this draft; just get your ideas down the best way you can without worrying about anything, particularly grammar, spelling, and such.
5. Leave your rough draft for at least a day. Then go over it and make necessary changes. To decide what changes to make, you can ask yourself the following questions:
   a. Is each idea clearly explained?
   b. Is each idea well developed (backed up with examples and/or explanation)?
   c. Are all ideas related to the topic?
   d. Do ideas appear in a logical order?
6. After making changes in your draft, recopy it and ask two classmates to read it and make suggestions.
7. Check your work for correct grammar, spelling, and punctuation.
8. Type or copy your essay carefully and proofread it for errors.

CHAPTER 2

Structuring the Essay

Prewriting is often disorganized. We make random associations, travel roundabout, double back over the same path, and test offbeat relationships. Illogical though it may seem on the surface, this process can be very productive—when we are discovering ideas. However, a reader cannot be expected to follow such twists, turns, repetitions, and leaps. Thus, once you have some ideas formed and have settled on which of them to include, you are obligated to help your reader by presenting those ideas in an orderly way.

FROM PREWRITING TO ORGANIZING

Before actively working to order your material, evaluate your ideas and make preliminary decisions about which to use and which to reject. Make these decisions on the basis of which ideas best develop your topic, suit your purpose, and accommodate your audience. After your evaluation, you may discover you have rejected quite a few ideas. Or you may decide to alter your topic, purpose, or audience. If this happens, more ideas may be needed and you can find yourself prewriting and evaluating again. Actually, this prewriting and evaluating process can occur any number of times until you are satisfied that your topic, purpose, audience, and ideas are established well enough to form a comfortable departure point. Then you can think about ways to organize your ideas.

The chart below shows what can occur before writers give serious thought to organizing.

HOW THE PROCESS WORKS

Prewriting

Idea Generation

1. Writer discovers subject.
2. Writer shapes topic.
3. Writer discovers ideas to develop topic.

Establishing Audience and Purpose

1. Writer may establish audience and/or purpose before, or at any point during, idea generation.
2. Writer may establish audience and/or purpose after idea generation.

Evaluation

1. Writer considers subject, topic, supporting ideas, audience, and purpose to be sure all are compatible with each other.
2. If necessary, writer adjusts subject, topic, supporting ideas, audience, or purpose (any or all) to make them compatible.
3. If changes are necessary, the writer may prewrite again to discover ideas for effecting these changes or adjusting material to accommodate them.

   NOTES:

   a. The process continues until the writer feels he or she has enough to proceed. How much of this framework must be in place before the writer advances will vary from writer to writer.
   b. Writers often step back before moving forward. This means that discovering ideas can lead to a new topic, establishing purpose can shift audience, and so on.

When to Move On

At some point during prewriting, you will feel "done." You will feel satisfied that you have a workable topic, a viable purpose, a clear and appropriate audience, and enough ideas to form a departure point.

Being "done" with prewriting means different things to different writers. Some writers cannot advance until they are certain of every idea they want to include and the method they will use to develop each of those ideas. For those writers, prewriting may take longer because it must yield more. Others require less of prewriting. These writers do better knowing some of the major points they will cover. Such writers feel constrained if they predetermine too much; they prefer to discover only some of their main points during prewriting (or maybe only one main point) and let the rest emerge in the flow of their later writing.

How much you require of prewriting only you can decide. You may already have a sense of how much groundwork you must lay before moving on. If not, try prewriting extensively and less extensively for separate writing tasks and evaluate which way works better. Keep one thing in mind, however: if you have trouble going forward, you probably have not laid enough groundwork. Try additional prewriting to advance more readily.

What to Move On To

Some writers can organize mentally by reviewing their ideas from prewriting and arranging them logically in their heads. This usually works when there are only a few ideas to deal with. Some writers organize as they write their first draft. They decide which idea to treat first, write through it, and then decide what comes next when they get there. Other writers are more successful if they plot their organization in a separate outlining step between prewriting and the first draft. Regardless of whether you go from prewriting to draft or from prewriting to outlining, at some point you will have to concern yourself with the logical organization of your ideas.

There is no single way to organize an essay, for many different organizational strategies are at the writer's disposal. You can even take the same ideas and organize them effectively in more than one way. Despite this variety, we can make many generalizations by discussing one useful pattern of organization. This pattern can be varied in many ways and even abandoned altogether, but a discussion of it serves two purposes. First, it provides a useful model because the pattern can serve in many situations. Second, the pattern provides a handy departure point. Understanding how it works can make you more aware of ways to vary your organization and still be logical and effective.

A USEFUL PATTERN OF ORGANIZATION

Here's something you already know: an essay has a beginning, a middle, and an end. In the pattern of organization presented here, the beginning is the introduction; the middle is the body; and the end is the conclusion. Let's take an overview of each of these three parts and then deal with each in more detail.

1. The first paragraph (or paragraphs) of the essay forms the **introduction**, which serves two purposes: it lets your reader know what your essay is about, and it arouses your reader's interest in your topic. That's your beginning.
2. Next comes the middle. This is two or more **body paragraphs.** The body paragraphs present detail to develop your topic. They form the real meat of the essay.
3. The end of your essay is the **conclusion**. This final paragraph (or paragraphs) brings your essay to a satisfying finish.

Before looking more closely at the function and structure of the three parts of the essay, read the student essay in the next section. It illustrates the pattern of organization that is discussed in the rest of this chapter. The notes in the margin call your attention to the structural features of the essay, features that will be referred to throughout the rest of this chapter.

All Creatures Great and Small

Paragraph 1 is the introduction. The last sentence is the thesis, which tells what the essay is about (bleacher creatures are vile, and Gladys's son had become one). The rest of the introduction stimulates reader interest with description.

1 Gladys Kline stared at her TV in abject horror. Before her eyes lay a gross caricature of a man. His face and hair were discolored, his body disfigured by grain alcohol. He seemed to be having a tantrum—jaw working wildly, arms flailing at his sides. That man was Gladys Kline's son. All at once, memories flooded through her mind—the banners in his bedroom, Saturday night football games, the subscription to *Sports Illustrated.* Like countless others, Gladys Kline never thought it would turn out this way. Nonetheless, it had happened: Her son had deteriorated into the vilest of all beings—a bleacher creature.

Paragraph 2 is a body paragraph. The first sentence is the topic sentence, which tells what the paragraph is about (the appearance of the bleacher creature). The rest of the paragraph is the supporting detail, which develops the topic sentence idea. In all, the paragraph helps support the thesis idea.

2 One of the first symptoms of the deterioration is his disgusting appearance. Let us consider Bobby Ray Kline as an example. Bobby Ray's sweatshirt always exposes about a 2-inch span of rather flaccid flesh protruding over his waistband. The front of his shirt is commonly adorned with today's stadium mustard and yesterday's spaghetti sauce. Bobby Ray's innovation in hair styling is to knot dog bones in his hair. He would advise you that the greasier your hair, the more manageable the style. In tribute to the Cleveland Browns, Bobby Ray had his hair dyed orange and white. Bobby Ray is very proud of his neon locks, for they help him get noticed by the television cameras—much to the chagrin of his mother. To top off his appearance, Bobby Ray applies makeup to his face. From the top of his forehead to the tip of his chin, urban graffiti is sprawled in vibrant colors. The obscene words Bobby Ray expertly sketches upon his skin would stop a nun dead in her tracks.

Paragraph 3 is a body paragraph. The topic sentence (the first) tells that the paragraph will focus on obscene speech. The rest of the paragraph (the supporting details) develops the topic sentence idea. The paragraph helps develop the thesis idea.

3 Under bleacher creature code, obscenity on the face must translate into profanity in speech. A bleacher creature must be well versed in the seven deadly words. Not only must he be familiar with the terms, he must be able to utilize them in a variety of ways. For instance, he must be able to apply the words to the mother, brother, or any living relative of the person he intends to insult. This task apparently becomes easier as the level of beer consumption rises. After downing the first twelve-pack, most creatures are considered to be at their verbal peak. During this stage, verbal barrages lasting 10 to 15 minutes are not uncommon. Usually, they are directed at some poor, unsuspecting line judge. There are exceptions to this rule, as when intercreature conflicts arise.

Paragraph 4 is the last body paragraph. Its topic sentence (the first) notes that the paragraph will discuss the creature's lack of consideration. The rest of the paragraph is supporting detail, which develops the topic sentence idea. The paragraph helps prove the thesis.

These conflicts bring into focus the major credo of the bleacher crea- 4
tures: Thou shalt show a consistent lack of consideration toward others. Under this rule, a blatant disregard for the neighbor is a must. A bleacher creature has to possess the ability to spill beer on many of his less fortunate counterparts at the same time he is whistling shrilly through his teeth. When throwing empty beer cans into the crowd, a very talented creature can make the containers ricochet off two or more spectators. Staggering back to the concession stand for refills, he then must proceed to knock down, knock into, or knock out any or all bystanders in his way. All these actions should be performed with gleeful smiles, to leave no doubt the creatures are sincere in what they do. There is a more tender side to these animals. When confronted by a member of the opposite sex, the creatures will begin burping loudly to gain the attention of the female. Virility is proven not only by the vulgarity of the burps, but by the rapid succession in which they are delivered. As for Bobby Ray, he has yet to muster the gastric power needed to be a contender in this field.

Paragraph 5, the conclusion, brings the essay to a satisfying finish.

At 33 years of age, Bobby Ray was sure his mother would miss him ter- 5
ribly if he ever married and left home. Little did he know that back at the Kline homestead, Gladys was busily throwing all his possessions on the front lawn. Her lease had a no-pets clause, and Gladys always followed the rules.

THE INTRODUCTION

First impressions are important because initial reactions often dictate our responses. Think about it a moment. Have you ever dropped a course after attending only one class session? Have you ever made an excuse to walk away from a person you have just met? Have you ever selected a restaurant on the basis of its name? We all do such things, and we do them in response to first impressions. Because first impressions are so important, the introduction of your essay must be carefully handled so that your reader's initial reaction is favorable. (Reread the introduction of "All Creatures Great and Small." Notice how well it stimulates reader interest.)

In addition to creating a first impression that can please or displease your reader, the introduction can serve another purpose. It can tell your reader what your essay is about by including a statement that reveals the topic. This statement is called a **thesis.** Below are three introductions written by students. In each introduction the thesis is underlined.

INTRODUCTION 1

Parents are always pushing their teenagers to get a job and that is understandable. Teens cost their folks a great deal of money, so naturally parents want them to help

> out with that paycheck from McDonalds. Nonetheless, teenagers should not be required to work during the school year.

The thesis indicates that the essay will discuss why teenagers should not have to work while they are going to school.

INTRODUCTION 2

> There was a blistering wind howling outside my van window as I was driving to my early-evening English class. The snow began to fall rapidly, blowing and swirling in the air before it reached the road in front of me. Once I had reached my destination, YSU's campus, I had to struggle to search out and snare a parking space.

The thesis indicates that the essay will explain what the writer went through trying to find a parking space on campus before English class.

INTRODUCTION 3

> What is a woman? If all that propaganda out there is correct, a woman is someone who delights in serving. Her husband, her children, her house--taking care of these is woman's ultimate purpose in life. If she doesn't relish it, then surely something is wrong--with her. Most women were brought up firmly grounded in the belief that their major role in life is to marry, have children, and keep a clean house and beautiful home. From the time little girls are big enough to mimic Mother, they are taught in subtle ways that the never-ending battle with dirt, dust, and grime should be their major concern in life. Nonetheless, I find housework frustrating.

The thesis indicates that the essay will discuss the fact that the writer finds housework frustrating.

Look again at the thesis statements in the above three introductions and notice that they present the writers' topics in a particular way: each thesis indicates the writer's broad subject and the narrow territory within that broad subject staked out for treatment. This is charted for you as follows:

Thesis 1
Broad subject: `teenagers`
Narrowing: `They should not work while attending school.`

Thesis 2
Broad subject: `campus parking`
Narrowing: `It is a struggle.`

Thesis 3
Broad subject: `housework`
Narrowing: `It is frustrating.`

You have probably noticed that in each example the thesis is the last sentence of the introduction. While the thesis can work well at the beginning or in the middle of the introduction, many writers find it convenient to place the thesis at the end.

Below are examples of introductions with thesis statements at the beginning and in the middle. The thesis statements are underlined for you.

INTRODUCTION 4

<u>If Marcus Norris wins the mayoral election, our city will not recover from its current economic slump.</u> Norris is on record as advocating layoffs of city workers, which will swell our unemployment ranks. He also favors increased deficit spending, which will strain our city budget to its limit. Most troubling of all, he plans to scrap the economic recovery program begun by our current mayor.

Introduction 5

Psychologists have devised many sophisticated tests for determining the kinds of personalities people have. They need not have bothered, for there is an easier way. <u>It is possible to determine people's personalities from the cars they drive.</u> Whether a person is aggressive, retiring, success-oriented, failure-prone, sexy, or drab--these traits and others are reflected in the individual's choice of automobile.

NOTE: Another useful approach to the thesis is to state the main points to be covered in the essay, like this.

```
Dr. Hernandez is an excellent professor because she is
patient, dedicated to students, and entertaining.
```

NOTE: Sometimes the introduction is written without a thesis. In such cases, the writer's subject and narrowing are strongly implied elsewhere in the essay. Usually, however, student writers are encouraged to include stated thesis sentences. (For an example of an essay with an implied thesis, see "Look Out, Here She Comes" on page 56.)

Shaping the Thesis

The thesis is important to both the writer and the reader. It is important to the writer because it provides the focus for the essay and hence guides the writer. A writer selecting details and deciding how to express those details will weigh them against the thesis to be sure everything functions to develop the thesis and fulfill its promise. Similarly, the thesis is important to the reader, who develops expectations for an essay according to what the thesis promises. Because the thesis is important to both writer and reader, you must shape it carefully. To do so, keep the following four points in mind.

1. AVOID BROAD STATEMENTS

In Chapter 1 you learned of the need for a narrow topic, and this applies directly to the thesis (see page 7). A thesis that is too broad will force the writer into a vague, superficial discussion that will never satisfy a reader because it will never get beyond statements of the obvious. The following thesis statement is too broad.

```
The role of women has changed drastically in the last fifty
years.
```

This broad thesis presents a problem for the writer. Fifty years is a long time; to discuss in-depth all the changes in that time span would require more pages than the typical college essay runs. If the essay were to run a more manageable length, the writer could do little more than skim the surface and state the obvious. Below is a more suitable thesis, one that is sufficiently narrow.

```
The leadership role of women in state politics has changed
drastically in the last ten years.
```

This thesis is better because it is narrowed to include only one role of women in one political arena and because the time span is more reasonable.

More than one subject or more than one narrowing may cause the thesis to be too broad, as the following chart shows:

Too Broad (two subjects)	*Better (one subject)*
The Nontraditional Student Center and the International Student Union are two university organizations that serve students well.	1. The Nontraditional Student Center serves students well. 2. The International Student Center serves students well.
Too Broad (two narrowings)	*Better (one narrowing)*
Divorce would be less traumatic if custody laws were revised and if attorneys counseled their clients more carefully.	1. Divorce would be less traumatic if custody laws were revised. 2. Divorce would be less traumatic if attorneys counseled their clients more carefully.

2. AVOID FACTUAL STATEMENTS

Factual thesis statements do not work because they leave the writer with nothing to say. Here are some examples of factual statements and suitable revisions.

Factual Statement	*Suitable Thesis*
1. The water department is considering a rate increase.	1. The water department's proposed rate increase is unnecessary.
2. Many network television programs are violent.	2. Television networks should reduce the amount of violence in their programs.
3. My parents own a beach house.	3. My happiest childhood memories are of the summers I spent at my parents' beach house.

3. EXPRESS THE NARROWING IN SPECIFIC WORDS

Because the reader relies on the thesis for a clear indication of what the essay is about, the narrowing should be expressed in specific words. Consider this thesis, for example:

It is interesting to consider the various meanings of love.

The word *interesting* is vague, so the reader cannot be sure how the writer is narrowing the subject. In the following revision, however, the narrowing is stated in specific terms, so the reader has a clear sense of the focus of the essay.

We apply the word love to a broad spectrum of emotions.

4. AVOID THE ANNOUNCEMENT

A thesis such as, "This paper will show why I've always hated team sports," is generally considered weak style. Notice the difference between the following announcements and acceptable thesis statements.

Announcement	*Better Thesis*
1. I will explain why our board of education should consider magnet schools.	1. Our board of education should consider magnet schools.
2. This essay will describe the best way to choose a major.	2. Students who are unsure of how to choose a major should follow my advice.
3. The next paragraphs will present the reasons Americans value youth.	3. Americans value youth for surprising reasons.

EXERCISE

The Thesis

1. In the following thesis statements, identify the broad subject and the narrowing.
   a. No experience is more exasperating than taking preschool children to the grocery store on a Saturday to do a week's worth of shopping.
   b. My brother, Jerry, taught me the meaning of courage.
   c. Television news does not adequately inform the U.S. public.
   d. It has been said that Benjamin Franklin was a great diplomat; however, no one is more skilled at diplomacy than people who make their living selling clothes.
   e. Many people believe a little white lie can be better than the truth, but even these seemingly harmless fibs can cause trouble.
2. Two of the following thesis statements are acceptable. Write *A* if the thesis is acceptable; *B* if it is too broad; *FS* if it is a factual statement; *V* if it is vague; *FA* if it is a formal announcement. Then rewrite the unacceptable thesis statements to make them suitable.
   a. There are many game shows on television.
   b. Schools should not be funded by property taxes.

c. The next paragraphs explain why I am an avid skier.
d. Higher education is in need of reform.
e. College students can learn to handle stress if they follow my advice.
f. My Christmas cruise to the Bahamas was nice.

3. Below are four broad subjects. Select two of them and write a thesis for an essay about each. Narrow so that you are treating a topic manageable in 500 to 700 words.

   example: Saturday morning cartoons: If parents took the time to watch Saturday morning cartoons with their children, they would be surprised at how violent these programs really are.

   a. sports
   b. large parties
   c. a childhood memory
   d. grades

Creating Interest in Your Topic

In addition to presenting your thesis, the introduction should arouse your reader's interest in your essay. Below are six approaches you can take to stimulate that interest. Each approach is illustrated with an introduction taken from a student essay.

APPROACH 1: PROVIDE BACKGROUND INFORMATION

> Rick was always taking crazy chances. Even in elementary school, he was the one to lock himself in the teacher's supply closet or lick a metal pole in the dead of a subzero winter. By high school, Rick had moved on to wilder things, but his drinking was the biggest concern. I guess that is why no one was really surprised when he drove off the road and killed himself the day after his eighteenth birthday.

NOTE: The essay with this introduction tells what happened the night Rick died.

APPROACH 2: TELL A PERTINENT STORY

> Last winter while home alone, I tripped on the garden hose and fell in my garage while the door was down. The pain was excruciating, and I could not move. I lay there for two hours, sobbing, until my son came home. Now, I am not an old woman; I am just 45. However, that experience made me feel fearful of growing old and living alone.

APPROACH 3: EXPLAIN WHY YOUR TOPIC IS IMPORTANT

The recent tuition hike proposed by the Board of Trustees has serious implications for everyone on this campus, students, faculty, and staff alike. If tuition goes up 45 percent as expected, fewer students will be able to attend school, which will mean fewer faculty and staff will be employed. Once the cost of school becomes prohibitive for all but the wealthy, then this university will begin a downward spiral that will eventually mean its demise. There is only one way to solve our economic woes. We must embark on an austerity program that makes the tuition hike unnecessary.

APPROACH 4: PRESENT SOME INTERESTING IMAGES OR USE DESCRIPTION

It was a cool, crisp October morning. Sunrise was complete, the countryside awake and responding to another day. As I turned and slowly made my way into the woods, I had no idea what lay ahead on the path I was to follow that day.

APPROACH 5: PRESENT AN INTRIGUING PROBLEM OR RAISE A PROVOCATIVE QUESTION

Are you a Dr. Jekyll who transforms into Mr. Hyde the minute you get behind the wheel of a car? Are you a kind little old lady who becomes Mario Andretti's pace car driver the instant you hit the freeway? Are you an Eagle Scout by day and a marauding motorist by night? The chances are you are because people's personalities change the moment they strap on that seat belt and head out on the highway.

APPROACH 6: PRESENT AN OPPOSING VIEWPOINT

People against putting warning labels on CDs with sexually explicit or otherwise offensive lyrics have their reasons. They cite free speech and they say teens will be encouraged to buy the CDs with the advisory labels. Even so, I favor warning labels on certain kinds of CDs.

NOTE: Avoid writing an introduction that refers to your title as if it were an integral part of the essay. Thus, if your title is "The Impact of the Information Highway," avoid beginning with "It will change the way we work and live." Instead, write "The information highway will change the way we work and live."

HOW THE STRUCTURE WORKS

Introductions

1. Your introduction is important because it forms your reader's first impression.
2. An introduction can
   a. Present your topic
   b. Arouse interest in your topic
3. The introduction can present your topic in a thesis.
   a. The thesis is often the last sentence of the introduction.
   b. The thesis presents your topic by stating your subject and your narrowing in specific terms.
   c. Both the subject and the narrowing must be restricted.
   d. Avoid a thesis that reads like an announcement or that is a factual statement.
4. Six ways to create interest in your topic are
   a. Providing background information
   b. Telling a story
   c. Explaining why your topic is important
   d. Presenting images or using description
   e. Presenting a problem or raising a question
   f. Presenting opposing views
5. Your approach to your introduction will, in part, be determined by your audience and purpose.

Introductions and the Writing Process

During prewriting you work to develop a thesis and ideas to support that thesis; you may not give much thought to an introduction. Thus, when you write a first draft you may be stumped about how to begin. So what do you do?

Actually, you have two choices. First, you can skip your introduction and begin with your second paragraph. By the time you finish your draft, an approach to your introduction may suggest itself. If you skip your introduction, you should draft a tentative thesis to provide a focus, something you can check your detail against so you do not drift into unrelated areas.

Your second choice is to prewrite for your introduction in a separate stage. (Of course, you can do this too if you skip your introduction and find when you return that you are still stuck.) To prewrite, try the following.

1. Write out your thesis.
2. Ask yourself whether your audience needs background information to appreciate your topic or view. If so, list the points needed.

3. Decide whether you could tell a brief story to interest your audience and pave the way for your thesis.
4. List the reasons your topic is important to you, and list the reasons it should be important to your reader.
5. Decide whether you can describe anything related to your topic to engage the interest of your reader.
6. Ask questions or raise problems that would interest or arouse the curiosity of your reader.
7. List any views that oppose your thesis.
8. Review your responses to numbers 2–7 and decide (considering your audience and purpose) which material will make the best introduction. That material, along with the thesis you wrote for number 1, should serve as a departure point for drafting your introduction.

Composing at the Computer

If you compose at the computer or word processor, the following techniques may prove particularly helpful.

If you cannot decide which approach to your introduction is the best, try windowing if your computer has that capability. To window, execute the keystrokes that allow you to divide the screen in half. Try a different approach to your introduction on each half of the screen and compare the two to decide which you like better. You can compare that approach to another that you write after erasing the half you didn't like as well.

Sometimes your conclusion can be turned into an excellent introduction with some reworking. Try moving your conclusion to the beginning of your essay to determine if it holds more promise as an introduction than as a conclusion.

GROUP EXERCISE

Three Introductions to Revise

Below are three introductions written by students. Each one has the potential to be effective, but each one has problems. Work with two or three classmates to revise each introduction so that it stimulates interest and has a suitable thesis.

1. It was snowing when I boarded the plane. But I was terrified. I have always been afraid of air travel, and hopefully I will someday overcome this fear.

Suggestions for revision: Create some images. Describe the weather in more detail. Specify the kind of airplane and explain more carefully the feeling of terror. Also, does the thesis present one or two narrowings? It should only present one.

2. I set the alarm two hours earlier than usual and spent the morning cleaning like crazy. At 11:00 I went to the grocery store and bought all the necessary food. All afternoon I

```
cooked; by 5:00 I was dressed and ready; but still the
first meal I cooked for my in-laws was terrible.
```

Suggestions for revision: Be more specific. What time did the alarm go off? Give an example or two of the cleaning you did. What food did you buy? Was it expensive? What did you cook? How bad was it? Can you find a word or words more specific than *terrible?*

```
3. Does crime pay? Does justice win out? Do the police always
   get their man? The day I shoplifted a box of candy I
   learned the answers to these questions.
```

Suggestions for revision: Substitute more interesting questions for these trite, rather boring ones—perhaps some questions that focus on the writer's feelings, such as: "Have you ever wondered what a criminal feels when he or she gets caught?" Create some interest by naming the brand or type of candy and giving its price and by giving the name of the store.

EXERCISE

Three Introductions to Write

1. Using one of the thesis statements you shaped when you responded to number 3 on page 37, establish an audience and purpose and write an introduction for an essay that might use that thesis. Feel free to alter the original thesis somewhat.
2. Below is a list of four subjects. Select one and shape a narrow topic from it. (If necessary, prewrite to find a suitable topic.) Then establish an audience and purpose. Next, write an introduction for an essay that discusses that topic.
   a. A first experience
   b. A disagreement with a friend
   c. A pleasant (or unpleasant) surprise
   d. The best (or worst) feature of your university
3. Write a second introduction using the thesis, audience, and purpose you shaped for number 2 above, only this time use a different approach. That is, if you told a story the first time, try something else—say, creating images—this time. If you wish, you may state your thesis differently in this second introduction. (As an alternative, select a subject different from what you used for number 2. Just be sure to narrow, establish audience and purpose, and use a different approach than you did for the first introduction.)

THE BODY PARAGRAPHS

The paragraphs after your introduction form the **body** of your essay. The purpose of the body paragraphs is to present the detail that supports, explains, defends, describes, illustrates, or otherwise develops the idea given in your thesis.

Obviously the body is the real core of an essay, for here you present the material to convince your reader of the validity of your thesis.

In the organizational pattern we are discussing in this chapter, each body paragraph has two parts: the topic sentence and the supporting detail.

The **topic sentence** provides focus by presenting the point the body paragraph will deal with. This point will be one aspect of the thesis. While the topic sentence can appear anywhere in the body paragraph, many student writers find it easiest to place the topic sentence first. After the topic sentence comes the **supporting detail.** This is all the information that explains, illustrates, defends, describes, supports, or otherwise develops the idea presented in the topic sentence. Look again at the body paragraphs of "All Creatures Great and Small," on page 30, and notice the topic sentence and supporting details.

Adequate Detail

You cannot expect a reader to understand and appreciate the view in your thesis if you do not provide enough convincing support for that view. Let's say someone walked up to you and said, "This town stinks." You respond by asking why. The first person replies, "It's awful here; I hate it. I'm going to leave, and you should too." Would you agree that the place is awful? I doubt it, because you were not given convincing evidence to support the claim that the place stinks. That is the way it is with supporting detail: if it is not adequate, no reader will accept as truth the idea in the thesis.

To ensure that you supply adequate detail, remember that you can't just *tell;* you must also *show*. Thus, the person who *told* by saying that the town stinks should also *show* by providing specific evidence, such as there is no symphony or museum, there is only one theater, the local government is corrupt, the public schools are poorly funded, the roads are in disrepair, and the people are snobs.

When writers show rather than tell, they are supporting generalizations. A **generalization** is a statement offered as truth. The support is what is offered as proof. Say, for example, that you believe registration at your school is too much of a hassle. That would be your generalization—your statement of truth. To convince me that registration is a hassle at your school, you would have to do more than just make the statement. After all, why should I accept your statement as fact just because you make it? If I am to believe registration is a hassle, you will have to prove it to me. Here is a list of some evidence you could provide to support your generalization about registration.

long lines
crowded facilities
too few classes offered
confusing procedures
inaccessible advisers

If you were writing an essay about the hassles of registration, you could write one body paragraph on each of the points in the above list. However, you would have to support every generalization in every body paragraph by showing in addition to telling. Thus, the paragraph about crowded facilities must describe the nature and extent of the crowding in enough detail to convince the reader that crowding really exists. This need to support generalizations holds for every generalization you make everywhere in the body of your essay.

Look again at "All Creatures Great and Small" on page 30. Notice that the author supports the thesis generalization by providing this evidence in the topic sentences of the body paragraphs.

The bleacher creature's appearance is disgusting.
The bleacher creature's speech is profane.
The bleacher creature lacks consideration for others.

Now look at the body paragraphs and notice how carefully the author develops each topic sentence generalization. For instance, to show that the bleacher creature's appearance is disgusting, the author makes these points.

Fat belly hangs exposed over the belt line.
Sweatshirt is food-stained, and not all the stains are fresh.
Dog bones are in hair.
Hair is greasy (unwashed).
Hair is dyed orange and white.
Obscene words are written on face.

Ways to Develop and Arrange Supporting Detail

To provide the adequate detail a reader requires, writers have a number of strategies at their disposal, and many of these are explained in Part II of this book. These strategies include:

Description: The writer can describe something.

Narration: The writer can tell a story.

Illustration: The writer can provide examples.

Process analysis: The writer can explain how something is made or done.

Comparison and contrast: The writer can point out similarities and differences.

Cause-and-effect analysis: The writer can explain the causes and effects of something.

Definition: The writer can explain what something means.

Classification: The writer can explain how items are grouped.

Regardless of the kind of details the writer provides, those details must be presented in a logical order so the reader can easily follow the sequence of ideas. Several arrangements are possible:

Chronological order: This is a time order. The writer begins with what happens first, moves to the second event, on to the third, and so on. This is a useful order for the storyteller.

Spatial order: With this arrangement, the writer moves across space in some logical way, say top to bottom, outside to inside, left to right, and so on. Writers who describe, frequently use a spatial arrangement.

Progressive order: With this order, the writer moves from the *least* compelling (important, surprising, convincing, or representative) idea to the most compelling. Writers who aim to persuade often use a progressive order to save the most compelling argument for last.

More specific information on arranging details is given in Part 2.

Relevant Detail

In addition to being adequate, your supporting detail must be *relevant.* This means that every detail in a body paragraph must be clearly related to the topic sentence of that paragraph. Thus in "All Creatures Great and Small," the first body paragraph (about disgusting appearance) could not describe clean, neat designer jeans and polished Italian shoes. Since these are not disgusting, they are not relevant. Sometimes writers include detail that is not relevant because they become so concerned about supplying *enough* detail that they overlook the need to include the *right* detail. You know the feeling, that sense that if you only write enough, in there somewhere you will say something terrific. This common impulse is a dangerous one that can lead you to write ideas that do not belong because they are not related to the topic sentence.

In addition to being sure that the detail in a paragraph is relevant to its topic sentence, a writer must be sure that each topic sentence is relevant to the thesis. If you have a topic sentence—and hence a paragraph—that does not pertain to the thesis, a portion of your essay will stray from the stated topic. Thus, "All Creatures Great and Small" cannot include a topic sentence that says bleacher creatures are nice to children—that statement would not be relevant to the thesis, which presents the creatures as vile.

To ensure relevance, think of your thesis as a contract between you and your reader. It guarantees that your essay will be about what the thesis says it will be about. Run a careful check on both your topic sentences and your supporting detail to be certain you have not violated the terms of the contract.

Take some time now and reread "All Creatures Great and Small" on page 30. Notice that every topic sentence is clearly relevant to the thesis. Also notice that all the supporting details in each body paragraph are directly related to the appropriate topic sentence.

When to Begin a Paragraph

Writers usually begin a new paragraph each time they begin discussion of a new point to develop the thesis, with the following exceptions.

1. If the discussion of a point requires a very long paragraph, the writer can break up the discussion into two or more paragraphs as a courtesy to the reader, who may find one very long paragraph taxing.
2. A writer can begin a paragraph to emphasize a point. If a point can appear in a paragraph along with other ideas but the writer wants that point to receive special emphasis, it can be placed in a paragraph of its own.
3. A writer may use one body paragraph to make a point and then illustrate that point with a long example or a series of short examples. If including the example or examples in the paragraph that makes the point would create an overly long paragraph, then the example(s) can appear in a separate paragraph.

HOW THE STRUCTURE WORKS

Body Paragraphs

1. Body paragraphs present detail to demonstrate the validity of the thesis.
2. In the pattern of organization discussed here, body paragraphs have two parts: the topic sentence and the supporting detail.
3. The topic sentence tells what the body paragraph is about; it presents the aspect of the thesis under discussion in the body paragraph.
   a. A topic sentence can appear anywhere in the body paragraph, but it is often convenient to place it first.
   b. The topic sentence must be relevant to the thesis.
4. The supporting detail develops the point presented in the topic sentence.
   a. The writer must support all generalizations by showing and not just telling.
   b. The supporting detail must be relevant to its topic sentence.
   c. Supporting details must be arranged in a logical order.

Evaluating Your Supporting Detail

How can writers be sure their detail is adequate and relevant? A number of ways to evaluate your detail are noted in Part II. For now, you might find the following evaluation techniques helpful.

TO EVALUATE THE ADEQUACY OF YOUR DETAIL

1. Underline every generalization and bracket off the specific details that support each generalization. Look at the bracketed material and ask yourself whether you are *showing* the truth of the generalization in enough detail.
2. Ask someone who can be objective to read your draft and note in the margin any additional information he or she needs to appreciate your view.
3. Count the number of sentences in each of your body paragraphs. If you have a paragraph with fewer than five sentences, ask yourself if you have developed your topic sentence adequately.
4. For each body paragraph in your draft, answer the following questions.
   a. Why would my reader find the information in this paragraph helpful?
   b. How does the information in this paragraph advance my purpose?
   If you cannot justify the inclusion of certain details, then these details are probably not appropriate.

TO EVALUATE THE RELEVANCE OF YOUR DETAIL

1. Examine each of your topic sentences against your thesis and ask yourself whether each is clearly related to the thesis.
2. Examine each sentence of every body paragraph and ask yourself whether each is clearly related to its topic sentence.
3. Ask someone who will be objective about your work to read your draft and underline any detail that does not seem relevant.

EXERCISE

Body Paragraphs to Evaluate

The following essay, written by a college freshman, has definite strengths as well as some problems. Read the essay and answer the questions after it. These questions are meant to help you understand the points made about body paragraphs.

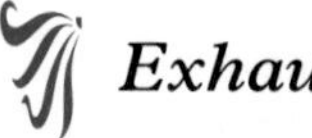

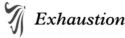

Exhaustion

All of my friends told me it would be hard for me to attend college at my age because I was eighteen years removed from any study habits that I may have once had. However, I'm finding that the hardest part of attending college is not lack of study habits but coping with the exhaustion from trying to keep up with attending classes, working 40 hours a week, raising a family of three exuberant boys, and taking care of household chores. *1*

A typical day starts for me at 6:00 in the morning when I crawl out of my toast-warm bed and stumble over the dog. Flicking on the lights in each of the boys' rooms, I grope my way carefully down the stairs, with eyes half open. My first encounter is with three hungry, mewling cats and a dog who lets me know he has to be let out. Next I grab a cup of coffee and gulp half of it down so I can pry my eyes open enough to take care of all the urgent matters of the morning. Gulping coffee and grabbing quick puffs of my cigarette, I stumble around packing school lunches. Now it's time for the real work, pushing the boys to get ready for school. "Greg, don't forget to brush your teeth." "Bob, take that shirt off. I don't care if it is your favorite; you wore it yesterday." "Mike, you can't comb your hair like that; it makes you look like Alfalfa." By the time I get them out the door, I'm ready to go back to bed, but work is waiting and I have no time to lose. Eight-thirty finds me on the job, brushed, curled, and ready to begin. *2*

The hands on the clock finally reach twelve and it's time for my lunch hour. Lunch? What is that? I have one hour to do my grocery shopping for the day and pay any bills that need paying. I rush home, put my milk and bread away, take care of the pets again, and hurry back to work by one o'clock. *3*

Work is filing, typing, taking payments, balancing my money drawer, and putting my data on the computer as fast and efficiently as possible so I can exit quickly at 4:30 p.m. *4*

My first class in the evenings at college starts at 5:40, and I live 40 miles from campus, so my trip usually takes 45 to 50 minutes. By the time I find a parking place, I barely make it to class on time. Algebra class is over at 9:30. I then have a 45-minute drive home. *5*

Packing lunches for the next day, bathing and washing my hair, finding something to eat, and relaxing enough to go to sleep usually puts me in bed as late as 1:00 a.m. Most of the time I fall asleep immediately because I am so worn out. *6*

I knew attending college and working would be hard, but I did not realize it would be this exhausting. However, I feel that when I graduate it will have been worth the exhaustion to achieve at last a degree which I have always wanted. *7*

---

1. What is the thesis of "Exhaustion"?
2. When you finished the essay, did you feel there was enough detail to demonstrate the validity of the thesis? That is, is the thesis adequately developed in the body paragraphs? Explain.
3. What is the topic sentence for each body paragraph? Are all these topic sentences relevant to the thesis?
4. Which topic sentence receives the most development?
5. Which topic sentence receives the least development? How do you react to the paragraph with that topic sentence?
6. Do any paragraphs need additional supporting detail because the author is telling without showing?
7. Are any details not relevant to the appropriate topic sentence?

EXERCISE

Two Body Paragraphs to Write

1. Assume you are writing an essay using one of the following thesis statements.
   The best thing about ____________________ is ____________________ (you fill in the blanks).
   The worst thing about ____________________ is ____________________ (you fill in the blanks).

   Decide which thesis you will use, and prewrite until you discover two main ideas for developing that thesis. For example, if your thesis is, "The best thing about college life is meeting interesting people," you might describe the people you meet in class and the people you meet in your dorm. Or develop one paragraph about Chris, the guy you met from Zimbabwe, and another about Dr. Sorenson, the prof who got you interested in cellular biology. Develop each main point in a body paragraph. (You may want to prewrite a second time to discover supporting detail.) You will probably revise your paragraphs (maybe more than once) before you are satisfied with them.
2. Bring your completed body paragraphs and thesis to class and exchange them with a classmate. After reading each other's work, write a note to the person whose paragraphs you read, and in the note, answer the following questions.
   a. Are the topic sentences relevant? If not, what specifically is the problem?
   b. Are all the supporting details relevant? If not, what detail is not relevant? Why?
   c. Is the supporting detail adequate in each paragraph? If not, where is the detail needed? What kind of detail should it be?
   d. Is the order of details logical? If not, what is wrong?
3. When you get back your paragraphs, study your classmate's responses. Decide whether you agree with the evaluation. If not, discuss your disagreement with your instructor.

THE CONCLUSION

The conclusion of an essay is important because it influences your reader's final impression. Have you seen a movie that starts out strong and then fizzles at the end? As you walked out of the theater, you probably talked about the disappointing ending, not the strong beginning or middle. Writing works the same way. Even if it has a strong introduction and body, an essay with a weak conclusion will leave your reader feeling let down. For this reason, the same care that goes into your introduction and body should also go into your conclusion.

Consider for a moment the conclusion a student wrote for an essay with the thesis, "The way Mr. Wang communicated with students, challenged them, and spent his own time with them made him the teacher I respected most." The essay with this thesis had three body paragraphs, one on communicating with students, one on challenging students, and one on spending his own time with students. The conclusion read like this:

> Therefore, Mr. Wang is the teacher I most respected because of the way he communicated with students, the way he challenged them, and the way he spent his own free time helping them.

How do you react to this conclusion? Do you find it boring? Are you annoyed by the repetition of the thesis? Boredom and annoyance are valid reactions to this conclusion. Actually, the student's essay was well organized, with interesting detail, but the writer did not craft his conclusion carefully, so the reader comes away feeling disappointed.

Now react to a conclusion handled with more care. This conclusion was for an essay describing a night spent at the beach. Throughout the essay the writer likened the beach to a lover. Here is the conclusion:

> As the sun rose to signal the start of a new day, I walked away, not feeling at all tired but instead fulfilled. The beach had offered me all of her beauty, and the night we spent together would remain a pleasant memory always.

This second conclusion is more interesting than the first, so a reader will leave the second essay with a better reaction. The point to be drawn from all this is that, like first impressions, final reactions are significant.

Now look again at "All Creatures Great and Small" on page 30. Is the conclusion effective? Why?

Ways to Handle the Conclusion

The conclusion can be handled a variety of ways. Some of these are described below.

1. LEAVE THE READER WITH AN OVERALL REACTION

With this approach, the writer extracts from the major points of the essay some overriding impression, observation, or reaction to leave the reader with a final sense of how the writer feels about things. The conclusion of "Shame" on page 00 is an example of this approach.

2. SUMMARIZE THE MAIN POINTS OF THE ESSAY

For this approach, the writer recaps the major ideas in the essay. However, the writer should save a summary conclusion for those times when a brief review would help the reader. If you have written a relatively short essay with easily understood and easily remembered ideas, your reader does not need a summary and may grow annoyed at unnecessary repetition. On the other hand, if your essay has many ideas, some of which are complex, your reader will appreciate a summary at the end. For an example of a summary conclusion, see "Ban Those Traps" on page 000.

3. INTRODUCE A RELATED IDEA

An effective conclusion can include an idea not appearing elsewhere in the essay. For this approach to work, the idea must be clearly and closely related to the ideas that appear in the body, or the reader will be caught offguard by an idea that seems to spring out of nowhere. The conclusion of "Seniors in the Night," on page 171, is an example of introducing a related idea.

4. MAKE A DETERMINATION

Frequently, the ideas in the body lead to some significant point or determination. When this is the case, the final paragraph(s) can be used to state and explain that point. This approach appears in "Friends at Work" on page 265.

5. RESTATE THE THESIS OR ANOTHER PORTION OF THE INTRODUCTION

You can conclude an essay by repeating the thesis or another part of the introduction. However, when this approach is used at the wrong times, the effect is unsatisfactory. The conclusion you read on page 49 (about Mr. Wang) seems lazy; it is certainly dull. Yet this approach *can* succeed if you keep two things in mind. First, if you repeat the thesis or another part of the introduction, restate the idea using different language. That is, restate the idea in a new way. Second, the restatement is best used to achieve the dramatic effect that comes from repetition. For an example of restatement in a new way, read "Horse Sense" on page 214.

6. COMBINE APPROACHES

Your conclusion can combine two or more strategies. You can restate the thesis and then summarize. You can make a determination and then give an overall reaction. A related idea can appear with a restatement. Any combination of approaches is possible. The conclusion of "The Human and the Superhuman" on page 240, includes a new and related idea and makes a determination.

The length of the conclusion varies. Sometimes a single sentence serves very well. Other times you may need a paragraph of several sentences. For a long essay, a conclusion of more than one paragraph may be in order. Regardless, the function of a conclusion is to bring your writing to a satisfying finish. Effective writing does not screech to a halt but closes off neatly.

There is another note on the conclusion: avoid beginning this final paragraph with "In conclusion." This phrase has become a cliché that can annoy a reader.

Conclusions and the Writing Process

If you have trouble with your conclusion, try the following procedure.

1. Ask yourself these questions:
   a. Would my reader appreciate a summary or find it unnecessary?
   b. Would a restatement of the thesis provide emphasis or dramatic effect? Or would it seem lazy and boring?
   c. Can I close with an overall reaction?
   d. What ideas related to my thesis do not appear in my introduction or body? Would closing with any of these ideas help my reader appreciate the significance of my topic or advance my purpose?
   e. Can I draw any conclusions from the points in my body paragraphs to help fulfill my purpose or to help my reader appreciate my view?
2. The answers to the questions above can help you discover suitable approaches to your conclusion. If more than one approach appears possible, consider combining approaches or choose the one you like best or the one that seems the easiest to handle.
3. When the conclusion proves troublesome, keep it brief—perhaps only one sentence.

HOW THE STRUCTURE WORKS

Conclusions

1. Because final impressions significantly influence your reader's reaction, your conclusions must be carefully crafted.
2. The function of a conclusion is to bring your essay to a satisfying finish.
3. Possible approaches to the conclusion include
   a. Leaving the reader with an overall reaction
   b. Summarizing your main points if your essay is long or has complex ideas
   c. Introducing a related idea
   d. Making a determination from the ideas in your essay
   e. Restating the thesis or another part of the introduction in a new way for emphasis or dramatic effect
   f. Combining approaches
4. The length of the conclusion can vary.
5. Avoid beginning with "In conclusion."

EXERCISE

Three Conclusions to Evaluate

Read "The Old Ball Game," on page 327, "What It Means to Be a Friend," on page 282, and "Fishing Woes," on page 195. Answer the following questions about the conclusion of each of these essays.

1. Does the conclusion bring the essay to a satisfying close? Explain.
2. What approach is used for the conclusion? Is this approach effective? If not, explain why.
3. Is the length of the conclusion appropriate? If not, explain why.
4. Does the conclusion leave you with a positive final impression? If not, explain why.

GROUP EXERCISE

A Conclusion to Write

Below is a clever essay written by a student. The conclusion has been omitted, so with two classmates write your own. In class take turns reading your conclusions and note the variety of approaches. You will find it interesting to see how many different ways the conclusion can be handled.

Beware the Body Brigade

I honestly believe that if all the health fanatics were piled in one big heap, the mound would make Mount Everest look like an anthill. These joggers and protein-poppers seem to be banding together armed with sweatsuits and wheat germ to descend upon the junk food junkies and those chumps whose only exercise is climbing in and out of bed morning and night. The poor slovenly souls in the latter group struggle to defend themselves against the psychological tactics of what I call the "Body Brigade." Disguised as run-of-the-mill let's-get-a-pizza people, they are actually brainwashers. Take your Big Mac and run the other way if you come face-to-face with a Body Brigader. The breed works in potent ways. *1*

Take for instance the health food nut. The health food nut will weaken your resistance and convert you to a Body Brigade Believer by threatening you with immediate, self-inflicted death if you continue eating "whatever that awful stuff is you're feeding yourself." As you open your lunchbox, empty stomach growling, and begin to gobble your bologna sandwich, he or she will grab your arm, yank the sandwich from between your teeth, and proclaim, "You're *killing* yourself eating that junk. Don't you know they put *rat meat* in bologna?" Because you now believe that you will not rise from the lunch table upon consuming your rat bologna, the carrot sticks and plain, natural yogurt your patron Brigader offers you begin to look appetizing. Watch out, Burger Barn addict—you are beginning to weaken. *2*

If you ever hear a pair of sneaker-clad feet running up behind you—don't turn around. You are being chased by the jogger. The jogger will snare you by pounding into your head the "I used to look *like you* before . . ." line. A common conversation goes something like this: "You take the bus to work? And it's only 5 miles to your office? You have to be kidding." Mr. Addidas here believes that you *3* should run the "short 5-mile jaunt" each morning, despite the fact that walking just the two blocks from your doorstep to the bus stop leaves you gasping for air. The next line is "I used to look *like you*" (and the Brigader puckers up his face on the "like you") "before I started running each morning. I used to have a pot belly just like you do, and look at me now." You do look at the jogger—no gut. You look at yourself—big gut. Never worried before about your pot belly, now you feel as if you have an overblown beachball beneath your shirt. The self-disgust maneuver is working on you, and you begin to feel inferior to the Brigader.

AN ILLUSTRATION OF THE USEFUL PATTERN OF ORGANIZATION

At the beginning of this chapter, the student essay "All Creatures Great and Small" (page 30) illustrates the pattern of organization we have been discussing. The following essay is another example of the pattern, only this time the essay was written by a professional. The notes in the margin will help you study the pattern.

Types of Consumer Buying Behavior

William M. Pride and O. C. Ferrell

Paragraph 1 is the introduction. It provides background information. The thesis is the last sentence. It presents the topic as consumer decisions and the writer's view that they can be classified into three categories.

Consumers usually want to create and maintain a collection of products that satisfy their needs and wants in both the present and future. To achieve this objective, consumers make many purchasing decisions. For example, people must make several decisions daily regarding food, clothing, shelter, medical care, education, recreation, or transportation. As they make these decisions, they engage in different decision-making behaviors. The amount of effort, both mental and physical, that buyers expend in decision making varies considerably from situation to situation. Consumer decisions can thus be classified into one of three broad categories: routine response behavior, limited decision making, and extensive decision making.[1] *1*

Paragraph 2 is a body paragraph. Sentence 1 is the topic sentence, which notes the first aspect of the thesis under consideration (routine response behavior.) The rest of the paragraph is supporting details that explain routine response behavior. The supporting details include examples.

A consumer practices *routine response behavior* when buying frequently purchased, low-cost items that need very little search and decision effort. When buying such items, a consumer may prefer a particular brand, but he or she is familiar with several brands in the product class and views more than one as being acceptable. The products that are bought through routine response behavior are purchased almost automatically. Most *2*

1. John A. Howard and Jagdish N. Sheth, *The Theory of Buyer Behavior* (New York: Wiley, 1969), pp. 27–28.

buyers, for example, do not spend much time or mental effort selecting a soft drink or a snack food. If the nearest soft-drink machine does not offer Sprite, they will quite likely choose a 7-Up or Slice instead.

Paragraph 3 is a body paragraph. Sentence 1 is the topic sentence, which notes the second aspect of the thesis to be discussed (limited decision making). The supporting details include examples.

Buyers engage in *limited decision making* when they buy products occasionally and when they need to obtain information about an unfamiliar brand in a familiar product category. This type of decision making requires a moderate amount of time for information gathering and deliberation. For example, if Procter & Gamble introduces an improved Tide laundry detergent, buyers will seek additional information about the new product, perhaps by asking a friend who has used the product or watching a commercial, before they make a trial purchase. 3

Paragraph 4 is a body paragraph. Sentence 1 is the topic sentence. It notes the third aspect of the thesis to be discussed (extensive decision making). The rest of the paragraph is supporting details to develop the topic sentence. The words "the most complex decision-making behavior" suggest a progressive order. The supporting detail is one sentence. Is that adequate?

The most complex decision-making behavior, *extensive decision making,* comes into play when a purchase involves unfamiliar, expensive, or infrequently bought products—for instance, cars, homes, or an education in a college or university. The buyer uses many criteria to evaluate alternative brands or choices and spends much time seeking information and deciding on the purchase. 4

Paragraph 5 is a body paragraph. The first sentence is the topic sentence, which presents the next aspect of the thesis under consideration (impulse buying). The rest of the paragraph is supporting details.

By contrast, *impulse buying* involves no conscious planning but rather a powerful, persistent urge to buy something immediately. For some individuals, impulse buying may be the dominant buying behavior. Impulse buying, however, often provokes emotional conflicts. For example, a man may want to have the new golf bag he just saw right away and so purchases it on the spot, but he also feels guilty because he knows his budget is limited that month. 5

Paragraph 6 is the conclusion. It ties off the essay with a related idea.

The purchase of a particular product does not always elicit the same type of decision-making behavior. In some instances, we engage in extensive decision making the first time we buy a certain kind of product but find that limited decision making suffices when we buy the product again. If a routinely purchased, formerly satisfying brand no longer pleases us, we may use limited or extensive decision processes to switch to a new brand. For example, if we notice that the gasoline brand we normally buy is making our automobile's engine knock, we may seek out a higher octane brand through limited or extensive decision making. 6

ADAPTING THE PATTERN

The pattern of organization described in this chapter works well in a variety of situations. However, you can also adapt the pattern to suit any piece you are working on. Below is a chart of common adaptations.

HOW THE STRUCTURE WORKS

Adapting the Useful Pattern

I. Introduction
   A. Sometimes there is no separate introduction; instead the essay begins with the writer's first main point.
      1. When there is no separate introduction, the thesis can be strongly implied in the rest of the essay or stated in the conclusion.
      2. Narrative essays (ones that tell stories) often begin with the first chronological event rather than a formal introduction.
   B. The thesis can be more than one sentence in the introduction.
   C. The thesis can be at the beginning or middle of the introduction rather than at the end.
   D. Sometimes the first paragraph begins with the thesis, and after the thesis the writer begins development of the first main point. This development forms the remainder of paragraph 1.

II. The Body
   A. Sometimes a body paragraph does not have a stated topic sentence. Instead, the aspect of the thesis under discussion is strongly implied.
   B. A stated topic sentence can appear in the middle or at the end of a body paragraph.
   C. A single aspect of the thesis can be discussed in two or more body paragraphs.
   D. Two closely related aspects of the thesis can be treated in the same body paragraph.

III. The Conclusion
   A. Sometimes there is no separate concluding paragraph.
      1. This can be the case when the discussion in the last body paragraph provides sufficient closure.
      2. This can also happen when a concluding sentence forms the last sentence of the last body paragraph.
   B. When there is no stated thesis in paragraph 1, the thesis can appear in the conclusion.
   C. The concluding paragraph can include the last (and frequently the most significant) point to develop the thesis.

ADAPTING THE PATTERN: ILLUSTRATIONS

To appreciate some of the ways writers can vary the pattern of organization described in this chapter, read the following three student essays. Notes in the margin call your attention to the adaptations.

Look Out, Here She Comes

Introduction has no specifically stated thesis that reveals the topic. Instead, it is implied that the essay is about Nora Tompkins in Valu King.

Every morning at 8:30 a.m., there enters a short, overweight, middle-aged woman through the front doors of the Valu King where I am employed, even though we do not officially open for business until 9:00. This lady is always dressed in the same out-of-style, dirty-looking outfit. Her hideous legs are so fat they are fortunate to be supported by a pair of old, black, high-heeled pump shoes. Her gray hair is unsuccessfully dyed with red. From her appearance you would assume that she can't afford new clothes or health and beauty care. The lady is Nora Tompkins. *1*

Nora starts every day off by browsing through the produce section, searching for discolored, old, or bruised fruits and vegetables. Once she has discovered some items, she asks us if she can have them reduced. Sometimes she practically begs us to mark the price down for her. If we do not mark the produce down enough to suit her, Nora throws the items back in the display and wheels her cart away in a huff. *2*

As Nora exits the produce section and enters my dairy department, she slowly grabs a few of my sale items, looking at them to see if they are her idea of real bargains. If she notices some milk products are reduced, she will usually buy all of them, even though the expiration date is near. *3*

The day-old bakery items are her favorites. Upon arriving at the day-old rack, she starts glancing over it for bargains. Most of the time, she fills her cart with these reduced items. But first she demands they be reduced even more. I have seen her stand there and argue about the price with the bakery women. She has even taken a swing at one of them for not reducing the day-old pastries more. *4*

There are only two things she looks at in the grocery department: generic products and sale items. These are the only items she will buy, and she usually does not want just one or two of each of these products. She usually asks us if she can buy a full case, regardless of what our ad says is the limited purchase on these items. *5*

Topic sentence of body paragraph is implied: Nora behaves just as badly in the meat department.

Inexpensive fresh cuts of meat are all she buys out of the meat cases. She picks up a piece of meat that she might want and inspects it better than a health inspector. The meat cutters have found meat packages with holes in them because of Nora's finger inspection. She even has enough nerve to ask the meat cutters to trim off minute pieces of fat for her. Other times she has asked them to cut one thick piece of beef into two thin pieces of meat for her. *6*

Over time, everyone in the store, including the cashiers, has come to hate Nora. Now most of the employees avoid her by staying in the back room or slipping into an aisle she has already passed. She wants to be friends with everyone so that she can save a penny, but no one even says hello to her anymore. More than once Nora has asked cashiers not to charge her for some of the food, but they do anyway. It's not a matter of honesty. They really hate the woman. *7*

Rather than a standard conclusion, final paragraph presents the last (and perhaps main) point of the essay.

We are all relieved when Nora leaves. When she finally does go, she takes all of this discount food to her $150,000 home in a suburban development. Then, after she cleans, cooks, or repacks most of the food, she drives out to a roadside stand, sells these lower-priced items to people at a higher price, and pockets the profit. 8

The Ball Game

Essay has a two-paragraph introduction that provides background information. There is no stated thesis.

It was midsummer and the Little League baseball playoffs had begun. Many teams from the area participated in them, including the one I coached. My team was made up of 9- and 10-year-olds, all relatively the same size and build, with one exception. Jimmy was much smaller and had much less athletic ability than the others. Still, he was very excited about the playoffs. Jimmy's father was also worked up over the playoffs, maybe too worked up. 1

When my team went on the field for the pregame warmups, it was easy to pick Jimmy out of the crowd. His uniform was much too big. He was always tripping over his long pants or pulling his sleeves up to throw the ball. His cap was continuously falling over his eyes, blocking his vision. Still, Jimmy was as proud and happy to be a part of that team as the next boy. He never complained about anything; he just went along with what was asked of him. 2

It was in the third inning of our first game that I sent Jimmy in to bat. He was so excited when I told him that he ran out on the field without the bat. But when he came back to get it, I reminded him to calm down and take his time. His first swing at the ball brought a solid single; it was his first hit all year. The big, gleaming smile on Jimmy's face showed how proud he was. But his father, who was watching the game from the side of the dugout, stood still. He neither clapped nor smiled. The look on his face seemed to say, "Is that all?" 3

Jimmy's second at-bat was not at all good. He struck out in three straight pitches. As he slowly turned around to make that lonely walk back to the dugout, I could see the disappointment all over his face. I went out to meet Jimmy and started to console him, when suddenly I was pushed from behind and knocked several feet away from him. It was Jimmy's dad who pushed me. It was also Jimmy's dad who was yelling and screaming at Jimmy in front of everyone in the ball park. Everyone tried to ignore the scene Jimmy's dad was making. The players in the dugout began to talk to each other, coaches looked at the roster sheets, fans stared up at the sky, and Jimmy just looked down at the ground, crying ever so slightly so no one would notice. 4

Body paragraph 5 has no stated topic sentence.

After several minutes, which seemed more like hours, Jimmy's dad finally walked off the field and left the park. Jimmy walked slowly 5 back to the dugout and sat on the end of the bench for the rest of the game. He stared blankly into the ground, not once looking up, as big round tears rolled slowly down his embarrassed cheeks.

Conclusion, paragraph 6, presents thesis idea: that a few minutes of yelling caused Jimmy to lose pride and confidence. A larger thesis is implied by the essay: Little League parents can do more harm than good.

We lost the playoff game that day, but no one seemed to mind that much. We all realized that Jimmy had lost something more important, something it would not be easy to get back. In just a few minutes of cruel and thoughtless yelling, the little bit of pride and confidence that Jimmy had gained was lost. 6

The Stranger from My Past

There is no separate introduction; the essay begins with the first event in the narration.

Would time never pass? The taunting chimes of the grandfather clock filled the room, and my eyes were drawn by its magnetic powers. I had been unable to keep from watching the hands slowly move around its face. Time had not moved so slowly in the past. I could no longer stand the loud ticking of the clock, so I stepped out through the door to await the arrival of my guest. 1

The body paragraphs do not have topic sentences; the time sequence of the narration provides structure and focus for the details.

The sun felt warm and soothing. My eyes squinted against the brightness of the afternoon, and as they slowly focused, I scoured the long gravel drive. Vague, shadowy images flickered in and out of my mind. What would he be like today? Was it age that put pressure on us to reunite, to bring our lives together once again? Why had we waited so long? 2

My mind traveled back over the years. I was walking to school. My head was bent to hide the tears hanging on my lashes. I felt frightened and alone. Then a hand lightly touched my shoulder, but I was afraid to look. I did not want a classmate to see the tears. I turned slowly and looked up into caring brown eyes of an unexpected friend. I tried to speak. He stopped me with a gentle smile of understanding. We continued to walk together, his gentle strength filling me with love and security. 3

The love we shared grew over the years. I marveled at the accomplishments he made in life. He became a man who would walk in places other men only dream of. Yet he remained the compassionate young man that had taken time to calm a little girl's fears. Nature etched and polished his qualities into a fine edge. Through the years his achievements led him down a different path, and my friend moved so far away. Suddenly a flash of light, reflecting off a car, snapped me back from the past. 4

The quiet hum of a car motor and crunching of tires on gravel filled my ears. My legs trembled as I approached the car. I saw his silhouette through the bright windshield. At last the motor was quiet, and the sound of the car door opening filled the air. As the car door swung slowly out, the man stood to reveal himself. Was this stranger my friend of long ago? 5

There is no separate conclusion; the last event of the story provides adequate closure.

My eyes took in every detail of the distinguished gray-haired man. He looked so different. I tried to conjure up those shadowy images to compare to this stranger. As I hesitated, he reached out and embraced me with loving arms. I still had doubts and did not respond. He stepped back holding my shoulders at arm's length. He looked at me with misty eyes and said, "Sis, do you not know your own brother?" Tears rushed forth as shadowy images of the past merged with the man before me. 6

WRITING ASSIGNMENT

You have read about how writers can generate and organize their ideas. Now it is time to try your hand at writing an essay. The broad subject for this essay is how you feel about writing and/or taking a writing course and why you feel as you do.

Your audience for this essay is your writing instructor, a person who is interested in your thoughts and feelings about this subject. The purpose of your writing is to communicate honestly and accurately the attitude you are bringing to your writing course in order to help your instructor better understand your feelings about your work.

Before you begin, review the following suggestions. You may want to try some of them, although you are not obligated to do so.

1. To generate ideas, consider your past experiences with writing and writing classes, whether you have enjoyed writing in the past, how successful your past writing has been, the kinds of writing you do and do not enjoy, what you hope to learn this term, what you see as your strengths and weaknesses, whether you are glad to be in a writing course, what you perceive as the purpose of your writing class, how good your previous writing instruction has been, what you think your chances of doing well are, and so on.
2. If you have trouble generating ideas for support, use some of the prewriting techniques described in Chapter 1.
3. Once you feel you have enough ideas to bring to a draft (and different writers will vary in their needs here), number your ideas in the order you wish to handle them.
4. Write your first draft, but let it be a rough one. Just get your ideas down the best way you can without worrying over anything. Try to go from start to finish in one sitting. If you have trouble getting started, skip your introduction and return to it after everything else is drafted.
5. After writing your draft, compare it against the charts on p. 39, p. 45, p. 51, and p. 55. Make any changes in your draft that you deem necessary after looking at these charts.

6. Type your reworked draft and ask two of your classmates to read it. Have your readers respond in writing to the following questions:
   a. Does the introduction hold your interest? If not, why?
   b. Is there a stated or strongly implied thesis? What is it?
   c. Are all generalizations adequately supported? If not, where is more detail needed?
   d. Are there any relevance problems? If so, what are they?
   e. Is there any detail not appropriate to the audience or purpose?
   f. Are there enough points to develop the thesis adequately?
   g. Is there anything you do not understand? If so, what?
   h. Does the conclusion leave you with a positive final impression? If not, what problems exist?
   i. What are the chief strengths of the draft?
7. Rework your draft, taking into consideration the reactions of your readers. If you question the validity of a reader response, ask for your instructor's opinion.
8. Check your essay slowly and carefully for spelling, punctuation, and grammar errors.
9. Type or copy your essay into its final form and then check it carefully for typing or transcription errors.

CHAPTER 3

From Ideas to Essay

Ask 20 successful writers what they do when they write, and you could get 20 different answers. This is because different people approach their writing in different ways. Ask one successful writer what happened when he or she wrote 20 different pieces, and once again you could get 20 different answers. This is because the same person does not always do the same things. Thus, we can make two important points about the writing process. First, there is no *one* process, and each varying approach can work well. Second, the same person does not always use the same procedures—an individual may change the process for a number of valid reasons.

Now what if I told you it is possible to identify steps in the writing process? "Ah," you might say, "this is not as tricky as I was starting to think. I just learn the steps and perform them in order, right?" Actually not. You see, the nature of the writing process is such that writers often find themselves stepping back before going forward. Let's say, for example, you have shaped a topic and generated ideas that please you, so you begin to consider ways to arrange your ideas. But while you are arranging, you discover a relationship between your ideas that had not occurred to you before. This discovery prompts you to go back and shape your topic a bit differently. You have stepped back before going forward, which illustrates that the writing process is not linear (advancing in a straight line through the steps) but **recursive** (advancing with some doubling back and more advancing—perhaps in a new direction).

What, then, can we say for sure about the writing process? Three things, actually, and they appear in the following chart.

HOW THE PROCESS WORKS

Safe Generalizations

1. The procedures writers follow vary from person to person.
2. The same person might use different procedures for different writing tasks.
3. The writing process is recursive rather than linear.

IMPROVING YOUR WRITING PROCESS

One goal of this text is to help you discover writing procedures that work for you. If you can learn what to do and when to do it, then your writing is bound to improve. A second goal of this text is to help you write efficiently, in ways that bring good results with a minimum of wheel spinning. To learn to write effectively *and* efficiently, you will be working toward discovering your own productive writing process.

You may be wondering how to discover which procedures work best for you, when the writing process varies from writer to writer. The answer lies in experimentation. This text describes a variety of ways to handle each aspect of writing. To discover your own effective, efficient writing process, you should sample several of the different techniques described. Afterwards, evaluate the success of what you sampled and make a decision about whether to retain a procedure because it worked well or try something else. If you experiment and evaluate in this fashion throughout the term, you will improve your writing process—and hence your writing.

Before discussing the writing process any further, you should identify what you currently do when you write by answering the following questionnaire.

A Writing Process Questionnaire

Answer the following questions as completely as possible.

1. How do you get ideas to include in your writing?
2. How do you establish your audience and purpose?
3. How do you decide what order your ideas should appear in? When do you decide this? Do you outline?
4. Do you typically write more than one draft? If so, how many?
5. How do you decide what changes to make in your drafts? At what point do you decide this?
6. Do you ask other people to read your work before you submit it? If so, who?
7. What do you do when you get stuck?
8. Under what circumstances do you produce your best work (in a quiet room, at night, a week before deadline, with a special pen, etc.)?
9. Do you write a piece all in one sitting or do you leave your work and come back to it? If you do the latter, when do you leave and when do you return?

Your answers to the questions above will tell you what you currently do when you write. However, you should also identify how successful your current process is by answering these questions.

1. Which features of your process (generating ideas, organizing, drafting, making changes) produce satisfactory results in a reasonable amount of time?
2. Which features of your process take too long or fail to produce satisfactory results?

Your response to question 2 indicates aspects of your process to improve. Keep a list of these aspects (perhaps in your journal), and the next time you write, try techniques described throughout this text to handle these aspects (consult the index to find the techniques under the following headings: Topic selection, Idea generation, Audience, Purpose, Outlining, First draft, Revising, Editing, Proofreading). After trying a new technique, evaluate its effectiveness, determine whether you need to experiment further, and choose the next technique you will try. (Again, you can do this in your journal.)

SIX AREAS OF THE WRITING PROCESS

Even though writers do different things when they write, most successful writers turn their attention to these six areas.

1. Generating ideas, establishing purpose, and identifying audience
2. Ordering ideas
3. Writing the first draft
4. Revising
5. Editing
6. Proofreading

Since we know that successful writers deal with these six areas, you may be wondering why there is so much variance among the writing processes of different writers. The explanation is that although successful writers attend to these six areas, they vary in the way they handle each area. Furthermore, they attend to these areas in different orders, and sometimes they attend to two areas at once. This variety is what explains the different approaches to writing.

Your efforts to discover the process that works best for you will involve you in understanding each of the six areas, becoming aware of the various approaches to handling each of the areas, and experimenting to learn which of the approaches works for you. Then you will have discovered your *own* effective, efficient process.

Now look again at the list of six areas, but this time let's group the areas to shed more light on the writing process.

WRITER-BASED	Prewriting	1. Generating ideas, establishing purpose, and identifying audience 2. Ordering ideas
	Writing	3. Writing the first draft
READER-BASED	Rewriting	4. Revising 5. Editing 6. Proofreading

The diagram above illustrates that the six areas in the process can be divided into two groups: *writer-based activities* and *reader-based activities*. In other words, as writers move from idea to finished piece, they first concentrate on what *they want* for their writing and then move to what their *readers need* in their writing. Of course, during writer-based activities the reader is still considered, just as the writer's orientation is a concern during reader-based activities. The division really represents the *primary* focus of each of the six areas of the process.

The chart also shows that the six areas can be grouped into three categories: **prewriting** (activities performed prior to writing the first draft), **writing** (writing the first draft), and **rewriting** (making changes in the first draft to get the piece ready for a reader). Prewriting and writing are primarily writer-based activities, while rewriting is primarily reader-based.

As you study the chart, remember the recursive nature of the writing process: you may not always move sequentially through the areas; instead your work in one area may prompt you to step back and make changes in an area handled earlier, and these changes will affect what you do when you go forward again.

This pretty much ends the safe generalizations about the writing process. Any further discussion gets us into the ways writers can deal with the six areas, and this is precisely what we will turn to next. As you read about these six areas and the ways they can be handled, do so with an eye toward techniques to try as you experiment to develop your own effective, efficient writing process.

Generating Ideas, Establishing Purpose, and Identifying Audience (Writer-Based/Prewriting)

As you recall from Chapter 1, the earliest stage of the writing process involves shaping a topic and generating support for that topic. To help you do these, several idea-generation techniques were described. As you work to develop your writing process, try several of these techniques to discover which are the most productive for you.

Generating ideas is a time of discovery, a time to learn what is at the front of the brain and what is lurking further back in the recesses. It is a time for shaking loose ideas to discover what you can and want to say. Obviously, then, idea generation is a highly writer-based activity because the focus is on discovering what the *writer* wants to say.

Yet this time before writing the first draft is not solely writer-oriented, for the writer must also consider who the reader will be and determine his or her needs. The nature of the writer's audience will significantly influence idea generation. For a review of how to establish and assess audience and a review of how audience affects detail, see the discussion beginning on page 25. Also, Part 2 describes specific techniques for establishing and assessing audience.

In addition to being affected by audience, idea generation is influenced by the writer's purpose. As you know from Chapter 1, a writer must decide the reason for his or her writing. Let's say you are discussing the writing program at your school. What is your purpose? Do you want to describe the program? Explain your experience in the program? Convince the reader that changes should occur in the program? Compare the program to another one? Do you want to share with the reader, inform the reader, or persuade the reader? Answering questions like these will help you discover your purpose, and your purpose, in turn, can affect the ideas you generate. Since you as the writer settle on the purpose you want, this is another writer-oriented activity. However, you may decide on your purpose with the reader in mind, which makes this a partially reader-based activity—as when you decide not to describe the program because your reader knows what it is like and choose instead to explain your experience so your reader can understand how the program affects students. For a review of purpose, see the discussion beginning on page 24. In addition, Part 2 describes specific techniques for establishing purpose.

Considering the Process

The following points identify some of the ways writers vary in their approaches to generating ideas, identifying audience, and establishing purpose. As you read, consider your own techniques to determine what, if anything, you might handle in a better way.

1. Writers vary in the number of ideas they must generate before they are comfortable moving on. Some writers determine main points without generating ideas for developing those main points. Other writers need to generate as many ideas as possible to develop their main points.
2. As a general rule, the more planning (prewriting) done prior to the first draft, the less reworking the draft will require. Some writers do better by putting more effort into prewriting, which usually means less revision, while others do better by putting less effort into prewriting and more into revising.
3. Some writers identify their audience and purpose when they shape their topic, while others do this in a separate step before or after idea genera-

tion. Some writers do not finalize their audience and purpose until they write their first draft.

4. Because the writing process is recursive, idea generation can prompt a change in topic, audience identification can necessitate additional idea generation, establishing a purpose can lead to selecting a different audience, and so on. In short, any one decision can mean a change in one or more aspects of topic, detail, audience, and purpose.
5. If you are not sure how to approach the first area of the writing process, try this sequence:

   a. Shape your topic.
   b. Establish purpose and identify audience (reshape topic if necessary after this).
   c. Generate enough ideas for your main points (alter topic, purpose, and/or audience if necessary after this).

ESSAY IN PROGRESS

Generating Ideas, Establishing Audience, and Determining Purpose

Directions: After completing this exercise, save your responses. They will be used later in this chapter as you work toward a completed essay.

1. Assume you have won a writer's contest. As first-prize winner, you may write a four-page, typed article that will be published in the magazine of your choice. You may write on any topic. What topic will you write about? (Remember to use the idea-generation techniques described in Chapter 1 if you have trouble shaping a topic.)
2. For what purpose will you write this article? (If necessary, determine your purpose by answering the questions on page 24.)
3. What magazine will you publish your article in?
4. What are the typical readers of this magazine like? (If necessary, answer the audience-assessment questions on page 25.)
5. Generate as many ideas as you can to include in this article. Try using at least two of the idea-generation techniques described in Chapter 1.
6. Study the ideas you have generated. Do they suggest you should alter your audience (magazine choice) or purpose in any way? If so, do that now.

Ordering Ideas (Writer-Based/Prewriting)

Ordering ideas is a writer-based activity because writers decide in what order *they* want to present their ideas. At the same time, however, deciding on order is partly reader-based because writers must find an arrangement that will help the reader appreciate the sequence of ideas and how they relate to each other.

The patterns of development you settle on often determine how you order your ideas. (See page 44 for a discussion of ways to order ideas.) If, for example, you use narration, then chronological order is suggested. If you describe, spatial order may be indicated. At other times, though, you will have to consider carefully to determine the most effective arrangement of details. (Part 2 gives additional information on ordering ideas.)

Outlining

Many student writers resist outlining because they see it as time-consuming, difficult, and somehow unnecessary. Yet outlining does not deserve this reputation. Because it helps writers organize their ideas before drafting, outlining can help ensure the success of an essay. Furthermore, any time and effort put into the outline is worthwhile because outlining makes drafting easier. You see, if you do not order and group your ideas prior to drafting with some kind of outline, you will have to order and group your ideas as you draft, which complicates the drafting process, causing writers to start over frequently and become frustrated as a result.

Outlines can be detailed or sketchy, formal or informal. The kind of outline you use will often be determined by your writing. Long, complex pieces often call for formal, detailed outlines, while briefer pieces can be planned with less detailed, informal outlines.

The detail you include in your outline—whether it be everything that will appear in your first draft or just the main points—will come from your prewriting ideas. However, since outlining stimulates thought, new ideas may occur to you. If so, include these ideas in your outline. Similarly, outlining may lead you to reject some of your prewriting ideas, and that is fine too. In other words, outlining does not mark the end of idea generation.

THE FORMAL OUTLINE

The formal outline, which is the most detailed, structured outline, allows writers to plot all their main points and major supporting details. This is the outline that uses roman numerals, letters, and arabic numbers. Main ideas that will serve as topic sentence ideas are designated with roman numerals; supporting details to develop a main idea are designated with capital letters; points to further develop supporting details are designated with arabic numbers. The format looks like some variation of this.

Thesis

I. Main idea
   A. Supporting detail
   B. Supporting detail
   C. Supporting detail

II. Main idea
  A. Supporting detail
    1. Further development
    2. Further development
  B. Supporting detail

Here is an example of a formal outline written for an essay about the attitudes of children toward food.

```
Thesis: Children can be taught to have healthy attitudes about
food.

  I. Parents should stress health and fitness.
     A. Teach nutrition.
     B. Serve healthy foods.
     C. Exercise with children.
     D. Set an example.
 II. Parents should make mealtimes pleasant.
     A. Keep conversation enjoyable.
        1. Avoid discussing problems.
        2. Avoid arguments about food.
     B. Serve balanced meals and let children choose
        quantities.
     C. Avoid eating in front of television.
III. Parents should not forbid children to eat certain foods.
     A. Children will want what they cannot have.
     B. Reasonable amounts of sugar and fat are not harmful.
 IV. Parents should praise children for their behavior, not
     their appearance.
     A. Children should take pride in what they do, not how
        thin they are.
     B. Those with a tendency toward carrying more weight need
        to like themselves.
```

NOTE: Sometimes a topic outline, rather than a sentence outline, works well. An outline for an essay on the causes of eating disorders could have a topic outline that looks like this in part.

```
I. Poor self-image
   A. Caused by media emphasis on thinness
   B. Caused by self-hatred
```

If you have trouble completing your outline, you may need to go back to prewriting to generate additional ideas. Once your formal outline is complete, however, you can check it to be sure your details are adequate, relevant, and in a logical order.

OUTLINE CARDS—METHOD I

Outline cards have many of the advantages of the formal outline, but they often simplify matters because the writer does not have to be concerned about roman numerals, letters, and numbers.

To outline using cards, you need several large index cards (or you can use sheets of paper). Use one card to plan your introduction, one separate card for each body paragraph, and one card for your conclusion. Each card will plot a separate section of your essay. On your introduction card, list the details you will include to arouse your reader's interest along with a preliminary version of your thesis. On each body-paragraph card, write a preliminary topic sentence along with a list of the points that will develop the topic sentence. On your conclusion card, list the details you will use to bring your essay to a satisfying close. On each of your cards you can list your details in the order they will appear in your first draft or not, as you prefer.

One advantage of cards is flexibility. A writer can easily shuffle body-paragraph cards into different sequences to examine alternative arrangements. Also, it is easier to rework parts of the outline when cards are used. A writer can throw out one or two cards and redo just those without having to rewrite the entire outline.

OUTLINE CARDS—METHOD II

An interesting form of outlining was shown to me by one of my students. She would take every idea she generated, whether a main point or a subpoint, and place it by itself on an index card. If she had 12 ideas, then she had 12 cards. Next she would examine each card and place it in a pile. A card with an idea related to something on another card would go in the same pile as that card. If she encountered a card that could go in more than one pile, she made the appropriate number of duplicate cards and placed them in the appropriate piles. After all her cards were sorted, she decided which pile to handle first, second, and so on. Then she studied the cards in the first pile to be handled and arranged them in the order she wanted the ideas to appear. This she did for each pile of cards. When an idea appeared in more than one pile, she decided which card to eliminate from which pile. Finally, she stacked her cards and wrote her draft from them. If she discovered her organization was not working, she would rearrange the order of her cards and try again.

OUTLINE WORKSHEET

The outline worksheet, like outline cards, allows writers to plot organization in as great or as little detail as they require. Also like outline cards, the worksheet does not make use of roman numerals, letters, and numbers. While it is not as easy to rework parts of the outline when the worksheet is used (this is the advantage of cards), it is easy to get a clear overview of your organization (this is one advantage of the formal outline).

The next page shows a sample outline worksheet. To use it, fill in the blanks with the amount of detail that works for you.

Sample Outline Worksheet

Introduction

Detail to generate reader interest ______________________________

____

____

Preliminary thesis ____

____

Body Paragraph

Preliminary topic sentence ______________________________________

____

Support ____

____

____

Body Paragraph

Preliminary topic sentence ______________________________________

____

Support ____

____

____

(NOTE: The number of body paragraph sections will correspond to the number of body paragraphs planned for the first draft.)

Conclusion

Detail to provide closure ____

____

____

THE OUTLINE TREE

An outline tree helps writers see the relationships among ideas. It also helps writers determine where more ideas are needed. The following example uses ideas discovered in the clustering on page 19.

To develop an outline tree, first write the central idea (this will be shaped into a thesis in the draft). Then place the first branches of the tree, using the ideas that can be main points or topic sentence ideas.

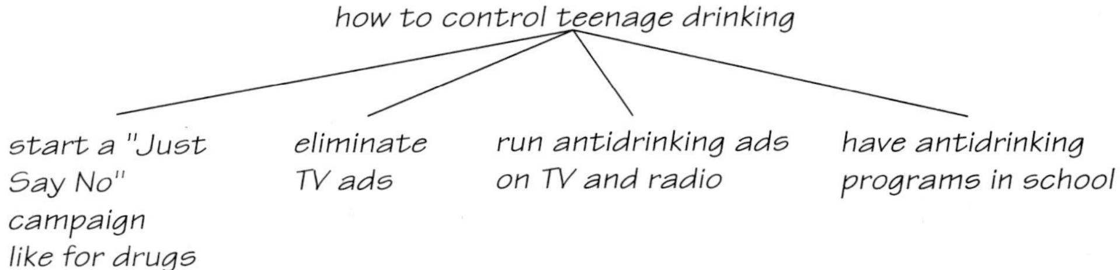

NOTE: Each of the first branches will be the focus of one or more body paragraphs.

Next, build the tree by adding additional branches.

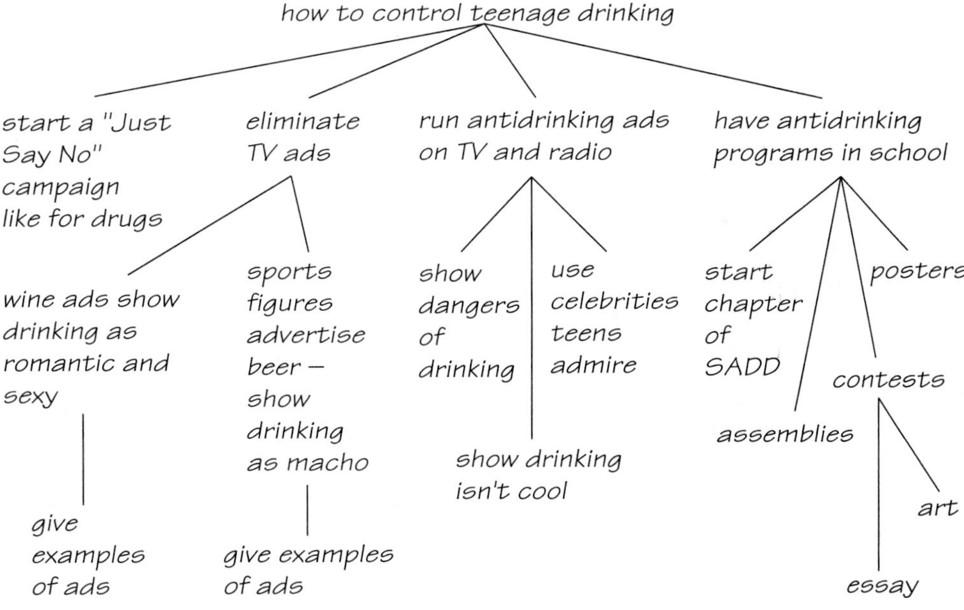

NOTE: The branches after the first level represent supporting detail to develop main points. You can study your outline tree to determine where detail is needed. For example, studying the above outline tree reveals that supporting details are needed to develop the main point that a "Just Say No" campaign could be started. If detail cannot be developed for this point, it should be eliminated or combined with "antidrinking programs in school." Further study of the outline tree shows that examples of wine ads and sports figures must be generated.

THE INFORMAL OUTLINE

The informal outline, sometimes called a scratch outline, is for writers who prefer to come to the first draft knowing only the main points that will be made and the order they will be made in. The informal outline does not usually include much of the detail that will develop main points, so writers who use it must have in mind how their ideas will be supported, or they must be capable of developing supporting ideas as they write the draft. Here is an informal outline that could have been put together by the student who wrote "All Creatures Great and Small" on page 30.

Bleacher creature is vile. (thesis)
Appearance is disgusting (describe hair, clothes, and makeup).
Bleacher creature swears a lot.
Bleacher creature is inconsiderate (give examples).
Bleacher creature gets thrown out of house (conclusion).

Notice that the outline suggests a thesis, major points to develop the thesis, and an approach to the conclusion. Nothing indicates how the reader's interest will be aroused, what development will be given the major points, where paragraphs begin and end, and specifically what will appear in the conclusion. For some writers, such an outline is not very helpful because too little is brought to the first draft. For others this is the preferred approach. These writers find a more detailed, structured outline constraining. They do better when less is determined prior to the first draft, and they can "create" as they go along.

Considering the Process

As you experiment and make decisions about your writing process, consider the following points about ordering ideas.

1. Writers vary in the amount of organizing they like to do before the first draft. Some writers require detailed outlines that amount to a blueprint of the essay, while others do better with only a rough sketch. Other writers prefer not to outline at all, feeling it stifles their creativity. These writers order their ideas the best way they can when they draft and then adjust their organization afterward as necessary.
2. Some writers like to write a formal outline after they have written their first draft to be sure everything has a logical placement. They do this

when they did not write an outline earlier, when they have deviated from their original outline, or when their original outline was sketchy or informal.

3. In general, the more detailed the outline, the more quickly the first draft goes and the less revision the draft requires.
4. During outlining writers often think of new ideas or make discoveries that cause them to step back and alter their topic, audience, purpose, ideas for support, or plan for organization.
5. You may have to revise your outline several times before you are ready to draft.

Composing at the Computer

If you compose at the computer or word processor, the following techniques may prove particularly helpful when you outline.

If you listed ideas for developing your topic, you can turn that list into a scratch outline. First, study the list to determine if you want to add or eliminate any ideas. Use your delete key to eliminate ideas, and then add any new ideas that occur to you. Using the copy-move command, you can then arrange your ideas in the order you want to treat them in your first draft.

If you like to outline your draft after it is written to check the order of ideas, try this. Create a second copy of your draft by renaming the file with an "out" extension (for "outline"). For example, a file named "essay" would be renamed "essay.out." Now go through that second file and identify the sentence in each paragraph that states the main idea and the sentences that give the major supporting details. Then delete everything else in the paragraph. Next, identify your thesis and move it to the top of the page. Now, using roman and arabic numbers and capital and lowercase letters, form the thesis and sentences into a formal outline. Study this outline to determine if any adjustments should be made in your draft.

ESSAY IN PROGRESS

Ordering Ideas

Directions: When you complete this exercise, save your responses. They will be used later in this chapter as you work toward a completed essay.

1. Select the outlining technique that most appeals to you and outline the ideas you generated when you completed the exercise on page 66.
2. Now select a different outlining technique and outline your ideas a second time.
3. Do you like one of the outlining techniques better than another? If so, which one and why? Do you think still another technique might work even better?

4. Do you think the outlining you did will help ensure a well-organized essay, or would you prefer to skip outlining and go on to drafting? Explain.
5. As a result of outlining, do you feel the need to return to an earlier stage of the process to alter topic, audience, or purpose or to generate ideas? If so, do that now.

Writing the First Draft (Writer-Based/Writing)

Regardless of your approach to prewriting, when your planning is complete, you are ready to write a first draft. Although drafting moves you out of prewriting and into writing, this activity is still writer-based because your focus is less on getting your writing ready for a reader than on expressing your ideas the best way you can at the time.

A first draft, commonly known as a **rough draft**, is an early effort to transform the prewriting ideas and outline into an essay, without worrying about grammar, usage, spelling, and such. This early effort is tentative, subject to changes of every kind. It can be loaded with errors and rough spots, but still it forms a base—material to shape and alter until the desired product is reached. By the time the final product *is* reached, so many changes may have occurred that it can bear little resemblance to the original draft.

Writers who work from highly detailed, formal outlines may have to do little idea generation and organizing while writing the first draft. However, the less detailed and structured the outline, the more ideas writers will have to develop while drafting and the more organizing they will become involved in.

When you write your draft, you may get stuck. That is common. Simply skip the troublesome section and go on, leaving space for the omitted part to be added later. Many writers use this strategy for their introductions. If you cannot get started, begin with body paragraphs and return to the introduction later. If you have an idea about how you want to approach a difficult part but you cannot get the words down, make a note in the margin to remind yourself later of what you had in mind. Also, if you cannot find the right word, leave a blank or use an alternative and underline it for later revision.

Skipping troublesome sections prevents you from becoming bogged down at any one point and slowing your progress. Also, if you skip a troublesome part, you may find when you return to it that somehow the words you needed surfaced while you were working on other parts of the essay.

Considering the Process

In addition to what you have already read about the first draft, the following points should be considered as you make decisions about your writing process.

1. Some writers do not handle a first draft as a rough draft; they prefer to revise as they go. Such writers really combine the first-draft and revision steps. They are uncomfortable with rough copy, and so they write

a paragraph or perhaps just a sentence or two and then go back over what they have to shape and refine it. These writers push on in better fashion when they know that what they have left behind is in pretty good shape.

2. Some writers have very strong feelings about their introductions. They have to get this opening paragraph close to perfect before they can go on comfortably. These writers will revise or start over repeatedly until they are satisfied with their introduction, and then they go on to produce the rest of the first draft in rougher form.
3. Idea generation occurs during first-draft writing, so be receptive to new ideas and discoveries, and be prepared to go back and alter decisions made before the first draft if necessary. Also, if you discover while drafting that you need more ideas, return to prewriting.
4. In general, the more planning done prior to the draft, the less revision the draft will need. This is not to say that it is better to plan extensively. What is best is what works for you.
5. Remember that first drafts are *supposed* to be rough. If you expect perfection at this point, you will become frustrated unnecessarily.

Composing at the Computer

If you write your draft at the computer or word processor, place your outline in a window or print it out to serve as a guide for your work. Remember, however, that the outline is not sacred. You can depart from it in response to new ideas.

If you have trouble expressing an idea, use the block-move sequence to insert the appropriate section of your outline into the draft to hold the place. You can work the troublesome part through later, when you revise.

ESSAY IN PROGRESS

Writing the First Draft

Directions: After completing this exercise, save your draft. You will use it later in this chapter as you work toward your completed essay.

1. Using one of the outlines you wrote when you completed the exercise on page 73, write a first (rough) draft in one sitting. Do not worry about getting anything down in perfect form; just write your ideas the best you can. Skip any troublesome sections.
2. Study your draft. Does it suggest that you should return to an earlier stage in the process? If so, which one(s) and why? Return to those stages now and do what is necessary.
3. Were you comfortable writing your first draft? If not, what will you do differently the next time you draft? Why?

Revising (Reader-Based/Rewriting)

The first draft completes the work that is primarily writer-based, so the writer can begin getting the piece ready for a reader. The job of rewriting (revision) begins.

No matter how rough the first draft is, it gives the writer raw material to work with. There it is on the page—the first expression of the writer's ideas, ready to be shaped into polished form. There are rough spots, gaps, errors, and lots of things that are not working, but it can be transformed into something that satisfies the writer and engages the reader. This process of reworking is **revision**.

Revision is the very essence of the writing process. There is simply no way to overemphasize its crucial role. Yet despite the importance of revision, not every writer understands its nature and function.

Many students, for example, say how frustrated they feel after completing a first draft, reading their work over, and discovering that it is nowhere near ready for a reader. They seem surprised that they have written so many pages but none of them is "right" yet, and they conclude that they cannot write. These students are expecting too much of themselves by looking for a finished product too soon. Only the rare writer gets it right the first time. The rest of us produce drafts that need a major overhaul.

Some writers recognize the need to revise but fail to appreciate how much time and effort must go into the process. They think that revising means going through the draft to fix spellings, insert some punctuation, and change a few words. Sure, a blessed few write quickly and produce near-perfect first drafts, but most people must make significant changes in content and wording before turning a piece over to the reader.

Evaluating Your Draft

The word *revision* (re-vision) means "seeing again." The revision process calls upon writers to look again at their work. However, because revision marks the point when writers cross the line from writer-based to reader-based activity, revision involves us in seeing our work from the reader's point of view.

How, you may be wondering, can writers view their work as their readers will? How do writers know what to change in their drafts? These questions go to the heart of the revision process, and the following suggestions will help you answer them.

1. Before revising, leave your work for a good chunk of time—several hours at least, a day or more if possible. In fact, the longer you can stay away, the better. Getting away is important because after generating ideas, outlining, and drafting, you know what you mean so well that you may not recognize when you have failed to clarify an idea for a reader who does not have the same awareness. Getting away is also important for helping you make the very important shift from writer to reader.
2. Your chief concerns should be *content, organization,* and *effective expression.* Take a hard look at your first draft to determine whether you have

met your reader's needs by expressing your ideas clearly, by providing enough detail, and by avoiding irrelevant detail. Be sure your organization is logical and effective and be sure each idea flows logically from the one before it. Finally, evaluate your sentences to be sure they are effective. (Chapter 4 discusses how to craft effective sentences.)

The revising checklist on page 80 notes what to look for during revision. As you use the list, notice that matters of grammar, usage, and punctuation are not included. These details are attended to later, during editing.

3. If you drafted with a pen or pencil, type your draft after it is written. Your essay will resemble printed matter, which makes it easier to view your writing as "someone else's work," an orientation that lends objectivity. Also, when you view your work in type, you can spot problems with detail, organization, and expression more easily. Sometimes such problems leap out at you, as when you see that a paragraph is running only two typed lines, an indication that your detail may not be adequate.
4. Another way to achieve a fresh perspective is to read your draft out loud and approach it from the sense of sound rather than sight. Writers often hear problems that they overlooked visually.
5. You may be tempted to overlook a problem, but do not allow yourself to do so. You may discover detail not relevant to your thesis but want to keep it anyway because you like the way the idea is expressed—well, show no mercy and strike the irrelevancy. You may notice that your organization could be improved, but you spent ages on your outline and you hate to redo it—well, redo it anyway. The harder you are on yourself, the better your essay will be.
6. Trust your instincts. If you sense a problem, the odds are high that a problem exists—even if you cannot give it a name.

Getting Reader Response

Writers can get valuable advice from others. As a matter of fact, professional writers make changes based on the responses of such readers as editors, reviewers, and proofreaders. You, too, can benefit from the reactions of others, but to do so, keep the following guidelines in mind.

1. Pick readers who will view your work objectively and who will not be afraid to offer constructive criticism. If your mother likes everything you do no matter what, then do not use her as a reader. If your roommate is uncomfortable giving criticism, that person will not be a helpful reader.
2. Choose readers who know the qualities of effective writing. A person who has failed English 101 three times may not be the best judge of what is right and wrong with your draft.
3. Evaluate your readers' responses carefully. Weigh the reactions and accept or reject them in a discriminating way. If you are unsure about the reliability of a particular response, ask your instructor to help you decide.

4. Give your draft to more than one person and look for consensus. When readers agree, their view is likely to be reliable. When readers disagree and you cannot make up your mind about who is right, seek guidance from your instructor or another knowledgeable reader.
5. Form a group with several classmates and exchange drafts regularly. Meet and discuss with this group several times while your work is in progress.
6. If your campus has a writing center, take your draft to be read there by a sensitive reader.

The following procedures may help you secure reliable reader response.

PROCEDURE 1

Give your reader a photocopy of your draft, and ask that person to indicate the chief strengths and weaknesses in a summary comment at the end. Ask your reader to be specific, using language like this: "Good intro—it gets my interest; I don't understand the point you are making in paragraph 2—an example would help; paragraph 3 reads well, but I'm not sure how it relates to your thesis; the description at the end is vivid and interesting."

PROCEDURE 2

Give your reader a photocopy of your draft, and ask that person to write comments directly on the draft and in the margin the way an instructor might. Ask your reader to note strengths and weaknesses.

PROCEDURE 3

Ask your reader to write out the answers to the following questions on a separate sheet of paper.

1. What is the thesis of the essay?
2. Is there anything that does not relate to the thesis?
3. Are any points unclear?
4. Do any points need more explanation?
5. Is there any place where the relationship between ideas is unclear?
6. Does the introduction engage interest?
7. Does the conclusion provide a satisfying finish?
8. What is the best part of the essay?
9. What is the weakest part of the essay?

PROCEDURE 4

Give your reader a list of questions that reflect the concerns you have about the draft, such as: "Does the introduction arouse interest?" "Is the example in paragraph 2 detailed enough?" "Is there a better approach to the conclusion?"

Considering the Process

As you experiment and make decisions about your writing process, consider the following points about revision in addition to what you have already learned.

1. Some writers move through their first draft evaluating and revising everything at once. For others revision goes better if the draft is examined for one or two things at a time. If you prefer to revise this way in stages, try the following sequence.
   a. Read through your draft and make any changes that can be easily handled.
   b. Check that everything is relevant to the thesis and appropriate topic sentence. If something is not relevant, strike it no matter how much it hurts.
   c. Check next to be sure all your points are clear and that all generalizations are supported.
   d. Be sure your points follow logically from one to the next.
   e. Look at your introduction and conclusion. Be sure the former creates interest and the latter brings the essay to a satisfying close.
   f. Go back and attend to anything you were unable to handle earlier.
   g. Finally, review your sentences for effectiveness. Chapter 4 explains the principles of sentence effectiveness.

   As an alternative to the above sequence, start at the top of the revising checklist on page 80, and rework your draft until you can answer yes to every question on the list.
2. Writers who revise in stages often leave their work after each stage or two to restore objectivity. When they return, they evaluate their revisions and make further changes before going on.
3. Some writers revise one paragraph at a time, evaluating and rewriting until one paragraph is polished before going on to the next.
4. Some writers make their changes directly on the first draft by crossing out, writing above lines and in margins, drawing arrows, and so on. These writers often write on every other line when they draft to allow room for their changes. Other writers revise by writing a second draft on fresh paper.
5. Writers often rewrite until they have completed several drafts. It is impossible to know how many drafts a person will write for a particular piece.
6. Some writers cut and tape when they revise. If they decide to alter the sequence of sentences or paragraphs, they can easily move them to a new location.
7. If you are unsure of the best revision process for you, experiment first by going through the revising checklist below. Follow this with asking three readers to react to your second draft by answering the questions on page 78.

REVISION CHECKLIST

Before you consider the revision process complete, you should be able to answer *yes* to every question on this checklist.

1. Did you leave your work before you began to revise and after each complete revision?
2. Did you view your work from your reader's point of view?
3. Is your introduction geared to engage your reader's interest?
4. Does your essay have a clear, narrow thesis (stated or implied) that accurately conveys what your essay is about?
5. Do you have at least two body paragraphs?
6. Does each body paragraph have a topic sentence (stated or implied) that clearly and accurately conveys what the paragraph is about? Is each topic sentence relevant to the thesis?
7. Are all your points suited to your audience and purpose?
8. Is your supporting detail in each body paragraph adequate? Have you supported every generalization?
9. Is your supporting detail relevant to its topic sentence?
10. Do you have enough support in the body paragraphs to adequately develop your thesis?
11. Are all your ideas clearly expressed?
12. Are the supporting details in a logical order?
13. Did you use transitions to link ideas? (See Chapter 4.)
14. Did you write a conclusion geared toward leaving your reader with a positive final impression?
15. Are your sentences as effective as you can make them? (See Chapter 4.)

Composing at the Computer

If you compose at the computer or word processor, the following tips may help you revise.

1. Because your screen displays only a small portion of your draft at a time, you should study a printed copy of your draft to get a good overall sense of how it is shaping up.
2. Place the revision checklist in a window to serve as a reminder of the revision concerns.
3. If you are unsure whether some parts of your draft need work, place those sections in boldface type to highlight them. Then print your draft and ask a reliable reader to react to the boldface portions.
4. Use your insert key to separate each of your topic sentences from its supporting detail with about five lines. With this visual separation, you can

better judge how much supporting detail you have for each topic sentence. Add detail as necessary and then reform your paragraphs.

ESSAY IN PROGRESS

Revising the Draft

Directions: After completing this exercise, save your revision. You will use it later in this chapter as you work toward your completed essay.

1. Review pages 76–79 and make a list of the revising techniques you would like to try—the ones that seem like they might work for you.
2. Use the techniques in your list to revise the draft you wrote in response to the exercise on page 75.
3. Did your revision activities prompt you to return to any earlier stages of the process? If so, which ones?
4. Were you comfortable with the revision procedures you followed? If not, what will you do differently the next time you revise? Why?

Editing (Reader-Based/Rewriting)

When you edit, you are looking for mistakes in grammar, usage, capitalization, punctuation, and spelling. Editing is a reader-based activity because even the most tolerant readers are dismayed by misspellings, lack of punctuation, incorrect verbs, and such. If your writing contains frequent or serious lapses in grammar and usage, your reader will doubt your ability and lose confidence in what you have to say. That is, once your reader questions your ability with grammar and usage, that person is a short hop from questioning the validity of your ideas. Furthermore, because many of the rules facilitate communication between writer and reader (the period tells when an idea ends, for example) breaking these rules will undermine your ability to get a message across.

Finding Errors

Before you edit, you should leave your work to clear your head and restore objectivity. By the time you reach the editing stage, you will be so aware of what you wanted to say that you may see it on the page whether it is there or not. Getting away will help compensate for this tendency.

When you return to your work, you will be looking for two kinds of errors: those you have a tendency to make and those that are just slips. Go over your work twice. The first time through, look for the kinds of mistakes you typically make (fragments, lack of parallelism, or whatever), and the second time through identify and edit careless errors. Part 3 of this book is an explanation of the more frequent errors in grammar and usage. Consult this section on points you are unsure of. In addition, the following suggestions can help you find your errors.

1. Read through your draft *slowly,* studying each word and punctuation mark. To keep your speed down and increase your chances of finding errors, point to each word or punctuation mark with a pen as you go. (Be sure your eyes do not stray past what you are pointing to.)
2. Read your work out loud or speak it into a tape recorder to listen for mistakes. Be very careful to speak *exactly* what appears on the page. It is easy to speak a plural form, for example, when a singular form was actually written; it is easy to speak the word *feel* when *fell* is on the page. To avoid such substitution, speak *very* slowly, focusing for a second on each word. If you choose to speak your words to check for error, remember that certain kinds of mistakes cannot be heard. You cannot hear misspellings, nor can you hear certain punctuation, so at least once you should go over your work to check for mistakes visually.
3. Edit typed copy because errors are much easier to spot that way. Handwriting, particularly if it is not the best, can be deceptive, causing you to overlook mistakes. Also, typed copy depersonalizes your work so you can view it more objectively.
4. Professional writers have copy editors who check for errors that the author may have overlooked. You can follow the professionals' lead by asking someone to review your work for mistakes. However, be sure your reader is knowledgeable enough to spot errors. Also, you cannot relinquish your own responsibility to learn and apply grammar and usage rules by assuming someone else can always correct your errors for you. Ultimately, the responsibility for finding your mistakes rests with you. A reliable reader functions only to catch the occasional errors that get by you.
5. Trust your instincts. If your internal alarm sounds, assume there is a problem. If you cannot identify or solve the problem, get help from your instructor or another knowledgeable reader, perhaps a writing center tutor.

After checking for grammar and usage mistakes and editing accordingly (this can usually be done directly on the revised draft), type or copy your work into its final form, the form for submission. If you are writing for an instructor, he or she may have requirements for the final manuscript. Be sure you understand and fulfill these requirements, which may speak to such things as margins, placement of name and title, the amount of crossing out permitted, the kind of ink and paper to be used (or whether the essay must be typed), and so on.

Considering the Process

As you experiment to improve your writing process, consider the following points about editing in addition to what you have already learned.

1. Some writers combine revising and editing. As they rework their first draft, they consider grammar and usage at the same time they deal with content, organization, and effective expression. To do this, a writer must have strong grammar and usage skills. A writer weak in grammar and

usage runs a risk by combining revising and editing because there is too much to examine at once and there is a danger of missing something.

2. Writers who rarely have trouble with grammar and usage may skip a separate editing stage and look for the occasional mistake during proofreading. However, those who make mistakes with some regularity should never bypass separate editing because there is too much risk that mistakes will go unnoticed.
3. Keep track of your mistakes to learn your pattern of error. If your instructor notes your tendency to misuse commas, you can study the comma rules in Part 3 of this text; if your instructor notes frequent misspellings, you can check your dictionary more often.

Composing at the Computer

If you compose at the computer or word processor, the following tips may help you edit.

1. If your word processing program has grammar and spelling checkers, use them, but understand their limitations. For example, your program cannot tell if you have used *their* and *there* correctly; it can only tell if your spelling of these words corresponds to what it has in its dictionary.
2. After revising, quadruple space your text. Finding errors may be easier that way because fewer words will enter your field of vision and distract you. After editing, reformat your text.
3. Edit one time looking at the screen and one time looking at printed copy.
4. If you have problems with specific points of grammar, check Part 3 for specific tips on editing with the computer or word processor.

Proofreading (Reader-Based/Rewriting)

After editing your writing and copying or typing it into its final manuscript form, you should run one last check for errors by proofreading. Proofreading is a necessary final step because writers make mistakes when copying or typing the edited work into its final form. It is easy to leave a word out, lapse into a misspelling, and so on.

Proofreading can be handled much the same way as editing. The first step is to leave the final version for a while, to clear the head and regain objectivity. Remember, at no other point are writers as close to their work as here at the end, and so the tendency to see what was *intended,* rather than what *is,* is now most pronounced.

Because of this tendency, you must proofread slowly, one word or punctuation mark at a time. A quick reading through of your work is not proofreading. Use your pen to point to each word and punctuation mark as you read to keep yourself from building up speed that can cause you to overlook an error.

If you discover a mistake while proofreading, most instructors will allow you to ink in the correction neatly. However, use your judgment. If you have many corrections on a page, copy or type it over. The overall appearance of your work can affect a reader's reaction. If you do recopy or retype a page, remember to proof the new page for mistakes.

ESSAY IN PROGRESS

Editing, Proofreading, and Evaluating Your Process

1. Consider how frequently you make errors in grammar, usage, spelling, capitalization, and punctuation. Do you make them often enough to warrant editing in a separate step?
2. If you do not need to edit in a separate step, which do you believe will be more efficient for you: combining editing with revising or combining editing with proofreading? Explain your answer.
3. Using procedures you already know work for you or ones described in this chapter, edit the draft you revised for the exercise on page 81.
4. Leave your edited draft for at least half a day and then recopy or type your essay. Proofread the final version using procedures proven successful for you or ones described in this chapter.
5. If you completed all the "Essay in Progress" exercises in this chapter, you sampled procedures for each stage of the writing process. Which of these procedures (if any) worked well enough for you to use in the future? Which of these procedures (if any) will you not use again? Which procedures might you try in place of the ones that did not work well for you?

NOTE: You instructor may ask you to submit your completed essay.

WRITING REALITIES

As you experiment to discover your own effective, efficient writing process, keep in mind the following "writing realities."

1. WRITING IS USUALLY HARD WORK

Sometimes students think that while they are straining over the page, the rest of the world is out there merrily writing away with no trouble. On the contrary, writing is seldom easy for anyone. Sure, there are a few who write easily and well, but they are the exception. For everyone else, writing is hard work.

2. WRITING TAKES TIME

Think for a minute about the writing process. If you are to attend to all the stages and leave your work at strategic intervals, you must have time on your side. Furthermore, you must have enough time to step back before going forward as necessary. If you wait until the last minute, you will build in frustration and failure.

3. EVERYONE GETS STUCK SOMETIMES

When this happens to you, leave your writing for a time and refresh yourself by doing other things. When you return to your work, you may have the solution to your problem. If not, try to discover why the problem exists by asking the following questions.

Is my topic too broad?
Am I trying to write about something I do not know enough about?
Am I worried about getting everything "right" too soon?
Do I need a different organization?

If these questions do not help you solve the problem, ask a reliable reader to review your work and identify a way around the problem. Also, Appendix 1 suggests strategies to try if you get stuck.

4. MORE THAN ANYTHING ELSE, WRITING MEANS REVISION

You are unfair to yourself if you expect your first efforts to be top-quality. Professional writers are always tinkering with their work or making wholesale changes as they strive for the results they are after, and if pros must revise, you should not expect to get it right the first time. Thus, if you look at an early effort and discover everything is not what it should be, do not despair or conclude that you cannot write. Instead, get in there and revise.

5. WRITING CAN START OUT AS ONE THING AND END UP AS ANOTHER

When you revise, you make changes and sometimes the changes are sweeping. Thus, when revision is complete, you may end up with something very different from what you initially had in mind.

6. SOMETIMES A WRITER MUST START OVER

Even though you planned carefully and executed your plan to the best of your ability, you may discover that what you have is not working. This unpleasant discovery can be made at any point in the writing process. When you realize you have major problems and no attempts at revision seem to help enough, you may have to begin again. This can be frustrating, but if you must start again, take comfort in the fact that writers often must discover what they do *not* want to do before they learn what they *do* want to do.

7. KEEP YOUR WRITING IN MIND WHILE YOU ARE DOING OTHER THINGS

It is not true that people write only at a desk. You can be thinking about your work while you are cleaning the bedroom, walking the dog, or stuck in a traffic jam. Anytime your mind is not fully occupied, you can think of ideas, toy with approaches to your introduction, consider different organizations, and so on. If you do this, you are mentally planning ahead, and when you do sit down to your paper, the writing will move along more smoothly. Thinking about your writing in this way can be especially helpful when you have hit a snag. As you pursue other activities, let a portion of your brain consider solutions to your problem.

8. WRITERS HAVE INSTINCTS THAT CAN BE SHARPENED AND RELIED ON

Over the years you have heard, read, spoken, and written the language so much that a great deal of what you know about it has been internalized. As a result, you sometimes function more by instinct than by conscious awareness. When it comes to writing and reading your own writing, you often have an intuitive sense of what is and is not working. Sometimes you may sense a trouble spot even if you cannot identify why the problem exists. Thus, you should trust your instincts and assume there is a problem when you sense one. If your intuitive sense could stand some sharpening, get in the habit of reading a little bit every day. Subscribe to a weekly newsmagazine or read books about subjects of interest to you. Regular exposure to effective writing will help you internalize awarenesses about our language and sharpen your instincts.

WRITERS ON WRITING

In the following selections, two professional writers comment on various aspects of writing and their writing processes. These selections make a number of important points you should keep in mind as you consider your own process and ways to improve it.

About "The Watcher at the Gates"

In "The Watcher at the Gates" Gail Godwin writes of the "inner critic," the restraining voice in writers that can interfere with inspiration and creativity if not held in check in the early stages of writing. Yet Godwin makes it clear that the inner critic should be set free to exercise vigilance during revision and editing. Finally, Godwin confesses to the reason she, like many student writers, errs by turning the inner critic loose too soon.

The Watcher at the Gates

Gail Godwin

I first realized I was not the only writer who had a restraining critic who lived inside me and sapped the juice from green inspirations when I was leafing through Freud's "Interpretation of Dreams" a few years ago. Ironically, it was my "inner critic" who had sent me to Freud. I was writing a novel, and my heroine was in the middle of a dream, and then I lost faith in my own invention and rushed to "an authority" to check whether she could have such a dream. In the chapter on dream interpretation, I came upon the following passage that has 1 helped me free myself, in some measure, from my critic and has led to many pleasant and interesting exchanges with other writers.

Freud quotes Schiller, who is writing a letter to a friend. The friend complains of his lack of creative power. Schiller replies with an allegory. He says it is not good if the intellect examines too closely the ideas pouring in at the gates. "In isolation, an idea may be quite insignificant, and venturesome in the extreme, but it may acquire importance from an idea which follows it. . . . In the case of a creative mind, it seems to me, the intellect has withdrawn its watchers from the gates, and the ideas rush in pell-mell, and only then does it review and inspect the multitude. You are ashamed or afraid of the momentary and passing madness which is found in all real creators, the longer or shorter duration of which distinguishes the thinking artist from the dreamer . . . you reject too soon and discriminate too severely." 2

So that's what I had: a Watcher at the Gates. I decided to get to know him better. I discussed him with other writers, who told me some of the quirks and habits of their Watchers, each of whom was as individual as his host, and all of whom seemed passionately dedicated to one goal: rejecting too soon and discriminating too severely. 3

It is amazing the lengths a Watcher will go to keep you from pursuing the flow of your imagination. Watchers are notorious pencil sharpeners, ribbon changers, plant waterers, home repairers and abhorrers of messy rooms or messy pages. They are compulsive looker-uppers. They are superstitious scaredy-cats. They cultivate self-important eccentricities they think are suitable for "writers." And they'd rather die (and kill your inspiration with them) than risk making a fool of themselves. 4

My Watcher has a wasteful penchant for 20-pound bond paper above and below the carbon of the first draft. "What's the good of writing out a whole page," he whispers begrudgingly, "if you just have to write it over again later? Get it perfect the first time!" My Watcher adores stopping in the middle of a morning's work to drive down to the library to check on the name of a flower or a World War II battle or a line of metaphysical poetry. "You can't possibly go on till you've got this right!" he admonishes. I go and get the car keys. 5

Other Watchers have informed their writers that: 6

"Whenever you get a really good sentence you should stop in the middle of it and go on tomorrow. Otherwise you might run dry." 7

"Don't try and continue with your book till your dental appointment is over. When you're worried about your teeth, you can't think about art." 8

Another Watcher makes his owner pin his finished pages to a clothesline and read them through binoculars "to see how they look from a distance." Countless other Watchers demand "bribes" for taking the day off: lethal doses of caffeine, alcoholic doses of Scotch or vodka or wine. 9

There are various ways to outsmart, pacify or coexist with your Watcher. Here are some I have tried, or my writer-friends have tried, with success: 10

Look for situations when he's likely to be off-guard. Write too fast for him in an unexpected place, at an unexpected time. (Virginia Woolf captured the "diamonds in the dustheap" by writing at a "rapid haphazard gallop" in her 11 diary.) Write when very tired. Write in purple ink on the back of a Master Charge statement. Write whatever comes into your mind while the kettle is boiling and make the steam whistle your deadline. (Deadlines are a great way to outdistance the Watcher.)

Disguise what you are writing. If your Watcher refuses to let you get on with your story or novel, write a "letter" instead, telling your "correspondent" what you are going to write in your story or next chapter. Dash off a "review" of your own unfinished opus. It will stand up like a bully to your Watcher the next time he throws obstacles in your path. If you write yourself a good one. 12

Get to know your Watcher. He's yours. Do a drawing of him (or her). Pin it to the wall of your study and turn it gently to the wall when necessary. Let your Watcher feel needed. Watchers are excellent critics after inspiration has been captured; they are dependable, sharp-eyed readers of things already set down. Keep your Watcher in shape and he'll have less time to keep you from shaping. If he's really ruining your whole working day sit down, as Jung did with his personal demons, and write him a letter. On a very bad day I once wrote my Watcher a letter. "Dear Watcher," I wrote, "What is it you're so afraid I'll do?" Then I held his pen for him, and he replied instantly with a candor that has kept me from truly despising him. 13

"Fail," he wrote back. 14

About "How I Wrote 'Fat Chance' "

In the following selection, Barbara Wright makes many important points about the writing process. She notes the occasional necessity to begin again, the reality of writer's block, the fact that writing is hard, the usefulness of writing ends before middles, the purpose and nature of revision, the fact that writing takes time, the need to distance, the unreliability of inspiration, the fact that writing is a form of discovery, the fact that final versions can vary greatly from first drafts, and the role of instinct and how to sharpen it.

How I Wrote "Fat Chance"

Barbara Wright

Writing a short story, I find myself changing things from the moment the first word is committed to paper until the last word of the final draft is typed. Even as I proofread, I see changes I want to make. The only thing that saves me is that I am too lazy to retype the story. Someone once said that a work of art is never finished, only abandoned. I agree. 1

Although the process of some writers seems to fit in neat categories with the first, second, and third drafts on pink, blue, and yellow paper, the process I go through is haphazard, totally chaotic. I usually start with an image of the main character and an ill-defined intent. I never know what is going to happen in my 2 stories until I have finished one draft, which takes an average of a month, writing three hours every day except Sunday.

In "Fat Chance" I started out to write a story with an unreliable narrator named Jenny, a nineteen-year-old, 250-pound woman who goes to a weight reduction clinic and meets one of the waiters in the dining hall, who she deludes herself into thinking is attracted to her. I wanted to make the reader know more than the first-person narrator, to play with the tension between Jenny's fantasy and the reality. 3

Before beginning I read several books on obesity to find out how fat men and women perceive the world, the prejudices they encounter, how they view their fatness, and the problems they have in trying to reduce. Then I sat down and in two three-hour sessions wrote fifteen pages on Jenny's childhood, how she was taken advantage of by people in her high school, how they would use her to tell all their problems to, but wouldn't invite her to go on beach weekends because, as they told her, they didn't think she could swim. I wrote of the time she passed an anti-abortion activist on the street who didn't hand her a pamphlet, assuming that no one would sleep with her, so she wouldn't need any information. 4

Rereading what I had written, I realized that all of this was background information. There was no story. Nothing had happened. Those pages were necessary for me to write in order to get to know the character better, but they had nothing to do with the story I was about to tell, although I didn't know what that story was. However, I did discard the idea of the unreliable narrator. The Jenny who emerged on the page was different from the character I originally intended to create. This character was vulnerable, and tried to cover her vulnerability with tough language and humor, but she was basically honest and would never delude herself into thinking someone liked her if he didn't. 5

What had happened thus far was this: I had started with an intent, but in writing, was forced to discard the intent, although I hadn't replaced it with another. So there I was with fifteen pages that had to be thrown out. 6

I was able to salvage about three pages from different parts of the original and started from there. Now came the difficult part. For the next month, I worked on the first draft. 7

To explain why it takes me so long to write, I must divulge one of my dirty little secrets: I have writer's block, a mild form that makes it difficult for me to sit down and commit myself to paper. 8

In *Writing with Power* (New York: Oxford University Press, 1981) Peter Elbow identifies two kinds of difficulties in writing. The first he compares to carrying an unwieldy load across a stream on slippery rocks. This is the most noble, productive difficulty because it involves working through language, figuring out thoughts, developing ideas. One is struggling with the writing itself, and the task of mastering words and ideas can be overwhelming, thus causing the block (p. 199). This kind of writer's block derives from the fear of the unknown. When I know that a good idea is being formed, however inchoate and messy, as new ideas always are, there is a sense of real engagement, but also a pulling back, a terror of the unknown that causes me to panic, afraid I am going to blow the idea. 9

The second kind of difficulty is more neurotic, and, sadly, I suffer from it 10
more than anything else. Peter Elbow describes it this way: "You are trying to fight your way out from under a huge deflated silk balloon—layers and layers of light gauzy material which you can bat away, but they always just flop back again and no movement or exertion gets you any closer to the open air" (p. 199). In this type of block, the writer has no sense of direction and keeps going around in circles. Elbow attributes this behavior to fear of the generalized audience some writers carry in their heads.

The dangerous audience in my head is composed of two factions. To stage 11
left are all my critics, past, present, and future: the junior-high-school English teacher who read one of my essays in a voice like Bullwinkle's; all the people who have looked at my work and said something noncommittal, unable to disguise the screaming subtext; my eighty-year-old Quaker grandmother, whose heart may not be able to withstand the shock of sex scenes and vile language; people who may think they recognize themselves among my characters.

To stage right are my supporters, equally dangerous. These are people who 12
think I have talent, who think I am going to make it. I am afraid I am going to disappoint them, make them reassess their view of me, expose the *real me*. Both these groups form a Gestapo, and I can't shake what one writer called "the feeling that the Gestapo is going to come to my door and arrest me for impersonating an intellectual."

So this is the audience for the drama that happens every morning as I sit 13
down to write. The principal actors are the angel, the demon, and me. The props: a desk and a typewriter.

Angel: It's nine o'clock. Time to sit down and write.

Me: But I can't think of anything to say. I have no idea what my character is going to do. I've got to get Jenny out of the fat farm and downtown so she can meet Marvin.

Demon: The plants need watering.

Angel: Don't do it. You know you'll waste ten minutes.

Demon: Well the least you can do is clean up this mess. I mean, it's disgusting—coffee stains, flakes from the white-out, eraser dust, paper on the floor. We can't write in this filth.

Angel: Don't listen to him. Why don't you just get started?

Me: I don't know. I sit down to write and nothing quite . . . you know . . . jells. Maybe if I clean up . . .

Angel: Try freewriting. You can throw it away. No one is going to see it but me and . . . (whispers) . . . him.

Me: It only depresses me. I sit down and write ten minutes worth of crap, and nothing can be salvaged. It only makes me feel worse.

Demon: You'd better check the mail. There's probably another rejection slip.

Angel: (Ignoring him) Okay, then just write one sentence and see if that leads you to another.

Me: I can't seem to do it. When I write letters, they are full of life, everyone loves to get them—and I'm not counting my mother. But when I write a story, it never quite . . .

Angel: So write some background information on Marvin. You don't know what kind of a guy he is yet.

Me: Okay. (Sigh. Write a sentence, rip it out of the typewriter carriage, crumple it up, aim at the wastebasket and miss.)

Demon: (Taunting) You're going to have to say something difficult, aren't you? You don't know if you have the talent to do it, do you? I saw that pitiful, decaffeinated sentence you just wrote. And you call yourself a WRITER? I've got news for you, Toots. That's never going to pass muster.

Angel: (To demon) Will you cut the clichés? (To me) If you absolutely have nothing to say, then just sit down and stare at the blank paper. It's not going to hurt. What is it that you're afraid you're going to do?

Demon: Fail.

Considering this daily drama, the brouhaha of the audience in my head, and my own expectations, which are always higher than I can ever meet, the wonder is not that I write so little, but that I write at all. *14*

For a long time I thought my difficulty with writing was nature's way of handing me a rejection slip, but I have since learned that others share this. When asked if he enjoyed writing, William Styron said, "I certainly don't. I get a fine warm feeling when I'm doing well, but that pleasure is pretty much negated by the pain of getting started each day. Let's face it, writing is hell."[1] *15*

Yet the fine warm feeling is worth the pain, especially when one has the heady experience of the writing taking over and writing itself. These rare moments, gifts from the unconscious, are to be cherished. In "Fat Chance" this happened to me on the last three pages. I had been working on the first part of the story, describing what goes on at Dr. Bonner's rice clinic where Jenny goes to reduce. I had also been tinkering with a later section in which Jenny meets a black waiter named Marvin in a railroad-car diner when she goes in to order black tea. Marvin was still vaguely defined and I didn't know exactly what was going to happen between him and Jenny, but I knew it would be something horrible to make her abandon her diet and go on a super-binge. For some reason, I felt I had to write the last scene before I could go on with the middle part. Every morning for two weeks I wrote and rewrote the ending. The results were abysmal, depressing. The garbage can was overflowing with discarded pages. I couldn't get it right. Not even one sentence was redeemable. For me it was not a problem of what to say, but how to say it; the two are indistinguishable in fiction. Some days I would sit for three hours and produce nothing. At this point in my life, nothing was going right. The freshman English classes I was teaching were uninspired, I was not doing good work in my graduate-school classes, and my personal life was dor- *16*

[1] *Writers at Work: The Paris Review Interviews* (First Series), ed. Malcolm Cowley (New York: Penguin Books, 1977), p. 271.

mant. All these problems were aggravated by my inability to produce even one good sentence after two weeks of solid work. I knew that I had to get the ending right before I could go on.

Then, one night after teaching, I came back from school and decided that instead of studying or reading I would take a walk to relax. I could feel the pressure building up from all points in my life. When I came back, I felt an urgency to sit down at the typewriter, even though I had already done my three-hour stint and rarely write twice a day. Typing as quickly as I could, I wrote the entire last scene in ten or fifteen minutes. It appears in the final draft almost exactly as I wrote it. I was typing full speed when suddenly, out of nowhere, the image of a phoenix tattooed on Jenny's stomach appeared. As she gorges herself on junk food, she imagines the red and green wings blurring as her stomach expands until the tattoo is no longer recognizable as a bird. Clacking along, I typed: "But no one would see it but me. No one would ever see it but me." I came to an abrupt stop. I knew that I had the last line. And I knew I had the ending to the story. There was an immediate feeling of ecstasy. One of those rare moments in writing that make up in intensity what they lack in frequency. *17*

Popular misconception has it that writers' inspiration falls from the sky and thwacks them over the head. Actually, the moments of clarity are born of hard work, false starts, discarded efforts. It is only through the struggle that what was brewing in the unconscious is able to shoulder its way through to consciousness. *18*

Often the conscious mind needs a rest, needs to regroup. When the final breakthrough occurs, it seems so simple, and we wonder how we could have been so stupid as to miss it. The reason is that we were not psychologically ready to see it. *19*

This is why I write every day. Inspiration is infrequent, and the periods of drought are frustrating and debilitating, but necessary to make creative breakthroughs possible. *20*

After the ending to "Fat Chance" was written, I had to create a catalyst for Jenny's binging. This time, the unconscious deserted me. The first draft ended up like this: Jenny and Marvin go to the movies. She invites him back to her room. On the way there, two thugs from the Ku Klux Klan stop them, insult Marvin, tell him he's hard-up to be going out with a fat woman, then beat him up. Jenny runs to call the police. By the time the police get there, Marvin has disappeared. He quits his job and won't talk to her. Jenny goes to his house but his sister slams the door in her face. Then she goes on the binge. *21*

By this time I had been working on the story so long I had lost all critical faculties, so I asked the help of a friend, an excellent critic whom I trust. She made the following observations: the voice was inconsistent, the first three pages, which were from the initial fifteen I had written, were irrelevant, and the whole bit about the thugs was fake and depended too much on plot. Also the symbolism of the tattoo didn't work. *22*

Armed with this information, I went back to work. Usually, after the painful first draft, I work more quickly. I started the story in the middle of page four. I rewrote sections to make the voice consistent and tried to make the tattoo work. *23*

In the first draft, I had written one paragraph about the one time Jenny had been rebellious and got a phoenix tattoo on her stomach. This didn't do the trick, my friend told me, because her motivation for doing so wasn't clear. Now I added a scene in which Jenny's mother takes her to the department store on her sixteenth birthday to buy her a dress. Jenny tries on the largest size, but it is too small. Her mother humiliates her in front of the clerk, saying that they would take the dress anyway, since it would give Jenny incentive to reduce. Jenny changes in the cubicle, leaves the dress in a heap on the floor, then leaves without her mother, taking the subway home. On the way, she passes a tattoo shop and decides to get a phoenix tattooed on her stomach.

In this version, her motivation was still not clear. So finally I added a section in which she looks in the window of the shop and sees a life-sized photo of an obese oriental man stripped to the waist with a two-headed dragon tattoo winding up his stomach. Jenny remembers her mother's looking at the photo several weeks before and saying, "Can you imagine anyone showing off their blubber like that?" Now, juxtaposed against the department-store scene and the fact that her mother is always taking potshots at fatsos, the motivation is—I hope—clear. It is an act of self-hatred to get back at her mother. *24*

To find the details of the tattooing, I called a friend who had had a tattoo put on her chest. She told me about the reclining dentist-type chair and how the needles sounded and felt. *25*

Next I completely rewrote the catalyst for Jenny's binge. Now she goes to the restaurant where Marvin works. They overhear his friends in a booth, saying he must be hard-up to be going out with an obese woman—and white at that. Marvin jerks his hand away from hers and goes to the front of the store. Jenny leaves and calls him from Pizza Hut, but he doesn't say anything and she can't think of anything to say either, so she hangs up. Trapped in Pizza Hut, thick with the smell of oregano, tomatoes, and dough, she thinks a fast food fix will make it easier for her to think clearly. This is the start of the binge. *26*

Most of what appears in the final draft was not in the first draft. Yet I was able to write it in two weeks. The first draft was so difficult because I didn't know what was going to happen, who the characters were, or even what my intent was. I started out with an intent, a preconception of what the work would be. But through writing I was constantly reassessing the intent, adapting and changing it to fit what the writing produced. At other times the preconception forced a revision of the writing. Each time I reworked a scene, a paragraph, or even a sentence, it caused a restructuring of the whole. Everything was in flux. Fiction writers, more than any other kind of writers, are familiar with Keats' negative capability and are used to swimming in uncertainty and doubt, without the ability to grasp onto something firm. *27*

After the first draft, when one aspect of the writing had stabilized—in this case, the intent—it was much easier for me to work. Thus, I was able to complete the second draft in half the time. *28*

In revision, the only help I have to make changes is an internal Geiger counter that registers when something is not quite right. This Geiger counter is partly intuitive, partly educable. When it starts registering dissonance, I have to *29* stop, diagnose the problem, and decide what to do about it: whether to modify the intent or the writing.

For example, toward the end of the first draft, I was having trouble revising 30 the scenes at Dr. Bonner's clinic. I tried to put them in past tense, but they seemed awkward and unnatural. So I asked myself to whom and how soon after the incident was Jenny relating the story. I realized that she had to be relating it soon after the binge because the sense of self-hatred that comes out in the scene would have to be relatively fresh. I decided that she was telling the story while she was still at the clinic, having had to stay longer after the setback of her super-binge. She would be telling the story to someone who hadn't been to the clinic, but who knew she was still there. Thus the reader would have to put himself in the position of being a confidant. Walter Ong talks of writers who "fictionalize their audiences, casting them in a made-up role and calling on them to play the role assigned."[2] In my case, this tactic is often intuitive. Only when problems arise do I consciously analyze these relationships.

The more I read literature and the more I work on my own fiction, the more 31 sensitive my Geiger counter becomes, and the more often it registers dissatisfaction. I feel worse about my writing after two years of graduate school than I did when I first started, because the development of my Geiger counter has outdistanced the development of my writing. I can see the possibilities of what can be done with the short story form, and have become increasingly frustrated with my inability to reach the goal.

In her study of children's rewriting strategies, Lucy Calkins found that one 32 group of third graders, whom she called transitional children, would start and abandon piece after piece of writing. Nothing seemed to satisfy them. Calkins writes: "As children develop high standards for themselves and become more self-critical, they become more and more frustrated with what they have done, and more and more unwilling to reread, recopy and refine what they view as 'lousy' to begin with."[3]

I find that when my freshman writing students do their best work at the end 33 of the semester, they are invariably the most uncertain, the most self-critical. This is because over the course of the semester, they have learned what good writing is and how to identify the problems, but are not yet confident of their ability to solve the problems. Their Geiger counters have developed more rapidly than the skills to quiet them.

Even though it seems the longer I write the more dissatisfied I become, I 34 know that my only chance is to write regularly to develop the craft.

---

[2]"The Writer's Audience Is Always a Fiction," *PMLA,* 90 (1975), p. 17.

[3]Lucy McCormick Calkins, "Children's Rewriting Strategies," unpublished manuscript, University of New Hampshire, p. 18.

CHAPTER 4

Revising for Sentence Effectiveness

Individual sentences contribute to an essay in several ways: they contribute to the adequacy of detail; they clarify organization; and they make for an appealing style. The next sections of this chapter examine each of these three aspects of sentence effectiveness.

SENTENCE EFFECTIVENESS AND ADEQUATE DETAIL

When you read about adequate detail (see pages 42–44), you learned that writers must do more than *tell* that something is so—they must *show* that it is so with specific details to support every generalization. One way writers can be specific is to craft sentences with specific words.

Use Specific Diction

Diction means "word choice." Some words are general and some are specific. *General words* present a broad (and often vague) sense of our ideas, while *specific words* present a more precise sense of our ideas. Here are some examples to help you appreciate the difference between general and specific words.

General Words	Specific Words
shoe	combat boot
hat	baseball cap
woman	Mrs. Hernandez
went	stormed out
nice	colorful

Most often, writers should use specific words because they give the reader a more precise understanding of the writer's ideas—and in this way specific diction contributes to adequate detail. Consider, for a moment, the following sentence.

```
I walked across campus, feeling good about the test I just
took.
```

The word *walked* is general and vague. Some of the more specific alternatives to *walked,* ones that would be accurate when combined with *feeling good,* include:

```
strolled     strutted    bounced
sauntered    trotted     lilted
```

If we pick a more specific word for *walked,* one sentence we could get is:

```
I strutted across campus, feeling good about the test I just
took.
```

Now we have a more accurate sense of how the writer moved across campus, because of more specific word choice. However, there is still room for improvement because *good* is vague and general. Here are some more specific alternatives.

```
positive    elated      at ease       delighted    jubilant
pleased     satisfied   exhilarated   cheerful     optimistic
```

Now let's select a word that works with *strutted.* We need something that conveys lots of good feeling because we strut when we are really feeling up. For example, if we select *exhilarated,* we get:

```
I strutted across campus, exhilarated by the test I just took.
```

Now that is a more effective sentence than what we started out with because it is more specific.

During drafting, you need not worry too much about specific word choice. Just get your ideas down the best way you can at the time. During revision, however, work to make your sentences more specific by focusing on nouns and verbs. Instead of general nouns like *magazine, hat,* and *dog,* use the more specific *Newsweek, stocking cap,* and *collie.* Instead of general verbs like *said, moved,* and *drank,* use the more specific *blurted out, bolted,* and *sipped.*

Adding and revising modifiers can also make a sentence more specific. For example, instead of "Cans and candy wrappers are on the floor," you can revise to get, "Smashed Coke cans and crumpled Milky Way wrappers are scattered across the floor."

Of course, you must be careful not to overdo because too much specific word choice, especially description, can create a bulky overwhelming sentence, like this:

> Dozens of smashed, twisted, red-and-white Coke cans, lying bent on their distorted sides and at least forty crumpled, brown, wadded-up, misshapen Milky Way wrappers representing two weeks of my traditional midnight sugar intake are scattered messily in heaps everywhere across the green, plush-carpeted floor of my small, third-floor bedroom with its green walls and white ceiling.

Composing at the Computer

If you compose at the computer or word processor, the following tips may help you revise for specific word choice.

Your word processing program may have a built-in thesaurus you can use to find more specific alternatives to general words in your draft, or you may be able to buy an add-on program. Be sure, however, that you understand the meanings of any words you take from this source.

Use your computer's search-and-replace function to locate general words you are in the habit of using, words like *good, great, nice, awful, and bad.* Once you have located these words, you can evaluate their appropriateness and make changes as necessary.

EXERCISE

Specific Diction

1. Write more specific alternatives to the following general words.

book	movie	worker	school
go	bad	said	car
room	good	coat	look

2. Below are sentences with vague, general words. Revise the sentences to create more effective ones by substituting specific words for the general ones. In some cases, you may want to substitute several words for one general word and add additional detail, as shown in the following example.

   example: The happy boy ran down the street.

   revision: The paper boy sprinted down Ford Avenue, excited that he had finished his route an hour early.

   a. The room was a mess.
   b. By afternoon the child was feeling terrible.
   c. The food tasted awful.
   d. The way that person was driving his car almost caused an accident.
   e. The sound of that baby's cry really got to me.

f. The movie was very good.
g. Carlotta watched the ballplayers practice.

3. Compose a sentence about something you saw, heard, tasted, smelled, or touched today. Revise that sentence until you are satisfied that the diction is specific enough.

GROUP EXERCISE

Specific Diction

With two classmates, write the following ideas in sentences with specific diction. (You may need to revise a number of times before you are satisfied.)

example: the pleasant ringing of church bells
sentence: `The melodious ring of St. John's bells announced the start of morning worship.`

1. a squirrel running back and forth across a branch
2. the smell of brownies baking in the oven
3. the sound of rain on a roof
4. a woman wearing too much floral-scented perfume
5. walking barefoot and stepping on a sharp stone

SENTENCE EFFECTIVENESS AND ORGANIZATION

Writers must make clear how one idea leads to the next. One way they can demonstrate the relationships among their ideas—and hence help the reader appreciate the order and grouping of details—is to write sentences using coordination, subordination, and transitions. These three techniques will be taken up next.

Use Coordination and Subordination

A group of words with both a subject and a verb is a **clause.** If the clause is complete enough to stand as a sentence, it is a **main clause**; if the clause cannot stand as a sentence, it is a **subordinate clause**.

Main clause: `this year's citrus crop was seriously damaged by the late frost`

Explanation: This word group has the subject *citrus crop* and the verb *was damaged.* It is complete enough to be a sentence when a capital letter and period are added.

Subordinate clause: `because this year's citrus crop was seriously damaged by the late frost`

Explanation: This word group has a subject and verb, but it is not complete enough to be a sentence.

Two main clauses can appear in the same sentence if they are connected by one of the following **coordinating conjunctions**.

and	nor
but	for
or	so
yet	

When writers connect two main clauses in the same sentence, the technique is called **coordination**. Coordination allows a writer to demonstrate a specific relationship between ideas in the clauses. This relationship is identified by the coordinating conjunction used to connect the clauses, as described below.

1. If the main clauses are connected by *and,* the idea in the second clause functions in addition to the idea in the first:

```
The mayor urged a 14 percent budget cut, and he suggested a
freeze on municipal hiring.
```

2. If the main clauses are connected by *but* or *yet,* the idea in the second clause shows contrast to the idea in the first:

```
The temperatures have been unusually warm for December, but
(yet) it may snow for Christmas.
```

3. If the main clauses are connected by *or,* the idea in the second main clause is an alternative to the idea in the first:

```
Your research papers must be handed in on time, or you will
be penalized.
```

4. If the main clauses are connected by *nor,* the idea in the second clause is a negative idea functioning in addition to the negative idea in the first clause:

```
Unless the levy is passed, the school board cannot be expected
to raise teacher salaries, nor can it renovate the high school
buildings.
```

5. If the main clauses are connected by *for,* the idea in the second clause tells why the idea in the first clause happened or should happen:

   Television talk shows are popular, for viewers never grow weary of watching celebrities talk about themselves.

6. If the main clauses are connected by *so,* the idea in the second clause functions as a result of the idea in the first clause:

   Dr. Wesson was ill last week, so our midterm exam is postponed until Thursday.

PUNCTUATION NOTE: As the previous examples show, when two main clauses are joined by a coordinating conjunction, a comma appears before the conjunction.

When writers connect a subordinate clause and a main clause in the same sentence, the technique is called **subordination**. Subordination allows a writer to demonstrate the specific relationship between the ideas in the two clauses. This relationship is identified by the subordinating conjunction used to introduce the subordinate clause. Below are some common subordinating conjunctions, the relationships they signal, and representative examples. Notice that subordinate clauses can come before or after main clauses.

Conjunctions	Relationship and example
because in order that since	To show why the idea in the main clause occurs or occurred: Because the traffic signal on Dearborn Street is out, cars are backed up for two blocks.
after whenever as while before when	To show when the idea in the main clause occurs or occurred: Before undergraduates can enroll in upper-division courses, they must get permission from their academic dean.
where wherever	To show where the idea in the main clause occurs or occurred: Janine always attracts attention wherever she goes.
as if as though	To show how the idea in the main clause occurs or occurred: Jim was out partying last night as if he didn't have any problems.

if provided once unless	To show under what condition the idea in the main clause occurs or occurred: `Once the additional computer terminals are in place, we can complete the mailing lists in half the time.`
although even though though	To admit a point: `Although enrollment in literature courses has been down in the last five years, the trend is beginning to reverse.`

PUNCTUATION NOTE: As the previous examples show, a subordinate clause at the beginning of a sentence is followed by a comma. When the subordinate clause comes at the end of the sentence, a comma is used before the clause if it shows separation from the rest of the sentence.

EXERCISE

Coordination and Subordination

For each general subject, write one sentence with coordination and one with subordination to demonstrate the specific relationships indicated. Try to place some of your subordinate clauses before the main clauses and some of them after. Also remember the punctuation notes on pages 100 and 101. The first one is done for you as an example.

1. *exams:* (a) coordinate to show contrast; (b) subordinate to admit a point

    a. I have three exams today, but I have time for lunch.

    b. Although Dr. Manolio is known for giving difficult tests, her exams are always fair.

2. *spring:* (a) coordinate to show addition; (b) subordinate to show when
3. *your best friend:* (a) coordinate to show contrast; (b) subordinate to admit a point
4. *your favorite restaurant:* (a) coordinate to show an alternative; (b) subordinate to show why
5. *your first day of college:* (a) coordinate to show a result; (b) subordinate to show when
6. *a miserable cold:* (a) coordinate to continue a negative idea; (b) subordinate to show under what condition
7. *the first day of summer vacation:* (a) coordinate to show why; (b) subordinate to show when
8. *a party:* (a) coordinate to show addition; (b) subordinate to show where
9. *your favorite teacher:* (a) coordinate to show why; (b) subordinate to show how

10. *a movie you have seen:* (a) coordinate to show result; (b) subordinate to admit a point
11. *a holiday celebration:* (a) coordinate to show contrast; (b) subordinate to show why

Use Transitions

Transitions are connective words and phrases that show the relationship between ideas. Because they show how ideas relate to each other, transitions aid organization and prevent abrupt, annoying shifts. Consider, for example, the following sentences taken from an essay a student wrote about what she experienced when her boyfriend, Dave, broke their engagement.

> For weeks I wondered what I had done wrong until friends helped me realize that I was not necessarily responsible. Dave's explanation that "people change" became more acceptable to me.

The movement from the first to the second sentence is abrupt and confusing. Look what happens, however, when a transitional phrase is used to bridge the gap between the two sentences and clarify the relationship between ideas.

> For weeks I wondered what I had done wrong, until friends helped me realize that I was not necessarily responsible. As a result, Dave's explanation that "people change" became more acceptable to me.

The transitional phrase *as a result* is added at the beginning of the second sentence to signal that the ideas in the first sentence function as a cause, and the ideas in the second sentence function as the effect of that cause. By demonstrating this cause-and-effect relationship, the transition smooths the flow of ideas and helps the reader understand how the writer is connecting thoughts.

In addition to connecting ideas in different sentences, transitions can clarify the relationship between ideas in the same sentence. The following sentence is an example of this.

> In her campaign speech, the senator claimed she favored economic aid to the unemployed and the elderly; however, her voting record demonstrates otherwise.

In this example the word *however* functions as a transition that indicates contrast. That is, the transition signals to the reader that what comes after it is in contrast to what comes before it.

Transitional words and phrases can signal a variety of relationships. Be sure to check the Transition Chart, on pages 104–105, which presents these relationships and some common transitions used to signal them.

Use Repetition to Achieve Transition

Another way to achieve transition is by repeating key words. At some point, you may have heard the caution against repetition. Repeating yourself, you may have been told, is annoying to the reader and a waste of words, and often this is true. However, at times deliberate repetition is appreciated by the reader because it clarifies the relationship between ideas, bridges gaps, and hence aids comprehension. Consider the following pair of sentences.

> Exam anxiety is more prevalent among students than many instructors realize. Many students who understand the material are prevented from demonstrating their knowledge.

These sentences have a relationship to each other (cause and effect), but that relationship is not revealed as clearly as it could be. Also, an awkward gap exists between the sentences. To alleviate these problems, strategic repetition can serve as a transition.

> Exam anxiety is more prevalent among students than many instructors realize. Such anxiety prevents many students who understand the material from demonstrating their knowledge.

The relationship between ideas is clarified by the repetition of the word *anxiety* at the beginning of the second sentence. In addition, this repetition smooths the flow from the first sentence to the second.

You can also create transitions by repeating a key idea rather than a key word. To understand this, first look at the following sentences.

> Mr. Ferguson, driving at close to 60 miles per hour, took his eyes off the road for only a second to light a cigarette. A three-car pileup put two people in the hospital.

The relationship between these two sentences is not as clear as it could and should be. Further, the gap creates an abrupt shift, and both of these facts undermine the effectiveness of the sentences. The repetition of a key idea can serve as a transition and solve these problems.

> Mr. Ferguson, driving at close to 60 miles per hour, took his eyes off the road for only a second to light a cigarette. This momentary lapse caused a three-car pileup that put two people in the hospital.

Transition Chart

Relationship Signaled	*Transitions That Signal the Relationship*	*Example*
addition	also, and, and then, too, in addition, furthermore, moreover, equally important, another, first, second, third . . .	The mayor fully expects the city council to approve her salary recommendations for city employees. <u>In addition</u>, she is certain she will gain support for her road-repair program.
time sequence	now, then, before, after, afterward, earlier, later, immediately, soon, next, meanwhile, gradually, suddenly, finally, previously, before, next, often, eventually	<u>Before</u> an agreement can be reached between the striking hospital workers and management, both sides must soften their stands on the economic issues.
spatial arrangement	near, near to, nearly, far, far from, beside, in front of, next to, beyond, above, below, to the right, to the left, around, surrounding, on one side, inside, outside, across, opposite to, far off, behind, alongside, there	As you leave the fair grounds, turn right on Route 76. <u>Just beyond</u> the junction sign is the turnoff you need.
comparison	in the same way, similarly, just like, just as, in like manner, likewise	The current administration must not abandon its commitment to the poor. <u>Similarly</u>, it must not forget its promise to the elderly.
contrast	but, still, however, on the other hand, yet, on the contrary, nevertheless, despite, in spite of	<u>In spite of</u> the currently depressed housing market, money can still be made in real estate.

At the beginning of the second sentence, the phrase *this momentary lapse* refers to Mr. Ferguson's eyes taken off the road for only a second. It repeats that idea to achieve transition.

One other way to achieve transition is to use synonyms to repeat an idea. Consider these sentences.

Transition Chart (cont.)

Relationship Signaled	*Transitions That Signal the Relationship*	*Example*
cause and effect	because, since, so, consequently, hence, as a result, therefore, thus, because of this	Because of this year's frost, almost 30 percent of the state's fruit crop was lost.
purpose	for this purpose, so that this may occur, in order to	In order to pass the school levy, the school board must make clear just how desperately additional money is needed.
emphasis	indeed, in fact, surely, undoubtedly, without a doubt, certainly, truly, to be sure, I am certain	Adolescence is not the carefree time some adults view it to be. In fact, it can be the most unsettled period in a person's life.
illustration	for example, for instance, as an illustration, specifically, to be specific, in particular	Most of the parents complained that the schools were not tough enough. They said, for example, that their children were rarely assigned homework.
summary or clarification	in summary, in conclusion, as I have shown, in brief, in short, in other words, all in all, that is	The used car Joshua bought required brake pads, shocks, and a fuel pump. In other words, it was in terrible shape.
admitting a point	although, while this may be true, granted, even though, while it is true that	While it is true that too many Americans cannot read and write, this country's literacy rate is among the best in the world.

> Jenny has been in bed with strep throat for a week. Her illness may force her to drop her courses this term.

Notice that the second sentence begins with *her illness*. The word *illness* is a synonym for *strep throat,* which appears in the first sentence. This synonym repeats a key idea to achieve transition.

Use Transitions to Connect Paragraphs

Transitions can link ideas between the end of one paragraph and the beginning of the next. When used in this way, transitions tighten organization by demonstrating how the ideas of one paragraph relate to those of another, and they improve the flow of paragraphs by eliminating any abrupt shifts.

The transitional devices you have learned so far—using transitional words and phrases, repetition of key words, repetition of key ideas, and using synonyms—can all be used to bridge paragraphs as the following examples show.

1. *End of one paragraph:* `The students believe that the proposed library will not meet their needs.`

   Beginning of next paragraph: `In addition, students oppose construction of the library for another reason.`

   Transitional device: The transitional phrase *in addition* signals that the idea in the second paragraph functions as a supplement to the idea in the first paragraph.

2. *End of one paragraph:* `Clearly, teacher burnout is a serious problem.`

   Beginning of next paragraph: `Unfortunately, teacher burnout is not the only serious problem facing our schools.`

   Transitional device: Repetition of the key words *teacher burnout* and *serious problem* signals the connection between the two paragraphs.

3. *End of one paragraph:* `For the first time in years, the American divorce rate is beginning to drop.`

   Beginning of next paragraph: `The reasons for this new trend deserve our attention.`

   Transitional device: In the second paragraph, *this new trend* is a repetition of the key idea in paragraph 1, *the American divorce rate is beginning to drop.*

4. *End of one paragraph:* `All signs indicate that the safety forces strike will continue for at least another week.`

   Beginning of next paragraph: `If the work stoppage does last seven more days, the effects will be devastating.`

   Transitional device: In the second paragraph, *work stoppage* is a synonym for *strike,* which appears in the first paragraph. Also, in the second paragraph, *seven more days* is a synonym for *another week,* which appears in the first paragraph.

EXERCISE

Transitions

1. Write sentences and supply transitions according to the directions given. The first one is done for you as an example.
   a. Write two sentences about the way women are portrayed in television commercials. Link the sentences with a transitional word or phrase signaling contrast. Underline the transition.
      example: `Television ads do not depict women realistically. However, today's commercials are an improvement over those of five years ago.`
   b. Write one sentence about exams that has a transitional word or phrase of addition to link two ideas. Underline the transition.
   c. Write two sentences about your favorite television show. Link the sentences with a transitional word or phrase signaling emphasis. Underline the transition.
   d. Write one sentence about Thanksgiving (or another holiday) that has a transitional word or phrase of contrast. Underline the transition.
   e. Write two sentences that describe the location of things in your bedroom. Link the sentences with a transitional word or phrase to signal spatial arrangement. Underline the transition.
   f. Write one sentence about a campus issue with a transitional word or phrase for admitting a point. Underline the transition.
   g. Write two sentences about someone you enjoy being with. Link the sentences with a transitional word or phrase of illustration. Underline the transition.
   h. Write two sentences, each about a different relative. Link the sentences with a transitional word or phrase of either comparison or contrast. Underline the transition.
   i. Write two sentences about what you do upon waking in the morning. Link the sentences with a transitional word or phrase to show time sequence. Underline the transition.
   j. Write two sentences about the toughest instructor you have had. Link the sentences with a transitional word or phrase of clarification. Underline the transition.
2. In the following sentences, fill in the blanks with one or more words according to the directions given. The first one is done for you as an example.
   a. *Repeat key word:* I am uncomfortable with the principle behind life insurance. Basically *such insurance* means I am betting some giant corporation that I will die before my time.
   b. *Repeat key word:* Over the years the registration process has become increasingly complex, causing students to become confused and frustrated. This ____________________ is now being studied by campus administrators in an effort to streamline procedures.
   c. *Use a synonym* for *additional week:* Because so many students found it impossible to complete their term papers by Friday, Dr. Rodriguez was willing to give an additional week to work on them. ____________________ helped everyone feel more comfortable with the assignment.

d. *Repeat key idea:* The Altmans returned from their weekend trip to discover that their house had been broken into and ransacked. ________________ was so extensive, it took them two full days to get everything back in order.
e. *Repeat key idea:* According to the current charter, the club's president can serve for only one term. ________________ was meant to ensure that there would be frequent change in leadership.

SENTENCE EFFECTIVENESS AND STYLE

The way writers craft their sentences is their **style**. To hold their readers' interest, writers must have an appealing style.

Actually, you have already learned two stylistic considerations. When you use specific diction, you improve your style by creating more vivid, interesting sentences. Also, when you use transitions to connect ideas, you improve the flow of your sentences, which improves your style. The next pages discuss additional ways you can improve your style and thereby increase sentence effectiveness.

Use Simple Diction

Some writers believe that effective, sophisticated sentences require big, $20-words. These are the people who use *pusillanimous* when *cowardly* would do just as well—even better, actually. If these writers do not have words like *egregious* or *inveigle* in their vocabularies, they pull them out of a dictionary or thesaurus and plunk them into their writing.

Writers who believe "the bigger the words, the better the sentence" have not considered that a sentence cannot be effective if the reader cannot understand it. Also, they do not appreciate that they can be specific and accurate by using the wealth of simple, clear words they have at their disposal. Consider for a moment the following sentences taken from student essays.

> The impetuous drive of youth mellows into the steady pull of maturity.
>
> The car vibrated to a halt.
>
> Unnoticed, light filters in beneath the blinds.

These sentences are interesting and clear. They are effective because of the specific word choice. Yet although specific, the words are simple ones that are part of our natural, everyday vocabularies. Words like *filters, mellows, impetuous, drive, pull, vibrated,* and *halt*—words as simple as these make effective sentences. You need not hunt for high-flown, $20-words, because specific yet simple words create an appealing style. On the other hand, when writers use unnecessarily big words, the reader is put off by a style that seems pretentious and unnatural.

Eliminate Wordiness

When you draft, you work to get your ideas down any way you can. Naturally, conciseness is not one of your concerns. However, when you revise for sentence effectiveness, you should improve your style by eliminating unnecessary words. The following seven tips can help.

1. *Reduce empty phrases to a single word.*

Phrase	Revision
at this point in time	now
in this day and age	now
due to the fact that	because
in many cases	often/frequently
on a frequent basis	often/frequently
has the ability to	can
at that time	then
in the event that	if
for the purpose of	so

wordy: The mayor has the ability to alter that policy.

revision: The mayor can alter that policy.

2. *Eliminate Redundancy.* A **redundancy** says the same thing more than once.

Redundancy	Revision
the color yellow	yellow
circle around	circle
mix together	mix
the reason why	the reason
very unique	unique
the final conclusion	the conclusion

wordy: The Joint Chiefs of Staff felt an increased military budget was very necessary.

revision: The Joint Chiefs of Staff felt an increased military budget was necessary.

3. *Eliminate deadwood.* Words that add no meaning are *deadwood,* and they should be stricken.

wordy: Joyce is a clever type of person.

revision: Joyce is a clever person. [Joyce is clever.]

wordy: This kind of question is difficult to answer.

revision: This question is difficult to answer. [This question is difficult.]

4. *Eliminate unnecessary repetition.*

wordy: The first car in the accident was smashed and destroyed.

revision: The first car in the accident was destroyed.

wordy: I think and believe the way you do.

revision: I think [believe] the way you do.

5. *Avoid opening with "there."*

wordy: There are many things we can do to help.

revision: We can do many things to help.

wordy: There was an interesting mix of people at the party.

revision: An interesting mix of people was at the party.

6. *Reduce the number of prepositional phrases.*

wordy: The increase of violence in this country points to a decline in moral values.

revision: This country's increasing violence points to moral decline.

7. *Reduce the number of "that" and "which" clauses.*

wordy: The students asked the instructor to repeat the explanation that she gave earlier.

revision: The students asked the instructor to repeat her earlier explanation.

wordy: The book which is on the table is yours.

revision: The book on the table is yours.

NOTE: Sometimes words that could be cut out are left in because the sentence works better that way with the sentences before and after it. The trick is to eliminate *annoying* wordiness while using words to achieve a readable style that comes from each sentence flowing well from the previous one. Thus whether a writer uses "Most people notice right off that Melanie is a sarcastic person" or, "Most notice immediately that Melanie is sarcastic" will depend in part on which reads better with the sentences before and after.

EXERCISE

Eliminating Wordiness

Revise the sentences to eliminate wordiness.

sample original: `The most frightening experience that I think I ever had occurred when I was 15.`

sample revision: `The most frightening experience I had occurred when I was 15. [My most frightening experience occurred when I was 15.]`

1. The only audible sound to be heard was the blower of the heater motor as it worked to produce a soft, low hum.
2. The reason I feel our nation is so great is that both men and women of the species have opportunities to excel.
3. Until that day I did not realize or consider that people such as Corey are the most dangerous of all because they are so extremely selfish.
4. In my opinion it seems that a physical education requirement for college students is a complete waste of time.
5. This particular kind of sport is ideal for the person who desires exercise but is not in the best physical condition in the world.
6. There are many reasons why beer commercials should be banned from television.
7. The explanation of my son for why he was home late was the same explanation that he gave me last Saturday night.
8. The small little package which Jimmy gave Conchetta for her birthday held the ring that was for her engagement.
9. In the event that I am unable to join you, please start and begin to eat without my presence.
10. There were six dogs that were roaming the neighborhood which the dog warden found it necessary to take to the city pound.

Avoid Clichés

A **cliché** is an overworked expression that people are weary of hearing and reading. At one time, a cliché was an interesting way to say something, but as a result of overuse, it has become worn and dull. Below is a list of some clichés you may have heard.

scarce as hen's teeth	black as night
sadder but wiser	over the hill
cold as ice	the quick and the dead
crawl out from under	free as a bird
dry as a bone	tried but true
free and easy	bright-eyed and bushy-tailed
cried like a baby	drank like a sailor
vim and vigor	soft as silk
clear as a bell	hard as nails

For the most part, you should avoid clichés and find a more interesting way to express your ideas. Take a look at the following student sentence.

```
When my father accepted a job in Ohio, my heart sank.
```

As readers we have no trouble determining what the writer of this sentence means: he felt bad about his father taking a job in Ohio. Still, the cliché *my heart sank* creates two problems. First, it is vague. Just how bad did the writer feel? Was the writer depressed, scared, or what? Second, the sentence lacks interest because the cliché is dull.

Now react to the following revision.

```
When my father accepted a job in Ohio, I lost sleep worrying
about whether I would be able to make new friends.
```

With this revision, the reader understands both the nature and the extent of the writer's negative feeling. Thus, the revision is the more effective sentence.

NOTE: Even if you do not view clichés as overworked expressions, keep in mind that a seasoned reader will, which is a good enough reason to avoid them.

EXERCISE

Revising Clichés

Revise the sentences to eliminate the italicized clichés. You may revise several times before your sentence reads the way you want it to. Also, feel free to add any detail you wish.

example: My sixth-grade teacher was *mad as a hatter.*

revision: `My sixth-grade teacher was so eccentric that she wore the same faded green dress from September until Christmas break.`

1. Cassandra is never bored because she is always *busy as a beaver.*
2. *It's a crying shame* that rainy weather spoiled your vacation.
3. Anyone who can sit through Professor James's lectures deserves a medal, because the man has a *voice that would shatter glass.*

4. Juan is *happy as a clam* because he got an *A* in calculus.
5. Poor Godfrey is so clumsy he is *like a bull in a china shop.*

Avoid Passive Voice

In the **active voice**, the subject of the sentence *acts.* In the **passive voice**, the subject of the sentence is *acted upon.*

active: `The optometrist examined the child's eyes.` (The subject, *optometrist,* performs the action of the verb, *examined.*)

passive: `The child's eyes were examined by the optometrist.` (The subject, *child's eyes,* is acted upon.)

Most of the time, a writer should use active voice rather than passive voice, because active voice is more vigorous and less wordy than passive voice, as the following examples reveal.

passive: `The ball was thrown into the end zone by the quarterback.`

active: `The quarterback threw the ball into the end zone.`

Another reason to favor active over passive voice is that the passive may not indicate who or what performed the action.

passive: `The workers were criticized for their high absentee rate.` (Who did the criticizing?)

active: `The new corporate vice president criticized the workers for their high absentee rate.` (Now we know who did the criticizing.)

Although you should usually choose active over passive voice, sometimes the passive voice is more appropriate, particularly when the performer of the action is either unknown or unimportant.

appropriate passive voice: `After germination, the plants are thinned so they are spaced 6 inches apart.` (Who thins the plants is not important.)

appropriate passive voice: `The chicken was baked until it was tough and tasteless.` (The person who baked the chicken is unknown.)

Sometimes a writer or speaker uses the passive voice to hide information. Be wary of this technique.

passive voice used to conceal: `I have been told that someone is stealing from the cash register.` (The writer or speaker does not want to reveal who did the telling.)

EXERCISE

Revising Inappropriate Passive Voice

Five of the following sentences are in the active voice; five are in the passive voice. Rewrite those written in the passive voice to change them to the active voice.

1. The elaborate sand castle was built by Tina, Jerry, and their father.
2. By noon, high tide had washed away most of their creation.
3. While I was shopping in the mall, my purse was snatched by a teenager dressed in torn blue jeans and a green sweatshirt.
4. The police reported that someone matching that description had stolen three other purses the same day.
5. The antique necklace I wear so often was given to me by my favorite aunt.
6. Aunt Sadie collected antique jewelry and gave me a piece every year for my birthday.
7. A surprise birthday party was thrown for Rhoda by three of her closest friends.
8. Unfortunately, Rhoda did not arrive when she was expected, so she ruined the surprise.
9. I asked my academic advisor how to improve my calculus grade.
10. I was told by my advisor to spend two hours a week in the math lab.

Use Parallel Structure

Parallelism means that coordinate sentence elements (elements of equal importance serving the same function) should have the same grammatical form. The following sentence, for example, has parallel structure.

`Mrs. Chen found the novel` <u>`outrageous`</u>`,` <u>`offbeat`</u>`, and` <u>`shocking`</u>`.`

The underlined words all have the same function (to describe *novel*) and they all have the same degree of importance in the sentence. To achieve parallelism, then, the words all take the same grammatical form—they are adjectives.

When writers fail to achieve parallelism, the result can be an awkward sentence that weakens style, as in the following example.

I have always liked hiking and to swim.

Because *hiking* and *to swim* have the same function (they serve as the object of the verb *have liked*), and because they are of equal importance, they should both have the same grammatical form. Yet one is an *-ing* verb form (present participle) and one is a *to* verb form (infinitive). To be parallel, both must be present participles or both must be infinitives.

I have always liked hiking and swimming.

I have always liked to hike and to swim.

Faulty parallelism occurs most often when writers place items in a series or a pair, when they compare or contrast, and when they use correlative conjunctions. These matters are discussed next.

1. Sentence elements forming a series or pair should have the same grammatical form.

nonparallel: You can get to Toronto by car, bus, or fly.

parallel: You can get to Toronto by car, bus, or plane.

explanation: The nonparallel series includes two nouns and a verb. Parallelism is achieved by revising to include three nouns.

nonparallel: Before my first date, Mother told me to be in by midnight and she said I was to be a gentleman.

parallel: Before my first date Mother told me to be in by midnight and to be a gentleman.

explanation: The nonparallel pair includes a verb (infinitive) phrase and a clause. Parallelism is achieved by revising to include two verb (infinitive) phrases.

2. Items compared or contrasted in a sentence should have the same grammatical form. Consider the following nonparallel sentence.

I love a day *at the beach* more than to spend a day in the country.

This sentence lacks parallelism because the noun phrase *a day at the beach* is contrasted with the verb phrase *to spend a day in the country.* To be parallel, the contrast should be expressed in one of the following ways.

> `I love a day at the beach more than a day in the country.` (Two noun phrases)
>
> or
>
> `I love spending a day at the beach more than spending a day in the country.` (Two *-ing* verb phrases)

Sometimes parallelism problems crop up because the writer fails to mention the second item being compared or contrasted, as in the following sentence.

> `I like small, intimate restaurants better.`

This sentence does not indicate what *small, intimate restaurants* is contrasted with. To solve the problem, add the missing contrast.

> `I like small, intimate restaurants better than crowded, noisy cafeterias. (Two noun phrases)`

3. **Correlative conjunctions** are conjunctions used in pairs. The following are correlative conjunctions.

either . . . or	both . . . and
neither . . . nor	not only . . . but [also]

To achieve parallelism with correlative conjunctions, be sure that the same grammatical structure that follows the first conjunction also follows the second.

nonparallel construction: `I want either to spend my vacation in New York City or in Bermuda.`

parallel construction: `I want to spend my vacation either in New York City or in Bermuda.`

explanation: In the nonparallel construction, a verb (infinitive) phrase appears after *either* and a prepositional phrase appears after *or*. In the parallel construction prepositional phrases appear after *either* and *or*.

nonparallel construction: `The ballet was both well performed and had lavish sets.`

parallel construction: `The ballet both was well performed and had lavish sets.`

explanation: In the nonparallel construction, *both* is followed by a modifier and *and* is followed by a verb phrase. In the parallel construction, *both* and *and* are followed by verb phrases.

EXERCISE

Parallelism

Rewrite the following sentences to achieve parallel structure.

1. The boutique is known for its variety of styles, for its haughty sales clerks, and daring new designs.
2. The police car sped up the street, its lights flashing, its siren wailing, and roaring its engine.
3. I find playing tennis to be better exercise than volleyball.
4. Kim not only has bought a tape deck but also a video recorder.
5. Susan is beautiful, arrogant, and has been spoiled by her parents.
6. My neighbor wants either to resurface his driveway or be painting his house.
7. Carlos plans to attend the university, study biology, and being accepted into medical school.
8. Neither is the newspaper column timely nor interesting.
9. Lisa enjoys working for a large corporation for its many chances for advancement, for its excitement, and because of its many fringe benefits.
10. The research paper was not acceptable because it was late, it was too short, and needed typing.

Eliminate Mixed Constructions

When a sentence starts out following a particular sentence pattern and midway switches to another pattern, the result is a problem called **mixed construction**. Consider the following sentences that express similar ideas, each following a different, acceptable sentence pattern.

```
By following my adviser's suggestions, I raised my grade-point average.
Following my adviser's suggestions raised my grade-point average.
```

If you form one sentence by mixing the patterns of these two sentences, the result is the following problem sentence.

```
By following my adviser's suggestions raised my grade-point
average.
```

Here is another sentence with mixed construction.

```
Although I need the money will not guarantee I will get the
scholarship.
```

To revise this problem sentence, separate the mixed constructions and use either one of the following improvements.

```
Although I need the money, I will not necessarily get the
scholarship.
Needing the money does not guarantee that I will get the
scholarship.
```

One way to find mixed constructions is to read your draft aloud or have someone to read it to you so that you can listen for this problem.

NOTE: A mixed construction is often the problem when you sense something is wrong but cannot give the problem a name.

EXERCISE

Revising Mixed Constructions

Read each sentence aloud to practice hearing mixed constructions, and then rewrite each sentence to eliminate the mixed patterns.

1. If we all pitch in and recycle is what will save our environment.
2. By getting a good night's sleep before an examination will improve a student's performance.
3. Because rain forests are vital to a stable ecology is the reason they must be protected.
4. In my residence hall, most of the basketball players live here.
5. In whole-language learning teaches children all subjects by using speech, reading, writing, and critical thinking.
6. When students do not pay attention in class causes instructors to lose their patience.
7. By expanding the mall's hours of operation during the holiday season is one way to increase sales.

8. Because the building contractor cut corners when he estimated the cost of the job caused a number of things to go wrong with the plumbing and the electrical work.
9. In assuming the worst will happen creates a self-fulfilling prophecy so the worst does happen.
10. By exercising regularly can promote psychological well-being as well as physical fitness.

Vary Sentence Structures

To achieve a pleasing rhythm, writers strive for **sentence variety** by varying sentence structures. Sentence variety improves style by helping writers avoid the monotonous rhythm that comes from too many sentences with the same pattern. For example, the following paragraph lacks the necessary sentence variety. As you read it, notice how you react.

> My son is in third grade. He told me yesterday that he was one of twelve students selected to take French. Greg is delighted about it. I am annoyed. I feel this way for several reasons. The French classes will be held three days a week. The students will have French instead of their usual reading class. I believe at the third-grade level, reading is more important than French. I do not want my son to miss his reading class. The teacher says Greg reads well enough for his age. I maintain that there is still room for improvement. Some people might say that learning French at an early age is a wonderful opportunity. They say students will be exposed to another language and culture. This will broaden their awareness. This may be so. I do not think students should be forced into French for this. They should have a choice of languages to study, the way they do in high school. Greg might be more interested in German. He cannot pick German now. He will learn French now. This means in high school he will probably pick French again. He will think it will be easier because he already knows some. He will never be exposed to German or whatever other language he might like. This is not broadening awareness. This is narrowing the field. I am concerned about a third-grader learning a new grammar. He does not have English grammar down pat yet. It would be better to

get one thing right before moving on to another. I suspect Greg will get the two grammars confused. Teaching French to third-graders in place of reading does not make sense to me.

The paragraph has an unsatisfactory rhythm because all the sentences begin the same way—with the subject. To achieve sentence variety and improve your style, include a mixture of sentence structures by following several of the suggestions below.

1. *Use coordination in some of your sentences.*

examples: Gregory is delighted to be learning French, but I am annoyed about it.

Third-graders are not ready for a foreign language, and I doubt they will profit much from it.

2. *Begin some sentences with subordinate clauses.*

examples: While I believe the study of French can be beneficial, I do not feel it should be taught to third-graders at the expense of reading instruction.

If my son is to learn another language, I prefer that he choose the one he wishes to study.

NOTE: For a more detailed discussion of coordination and subordination, see pages 98–102.

3. *Begin some sentences with one or two "-ly" words (adverbs).* When you use two *-ly* words to begin a sentence, these words may be separated in one of four ways: with a comma, with *and,* with *but,* or with *yet.*

examples: Excitedly, Greg told me of his opportunity to take French.

Patiently but [yet] firmly, I told Greg I did not want him to take French.

Loudly and angrily, I told Greg's teacher I did not want Greg to take French.

Slowly, thoroughly, Greg's teacher explained why Greg should take French.

punctuation note: Two *-ly* words are separated by a comma when *and, but,* or *yet* is not used. If one of these words appears, no comma is placed. In addition, an introductory *-ly* word or a pair of *two* introductory *-ly* words is followed by a comma.

examples: Wearily, I explained to Greg for the fifth time why he would not be taking French.

Loudly and irritably, I argued with the principal about the wisdom of teaching French to third-graders.

4. *Begin some sentences with the -ing form of a verb.* The *-ing* form of a verb is the **present participle**, and it can appear alone, in a pair, or with a phrase.

examples: Sobbing, Greg explained that all his friends were taking French, and he wanted to also.

Whining and crying, Greg left the room convinced that I was a cruel mother.

Understanding his disappointment, I finally agreed to the French instruction.

caution: When you begin a sentence with a present participle—whether it appears alone, in a pair, or with a phrase—be sure the participle and any accompanying words are immediately followed by a word or word group the participle can logically refer to. Otherwise you will create an illogical or even silly sentence.

example: Still having trouble with English grammar, it is not the time for Greg to learn French.

correction: Still having trouble with English grammar, Greg is not ready to learn French.

explanation: In the first sentence, the participle and phrase refer to *it,* which causes the sentence to express the idea that *it* was having trouble with English grammar. However, Greg was the one having trouble, so the word *Greg* must appear just after the participle phrase.

5. *Begin some sentences with "-ed," "-en," "-n," or "-t" verb forms.* These verb forms are the **past participle** forms of verbs, and they can function alone, in a pair, or with a phrase.

examples: Exasperated, Greg stormed from the room.

Spent from the long discussion with Greg, I took a nap for an hour.

Stricken with grief, Greg cried for an hour because he could not take French.

Frustrated and defeated, I finally allowed Greg to take the French class.

caution: When you begin a sentence with a past participle, whether it is alone, part of a pair, or in a phrase, be sure the word or word group immediately following the structure is something the participle can logically refer to. Otherwise the result will be a silly, illogical sentence.

example: `Delighted by the idea of learning a new language, French class was something Greg looked forward to.`

correction: `Delighted by the idea of learning a new language, Greg looked forward to French class.`

explanation: In the first sentence, *French class* appears just after the past participle with its phrase. As a result, it seems that the French class was delighted. In the revision, a word that the participle can sensibly refer to appears after the phrase.

punctuation note: An introductory participle—whether alone, in a pair, or with a phrase—is followed by a comma.

6. *Begin some sentences with "to" and a present-tense verb.* When *to* is used with the present-tense verb form, the structure is called an **infinitive**. Infinitives can appear alone, in pairs, or in phrases, but often they appear in phrases.

examples: `To understand my reaction, you must realize that I value reading above all other school subjects.`

`To be effective, a foreign language curriculum should offer students a choice of languages to study.`

`To appreciate and to accept my view, you must agree with me that reading is more important than French.`

punctuation note: An introductory infinitive—whether alone, in a pair, with a phrase, or with a modifier—is followed by a comma only if the infinitive and any accompanying words are followed by a main clause.

examples: `To study French in third grade, Greg would have to miss his reading class.`

`To study French in third grade seems foolish to me.`

explanation: In the first sentence the infinitive phrase *(to study French in third grade)* is followed by a main clause, and so a comma is used after the infinitive phrase. In the second sentence the infinitive phrase *(to study French in third grade)* is not followed by a main clause, so no comma is used after the phrase.

7. *Begin some sentences with a prepositional phrase.* A **preposition** is a word that signals direction, placement, or connection. Some of the common prepositions include the following.

about	among	between	from	of	over	under
above	around	by	in	off	through	with
across	before	during	inside	on	to	within
along	behind	for	into	out	toward	without

A **prepositional phrase** is a preposition plus the words that are functioning with it. Here are some examples.

across the bay	of the United States
before the rush hour	to me
at the new shopping mall	without the slightest doubt

To achieve sentence variety, you can begin some of your sentences with one or more prepositional phrases.

examples: `For a number of reasons, I oppose French instruction at the third-grade level.`

`By my standards, reading is more important than French for third-graders.`

8. *Vary the placement of transitional words and phrases.* Many transitions can function either at the beginning, in the middle, or at the end of a sentence. To achieve sentence variety, vary the placement of these structures.

examples: `Indeed, Greg was disappointed that I would not allow him to take French.`

`He was so disappointed, in fact, that I felt compelled to give in.`

`This does not mean my belief has changed, however.`

9. *Begin some sentences with the subject.* Sentence variety refers to mixing sentence structures to avoid the monotony of repetition. So by all means, begin some of your sentences with the subject.

10. *Strike a balance between long and short sentences.* Follow a long sentence with a much shorter one, or a short sentence with a longer one. While it is never

necessary to follow this pattern throughout an essay, on occasion it can enhance rhythm and flow.

examples: Although I explained to Greg repeatedly why I believed he was better off taking reading rather than French, he never understood my point of view. Instead, he was heartbroken.

I did my best. I reasoned with him, bribed him, and became angry with him, but still I could not convince Greg that he would be better off to wait a few years before studying a foreign language.

EXERCISE

Revising for Sentence Variety

Rewrite the paragraph on pages 119–120 to give it the sentence variety it needs. Strive for an adequate mix of structures, using as many patterns as you find necessary. Also, you may alter the existing wording somewhat, and you may add words (transitions, for example). Of course, there is no one way to revise the paragraph. There may be as many different effective revisions written as there are people in your class.

PART 2

Patterns of Development

CHAPTER 5

Description

Description creates pictures in the reader's mind. Sometimes writers use observable, factual details expressed in unemotional language to create an **objective description.** For example, a real estate appraiser who describes a house to determine its fair market value would write an objective description of the house. Other times, writers want to include their feelings about what they are describing, or they want to create certain feelings in the reader. At such times, writers use more emotional or expressive language to describe. This is **subjective description.**

Notice the difference between the factual language of objective description and the expressive language of subjective description in these two examples, taken from selections in this chapter.

objective description: It was like every other house in Jalco, probably larger. The adobe walls were thick, a foot or more, with patches of whitewash where the thatched overhang protected the adobe from the rain. There were no windows. The entrance doorway was at one end of the front wall, and directly opposite the door that led to the corral. ("A Mexican House")

subjective description: The kitchen was the great machine that set our lives running; it whirred down a little only on Saturdays and holy days. From my mother's kitchen I gained my first picture of life as a white, overheated, starkly lit workshop redolent with Jewish cooking, crowded with women in housedresses, strewn with fashion magazines . . . at whose center, so lashed to her machine that bolts of energy seemed to dance out of her hands and feet as she worked, my mother . . . beat out the first rhythm of the world for me. ("The Kitchen")

An essay can include both objective and subjective description. In fact, a single sentence can combine both, as the following example from an essay in this chapter reveals.

combined objective and subjective description: `She was only about five feet tall and probably never weighed more than 110 pounds, but Miss Bessie was a towering presence in the classroom. ("Unforgettable Miss Bessie")`

Description can form part of an essay that is predominantly developed with some other pattern, say narration or illustration. In this case, the description creates vividness, adds specific detail, provides vitality, or creates context. Other times, the description is the chief method of development. While the principles of descriptive writing discussed in this chapter hold true in either case, we will discuss description as the primary pattern of development.

PURPOSE

Writers often describe to share their perceptions with their reader. Sometimes writers want the reader to understand *why* their perception is what it is, and sometimes they want the reader to understand the effects the perception has on them. Writers can also describe in order to inform the reader, perhaps by helping their audience experience something new or come to a fresh appreciation of the familiar. Finally, writers can describe for a persuasive purpose—to convince a reader to view something the same way they do.

The purpose for your description will influence your detail selection. Let's say, for example, you wish to describe your car, and let's also say that you want your reader to understand that the car is a reflection of your outgoing personality. In this case, you might describe the flashy colors, custom dash, unusual hood ornament, elaborate sound system, and so forth. Now let's say you want your reader to come to a fresh appreciation of the familiar. In this case you might describe the features of your car that show it to be a marvel of engineering. If, however, you want to convince your reader to view your car as you do (as, say, something that does more harm than good), you might describe the features that contribute to air and noise pollution, that contribute to laziness, that can kill, and so on.

To determine the purpose or combination of purposes for your descriptive essay, you can ask yourself the following questions.

1. Can I help my reader understand why I perceive my subject a particular way?
2. Can I help my reader understand the effect my perception has on me?

3. Can I help my reader appreciate something he or she has not experienced before?
4. Can I help my reader achieve a fresh appreciation for something familiar?
5. Can I convince my reader to view something the same way I do?

AUDIENCE

Audience, like purpose, affects detail selection. How much your reader knows about your subject, how your reader feels about your subject, how interested your reader is in your subject—these factors influence your choice of details. For example, say you plan to describe the beauty of your campus commons in winter. If your reader is from a warm climate and has never seen snow, you will have to provide more details to create mental images than you would if your reader were familiar with snow. If your reader hates winter, you will have to work harder to help him or her appreciate the beauty than you would if your reader enjoyed winter.

To establish an audience for your description, you can ask yourself these questions.

1. Who would enjoy reading my description?
2. Who would learn something from my description?
3. Who shares an interest in my subject?
4. Who could be persuaded to view my subject as I do?
5. Who would I like to share my perceptions with?
6. Who would find my subject important?
7. Who could come to appreciate my subject as a result of reading my essay?

So that you can gear your detail to your reader's needs, answer the following questions.

1. How much experience has my reader had with my subject?
2. How does my reader currently view my subject?
3. What does my reader need to know about my subject?
4. What strong feelings does my reader have about my subject?
5. How much interest does my reader have in my subject?
6. How receptive will my reader be to my point of view?

SELECTING DETAIL

Let's say that the attic of your grandmother's house has intrigued you since you were a small child, so you decide to write a descriptive essay about it. Or let's assume that your grandmother herself has always interested you, so you decide to describe *her* in an essay. Either way, one thing is clear: you cannot describe *every-*

thing about your subject. If you tried to include every detail about your grandmother or her attic, the result would be an unwieldy essay. Then how do writers decide what to include and what to omit? You already know part of the answer: writers base their detail selection on their audience and purpose.

Something else you can do to avoid describing everything about your subject is to settle on one impression and describe only those features that contribute to that impression. For example, if your grandmother's attic has always intrigued you because it is eerie, full of reminders of the past, and unusual, pick one of these three impressions to form the focus of your description. Then describe only those features of the attic that convey the impression you have settled on. Similarly, if your grandmother is interesting because she is enthusiastic, eccentric, and young at heart, decide which of these three qualities will be your focus and then describe only features that convey that impression. (Settling on a single impression can be particularly helpful when you write subjective description.)

To see how description can focus on one impression, read the following paragraph written by a student.

The Fruit Cellar

It was late last night as I reluctantly took the steps down to the gloomy fruit cellar. *1*
Its dark, dusty shelves are located behind the crumbling basement walls. I fumbled in the dark for the lifeless screw-in light bulb and managed to twist it to a faint glow. With that the musty room was dimly lit, and long dark shadows lurked on the ceiling, picturing enlarged, misshapen jars of fruit. Water condensed and dripped from the ceiling, shattering the eerie silence. Cobwebs suspended in every corner hid their makers in a gray crisscross of lines. Hesitantly I took a step, my sneakers soaking up the black water lying 2 inches deep on the floor. A rat darted through a hole in the wall, and jars of fruit peered at me with their glassy eyes. The rotting shelves looked as if at any moment they would fall to the floor. The cold, gray walls reminded me of an Egyptian tomb forgotten long ago. Yet mummies don't decay, and I distinctly smelled the odor of something rotting.

"The Fruit Cellar" illustrates how descriptive detail can convey a single impression. In this case, the student writer's impression of the fruit cellar is that it is gloomy, so the writer describes only those aspects of the cellar that convey that sense of gloom.

If you have trouble determining an impression to convey, try filling in the blanks in the following sentences.

1. My subject makes me feel ____________________.
2. My subject is important to me because ____________________.
3. My first impression of my subject is ____________________.
4. The word that best describes my subject is ____________________.
5. When I am near my subject, my mood is ____________________.

Concrete Sensory Detail

To create vivid mental images (pictures in the mind) for the reader, description includes **concrete sensory detail,** which is specific words that appeal to the senses (sight, sound, taste, smell, touch). Look back at "The Fruit Cellar" and notice the many strong mental images created with concrete sensory detail. Take, for example, the sentence, "Cobwebs suspended in every corner hid their makers in a gray crisscross of lines." The detail here is *sensory* because it appeals to the sense of sight. It is also *concrete* (specific) because of such specific words as *suspended* and *crisscross of lines*. This specific detail that appeals to the sense of sight creates a clear picture in the mind of the reader, a picture much more vivid than one that would be formed from something like "cobwebs were in every corner hiding their spiders."

Notice too in "The Fruit Cellar" that the writer employs more than just the sense of sight. He also includes sound (water "shattering the eerie silence"), smell ("the odor of something rotting"), and touch ("feeling the dampness at my back"). While description typically relies more on one sense than the others, impressions are most clearly conveyed when the writer brings in as many senses as are pertinent to what is being described. Be careful, though. Too much concrete sensory detail bombards your reader with mental images; too much of it and your reader will think, "Enough already; give it a rest." To realize that this is true, read and react to the following sentence:

> The small, fluffy, gray terrier danced and jumped with excitement and pleasure as her master took the hard, crunchy, brown dog biscuit from the large red-and-white sack.

This overdone sentence illustrates that descriptive writers must exercise some restraint and recognize when enough is enough. This same principle of restraint holds true in paragraphs as well. Often when you have a complex, highly descriptive sentence in a paragraph, you should have a more simple, less descriptive one next to it. Take, for example, the following two sentences which appear together in "The Sounds of the City," on page 134.

> Trash cans rattle outside restaurants. Metallic jaws on sanitation trucks gulp and masticate the residue of daily living, then digest it with a satisfied groan of gears.

Notice that the second, very descriptive sentence appears next to a first, shorter and less descriptive one to create balance and prevent the reader from feeling there is too much.

NOTE: Concrete sensory detail is best achieved with specific, simple diction, which is explained on page 95.

ARRANGING DETAIL

The thesis for a descriptive essay can note what you are describing and the impression you have formed about what you are describing, like this.

> As a child, and now as an adult, I have always been drawn to Grandma's attic because it is filled with reminders of the past.

The thesis indicates that Grandma's attic will be described, and the impression is that it is filled with reminders of the past.

When you form your thesis, express your impression in specific language. Impressions expressed in words like *nice, great, wonderful, awful, terrible,* and *bad* are vague and do not tell the reader much. However, words like *relaxing, scenic, cheerful, depressing, congested,* and *unnerving* are specific and give the reader a clearer understanding of how you feel about what you are describing.

As an alternative, your introduction can state what you are describing *without* specifying your impression. With this technique, the reader gathers the impression from the details in the body.

Of course, your body paragraphs form the heart of your essay. Here you provide the descriptive details that bear out your impression of your subject. You can approach the arrangement of descriptive details several ways. If you are describing a place, **spatial order** is useful. You can move from left to right, top to bottom, near to far, the center to the periphery, or the inside to the outside. Sometimes a **progressive order** is effective. You can arrange your details so that they build to the features that most clearly or strikingly convey your impression. A **chronological order** can even be effective at times, as when you are describing what you see as you move through a place.

When you are describing a person, a progressive arrangement can be useful. You can move from the least to most telling features. Chronological arrangement is also possible. You can move from a description of past actions to more current ones, for example. You can also find some other logical arrangement, say moving from a physical description to a description of character to a description of actions.

TRYOUT To help you appreciate the difference between objective and subjective description, try this: Form a group with three or four classmates and together write a one-paragraph *objective* description of some part of your writing classroom. Then on a separate sheet, write a one-paragraph *subjective* description of the same thing. Trade paragraphs with at least one other group and note the chief strengths and weaknesses of the paragraphs you receive. Pay particular attention to simple, specific word choice, strong mental images, and ordering strategies.

PROFESSIONAL ESSAYS

The Sounds of the City

James Tuite

To create vivid mental images, writers usually rely heavily on the sense of sight. However, author James Tuite does something more unusual: he relies on the sense of sound to describe a city teeming with activity day and night.

New York is a city of sounds: muted sounds and shrill sounds; shattering sounds and soothing sounds; urgent sounds and aimless sounds. The cliff dwellers of Manhattan—who would be racked by the silence of the lonely woods—do not hear these sounds because they are constant and eternally urban. 1

The visitor to the city can hear them, though, just as some animals can hear a high-pitched whistle inaudible to humans. To the casual caller to Manhattan, lying restive and sleepless in a hotel twenty or thirty floors above the street, they tell a story as fascinating as life itself. And back of the sounds broods the silence. 2

Night in midtown is the noise of tinseled honky-tonk and violence. Thin strains of music, usually the firm beat of rock 'n' roll or the frenzied outbursts of the discotheque, rise from ground level. This is the cacophony, the discordance of youth, and it comes on strongest when nights are hot and young blood restless. 3

Somewhere in the canyons below there is shrill laughter or raucous shouting. A bottle shatters against concrete. The whine of a police siren slices through the night, moving ever closer, until an eerie Doppler effect* brings it to a guttural halt. 4

There are few sounds so exciting in Manhattan as those of fire apparatus dashing through the night. At the outset there is the tentative hint of the first-due company bullying his way through midtown traffic. Now a fire whistle from the opposite direction affirms that trouble is, indeed, afoot. In seconds, other sirens converging from other streets help the skytop listener focus on the scene of excitement. 5

But he can only hear and not see, and imagination takes flight. Are the flames and smoke gushing from windows not far away? Are victims trapped there, crying out for help? Is it a conflagration, or only a trash-basket fire? Or, perhaps, it is merely a false alarm. 6

The questions go unanswered and the urgency of the moment dissolves. Now the mind and the ear detect the snarling, arrogant bickering of automobile horns. People in a hurry. Taxicabs blaring, insisting on their checkered priority. 7

Even the taxi horns dwindle down to a precocious few in the gray and pink moments of dawn. Suddenly there is another sound, a morning sound that taunts the memory for recognition. The growl of a predatory monster? No, just garbage trucks that have begun a day of scavenging. 8

*The drop in pitch that occurs as a source of sound quickly passes by a listener.

Trash cans rattle outside restaurants. Metallic jaws on sanitation trucks gulp and masticate the residue of daily living, then digest it with a satisfied groan of gears. The sounds of the new day are businesslike. The growl of buses, so scattered and distant at night, becomes a demanding part of the traffic bedlam. An occasional jet or helicopter injects an exclamation point from an unexpected quarter. When the wind is right, the vibrant bellow of an ocean liner can be heard. 9

The sounds of the day are as jarring as the glare of a sun that outlines the canyons of midtown in drab relief. A pneumatic drill frays countless nerves with its rat-a-tat-tat, for dig they must to perpetuate the city's dizzy motion. After each screech of brakes there is a moment of suspension, of waiting for the thud or crash that never seems to follow. 10

The whistles of traffic policemen and hotel doormen chirp from all sides, like birds calling for their mates across a frenzied aviary. And all of these sounds are adult sounds, for childish laughter has no place in these canyons. 11

Night falls again, the cycle is complete, but there is no surcease from sound. For the beautiful dreamers, perhaps, the "sounds of the rude world heard in the day, lulled by the moonlight have all passed away," but this is not so in the city. 12

Too many New Yorkers accept the sounds about them as bland parts of everyday existence. They seldom stop to listen to the sounds, to think about them, to be appalled or enchanted by them. In the big city, sounds are life. 13

Questions on Technique

1. Paragraphs 1 and 2 form the introduction. While the two-paragraph introduction varies from the one-paragraph format discussed in Chapter 2, it is not an uncommon technique. Although it is two paragraphs, this introduction still presents the subject of the essay and the writer's impression. What is the subject and what is the impression?
2. In what kind of order does Tuite arrange his details?
3. Most of Tuite's descriptive details appeal to the sense of sound. What do all these sounds have in common? Is the description subjective or objective?
4. Tuite's concrete sensory detail appeals to our sense of hearing, but it still creates visual mental images. For example, "Taxicabs blaring, insisting on their checkered priority" is auditory detail that evokes a visual image of Manhattan traffic. Cite another example of concrete sensory detail that plays at once on the auditory and the visual.
5. The effectiveness of Tuite's description comes in large part from effective word choice. His verbs, for example, are simple, clear, and specific, as in "a police siren slices through the night." Cite four verbs that particularly appeal to you.
6. Tuite's nouns are well chosen. Notice, for example, *bickering* in "arrogant bickering of automobile horns." Cite two other simple, specific nouns.
7. Tuite's modifiers are simple and specific. Notice, for example, *frenzied* in "frenzied outbursts of the discotheque." Cite four other effective modifiers.

8. Cite two descriptions that particularly appeal to you and explain why you like them.
9. What approach is used for the conclusion?

For Group Discussion or Journal Writing

Does Tuite make New York City seem like a city you would like to spend time in? Refer to specific descriptions to support your reaction.

The Kitchen

Alfred Kazin

Alfred Kazin describes "the largest room and the center of the household" and includes a loving portrait of his mother. Both reveal that for those seeking a new life in America, times were not always easy.

In Brownsville tenements the kitchen is always the largest room and the center of the household. As a child I felt that we lived in a kitchen to which four other rooms were annexed. My mother, a "home" dressmaker, had her workshop in the kitchen. She told me once that she had begun dressmaking in Poland at thirteen; as far back as I can remember, she was always making dresses for the local women. She had an innate sense of design, a quick eye for all the subtleties in the latest fashions, even when she despised them, and great boldness. For three or four dollars she would study the fashion magazines with a customer, go with the customer to the remnants store on Belmont Avenue to pick out the material, argue the owner down—all remnants stores, for some reason, were supposed to be shady, as if the owners dealt in stolen goods—and then for days would patiently fit and baste and sew and fit again. Our apartment was always full of women in their housedresses sitting around the kitchen table waiting for a fitting. My little bedroom next to the kitchen was the fitting room. The sewing machine, an old nut-brown Singer with golden scrolls painted along the black arm and engraved along the two tiers of little drawers massed with needles and thread on each side of the treadle, stood next to the window and the great coalblack stove which up to my last year in college was our main source of heat. By December the two outer bedrooms were closed off, and used to chill bottles of milk and cream, cold borscht and jellied calves' feet. *1*

The kitchen held our lives together. My mother worked in it all day long, we ate in it almost all meals except the Passover *seder,* I did my homework and first writing at the kitchen table, and in winter I often had a bed made up for me on three kitchen chairs near the stove. On the wall just over the table hung a long horizontal mirror that sloped to a ship's prow at each end and was lined in cherry wood. It took the whole wall, and drew every object in the kitchen to itself. The walls were a fiercely stippled whitewash, so often rewhitened by my father in slack seasons that the paint looked as if it had been squeezed and cracked into the walls. *2*

A large electric bulb hung down the center of the kitchen at the end of a chain that had been hooked into the ceiling; the old gas ring and key still jutted out of the wall like antlers. In the corner next to the toilet was the sink at which we washed, and the square tub in which my mother did our clothes. Above it, tacked to the shelf on which were pleasantly ranged square, blue-bordered white sugar and spice jars, hung calendars from the Public National Bank on Pitkin Avenue and the Minsker Progressive Branch of the Workman's Circle; receipts for the payment of insurance premiums, and household bills on a spindle; two little boxes engraved with Hebrew letters. One of these was for the poor, the other to buy back the Land of Israel. Each spring a bearded little man would suddenly appear in our kitchen, salute us with a hurried Hebrew blessing, empty the boxes (sometimes with a sidelong look of disdain if they were not full), hurriedly bless us again for remembering our less fortunate Jewish brothers and sisters, and so take his departure until the next spring, after vainly trying to persuade my mother to take still another box. We did occasionally remember to drop coins in the boxes, but this was usually only on the dreaded morning of "midterms" and final examinations, because my mother thought it would bring me luck. She was extremely superstitious, but embarrassed about it, and always laughed at herself whenever, on the morning of an examination, she counseled me to leave the house on my right foot. "I know it's silly," her smile seemed to say, "but what harm can it do? It may calm God down."

The kitchen gave a special character to our lives; my mother's character. All 3
my memories of that kitchen are dominated by the nearness of my mother sitting all day long at her sewing machine, by the clacking of the treadle against the linoleum floor, by the patient twist of her right shoulder as she automatically pushed at the wheel with one hand or lifted the foot to free the needle where it had got stuck in a thick piece of material. The kitchen was her life. Year by year, as I began to take in her fantastic capacity for labor and her anxious zeal, I realized it was ourselves she kept stitched together. I can never remember a time when she was not working. She worked because the law of her life was work, work and anxiety; she worked because she would have found life meaningless without work. She read almost no English; she could read the Yiddish paper, but never felt she had time to. We were always talking of a time when I would teach her how to read, but somehow there was never time. When I awoke in the morning she was already at her machine, or in the great morning crowd of housewives at the grocery getting fresh rolls for breakfast. When I returned from school she was at her machine, or conferring over *McCall's* with some neighborhood woman who had come in pointing hopefully to an illustration—"Mrs. Kazin! Mrs. Kazin! Make me a dress like it shows here in the picture!" When my father came home from work she had somehow mysteriously interrupted herself to make supper for us, and the dishes cleared and washed, was back at her machine. When I went to bed at night, often she was still there, pounding away at the treadle, hunched over the wheel, her hands steering a piece of gauze under the needle with a finesse that always contrasted sharply with her swollen hands and broken nails. Her left hand had been pierced through when as a girl she had worked in the infamous Triangle Shirtwaist Factory on the East Side. A needle had gone straight through the palm,

severing a large vein. They had sewn it up for her so clumsily that a tuft of flesh always lay folded over the palm.

The kitchen was the great machine that set our lives running; it whirred down a little only on Saturdays and holy days. From my mother's kitchen I gained my first picture of life as a white, overheated, starkly lit workshop redolent with Jewish cooking, crowded with women in housedresses, strewn with fashion magazines, patterns, dress material, spools of thread—and at whose center, so lashed to her machine that bolts of energy seemed to dance out of her hands and feet as she worked, my mother stamped the treadle hard against the floor, hard, hard, and silently, grimly at war, beat out the first rhythm of the world for me. *4*

Every sound from the street roared and trembled at our windows—a mother feeding her child on the doorstep, the screech of the trolley cars on Rockaway Avenue, the eternal smash of a handball against the wall of our house, the clatter of *der Italyéner's* cart packed with watermelons, the sing-song of the old-clothes men walking Chester Street, the cries *"Arbes! Arbes! Kinder! Kinder! Heyse gute árbes!"* All day long people streamed into our apartment as a matter of course—"customers," upstairs neighbors, downstairs neighbors, women who would stop in for a half-hour's talk, salesmen, relatives, insurance agents. Usually they came in without ringing the bell—everyone knew my mother was always at home. I would hear the front door opening, the wind whistling through our front hall, and then some familiar face would appear in our kitchen with the same bland, matter-of-fact inquiring look: no need to stand on ceremony: my mother and her kitchen were available to everyone all day long. *5*

At night the kitchen contracted around the blaze of light on the cloth, the patterns, the ironing board where the iron had burned a black border around the tear in the muslin cover; the finished dresses looked so frilly as they jostled on their wire hangers after all the work my mother had put into them. And then I would get that strangely ominous smell of tension from the dress fabrics and the burn in the cover of the ironing board—as if each piece of cloth and paper crushed with light under the naked bulb might suddenly go up in flames. Whenever I pass some small tailoring shop still lit up at night and see the owner hunched over his steam press; whenever in some poorer neighborhood of the city I see through a window some small crowded kitchen naked under the harsh light glittering in the ceiling, I still smell that fiery breath, that warning of imminent fire. I was always holding my breath. What I must have felt most about ourselves, I see now, was that we ourselves were like kindling—that all the hard-pressed pieces of ourselves and all the hard-used objects in that kitchen were like so many slivers of wood that might go up in flames if we came too near the white-blazing filaments in that naked bulb. Our tension itself was fire, we ourselves were forever burning—to live, to get down the foreboding in our souls, to make good. *6*

Twice a year, on the anniversaries of her parents' deaths, my mother placed on top of the ice-box an ordinary kitchen glass packed with wax, the *yortsayt,* and lit the candle in it. Sitting at the kitchen table over my homework, I would look across the threshold to that mourning-glass, and sense that for my mother the distance from our kitchen to *der heym,* from life to death, was only a flame's length *7* away. Poor as we were, it was not poverty that drove my mother so hard; it was loneliness—some endless bitter brooding over all those left behind, dead or dying or soon to die; a loneliness locked up in her kitchen that dwelt every day on the hazardousness of life and the nearness of death, but still kept struggling in the lock, trying to get us through by endless labor.

With us, life started up again only on the last shore. There seemed to be no 8
middle ground between despair and the fury of our ambition. Whenever my mother spoke of her hopes for us, it was with such unbelievingness that the likes of us would ever come to anything, such abashed hope and readiness for pain, that I finally came to see in the flame burning on top of the ice-box death itself burning away the bones of poor Jews, burning out in us everything but courage, the blind resolution to live. In the light of that mourning-candle, there were ranged around me how many dead and dying—how many eras of pain, of exile, of dispersion, of cringing before the powers of this world!

It was always at dusk that my mother's loneliness came home most to me. 9
Painfully alert to every shift in the light at her window, she would suddenly confess her fatigue by removing her pince-nez, and then wearily pushing aside the great mound of fabrics on her machine, would stare at the street as if to warm herself in the last of the sun. "How sad it is!" I once heard her say. "It grips me! It grips me!" Twilight was the bottommost part of the day, the chillest and loneliest time for her. Always so near to her moods, I knew she was fighting some deep inner dread, struggling against the returning tide of darkness along the streets that invariably assailed her heart with the same foreboding—Where? Where now? Where is the day taking us now?

Yet one good look at the street would revive her. I see her now, perched 10
against the windowsill, with her face against the glass, her eyes almost asleep in enjoyment, just as she starts up with the guilty cry—"What foolishness is this in me!"—and goes to the stove to prepare supper for us: a moment, only a moment, watching the evening crowd of women gathering at the grocery for fresh bread and milk. But between my mother's pent-up face at the window and the winter sun dying in the fabrics—"Alfred, see how beautiful!"—she has drawn for me one single line of sentience.

Questions on Technique

1. The thesis of "The Kitchen" does not appear in the first paragraph. What is the thesis? What does the thesis indicate will be described, and what is the author's impression of what will be described?
2. In paragraph 1, what approach does Kazin take to the introduction?
3. Why does Kazin describe his mother's sewing activities in such detail?
4. Is it possible to view "The Kitchen" as a description of Kazin's mother? Explain.
5. What senses are appealed to? Cite an example of a description that appeals to each of these senses.
6. Cite one example each of an effective noun, verb, and modifier.
7. Cite a mental image that you find particularly appealing.

8. For what purpose do you think Kazin wrote his description?
9. Is the description primarily objective or subjective?

For Group Discussion or Journal Writing

In paragraph 2, Kazin says, "The kitchen held our lives together." Consider what you think he means and why he feels the way he does.

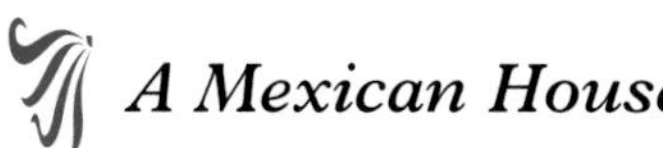

A Mexican House

Ernesto Galarza

Born in Mexico and relocated to California, Ernesto Galarza describes his one-room house in this exerpt from his autobiography Barrio Boy.

Our adobe cottage was on the side of the street away from the *arroyo.* It was the last house if you were going to Miramar. About fifty yards behind the corral, the forest closed in. 1

It was like every other house in Jalco, probably larger. The adobe walls were thick, a foot or more, with patches of whitewash where the thatched overhang protected the adobe from the rain. There were no windows. The entrance doorway was at one end of the front wall, and directly opposite the door that led to the corral. The doors were made of planks axed smooth from tree trunks and joined with two cross pieces and a diagonal brace between them hammered together with large nails bent into the wood on the inside. Next to each door and always handy for instant use, there was the cross bar, the *tranca.* On both sides of the door frame there was a notched stub, mortared into the adobe bricks and about six inches long. The door was secured from the inside by dropping the *tranca* into the two notches. 2

All the living space for the family was in the one large room, about twelve feet wide and three times as long. Against the wall between the two doorways was the *pretil,* a bank of adobe bricks three feet high, three across, and two feet deep. In the center of the *pretil* was the main fire pit. Two smaller hollows, one on either side of the large one, made it a three-burner stove. On a row of pegs above the *pretil* hung the clay pans and other cooking utensils, bottom-side out, the soot baked into the red clay. A low bench next to the *pretil,* also made of adobe, served as a table and shelf for the cups, pots, and plates. 3

The rest of the ground floor was divided by a curtain hung from one of the hand-hewn log beams, making two bedrooms. Above them, secured to the beams, was the *tapanco,* a platform the size of a double bed made of thin saplings tied together with pieces of rawhide. The top of a notched pole, braced against the foot of the back wall of the cottage, rested against the side of the *tapanco,* serving as a ladder. Along the wall opposite the *pretil,* in the darkest and coolest part of the house, were the big *cantaros,* the red clay jars; the *canastos,* tall baskets made of woven reeds; the rolled straw *petates* to cover the dirt floor where people walked or sat; and the hoes and other work tools. 4

There was no ceiling other than the underside of the thatch, which was tied to the pole rafters. On top of these, several layers of thatch were laid, making a waterproof cover thicker than the span of a man's hand. The rafters were notched and tied to the ridgepole and mortared on the lower end to the top of the walls. Between the top of the walls and the overhang there was an open space a few inches wide. Through this strip the smoke from the *pretil* went out and the fresh air came in. 5

It was the roof that gave space and lift to the single room that served as kitchen, bedroom, parlor, pantry, closet, storeroom, and tool shed. The slender rafters pointed upward in sharp triangles tied at the peak with bows of dark brown rawhide that had dried as tight as steel straps. Strings of thatch hung from the ceiling like the fringe of a buggy top, making it appear that the heavy matting of grass did not rest on the rafters but tiptoed on hundreds of threads. It was always half dark up there. My cousins, Jesus and Catarino, and I slept in the *tapanco*. More than a bedroom, to us it was a half-lighted hideaway out of sight of parents, uncles, aunts, and other meddlesome people. 6

Questions on Technique

1. Is Galarza's description primarily objective or subjective?
2. Cite three examples of concrete sensory details that create clear mental images.
3. Cite one example each of a specific yet simple noun, verb, and modifier.
4. In what kind of order are the details arranged? Cite three transitions that signal this order.
5. What do you judge to be Galaraza's purpose? Who do you think his intended audience is?

For Group Discussion or Journal Writing

Both Kazin ("The Kitchen" on page 135) and Galarza describe their houses. However, Kazin uses subjective description and Galarza uses objective description. Do you react differently to the different kinds of details? Explain. Why do you think each writer chose the kind of details he did?

Unforgettable Miss Bessie

Carl T. Rowen

Newspaper columnist Carl Rowen was profoundly affected by his high school teacher, Miss Bessie, and this description makes it easy to understand why.

She was only about five feet tall and probably never weighed more than 110 pounds, but Miss Bessie was a towering presence in the classroom. She was the only woman tough enough to make me read *Beowulf* and think for a few foolish days that I liked it. From 1938 to 1942, when I attended Bernard High School in 1

McMinnville, Tenn., she taught me English, history, civics—and a lot more than I realized.

I shall never forget the day she scolded me into reading *Beowulf.* 2

"But Miss Bessie," I complained, "I ain't much interested in it." 3

Her large brown eyes became daggerish slits. "Boy," she said, "how dare 4
you say 'ain't' to me! I've taught you better than that."

"Miss Bessie," I pleaded, "I'm trying to make first-string end on the football 5
team, and if I go around saying 'it isn't' and 'they aren't,' the guys are gonna laugh me off the squad."

"Boy," she responded, "you'll play football because you have guts. But do 6
you know what *really* takes guts? Refusing to lower your standards to those of the crowd. It takes guts to say you've got to live and be somebody fifty years after all the football games are over."

I started saying "it isn't" and "they aren't," and I still made first-string 7
end—and class valedictorian—without losing my buddies' respect.

During her remarkable 44-year career, Mrs. Bessie Taylor Gwynn taught 8
hundreds of economically deprived black youngsters—including my mother, my brother, my sisters and me. I remember her now with gratitude and affection—especially in this era when Americans are so wrought-up about a "rising tide of mediocrity" in public education and the problems of finding competent, caring teachers. Miss Bessie was an example of an informed, dedicated teacher, a blessing to children and an asset to the nation.

Born in 1895, in poverty, she grew up in Athens, Ala., where there was no 9
public school for blacks. She attended Trinity School, a private institution for blacks run by the American Missionary Association, and in 1911 graduated from the Normal School (a "super" high school) at Fisk University in Nashville. Mrs. Gwynn, the essence of pride and privacy, never talked about her years in Athens; only in the months before her death did she reveal that she had never attended Fisk University itself because she could not afford the four-year course.

At Normal School she learned a lot about Shakespeare, but most of all about 10
the profound importance of education—especially, for a people trying to move up from slavery. "What you put in your head, boy," she once said, "can never be pulled out by the Ku Klux Klan, the Congress or anybody."

Miss Bessie's bearing of dignity told anyone who met her that she was "edu- 11
cated" in the best sense of the word. There was never a discipline problem in her classes. We didn't dare mess with a woman who knew about the Battle of Hastings, the Magna Carta and the Bill of Rights—and who could also play the piano.

This frail-looking woman could make sense of Shakespeare, Milton, 12
Voltaire, and bring to life Booker T. Washington and W. E. B. DuBois. Believing that it was important to know who the officials were that spent taxpayers' money and made public policy, she made us memorize the names of everyone on the Supreme Court and in the President's Cabinet. It could be embarrassing to be unprepared when Miss Bessie said, "Get up and tell the class who Frances Perkins is and what you think about her."

Miss Bessie knew that my family, like so many others during the Depres- 13
sion, couldn't afford to subscribe to a newspaper. She knew we didn't even own a

radio. Still, she prodded me to "look out for your future and find some way to keep up with what's going on in the world." So I became a delivery boy for the Chattanooga *Times*. I rarely made a dollar a week, but I got to read a newspaper every day.

Miss Bessie noticed things that had nothing to do with schoolwork, but were vital to a youngster's development. Once a few classmates made fun of my frayed, hand-me-down overcoat, calling me "Strings." As I was leaving school, Miss Bessie patted me on the back of that old overcoat and said, "Carl, never fret about what you *don't* have. Just make the most of what you *do* have—a brain." 14

Among the things that I did not have was electricity in the little frame house that my father had built for $400 with his World War I bonus. But because of her inspiration, I spent many hours squinting beside a kerosene lamp reading Shakespeare and Thoreau, Samuel Pepys and William Cullen Bryant. 15

No one in my family had ever graduated from high school, so there was no tradition of commitment to learning for me to lean on. Like millions of youngsters in today's ghettos and barrios, I needed the push and stimulation of a teacher who truly cared. Miss Bessie gave plenty of both, as she immersed me in a wonderful world of similes, metaphors and even onomatopoeia. She led me to believe that I could write sonnets as well as Shakespeare, or iambic-pentameter verse to put Alexander Pope to shame. 16

In those days the McMinnville school system was rigidly "Jim Crow," and poor black children had to struggle to put anything in their heads. Our high school was only slightly larger than the once-typical little red schoolhouse, and its library was outrageously inadequate—so small, I like to say, that if two students were in it and one wanted to turn a page, the other one had to step outside. 17

Negroes, as we were called then, were not allowed in the town library, except to mop floors or dust tables. But through one of those secret Old South arrangements between whites of conscience and blacks of stature, Miss Bessie kept getting books smuggled out of the white library. That is how she introduced me to the Brontës, Byron, Coleridge, Keats and Tennyson. "If you don't read, you can't write, and if you can't write, you might as well stop dreaming," Miss Bessie once told me. 18

So I read whatever Miss Bessie told me to, and tried to remember the things she insisted that I store away. Forty-five years later, I can still recite her "truths to live by," such as Henry Wadsworth Longfellow's lines from "The Ladder of St. Augustine": 19

The heights by great men reached and kept
Were not attained by sudden flight.
But they, while their companions slept,
Were toiling upward in the night.

Years later, her inspiration, prodding, anger, cajoling and almost osmotic infusion of learning finally led to that lovely day when Miss Bessie dropped me a note saying, "I'm so proud to read your column in the Nashville *Tennessean*." 20

Miss Bessie was a spry 80 when I went back to McMinnville and visited her in a senior citizens' apartment building. Pointing out proudly that her building 21 was racially integrated, she reached for two glasses and a pint of bourbon. I was momentarily shocked, because it would have been scandalous in the 1930s and '40s for word to get out that a teacher drank, and nobody had ever raised a rumor that Miss Bessie did.

I felt a new sense of equality as she lifted her glass to mine. Then she 22
revealed a softness and compassion that I had never known as a student.

"I've never forgotten that examination day," she said, "when Buster Martin 23
held up seven fingers, obviously asking you for help with question number seven, 'Name a common carrier.' I can still picture you looking at your exam paper and humming a few bars of 'Chattanooga Choo Choo.' I was so tickled, I couldn't punish either of you."

Miss Bessie was telling me, with bourbon-laced grace, that I never fooled 24
her for a moment.

When Miss Bessie died in 1980, at age 85, hundreds of her former students 25
mourned. They knew the measure of a great teacher: love and motivation. Her wisdom and influence had rippled out across generations.

Some of her students who might normally have been doomed to poverty 26
went on to become doctors, dentists and college professors. Many, guided by Miss Bessie's example, became public-school teachers.

"The memory of Miss Bessie and how she conducted her classroom did 27
more for me than anything I learned in college," recalls Gladys Wood of Knoxville, Tenn., a highly respected English teacher who spent 43 years in the state's school system. "So many times, when I faced a difficult classroom problem, I asked myself, *How would Miss Bessie deal with this?* And I'd remember that she would handle it with laughter and love."

No child can get all the necessary support at home, and millions of poor 28
children get *no* support at all. This is what makes a wise, educated, warm-hearted teacher like Miss Bessie so vital to the minds, hearts and souls of this country's children.

Questions on Technique

1. Rowen's thesis is delayed for several paragraphs. What is his thesis? According to the thesis, what is the subject of the description and what is the author's impression?
2. Why does Rowen begin "Unforgettable Miss Bessie" with a description of Miss Bessie's size?
3. Paragraphs 2 to 6 tell a story. What purpose does this narration serve?
4. What purpose does the conversation serve?
5. Paragraphs 9 and 10 reveal something of Miss Bessie's past. What purpose does this background information serve?
6. Rowen notes the effects Miss Bessie had on him. What were those effects?
7. Rowen uses both objective and subjective description. Cite an example of each.
8. What approach does Rowen take to the conclusion?

For Group Discussion or Journal Writing

Miss Bessie explained that real courage was "refusing to lower your standards to those of the crowd" (paragraph 6). Do you agree or disagree with Miss Bessie's statement? Draw on your own experience and observation to provide examples that illustrate your view.

STUDENT ESSAYS TO READ AND EVALUATE

Below are four descriptive essays written by students. Some of the pieces are better than others, but each essay has definite strengths along with areas that could be improved with revision. As you read these essays, consider their strengths and weaknesses.

Following the student writings is an evaluation activity to give you practice analyzing writing. This practice will help you identify successful techniques to include in your own writing and less successful ones to avoid. Also, this practice will help you improve your sense of what does and does not succeed in writing so you can develop a sharp critical ability. Once you become a reliable critic—a critic whose judgments are accurate—you can make sound decisions about your own writing.

A Child's Room

I avoid going into my son's domain as often as I can. I like to keep life and limb intact, but there are times when it is impossible to escape the risk. One such time is in the evening when I have to carry him to his bed after he has fallen asleep in mine. Then, armed with a soporific child and a will to come out unharmed, I reluctantly approach his door and push it open. The sight that greets me is one of methodical disorder. 1

On the floor, a battle is being fought between the Super Heroes and the Ghostbusters. Superman, in his red silk shorts and flame red cape, is mounting the steps of the enemy's headquarters as the Marshmallow Man looms down at him from high atop the chimney. He-Man is fighting a green plastic dragon under a corner of the bed. The wail of a train whistle is heard as the 550 Express bears down on them on its endless journey around the room. Spilling out of one corner is the largest auto salvage yard in the United States. Matchbox cars are everywhere, and they are in every stage of disrepair. A rusted station wagon is missing a wheel, and next to it is a little red Volkswagon minus its hood and a door. A dilapidated wrecker has backed up to a worn-out bus and attempts to haul it away. 2

Another corner boasts an arsenal big enough to appeal to a hostile nation. Water guns, submachine guns, and popguns line the wall expectantly awaiting the next encounter with the enemy. Strewn across the floor are grenades and spent shotgun shells; they lay claim to the proximity of the battleground. A forgotten 3 leather holster dangles from his hobby horse. This is all evidence of a hurried retreat.

Still warily treading my way across the room, and with my eyes darting between the floor and the bed, I spot his bureau out of the corner of my eye. The bureau is a tall, stately antique with a large fuzzy mirror, and it is too short on drawers. It seems to be leaning ever so slightly to the right, as if ready to call it a day, or maybe just to rest its load. The load is made up of various articles of clothing. A grimy baseball shirt hangs from the top of the mirror, and muddy, stinky, rolled-up socks have been tossed about the marble top. Underwear, new and used, hangs from every knob. Clean clothes, half folded, have been tossed out of drawers and left in heaps on the floor. Worn and tired jeans hang from belts caught by the corners of the tall bureau. It pleads to be released from its burden. 4

His rumpled bed is within reach at last. As I get ready to lighten my load, I see that it is still impossible. His bed has been taken over by the Cleveland Zoo. A woolly bear is curled up at the bottom of the bed. A monkey and an elephant fight for a spot next to him. The soulful eyes of a stuffed beagle look up at me as if to say, "Don't move me." Three pigs are nestled between the pillows, and on top of one pillow is a white furry kitten already in a world of dreams. A large teddy bear reigns over the other pillow and spins his tales of adventure to a crowd of chipmunks. I hold my precious bundle with one hand, and I make a clean sweep of the animals with the other hand only to find sticky candy wrappers, half-eaten candy bars, and more surprises waiting for me under the covers. 5

At last the moment arrives, and I can gently lay him down and tuck him in against the night. I turn around and creep out of this room past all the toys in their various states of play, and I know that tomorrow will bring more imaginative play and a bigger mess for me to wade through. 6

Our Lake

Two weeks before I left for college, my boyfriend Steve told me that he had a surprise for me. On a Saturday afternoon we set out for what we now call "Our Lake." The lake and the woods that lead us to it provided the most beautiful and romantic scenery I have ever seen. 1

The woods were dim and chilly. The black trees stretched above Steve and me. Their leaves spread a blanket of shadow on the mossy carpet of the forest. Leaves of late summer surrounded us in earth shades as we wandered through. The primary colors of the spectrum were scattered kindly by Mother Nature, with a small bird providing a touch of blue. 2

I closed my eyes and let Steve's hand lead me while I inhaled deeply. A slight breeze carried the scent of pine, and thoughts of Christmas were handed to me like gifts for the holiday. The less distinct odor of rotting wood made me think of summers past. Suddenly, I was with old friends; we were together again in familiar places. 3

We kept walking. Our footfalls snapped at the ground angrily, and the 4 robins argued back. When we stopped to rest our bodies and cool our red cheeks, I noticed a patch of hot sunlight forcing its way through an opening in the trees ahead. I looked at Steve with eyes of inquiry. He nodded and said, "There it is."

5 Steve and I entered the electric doorway. Once through, I squinted at the contrast in light. When I was able to open my eyes, I smiled at the scene. A small creek that fed crystal water into the lake twisted behind a wall of trees until it was out of sight. Bright green grass timidly greeted the evergreens at a designated meeting point. Compared to the conversations of the menagerie living in the forest, the area surrounding the lake was so quiet that we could have heard a spider spinning her silver web.

6 On one side of the water was a slab of light grey rock supported by the shore and two stumps jutting out of the shallow water. Steve and I walked toward this resting place. The freshly mown grass tickled the bottom of my bare feet; its scent drifted to my nose. A bee that had been lazily munching on dandelion pollen curiously followed us after we passed. Its drone next to my ear sounded like the snore of an exhausted drunk.

7 When we reached the shelf of stone, I sat down and wiggled to the edge to dangle my tired feet in the water. My toes separated from the rest of my foot and waved happily to me.

8 Steve, who had been busy scaring crayfish into their tiny homes, came over to me and sat down. We were silent for almost an hour, but maybe our thoughts touched once or twice.

9 Meanwhile, the clouds had gathered together for a meeting. I shivered and suggested that we head back. Steve and I collected our shoes and left. The doorway to the dark colony of trees beckoned to us with inky maple fingers.

10 We set off for civilization with regret. The beauty of the scenery at "Our Lake" will never escape my memories.

Never Intrude

1 It was early morning, and I was diving just off the shores of Grand Cayman Island when I swam through an opening in the coral. At first I could only hear the intermittent gurgle of exhaust air, but as my eyes adjusted to the dim light, I was astonished by the assortment of life in what appeared to be a coral room.

2 There in the middle of the floor, caught by surprise, a crab shuttled from side to side unable to decide which way to go, yet unbothered nearby, a rust-red starfish worried at a clam it was trying to pry open. Deadman's fingers, a well-named rubbery sponge that was dangling from the ceiling, brushed my back. As I hung suspended just above the floor careful to avoid touching the few black sea urchins below. Fascinated, I watched as thousands of shrimp fry floated by like dust on a ray of sunlight, while hundreds of small fish, called neons, flitted in and out of the walls, their iridescent bodies giving the room a psychedelic effect. I looked at the wall on my right. There in a cubbyhole a porcupine fish had puffed itself up at least twice his normal size and was wedged tightly into his hole.

Bothered by my intrusion, a spotted jewfish loomed from the shadows to assert his territorial rights; when he swam towards me, lime-green anemones popped shut as if from fear. I could understand their concern, for he must have weighed over 100 pounds. When I raised my prod-rod, he seemed to reconsider his approach. With things at an impasse I had time to think of the position that I was in. Here in a room with jagged walls of blush pink, their white tips announcing it was fire coral. If he rammed me that coral would cut right through my wet suit and at best leave me with a nasty infection. Since I was the intruder, I carefully backed out into the open. Glad to be out of the confines of the coral room. 3

Miss Davis

Strangely, very little of my high school years stands out vividly. Yet I can recall just about everything about Miss Davis. Impeccably dressed, every hair in place, with eyes gleaming, she firmly yet fairly taught senior English. 1

That year, my last in high school, marked the beginning of a new era; North Lima and Greenford Schools had consolidated to become South Range. As if we heard a bugle sound the battle cry, we seniors resentfully marched in taking seats on each side of the room. "My initial requirement is assigned seats," Miss Davis ordered. "To make this consolidation successful, I insist you make new acquaintances. Rotating North Lima–Greenford, North Lima–Greenford, seat yourselves accordingly." Quietly protesting, we followed her command. The wall we had determined to fortify, she forcibly crushed in her domain. Continuing down the list of objectives for the year, she concluded that first eventful day, victor in the skirmish. 2

Poetry! We objected; we had no more interest in reading poetry than we had in becoming friends with the enemy camp from Greenford. Introducing us to her friends (the poets Kilmer, Sandburg, and Frost), she took us as hostages on a journey. While climbing trees, venturing through Spoon River, and choosing which path to take in those precarious Vermont woods, she bared her soul. Soon we comprehended the significance of these men to her. Any male suitor would be forced to joust with these idolized poets for her love. Secretly, we began to wonder if she had strolled hand-in-hand in those woods with Robert Frost. Her love for poetry was contagious. When making decisions now, I still see the options as "paths." 3

Miss Davis proved to be a guiding influence outside the classroom as well. Inflating like a hot air balloon, I vividly remember a scandal that had arisen. It created a dark, ominous cloud that seemed to bring school work to a halt. A National Honor Society student was accused of publicly flirting with a married bus driver. As senior advisor, with power similar to a Supreme Court Justice, Miss Davis pronounced the verdict. Accusations were not proof. Innocent until proven guilty, the student would remain an "honorable" member of the society. 4

As the furor subsided, we continued to master objectives. For the first composition assignment, we were to write a complaint letter for damaged merchandise 5 we had received. "Easy *A*," I thought. "Venting my hostility is effortless." When the letter was returned, I learned a painful lesson. She wrote on the top, "Disrespectful; learn to express yourself without damaging another's self-esteem." Often I have remembered this advice.

Most of the remaining term was spent writing a research paper. This loomed as an unattainable task. Other students had warned us of the horrors of writing a research paper. Yet as a result of her nurturing guidance, our papers developed. Nearly effortlessly, we scaled small hillocks while striving toward the summit. We climbed slowly, accomplishing one step at a time. Finally, we reached what heights we never thought possible. 6

We began counting the days until graduation. Yet we had one last requirement to fulfill. Miss Davis emphatically insisted we master her "Minimum Essential" test with a 100%. Diplomas would be retained until this milestone was accomplished. This test measured usage skills, such as correct use of homonyms. Many of us accomplished mastery initially. However, our classmate Mike took the test in repeated agony four times the final day of class. 7

While I cannot recall other teachers' names, Miss Davis's comes to life before me. Those she touched were firmly directed down paths they never would have chosen. She gave us confidence and skills that have proven to be "minimum essentials" for living. 8

Becoming a Reliable Critic by Evaluating Writing

One goal of this book is to help you become a reliable critic—someone who judges writing well—so you can make decisions about your own drafts with confidence. To that end, the activity in this section gives you practice evaluating writing and supporting your conclusions.

Form a group with several classmates and read all the student essays in this chapter. Then select one essay to evaluate (or use the one your instructor assigns). As a group, make decisions about the strengths and weaknesses of the essay by answering the evaluation questions that follow. One person should be designated the recorder and write down the group's responses. If group members disagree on some points, the recorder should make note of that disagreement and the reasons for it.

When deliberations are complete, one member of each group should report the group's findings to the rest of the class.

Evaluation Questions

1. The Thesis
   What subject and impression are presented? Are these stated or implied? Is the language specific enough?
2. The Introduction
   What do you think of the opening? Does it engage your interest?

3. Supporting Details
   Note any points you do not understand. Note any points that are not relevant. Is the language specific yet simple? Cite a mental image you like. Comment on the use of concrete sensory details. Note any striking problems with word choice.
4. Organization
   Are the details in a logical order? Evaluate the use of transitions.
5. The Conclusion
   Does the essay come to a satisfying end? Explain.
6. Overview
   What do you like best about the essay? What is the single most important revision the author should make?

Essay Topics: Description

1. In "The Sounds of the City" (page 133) Tuite captures the flavor of big-city life by recording the sounds heard in a 24-hour period. Try capturing the essence of some locale by relying predominantly on one sense.
2. In "Unforgettable Miss Bessie" (page 140) Rowen relies heavily on anecdotes to convey his impression of Miss Bessie. Describe a person and convey a dominant impression by using anecdotes.
3. Describe a person and convey what sets that person apart from many others.
4. Like Rowen (page 140), describe a teacher and focus on the effect she or he had on you.
5. Like Kazin (page 135), describe a room in the house you grew up in and reveal the memories the room evokes.
6. Write a piece describing an unforgettable person.
7. Describe your favorite (or most hated or feared) teacher, coach, scout leader, or clergyperson.
8. Describe the most popular student in your high school.
9. Describe the place you go when you are seeking solitude.
10. Describe a room where you live.
11. Describe the student cafeteria during the rush hour.
12. Describe your favorite outdoor spot on campus.
13. Describe the view from a rooftop or window.
14. Describe a place or scene where you work.
15. Describe a person you admire (or have little respect for).
16. Describe your campus library's reference room.
17. Describe a child busy at play.
18. Describe an employer or someone you work with.
19. Describe a bus, air, or train terminal.
20. Describe a schoolyard at recess, before school, or after school.
21. Describe your favorite night spot.
22. Describe someone you know who is eccentric (or daring or shy).

23. Describe a person who has had a lasting impact on you.
24. Describe your living room after a big party.
25. Like Galarza (page 139), use objective description to describe a place for an audience unfamiliar with it.

Thematic Topics

1. Galarza describes his one-room house (page 135). Kazin describes his boyhood kitchen (page 135). Think about the dwelling you grew up in and then write how you were affected by the living conditions it created.
2. The authors of "Unforgettable Miss Bessie" (page 140) and "Miss Davis" (page 147) describe how their teachers affected them. Explain how some aspect of your school experience had a lasting effect on you.
3. Drawing on the information in "Unforgettable Miss Bessie" and "Miss Davis," along with your own experience and observation, give and explain the qualities of an effective teacher.

Writing Strategies

Improving your writing process involves experimentation. You must first identify what you currently do when you write, and then you must determine which facets of your process need to be improved. Finally, you must try alternative approaches to the less successful features of your process, evaluate their effectiveness, and then go on to experiment further if necessary.

Chapters 1 to 3 suggest techniques you can experiment with. In addition, you can try the following strategies.

Topic Selection

1. To decide on a person or place to describe and on your impression of your subject, fill in the blanks in the following sentence: ________________ is the most ________________ I know. Fill in the first blank with a person or place (your subject), and fill in the second blank with a characteristic (your impression). You will get something like "The student cafeteria at noon is the most hectic place I know," which will lead to a description of the hectic nature of the cafeteria at 12:00. Or you might get something like "Uncle Nathan is the most eccentric person I know," which will lead to a description of Uncle Nathan's eccentricity. Be careful to use specific words to fill in your blanks and to pick manageable subjects, so you do not end up with something too broad or vague, something like "Wichita is the most interesting city I know." All of *Wichita* is too much to handle in one essay, and *interesting* is too vague to be useful to the reader.
2. If you are describing a place, select one that you can visit and observe. If this is not possible, select one that is fresh and detailed in your memory.
3. If you have trouble settling on the impression, complete the sentences on page 130.

Idea Generation

List writing can be an effective idea-generation technique. When describing a place, make your list at that place. If you are describing a person, observe the person before describing physical appearance and mannerisms. As you write your list, do not worry about effective sentences, mental images, organization, and such; simply get down as best you can and as quickly as you can the details that convey your impression. You would not, for example, list your grandmother's sparkling eyes if you wished to show her as intimidating, but you might want to list her hands gnarled with arthritis. A list for an essay about your intimidating grandmother might read, in part, like this:

gnarled hands
wrinkled, scary face
powerful voice
won't take no for an answer
pinches my shoulder when angry
fearsome eyes

Reader Response

If you like to secure reader response before revising, see page 77. In addition, ask your reader to circle words and concrete sensory detail that should be reconsidered and place a checkmark next to words and concrete sensory detail that are particularly effective.

REVISION CHECKLIST

In addition to the checklist on page 80, you can use this checklist for revising a descriptive essay.

1. Does your thesis (stated or implied) include both a subject to be described and an impression?
2. If stated, is your impression expressed in specific language?
3. Given your thesis, audience, and purpose, is your detail appropriately subjective or objective?
4. Are all your supporting details relevant to your subject and impression?
5. Have you used concrete sensory detail to create vivid mental images? Is your concrete sensory detail restrained when necessary?

CHAPTER 6

Narration

"So tell me what happened." We respond to that request by telling a story—by relating the events that occurred, where they occurred, when they occurred, and who was involved. In writing, such a story is called a **narration**.

DETAIL

Let's say two friends run into each other on campus and one says to the other, "What happened? You look terrible." Then the second friend replies, "I just went through the worst registration ever." The conversation that might follow reveals much about story-telling.

JOHN: What happened? You look terrible.

MARSHA: I just went through the worst registration ever.

JOHN: Why? What happened?

MARSHA: Well, I stood in line for twenty minutes, and when it was my turn I got turned away because I hadn't paid a library fine. So I went to the library and paid my $1.50, went back to registration, and stood in line for twenty minutes again, except this time when it was my turn the woman at the desk gave me a hard time.

JOHN: Why? What did she say?

MARSHA: She told me I needed the biology chairman's permission to take this biology course I wanted. I told her he already said it was OK, but she made a big deal about how I needed his signature on my schedule card. I got ticked and told her off.

JOHN: Why so angry?

MARSHA: Well, I'd already wasted over a half hour and didn't have one class scheduled, and I wasn't crazy about trying to run down Dr.

Ingles all over again. Anyhow, I went to the biology department and got Ingles's signature. By the way, I saw Lorenzo there and he's leaving for Florida on break.

JOHN: Forget Lorenzo and finish the story.

MARSHA: Yeah, well I went back to registration, stood in line again, for ten minutes this time, and you won't believe what happened when it was my turn.

JOHN: I give up, what?

MARSHA: The same woman was there and she told me to wait a minute—oh I forgot to tell you, this woman told me before that I better straighten out my act or I'd be in trouble.

JOHN: Wait a minute—when? The first or second time? You're losing me.

MARSHA: The second time, when I told her off. Anyway, when I got to her desk . . .

JOHN: The third time?

MARSHA: Yeah. When I got to her desk, she told me to wait—like I hadn't already done enough of that, you know. So I waited, and next thing I know, she's dragging some security guard over to me. And you know what he says?

JOHN: Will you tell the story already?

MARSHA: He tells me that unless I can act like an adult, I won't be allowed to register.

JOHN: Why did he say that?

MARSHA: I guess because when she made me get Ingles's signature, I called her a dumb broad.

JOHN: Why didn't you tell me that before? Sounds to me like you got what you deserved.

MARSHA: Yeah, I suppose.

The conversation between John and Marsha raises several points about effective narration. First, a good narration must include all the significant events. When Marsha neglects to tell John why she was angry, he asks her to supply this information. When she neglects to say that she called the woman a dumb broad, John is annoyed.

Second, an effective narration does not bring up unrelated points. When Marsha starts to speak of Lorenzo, John tells her to get back to the matter at hand.

Third, good narration follows a logical time sequence. When Marsha confuses the time she was told to straighten out her act and the time she got to the desk, John has to ask a question to get things clear.

Fourth, interesting narration does not drag on; its pace is brisk. When Marsha begins to bog down, John tells her to move the story along.

Finally, good narration usually has a point that can be drawn from the story.

John and Marsha both conclude that she acted badly and deserved to be chastised by the security guard.

The dialogue between John and Marsha illustrates the following points about narration.

1. All the significant details must be supplied.
2. Irrelevant details should be left out.
3. The story should be presented in a logical, understandable time sequence.
4. The story should be paced so it does not drag.
5. The story should make a point or lead to a conclusion.

SELECTING DETAIL

The five points made so far about narration, the ones listed above, really pertain to the selection of details to include in your story and the order to present these details in.

When deciding what to include in your narration, you can answer the standard journalist's questions: *who? what? when? where? why? how?* Most readers will want to know what happened, when it happened, where it happened, why it happened, how it happened, and who was involved. If you respond to each of these questions, you are likely to include all the significant information.

As you provide all the significant details, however, do not get carried away and include ideas not pertinent to the who, what, when, where, why, and how of your narration, or your reader will grow impatient. We have all seen movies that drag because of unnecessary detail, action, explanation, or dialogue. Such movies are boring. To avoid boring your reader, maintain a brisk pace by including only the significant details.

In addition to identifying significant details, you must determine which of these details require major emphasis. For some narrations, the who and where may deserve extended treatment, while the why, when, and how merit less development. Other narrations may dictate detailed discussion of the why. Which details you emphasize will be determined by the purpose of your narration and your audience.

PURPOSE

The detail you include and the journalist's questions you emphasize will be influenced by your purpose. Remember, a narration does more than tell a story; it makes a point with that story for a particular purpose. Let's say you tell the story about the time your psychology teacher was unfair to you. If your purpose is to vent your anger, you might focus on yourself and your feelings. If your purpose is to convince your reader that students need a grievance procedure, you might focus more on what happened. If your purpose is to inform your reader that even the best profs have their bad moments, you might emphasize the what and why of the event and the instructor involved. For this purpose, you might also describe the instructor as a typically fair one, which is something you would not do for the first two purposes.

To establish a purpose for your narration, you can ask these questions.

1. What point do I want my narration to make?
2. Does my point allow me to share part of my experience with a reader?
3. Does my point allow me to inform my reader? If so, of what?
4. Does my point allow me to persuade my reader? If so, of what?
5. Does my point allow me to entertain my reader?

AUDIENCE

Like your purpose, your audience will influence the detail you include and the journalist's questions you emphasize. Let's return to the story of the psychology professor who was unfair to you to illustrate this. If your reader knows little about the workings of a college classroom, you might include more explanatory detail than if your reader is currently attending the university. If your audience is a classmate who witnessed the incident, you might emphasize what happened less than if your audience is someone who did not witness the event.

To settle on an audience, you can ask these questions.

1. Who would be interested in my story?
2. Who could learn something from my story?
3. Who could be influenced by my story?
4. Who would I like to share my experience with?

To assess the nature of your audience so that you know what kind of detail your reader requires, you can ask these questions.

1. Are there any of the who, what, when, where, why, how questions my reader already knows the answers to?
2. Does my reader have any strong feelings that will influence reaction to my narration?
3. What must my reader know to appreciate my point?
4. Has my reader had an experience similar to the one I am narrating?

ARRANGING DETAIL

Narrative details are arranged in *chronological* (time) order. Usually, you start with what happened first, move to what happened next, and so forth. However, this is not the only chronology available. You can also begin at the end and flash back to the first event and proceed in chronological order from there. Similarly, you can begin somewhere in the middle of a story and then flash back to the beginning.

Let's say I want to narrate an account of preparing for and taking a final exam. If I want to begin with the first event and move chronologically, I might begin this way.

> I filled the kettle with water enough to keep me in coffee for the rest of the night, opened a 16-ounce bag of Fritos, arranged my statistics notes next to my text, and I was ready to make sense of T-scores and chi-squares.

After this opening sentence, I would describe the night of study, explaining events in the order they occurred. Then I would move on to the next morning and how I felt on the way to the exam. From there I would narrate the events of the exam.

But I could follow a different time sequence: I could begin in the middle.

> The alarm jarred me from a fitful 3 hours' sleep, and I knew the time for preparation was gone. In just 2 hours I would be sweating over my statistics exam, "Well, old girl," I tried to reassure myself, "you certainly studied hard enough." Yes, I put in some kind of night preparing for the test.

From here I could flash back to narrate the night of study, return to the time I woke up, and move through the events up to and including the exam.

Or I could start at the end in this fashion.

> As I left the classroom, I knew I would be lucky to get a C− on my stat exam. Anything higher would call for divine intervention. Yet, it wasn't like I hadn't prepared for the test.

From this point I could flash back to the night of study and detail the events chronologically up to and including the exam.

The fact that narration has a logical chronology that is readily recognized by the reader can greatly influence the structure of a narrative piece. For example, topic sentences are not always necessary or desirable because the chronology is often enough to hold details together and give them a logical presentation. Once the reader grasps the time sequence at work, he or she easily understands why ideas are grouped and presented in the order that they are: they follow the governing chronology.

You can also write a narration without traditional paragraphs of introduction and conclusion. This is particularly true when the events in the narration speak so well for themselves that no formal working up to them (introduction) or tying off of them (conclusion) is necessary. Often, however, writers of narration feel the need for an introductory remark, so they precede their narration with a one- or two-sentence introduction before presenting the first chronological event. Sometimes this preliminary material presents the point of the narration.

Similarly, instead of a concluding paragraph, writers may tie things off with a brief one- or two-sentence closing, which may draw a conclusion from the narration or present something that occurred after the events narrated. However, this is not to say that narration cannot have an introduction with thesis and a concluding paragraph.

Finally, writers sometimes comment on the significant aspects of their narrations. Sometimes an event, person, location, or time holds a significance that is not obvious from the story, or a writer may wish to underscore something in the story. This can be handled in a number of ways. The writer can state the significance in the thesis, in the introductory remarks, in the conclusion, or at a logical point in the narration.

USING DESCRIPTION

Memorable narrations include specific, descriptive details to make the story vivid. Important details of scene are often described, as are key people and events. To appreciate the importance of description, compare these two versions of a narration.

> The child drove his tricycle down the driveway into the path of an oncoming car. Fortunately, the driver, who was speeding, was able to swerve in time to avoid a collision.
>
> Four-year-old Ishmael hopped on his racing red tricycle and began pedalling furiously down his driveway. By the time he reached the end, he had gathered too much speed to stop. With fear in his eyes, he screamed mightily as his out-of-control trike headed into the path of a speeding Chevy Lumina. The teenage driver, startled into action, swerved just in time to avert disaster.

You probably found the second version more interesting because of the specific detail and description. (For a review of how to include specific, descriptive details, see the discussion of specific diction on page 95 and concrete sensory detail on page 131.)

USING CONVERSATION

Writers use conversation because what people said can be important to the advancement and meaning of the story. Another reason writers use conversation is that it can add vitality to an essay. To appreciate this, consider the following two sentences.

```
The coach shouted that we should get in there and hustle.

The coach shouted at us, "Get in there and hustle!"
```

The second sentence has more power than the first because the coach's exact words appear. As a result, this sentence will have greater impact on the reader and create more interest.

Typically, sentences that contain conversation have two parts: a part that notes what was said, and a part that indicates who did the speaking. How you punctuate depends on where these parts appear.

When the spoken words come before the statement of who spoke, the sentence looks like this.

```
"Get out of here while you have the chance," the stranger
warned.
```

1. Spoken words are enclosed in quotation marks.
2. Spoken words are followed by a comma, which appears before the final quotation marks. If a question is asked, then a question mark is used.

```
"What chance do I have?" Joyce wondered.
```

3. The first of the words showing who spoke begins with a lower-case letter unless it is a proper noun (such as *Ed*) or a word always capitalized (such as *I*).

When the statement of who spoke comes before the words spoken, the sentence looks like this.

```
Alex responded quietly, "My sister is the one to blame."
```

1. The statement of who spoke is followed by a comma.
2. The spoken words appear in quotation marks.
3. The first of the spoken words is capitalized.
4. The spoken words are followed by a period, which appears before the final quotation marks.

When the spoken words come both before and after the statement of who spoke, the sentence will look like one of the following:

```
"I wish I knew," Paulette sighed, "why I always end up doing
most of the work."

"Please be here by 8:00," Dad cautioned. "We don't want to get
a late start."
```

1. The first and second groups of spoken words appear inside separate sets of quotation marks.
2. The first group of spoken words is followed by a comma.
3. If the first group of spoken words is not a sentence, a comma appears after the statement of who spoke.
4. If the first group of spoken words is not a sentence, the second group of spoken words does not begin with a capital letter.
5. If the first group of spoken words forms a sentence, the statement of who spoke is followed by a period, and the second group of spoken words begins with a capital letter.
6. The second group of spoken words is followed by a period, which appears inside the final quotation marks.

When the spoken words form a question, a question mark is used instead of the period or comma after the spoken words:

Malcolm asked, "Where did you park my van?"

"When is the last day of the book sale?" Carla questioned.

"Can we go now," Sis asked, "or do we still have to wait for Joe?"

1. In each case above, the question mark replaces the period or comma because the spoken words form a question.
2. The question mark appears inside the quotation marks.

When the entire sentence, rather than just the spoken words, is forming the question, the question mark appears outside of the quotation marks:

Can you believe that Professor Golden said, "If you want, we will postpone the test until Monday"?

The question mark is outside the quotation marks because the entire sentence, not the spoken words, forms the question.

When you use quotation marks to signal the use of conversation, be careful that you really do have spoken words. Notice the two sentences below:

Maria announced that she was quitting her job to attend school full-time.

Maria announced, "I'm quitting my job to attend school full-time."

1. Although it is tempting to use quotation marks in the first sentence, no spoken words appear there.

2. Since the second sentence does have spoken words, quotation marks are necessary.

A person's thoughts are often punctuated the same way as spoken words.

```
Joshua thought to himself, "I'm sure I can win this event if
I get a fast start."
```

To be more precise and to increase the vitality of your writing, consider these substitutions for *said* and *asked.*

responded	whispered	explained
replied	whimpered	questioned
shouted	announced	inquired
cried	blurted out	wondered
snapped		

TRYOUT Reread the dialogue between John and Marsha on page 152 and then write a narrative paragraph or two telling what happened when Marsha went to register for classes. Use the details given in the dialogue and any other details that you care to add. Arrange the details in chronological order, and use some description and conversation. Be sure to answer all the journalist's questions.

PROFESSIONAL ESSAYS

Looking for Work

Gary Soto

In striking clarity and detail, Gary Soto narrates the events of a July day of his youth. From his account, the reader learns something of the dreams and reality of a young Mexican-American boy.

One July, while killing ants on the kitchen sink with a rolled newspaper, I had a nine-year-old's vision of wealth that would save us from ourselves. For weeks I had drunk Kool-Aid and watched morning reruns of *Father Knows Best,* whose family was so uncomplicated in its routine that I very much wanted to imitate it. The first step was to get my brother and sister to wear shoes at dinner. 1

"Come on, Rick—come on, Deb," I whined. But Rick mimicked me and the same day that I asked him to wear shoes he came to the dinner table in only his swim trunks. My mother didn't notice, nor did my sister, as we sat to eat our beans and tortillas in the stifling heat of our kitchen. We all gleamed like cello- 2 phane, wiping the sweat from our brows with the backs of our hands as we talked about the day: Frankie our neighbor was beat up by Faustino; the swimming pool at the playground would be closed for a day because the pump was broken.

Such was our life. So that morning, while doing-in the train of ants which arrived each day, I decided to become wealthy, and right away! After downing a bowl of cereal. I took a rake from the garage and started up the block to look for work. 3

We lived on an ordinary block of mostly working class people: warehousemen, egg candlers,[1] welders, mechanics, and a union plumber. And there were many retired people who kept their lawns green and the gutters uncluttered of the chewing gum wrappers we dropped as we rode by on our bikes. They bent down to gather our litter, muttering at our evilness. 4

At the corner house I rapped the screen door and a very large woman in a muu-muu answered. She sized me up and then asked what I could do. 5

"Rake leaves," I answered smiling. 6

"It's summer, and there ain't no leaves," she countered. Her face was pinched with lines; fat jiggled under her chin. She pointed to the lawn, then the flower bed, and said: "You see any leaves there—or there?" I followed her pointing arm, stupidly. But she had a job for me and that was to get her a Coke at the liquor store. She gave me twenty cents, and after ditching my rake in a bush, off I ran. I returned with an unbagged Pepsi, for which she thanked me and gave me a nickel from her apron. 7

I skipped off her porch, fetched my rake, and crossed the street to the next block where Mrs. Moore, mother of Earl the retarded man, let me weed a flower bed. She handed me a trowel and for a good part of the morning my fingers dipped into the moist dirt, ripping up runners of Bermuda grass. Worms surfaced in my search for deep roots, and I cut them in halves, tossing them to Mrs. Moore's cat who pawed them playfully as they dried in the sun. I made out Earl whose face was pressed to the back window of the house, and although he was calling to me I couldn't understand what he was trying to say. Embarrassed, I worked without looking up, but I imagined his contorted mouth and the ring of keys attached to his belt—keys that jingled with each palsied step. He scared me and I worked quickly to finish the flower bed. When I did finish Mrs. Moore gave me a quarter and two peaches from her tree, which I washed there but ate in the alley behind my house. 8

I was sucking on the second one, a bit of juice staining the front of my T-shirt, when Little John, my best friend, came walking down the alley with a baseball bat over his shoulder, knocking over trash cans as he made his way toward me. 9

Little John and I went to St. John's Catholic School, where we sat among the "stupids." Miss Marino, our teacher, alternated the rows of good students with the bad, hoping that by sitting side-by-side with the bright students the stupids might become more intelligent, as though intelligence were contagious. But we didn't progress as she had hoped. She grew frustrated when one day, while dis- 10

[1]*egg candler:* one who inspects eggs by holding them up to a light.

missing class for recess, Little John couldn't get up because his arms were stuck in the slats of the chair's backrest. She scolded us with a shaking finger when we knocked over the globe, denting the already troubled Africa. She muttered curses when Leroy White, a real stupid but a great softball player with the gift to hit to all fields, openly chewed his host[2] when he made his First Communion; his hands swung at his sides as he returned to the pew looking around with a big smile.

Little John asked what I was doing, and I told him that I was taking a break from work, as I sat comfortably among high weeds. He wanted to join me, but I reminded him that the last time he'd gone door-to-door asking for work his mother had whipped him. I was with him when his mother, a New Jersey Italian who could rise up in anger one moment and love the next, told me in a polite but matter-of-fact voice that I had to leave because she was going to beat her son. She gave me a homemade popsicle, ushered me to the door, and said that I could see Little John the next day. But it was sooner than that. I went around to his bedroom window to suck my popsicle and watch Little John dodge his mother's blows, a few hitting their mark but many whirring air. 11

It was midday when Little John and I converged in the alley, the sun blazing in the high nineties, and he suggested that we go to Roosevelt High School to swim. He needed five cents to make fifteen, the cost of admission, and I lent him a nickel. We ran home for my bike and when my sister found out that we were going swimming, she started to cry because she didn't have the fifteen cents but only an empty Coke bottle. I waved for her to come and three of us mounted the bike—Debra on the cross bar, Little John on the handle bars and holding the Coke bottle which we would cash for a nickel and make up the difference that would allow all of us to get in, and me pumping up the crooked streets, dodging cars and pot holes. We spent the day swimming under the afternoon sun, so that when we got home our mom asked us what was darker, the floor or us? She feigned a stern posture, her hands on her hips and her mouth puckered. We played along. Looking down, Debbie and I said in unison, "Us." 12

That evening at dinner we all sat down in our bathing suits to eat our beans, laughing and chewing loudly. Our mom was in a good mood, so I took a risk and asked her if sometime we could have turtle soup. A few days before I had watched a television program in which a Polynesian tribe killed a large turtle, gutted it, and then stewed it over an open fire. The turtle, basted in a sugary sauce, looked delicious as I ate an afternoon bowl of cereal, but my sister, who was watching the program with a glass of Kool-Aid between her knees, said, "Caca." 13

My mother looked at me in bewilderment. "Boy, are you a crazy Mexican. Where did you get the idea that people eat turtles?" 14

"On television," I said, explaining the program. Then I took it a step further. "Mom, do you think we could get dressed up for dinner one of these days? David King does." 15

"Ay, Dios," my mother laughed. She started collecting the dinner plates, but my brother wouldn't let go of his. He was still drawing a picture in the bean sauce. 16

[2]*his host:* the wafer that represents, in the Catholic sacrament of Communion, the bread of the Last Supper and the body of Christ.

Giggling, he said it was me, but I didn't want to listen because I wanted an answer from Mom. This was the summer when I spent the mornings in front of the television that showed the comfortable lives of white kids. There were no beatings, no rifts in the family. They wore bright clothes; toys tumbled from their closets. They hopped into bed with kisses and woke to glasses of fresh orange juice, and to a father sitting before his morning coffee while the mother buttered his toast. They hurried through the day making friends and gobs of money, returning home to a warmly lit living room, and then dinner. *Leave It to Beaver* was the program I replayed in my mind:

"May I have the mashed potatoes?" asks Beaver with a smile. 17

Sure, Beav," replies Wally as he taps the corners of his mouth with a 18
starched napkin.

The father looks on in his suit. The mother, decked out in earrings and a 19
pearl necklace, cuts into her steak and blushes. Their conversation is politely clipped.

"Swell," says Beaver, his cheeks puffed with food. 20

Our own talk at dinner was loud with belly laughs and marked by our point- 21
ing forks at one another. The subjects were commonplace.

"Gary, let's go to the ditch tomorrow," my brother suggests. He explains 22
that he has made a life preserver out of four empty detergent bottles strung together with twine and that he will make me one if I can find more bottles. "No way are we going to drown."

"Yeah, then we could have a dirt clod fight," I reply, so happy to be alive. 23

Whereas the Beaver's family enjoyed dessert in dishes at the table, our mom 24
sent us outside, and more often than not I went into the alley to peek over the neighbor's fences and spy out fruit, apricot or peaches.

I had asked my mom and again she laughed that I was a crazy *chavalo*[3] as 25
she stood in front of the sink, her arms rising and falling with suds, face glistening from the heat. She sent me outside where my brother and sister were sitting in the shade that the fence threw out like a blanket. They were talking about me when I plopped down next to them. They looked at one another and then Debbie, my eight-year-old sister, started in.

"What's this crap about getting dressed up?" 26

She had entered her *profanity* stage. A year later she would give up such 27
words and slip into her Catholic uniform, and into squealing on my brother and me when we "cussed this" and "cussed that."

I tried to convince them that if we improved the way we looked we might get 28
along better in life. White people would like us more. They might invite us to places, like their homes or front yards. They might not hate us so much.

My sister called me a "craphead," and got up to leave with a stalk of grass 29
dangling from her mouth. "They'll never like us."

My brother's mood lightened as he talked about the ditch—the white water, 30
the broken pieces of glass, and the rusted car fenders that awaited our knees. There would be toads, and rocks to smash them.

[3]*chavalo:* kid.

David King, the only person we knew who resembled the middle class, called from over the fence. David was Catholic, of Armenian and French descent, and his closet was filled with toys. A bear-shaped cookie jar, like the ones on television, sat on the kitchen counter. His mother was remarkably kind while she put up with the racket we made on the street. Evenings, she often watered the front yard and it must have upset her to see us—my brother and I and others—jump from trees laughing, the unkillable kids of the very poor, who got up unshaken, brushed off, and climbed into another one to try again. 31

David called again. Rick got up and slapped grass from his pants. When I asked if I could come along he said no. David said no. They were two years older so their affairs were different from mine. They greeted one another with foul names and took off down the alley to look for trouble. 32

I went inside the house, turned on the television, and was about to sit down with a glass of Kool-Aid when Mom shooed me outside. 33

"It's still light," she said. "Later you'll bug me to let you stay out longer. So go on." 34

I downed my Kool-Aid and went outside to the front yard. No one was around. The day had cooled and a breeze rustled the trees. Mr. Jackson, the plumber, was watering his lawn and when he saw me he turned away to wash off his front steps. There was more than an hour of light left, so I took advantage of it and decided to look for work. I felt suddenly alive as I skipped down the block in search of an overgrown flower bed and the dime that would end the day right. 35

Questions on Technique

1. For what purpose do you think Soto wrote "Looking for Work"? Who would you judge to be his intended audience?
2. What point does Soto's narration make? Is that point stated or implied?
3. "Looking for Work" lacks a separate introduction with thesis. Is that a problem? Explain.
4. In what paragraphs does Soto explain an event or its significance?
5. Soto uses a great deal of description. What does this description contribute? Cite two examples of description that you find effective. Cite three examples of specific diction that appeal to you.
6. What does the conversation contribute to the essay?
7. In what paragraphs does Soto use a flashback technique?
8. Which of the journalist's questions are emphasized?
9. What approach does Soto take to his conclusion?

For Group Discussion or Journal Writing

As a youth, Gary Soto longed for a life like the ones he saw in television shows like *Leave It to Beaver* and *Father Knows Best*. If you have seen these shows, explain why they appealed to Soto. If you have not seen these shows, describe the kind of life Soto longed for.

Shame

Dick Gregory

The following narration, taken from the author's autobiography, tells how Dick Gregory learned to feel shame and the effect that emotion had on him.

I never learned hate at home, or shame. I had to go to school for that. I was about seven years old when I got my first big lesson. I was in love with a little girl named Helene Tucker, a light-complected little girl with pigtails and nice manners. She was always clean and she was smart in school. I think I went to school mostly to look at her. I brushed my hair and even got me a little old handkerchief. It was a lady's handkerchief, but I didn't want Helene to see me wipe my nose on my hand. The pipes were frozen again, there was no water in the house, but I washed my socks and shirt every night. I'd get a pot, and go over to Mr. Ben's grocery store, and stick my pot down into his soda machine. Scoop out some chopped ice. By evening the ice melted to water for washing. I got sick a lot that winter because the fire would go out at night before the clothes were dry. In the morning I'd put them on, wet or dry, because they were the only clothes I had. 1

Everybody's got a Helene Tucker, a symbol of everything you want. I loved her for her goodness, her cleanliness, her popularity. She'd walk down my street and my brothers and sisters would yell, "Here comes Helene," and I'd rub my tennis sneakers on the back of my pants and wish my hair wasn't so nappy and the white folks' shirt fit me better. I'd run out on the street. If I knew my place and didn't come too close, she'd wink at me and say hello. That was a good feeling. Sometimes I'd follow her all the way home, and shovel the snow off her walk and try to make friends with her Momma and her aunts. I'd drop money on her stoop late at night on my way back from shining shoes in the taverns. And she had a Daddy, and he had a good job. He was a paper hanger. 2

I guess I would have gotten over Helene by summertime, but something happened in that classroom that made her face hang in front of me for the next twenty-two years. When I played the drums in high school it was for Helene and when I broke track records in college it was for Helene and when I started standing behind microphones and heard applause I wished Helene could hear it, too. It wasn't until I was twenty-nine years old and married and making money that I really got her out of my system. Helene was sitting in that classroom when I learned to be ashamed of myself. 3

It was on a Thursday. I was sitting in the back of the room, in a seat with a chalk circle drawn around it. The idiot's seat, the troublemaker's seat. 4

The teacher thought I was stupid. Couldn't spell, couldn't read, couldn't do arithmetic. Just stupid. Teachers were never interested in finding out that you couldn't concentrate because you were so hungry, because you hadn't had any breakfast. All you could think about was noontime, would it ever come? Maybe you could sneak into the cloakroom and steal a bite of some kid's lunch out of a coat pocket. A bite of something. Paste. You can't really make a meal out of paste, or put it on bread for a sandwich, but sometimes I'd scoop a few spoonfuls out of 5 the paste jar in the back of the room. Pregnant people get strange tastes. I was pregnant with poverty. Pregnant with dirt and pregnant with smells that made people turn away, pregnant with cold and pregnant with shoes that were never bought for me, pregnant with five other people in my bed and no Daddy in the next room, and pregnant with hunger. Paste doesn't taste too bad when you're hungry.

The teacher thought I was a troublemaker. All she saw from the front of the room was a little black boy who squirmed in his idiot's seat and made noises and poked the kids around him. I guess she couldn't see a kid who made noises because he wanted someone to know he was there. 6

It was on a Thursday, the day before the Negro payday. The eagle always flew on Friday. The teacher was asking each student how much his father would give to the Community Chest. On Friday night, each kid would get the money from his father, and on Monday he would bring it to the school. I decided I was going to buy me a Daddy right then. I had money in my pocket from shining shoes and selling papers and whatever Helene Tucker pledged for her Daddy I was going to top it. And I'd hand the money right in. I wasn't going to wait until Monday to buy me a Daddy. 7

I was shaking, scared to death. The teacher opened her book and started calling our names alphabetically. 8

"Helene Tucker?" 9

"My Daddy said he'd give two dollars and fifty cents." 10

"That's very nice, Helene. Very, very nice indeed." 11

That made me feel pretty good. It wouldn't take too much to top that. I had almost three dollars in dimes and quarters in my pocket. I stuck my hand in my pocket and held onto the money, waiting for her to call my name. But the teacher closed her book after she called everybody else in the class. 12

I stood up and raised my hand. 13

"What is it now?" 14

"You forgot me." 15

She turned toward the blackboard. "I don't have time to be playing with you, Richard." 16

"My Daddy said he'd . . ." 17

"Sit down, Richard, you're disturbing the class." 18

"My Daddy said he'd give . . . fifteen dollars." 19

She turned around and looked mad. "We are collecting this money for you and your kind, Richard Gregory. If your Daddy can give fifteen dollars you have no business being on relief." 20

"I got it right now, I got it right now, my Daddy gave it to me to turn in today, my Daddy said . . ." 21

"And furthermore," she said, looking right at me, her nostrils getting big and her lips getting thin and her eyes opening wide, "we know you don't have a Daddy." 22

Helene Tucker turned around, her eyes full of tears. She felt sorry for me. Then I couldn't see her too well because I was crying, too. 23

"Sit down, Richard." 24

And I always thought the teacher kind of liked me. She always picked me to wash the blackboard on Friday, after school. That was a big thrill, it made me feel important. If I didn't wash it, come Monday the school might not function right. 25

"Where are you going, Richard?" 26

I walked out of school that day, and for a long time I didn't go back very often. There was shame there. 27

Now there was shame everywhere. It seemed like the whole world had been inside that classroom, everyone had heard what the teacher had said, everyone had turned around and felt sorry for me. There was shame in going to the Worthy Boys Annual Christmas Dinner for you and your kind, because everybody knew what a worthy boy was. Why couldn't they just call it the Boys Annual Dinner, why'd they have to give it a name? There was shame in wearing the brown and orange and white plaid mackinaw the welfare gave to 3,000 boys. Why'd it have to be the same for everybody so when you walked down the street the people could see you were on relief? It was a nice warm mackinaw and it had a hood, and my Momma beat me and called me a little rat when she found out I stuffed it in the bottom of a pail full of garbage way over on Cottage Street. There was shame in running over to Mister Ben's at the end of the day and asking for his rotten peaches, there was shame in asking Mrs. Simmons for a spoonful of sugar, there was shame in running out to meet the relief truck. I hated that truck, full of food for you and your kind. I ran into the house and hid when it came. And then I started to sneak through alleys, to take the long way home so people going into White's Eat Shop wouldn't see me. Yeah, the whole world heard the teacher that day, we all know you don't have a Daddy. 28

Questions on Technique

1. What sentence begins the actual narration?
2. What two purposes does the material before the opening of the narration serve?
3. This narration includes explanatory detail. For example, the author departs from his narration to explain why he ate paste and how he managed to wash his clothes. What other examples of explanation can you find?
4. What purpose do the explanations serve?
5. The author comments on the significance of certain aspects of his narration. For example, he says, "Everybody's got a Helene Tucker, a symbol of everything you want." What other commentary appears?
6. What does the conversation contribute?
7. What points does the narration make? Are the points stated or implied?
8. What kind of conclusion is used? Is it effective? Why?
9. In "Shame" we are not told why the teacher humiliated Gregory. Why not? Is this omission a strength or a weakness in the narration? Why?
10. What would you judge to be the purpose of Gregory's narration?

For Group Discussion or Journal Writing

Dick Gregory says, "Everybody's got a Helene Tucker, a symbol of everything you want" (paragraph 2). What is your symbol of everything you want? Do you think that symbol is also a symbol for what other people want? Explain.

The Girl in Gift Wrap

Paul Hemphill

He worked in men's shoes, and she worked in gift wrap. Could he find the courage to speak to her?

He worked in Men's Shoes and she worked in Gift Wrap, and he considered it the best part-time job he had ever had during any Christmas holiday. All day long, while he fitted feet to shoes and she wrapped Christmas gifts, they were no more than thirty feet apart. There were only thirty feet separating him and the most beautiful girl he had ever seen, and maybe it would have been better if he had a job on another floor, because the thought of being so close to her but never having spoken to her was driving him out of his mind. 1

The first thing he had noticed about her was the way she looked at the customers with her eyes. They were the most beautiful eyes in the world. They were dark blue, a very dark blue, with long, black eyelashes protecting them. He would go home every night remembering how she teased people by looking up at them through those long, black eyelashes. Her hair was black, too, a silken, shimmering black streaming down over her shoulders. And her face was soft and white, and her figure was like a ballet dancer's, and every day she wore baby blue or desert tan or mint green to promote all of this to the fullest. Here he was, working thirty feet away, and he did not know how much longer he could stand being so close, yet so far away. It really was a wonderfully painful kind of job, being in Men's Shoes while she was in Gift Wrap. 2

And now it was the last week before Christmas. He knew he was going to have to find some way to talk to her before they both went back to school, if she went to school at all, and he did not know how he was going to do it. 3

Once, he thought he was in love with a girl in high school. That was his senior year. All year long he tried to sit near her and her dates during the football and basketball games, and he even prayed he would be in the same classes with her. She had a lot of dates, and this discouraged him, so he never got around to asking her for a date. It wasn't until he had graduated and gone to college that he learned why she had been so popular, and because he had not dreamed she was that kind of girl, that made him feel even more awkward. 4

But now the Christmas holidays were almost over. The crowds of shoppers were thinning. Those who came now were men buying at the last minute for their wives. There were only three more shopping days until Christmas. Three more days to do something. And he chose to make his move on her coffee break. 5

The snack bar where she always went for her break was not crowded. That 6 would make it easier for him. He had waited for her to leave, and then he had followed her, and when she took one of the stools at the counter he took another, leaving one stool between them, and after their snacks had come, he cleared his throat and said, "Well, it's almost over now."

"Yes, and I hope I never see another package," she said. "I work in Gift 7
Wrap."

"I know. I work in Men's Shoes. Next to you," he said. She seemed friendly 8
enough. And her eyes really were beautiful.

"Ah, do you go to school?" he asked her. 9

"No. I'm just trying to make some money for Christmas." 10

"Yeah. Me, too. I'm in college." 11

"What are you studying?" 12

"Engineering. I'm going to be an engineer." 13

"That's wonderful. That's a good profession, isn't it?" 14

"It sure is," he said, looking into her beautiful blue eyes. 15

She said, "What's Santa Claus going to bring you for Christmas?" She 16
laughed, a very nice laugh, when she said it.

"Oh, I don't know. Clothes, I guess. How about you?" 17

She answered so quickly and easily and pleasantly. That is what made it 18
hurt. "An engagement ring," she said.

"Oh," he said. And he went back to Men's Shoes, and she to Gift Wrap. 19
She was only thirty feet away. There were three miserable days to go.

Questions on Technique

1. Which of the *who, what, when, where, why,* or *how* questions does Hemphill emphasize the most?
2. What elements of description appear in the narration? What purpose does the description serve?
3. What purpose does the conversation serve?
4. Where in the essay is there a statement of the narration's significance?
5. The narration teaches a lesson. What is that lesson?
6. What element of contrast appears in the narration?
7. What do you judge to be Hemphill's audience and purpose?
8. What approach does the author take to the conclusion?

For Group Discussion or Journal Writing

Using the evidence in the essay for clues, write a list of words that describe the college student who worked in men's shoes.

STUDENT ESSAYS TO READ AND EVALUATE

The following narrations, written by students, have both strengths and weaknesses. As you read, try to determine what works well and what does not. Doing so will help you become a reliable critic so you can make accurate judgments about your own writing. Studying these essays will make you aware of successful techniques to incorporate into your own writing as well as less successful techniques to avoid. The evaluation activity after the readings will help you examine the important features of the essays.

Lots of Locks

I was 12 years old at the time. It was the summer before I was to enter junior high school. I sat in the beautician's chair, awaiting the first haircut of my life. I stared at my long braided hair stretching down the middle of my back, the tip making a relaxed curl at my waist. As far back as I could remember, my hair had always been that long. Even old photographs of me at the age of 3 or 4 showed long locks of hair cascading over my shoulders and covering most of me. What a hastle those locks had been over the years. Most people had nightmares of assailants coming at them with a knife or gun. In my nightmares, I saw my mom coming at me with a wide-tooth comb. 1

Combing my hair was always such a huge task. I remember my mom standing me on an old wooden kitchen chair. Then she'd start combing. She'd angle the comb at the top of my head, ever so gently, then pull, tug, and yank until the comb made a jerky exit at the ends of my long strands. 2

"Ow," I'd holler. "That hurts!" "Use the brush," I'd plead. 3

"Now honey," she'd say calmly, "you know that brush won't get the tangles out." 4

"I don't care!" I'd start crying, hoping to change her mind. 5

Of course my whining didn't do a bit of good. My sisters, the brats that they were, hung around just to tease me. 6

"Whiney Caroliney, Whiney Caroliney," they'd taunt in unison and almost perfect harmony. 7

I'd cry even harder, and my mom would take a quick swat at them. She'd try to shut me up by cooing. 8

"Look honey at this big rats' nest I got out of your hair. You know that's what these tangles really are, don't you? If we don't get those buggers out of your hair today, there'll be twice as many in there tomorrow." 9

I would look at the knotted ball of hair wrapped around the teeth of the comb, with its stragley ends sticking out all over, and my childlike gullibility would lead me to believe her fabrication. When she finished, I imagined what a chicken might feel like after having all its feathers plucked. 10

I thought about other times when having long hair was a real pain (in a different sense of the word). Some mornings my mom would fix my hair into two long braids. Not only would family and friends give them a tug, but even an occasional stranger could not resist the urge to pull on my braids. It was as impossible as trying to resist the urge to "squeeze the Charmin." Another hairdo she liked to deck me out in was the crisscrossing of the two braids on the top of my head. I hated my hair like that. I felt I looked like the old woman in the T.V. series, *I* 11

Remember Mamma (popular in the 50's). Since I was a tomboy, most of the time I just wore my hair in a ponytail. Still my hair would fly around and slap me in the face while playing kick the can, or homerun derby, like a horse's tail swatting flies. I would be glad to get rid of the nuisance. Who wouldn't be? My long locks were way overdue for a trimming.

Finally, the beautician entered the room. She picked up a pair of scissors 12
larger than any I had ever seen. I felt one last, long tug on my hair and heard the muffled cutting sounds of the scissors. My long lifeless braid fell limp to the floor.

"Free at last!" I thought. "No more long tangle sessions," I sighed to myself. 13
"No one would pull on my hair now," I mused. "How happy could any one person be?" I wondered.

At that moment, I felt a tear forming in the corner of my eye and I wondered 14
why.

Seniors in the Night

As we go through life, few of us give much thought to what will become of us 1
should we not be able to care for ourselves in our golden years. I, for one, would not mind living in a boarding home that had the atmosphere of Kay's Boarding Home for the Elderly. I worked for Kay, and I'll never forget the childlike innocence that engulfed the elderly who lived there.

I had the opportunity to work both day and night shifts at Kay's. Day turn 2
consisted of basic care, giving baths, changing beds, light housekeeping, preparation and serving the meals, and making sure nobody slipped out the door to "go home." The patients were pretty much the typical vaguely senile senior citizens. A challenge to the workers' nerves at times, too. As the sun set, the patients would begin to scurry around and slip into PJs and beds. Everyone would be in bed by 9:00 P.M., donning their chameleon skins and waiting for me, the sole employee of midnight turn.

As I clocked in at 11:00 P.M., I knew the night would hold plenty of action 3
for me before the sun would rise up in the morning. The intercom throughout the house let me hear every sound made by any of my 14 charges. Each patient had their own night time sound, so as I would go about my duties I could keep audio tabs on all.

Running up and down the basement stairs doing laundry, I would stop at 4
intervals to listen for the slow, deep rasp of Bertha's snore—the night wouldn't be complete without it.

Working in the kitchen, I would hear the familiar squeak-creak, squeak- 5
creak of the floor boards at the end of the hall indicating that I was right on schedule because Jr. met me each night around midnight to check on the time. "It's 12:15, Jr.," I'd tell him, but still hour by hour Jr. would be up throughout the night checking on the time. He had a phobia of missing breakfast—fat chance. After promising Jr. to wake him first in the morning, I'd give him a hug and tuck him back into bed, for the first of many times of the night.

About a half-hour later I'd see an awkward, eerily shaped shadow coming toward me—it's Uncle Alf taking his bihourly trip to the john. He'd do this all night, I think, so that he could fuss and holler all the next day that he didn't sleep well. 6

Upon completion of my hourly checks (making sure that no one "checked out" since the previous hour), a slow moving shadow is again making its way down the hall, only this time it would be Pappy. Always fully attired in overalls, flannel shirt, boots, and a hunter's cap. Pappy was up and at 'em at 4:30 A.M. like clockwork ready for chores. After 5 or 10 minutes of persuasive arguments that there are no farms within hollering distance, he would finally go back to bed. Okay, so I promised that "the eggs had been gathered and the cows had been milked"; they had been—many years ago. 7

As 7:00 A.M. rolled around I would prepare to leave my little darlings, but not until I'd seen the twinkle in each of their eyes. Most of them would refer to me as "The Girl in the Night," just as if it was my name. Whatever they chose to call me, I can only hope that those who are capable of any memory at all are able to recall me with half the fondness as I have of them. Each of the night stalkers was me—yet to come. 8

I Learned to March

I can still see it clearly even after all these years. A bright cheerful fourth-grade room filled with thirty eager children of all varieties of body and mind. I can also hear it as if it enveloped me. The music of John Philip Sousa stays with me even today. 1

She played the records every day, that staunch old woman. Miss Thompson was a matriarch. She was close to retirement that year, and feared by every third-grader walking the halls of Walker Elementary School. The summer before my fourth school year was one of great anticipation. Miss Thompson was a legend with a bifurcated image. She was feared due to her demanding nature, and respected for her strength. Miss Thompson was crippled. She had survived polio as a child and as a result walked with the aid of a cane and was marked with a deformed left foot and leg. The day those fourth-grade room assignments arrived the phone lines were jammed. Mary called Cindy, Cindy called Susie, and Susie called me. I alone, of all my friends, had been placed in Miss Thompson's class. 2

I wanted to cry, to scream of the injustice of it all. I knew what lay ahead. I could feel it in every nerve cell of my body. It was not the homework; it was not her demand to perform with above-average capabilities; it was that damned marching! 3

Everyday through the small glass window of Room 11, the students of Miss Thompson could be seen marching round the room, knees up high, heads back, chests out, marching to the music of "Stars and Stripes Forever." Worse, though, was the fact that the students of Room 11 could see the jeering faces of the crowds 4 in the hallway. They laughed and snickered and even pointed! I could feel the shame even then, reading that small card with her name so stately printed upon it. I knew how I would look to them!

Yet, deep inside of me, slowly nurturing, was a slight sense of titillation. I 5
was an extremely shy child. Having no brothers or sisters and an introverted mother, I too became quiet and reserved. Still, I was curious about this new twist in my life.

I survived the remainder of the summer by doing deep-breathing exercises, 6
and arrived at school on the first day of fourth grade a total nervous wreck. I seated myself in the back of the room, unable at any time to remove my gaze from this silver-haired woman sitting perfectly erect at her desk.

How I learned that first day. I learned of consistent demand topped with a 7
dollop of love; I learned to respect the grace of a woman who had midmorning tea brewed in a cup with a strange heating coil; I learned that indeed my back did feel better if I sat erect in my chair; and I learned to march—with my knees high, my head back, and my chest out, to John Philip Sousa's classic piece, "Stars and Stripes Forever."

Friends

Carrie, Lesley, Joel, Mark, and I were friends for as long as any of us could 1
remember. We played together as young children and went out together as young adults. We were inseparable; we did everything together—until we all got sick and watched each other die.

Joel died first. He's not physically dead, but he has no life. Drugs created a 2
chemical imbalance in his brain. Joel is a complete and total vegetable. He doesn't recognize any of us. He doesn't even recognize his mother and father. He probably never will.

Lesley died around three o'clock in the morning. Her parents found her at 3
six thirty on December 3. At seven thirty I received a phone call stating that Lesley was dead. I laughed and hung up the phone and waited for my best friend Lesley to come pick me up for school.

At 8:01 the first newspaper called me. The reporter wanted to ask questions 4
about her overdose and about her friends who had all been in drug clinics at one time or another. They wanted to know why we let two of our friends ruin their lives. They wanted to know why our group of friends never told anyone about Joel and Lesley's addictions. The reporters asked who was going to die next. People I didn't even know called and asked how I planned on dying. They said I could go Joel's way or Lesley's way or choose my own way. Newspapers said that other high school students were making bets on who was going to die next. They said the odds were with me.

The day of the funeral was the worst day of my life. Mark picked us all up 5
for the service. When we pulled into the church we could see a huge crowd of

people standing in the church yard. Curt, Carrie, Mark, and I got out of the car and began walking towards the church. Curt and Mark placed Carrie and me between them. As soon as the reporters saw us they started screaming questions. People grabbed at us and tried to separate our tiny group. Carrie got questions about Joel, while Curt got questions about Lesley. Most of the questions were general and not meant to upset either of the two. When they asked me a question, it was a different story. I seemed to be their scapegoat. Mark thought it was because my boyfriend was still alive, and I was the only one with my partner still alive. Since Mark was never addicted to drugs or in a drug rehab, he didn't get the same treatment.

The four of us walked down the church aisle hand-in-hand. We sat in 6
a pew near the front of the church. As people came in, they pointed and whispered about our tiny little group of friends. They said, "That's Lesley's boyfriend" as they pointed to Curt. "Carrie," they would say staring in her direction trying to be discrete with their pointing, "she's Joel's girlfriend. You know, the boy in the mental hospital." Then it was Mark's and my turn to be put under the microscope. Mark was called the sober person in our group. He was much more responsible than the rest of us. When my name came up, it was always: "Wasn't she the one who took Joel to the hospital?" They said I was sure to be next. Some even said I should be in the coffin instead of Lesley.

At the end of the service, we walked toward Lesley's coffin. Concentrating 7
on getting to Lesley, we didn't notice her parents walking towards us. I glanced up just in time to see Lesley's dad grab Curt's arm. I looked up and saw Lesley's mother mouth the words, "You killed my daughter." Her father looked at all of us. "You're all going to die. First, Joel, then Lesley, who's next?" They walked away leaving us standing there shocked and upset.

Reaching Lesley's dead body sent Carrie and me into hysterics. "Wake 8
up," I heard myself whisper. "Wake up, Les!" I yelled suddenly terrified that they were going to bury her alive. I took a step toward the coffin and grabbed her stiff, cold body. I could hear Carrie call her dead friend and saw her grab Lesley's arm.

"She's dead, Mo," said Mark's voice. I turned angrily on Mark. I couldn't 9
believe he thought she was dead. I knew she was alive. Tears poured down my face as I stared at my boyfriend thinking only that he betrayed our group.

"Les is dead, Mo," said Curt. I turned to see Curt crying. I saw big tears 10
pour down his face and somehow I realized that Lesley was dead. I immediately fainted to the floor and Carrie followed close after.

The newspapers showed pictures of Carrie and me getting carried out of the 11
church. Jackets covered our faces, but it was clearly us and clearly Mark and Curt carrying us out.

Eventually, all of us stopped using drugs. We all go visit Joel, but he does- 12
n't seem to see us. Lesley's grave is always covered with flowers. I go to talk to her whenever I can. Mark and I got to tell her we were engaged. We saw her parents as we were leaving. They said they were happy they could come to

our wedding instead of our funerals. They only wished that their daughter could have lived to see her childhood friends get married. I wish she could be there too.

Becoming a Reliable Critic by Evaluating Writing

Form a group with several classmates and select one of the previous student writings (or use one your instructor assigns). Designate one person to record the group's findings and another to report those findings to the class. Then read the essay closely and answer the evaluation questions below. Answering these questions will help you appreciate how each aspect of an essay contributes to or detracts from its overall quality, and it will point out successful techniques you may want to bring to your own writing as well as less successful techniques to avoid.

Evaluation Questions

1. The Opening
   Does the opening engage your interest? Why or why not?
2. Supporting Details
   Which journalist's questions are answered? Are any treated in too much or too little detail? Note any points that you do not understand.
   Does the writer interrupt the narration to explain?
   Evaluate the effectiveness of this technique.
   Evaluate the use of conversation and description.
3. Organization
   Does the writer use or omit an introduction, stated thesis, topic sentences, and conclusion paragraph effectively? Explain. What chronology is followed? Is the time sequence easy to follow? Evaluate the use of transitions.
4. The Closing
   Does the narration end in a satisfying way? Explain.
5. Overview
   What do you like best about the essay? What is the single most important revision the author should make?

Essay Topics: Narration

1. Relate an occurrence that caused you to change your view of someone or something, making sure you note your view both before and after the event. If you like, you can tell why the occurrence caused you to change your view.
2. Tell of an event that had a significant impact on you. Make clear what the impact was/is. You can also tell why the event affected you as it did.

3. Tell a story that describes a single, specific school experience. While it is not necessary, you can use a humorous approach.
4. Narrate an event or moment that was embarrassing, amusing, distressing, or puzzling to you or someone else.
5. Tell of a time when things did not go as you, or another, expected them to. Make clear what the expectation was and comment on why things did not go as planned.
6. Write a narration about a specific job experience you have had.
7. Narrate a childhood memory.
8. Tell the story of a time you were happy or unhappy with your family life.
9. Narrate a moment or event that marked a turning point in your life.
10. Tell of a time when you (or another) were treated unjustly.
11. Write an account of the time you were the angriest you have ever been.
12. Tell of an event that caused you to feel regret.
13. Narrate the happiest moment you have had with a friend or member of your family.
14. Relate an incident that caused you to realize something for the first time. Explain what the effect of that realization has been.
15. Tell a story of a time you witnessed (or displayed) courage.
16. Relate a memorable experience you have had in a sports competition.
17. Tell the story of some first-time experience.
18. Write of a time when a friend or relative disappointed you.
19. Write an account of your happiest birthday.
20. Narrate your proudest moment.

Thematic Topics

1. In "Looking for Work" (page 160), Gary Soto says he wanted his family to be more like families on television. To what extent do you think television influences our desires? Is this influence largely positive or negative?
2. In "Shame" (page 165), Dick Gregory tells of learning shame in the classroom. In "I Learned to March" (page 172), the student author tells of learning more positive things. Explain whether your classroom experience was more like Gregory's or the student author's. Be sure to explain why you view your experience the way you do.
3. School affects people in ways unrelated to learning subject matter. Explain and illustrate one or more of these ways, drawing on any or all of the following: "Shame," "I Learned to March," "Unforgettable Miss Bessie" (page 140), and your own experience and observation.

Writing Strategies

As you write your narrative essay, continue experimenting to improve your writing process. Chapters 1 to 3 describe techniques you can try. In addition, the following procedures may prove useful.

Topic Selection

If you are having trouble settling on the story you want to tell, fill in the blanks in one of the following sentences:

1. I'll never forget the time I ______________________________.
2. I was never so embarrassed as when ______________________________.
3. The first time I ____________________ I learned ____________________.

Idea Generation

To generate ideas, answer the following questions:

1. Who was involved?
2. What happened?
3. When did it happen?
4. Where did it happen?
5. Why did it happen?
6. What was the effect?
7. Who was affected?
8. How did it happen?
9. Could it happen again?
10. Why is it important?
11. What was learned?
12. Was it expected to happen?

First Draft

Write out in essay form what happened first, second, third, and so on. Simply begin at the beginning and write through to the last element of the story. Do not worry about grammar, spelling, punctuation, sentence effectiveness, or anything else except getting every occurrence in chronological order. Comment on and/or explain points if it occurs to you to do so, and use conversation and description when this comes naturally and seems fitting. Do not worry at this point about an introduction, thesis, or conclusion.

Reader Response

If you like to secure reader response as part of your revising process, see page 77. In addition, ask your reader to note any places on the draft where you should comment on or explain the significance of an event. Then ask that person to write out the point your narration makes so you can be sure you are expressing what you want to express.

REVISION CHECKLIST

In addition to the checklist on page 8, you can use this checklist to help you revise your narration.

1. Does your narration make a specific point that is stated or strongly implied? What is that point?
2. Have you answered all the journalist's questions? Have you emphasized the answers to some questions as your audience and purpose warrant?
3. Is the narration well paced and free of irrelevant detail?
4. Are details arranged chronologically, with or without flashbacks?
5. If you have omitted a formal introduction, stated thesis, topic sentences, and/or concluding paragraph, have you done so judiciously?
6. When necessary for clarity, have you interrupted the narration to comment on an event or explain its significance?
7. Have you used conversation, specific diction, and description as necessary for vividness?
8. Read your draft aloud to listen for places where transitions or sentence variety are needed.

CHAPTER 7

Illustration

An illustration is an example—and nothing helps a reader understand a writer's point better than an example. Think about a time when you were reading and feeling unsure about what the writer meant. Just when you were feeling the most uncertain, you may have come across the words, "for example." Remember how hopeful you felt when you read those words, knowing they were introducing an illustration that would clarify things? Remember how much better you understood the writer's point after you read the example? That is because a well-chosen illustration can crystallize meaning. In short, one carefully selected example can be worth hundreds of words of explanation.

DETAIL

Even our most routine communications rely heavily on examples to make their point. Let's say a friend asked you who to take for geology and you replied, "Take Chung; he's the most reasonable." Well, your friend would probably want you to clarify why Chung is the most reasonable, and you might explain by providing examples. "His tests are graded on the curve, he requires only one research paper, and he's always in his office to help students." Even the question, "What do you want to do tonight?" can prompt the use of examples. If you replied, "Something relaxing," you would not be as clear as if you added examples. "Something relaxing like a movie or a quiet dinner at Alonzo's."

Illustration adds clarity because it makes the general more specific; it allows the writer to nail down a generalization by providing specific instances of ways that generalization is true. Consider, for example, the following four sentences.

> It is not easy today for a young married couple to get off to a good start. House prices are high, making home ownership almost impossible, so the couple may spend many

> years in a cramped apartment. Unemployment is high, so many couples cannot find the jobs they need to secure their income. Perhaps most significantly, young marrieds find that financial worries cause tensions that strain the marriage bond.

In the above example, the first sentence expresses a generalization. The three sentences after that provide illustrations that bear out the generalization. In Chapter 2, when supporting detail was discussed, you were cautioned to *show* rather than *tell* (see page 42). Very often, illustrations help you do that by providing instances to make generalizations concrete.

In addition to providing clarity and concreteness, illustrations add interest. Writing that never goes beyond generalizations is often dull. Yet carefully chosen examples add vitality and create reader interest by bringing things down from the abstract level to a more specific, easily understood one.

Because illustrations add clarity, concreteness, and interest, they are a frequent component of writing, regardless of the dominant pattern of development. Essays developed primarily with description, narration, comparison and contrast, or any other pattern can make liberal use of examples. This chapter, however, will discuss illustration as the primary pattern of development.

PURPOSE

Let's say you plan to write an essay that illustrates the benefits of running. You could do this for a number of reasons. Perhaps you want to influence your reader to take up running, or maybe you want your reader to understand why running is such an important part of your life, or perhaps you wish to make your reader aware that running provides more than physical exercise, or maybe you want your reader to understand what distinguishes running from other forms of exercise.

You can determine your purpose by asking these questions.

1. Do I want to share my reaction to or feeling about my subject?
2. Do I want to help my reader understand why I respond to my subject as I do?
3. Do I want to clarify the nature of my subject?
4. Do I want to convince my reader of something?

Let's return to the essay about the benefits of running to see how these questions can help a writer establish purpose. Say I run 4 miles every day, regardless of the weather, and many of my friends have considered me odd for this. I might want to help my friends understand my dedication to running so they will alter their view of me. Thus, my purpose (as a result of answering question 2 above) could be to illustrate what motivates me by giving examples of the psychological benefits I get from running. This I would do in hopes of earning my friends' understanding.

Now let's assume I have a friend who is depressed and tense much of the time. After answering question 4, I might decide to illustrate the ways running can decrease depression and tension. This I could do in an effort to convince my friend to begin running to improve his state of mind.

My purpose will partly dictate what illustrations I use. For the first essay I would provide examples of all the benefits important to me, but in the second I would provide only examples of ways running combats depression and tension.

AUDIENCE

To determine your audience, you can answer the following questions.

1. With whom do I want to share? Or whom do I want to entertain, inform, or convince?
2. Who would benefit from reading about my subject?
3. Who does not know enough about my subject?
4. Who sees my subject differently than I do?
5. Who would be influenced by reading about my subject?

Once audience is identified, you should determine the nature of that audience by answering questions like these.

1. How much does my reader know about my subject?
2. Is my reader's knowledge of my subject firsthand?
3. Does my reader have any strong feelings about my subject?
4. Does my reader have an interest in my subject?
5. Is my subject important to my reader?

To appreciate how audience influences the choice of examples, assume you are writing a piece about why your college is a good one, and in it you plan to present examples to illustrate some of your school's strengths. If you are writing for an academically oriented audience that does not care much for sports, you would not cite as an example that your football team is the conference champion. Similarly, a paper aimed at parents of prospective freshmen should not cite as an example the wild parties on Saturday nights. Thus, when you select your examples, keep your reader in mind.

THE NATURE AND NUMBER OF ILLUSTRATIONS

How many examples to use is a key decision. With too few examples you can fail to clarify your generalization and provide the necessary concreteness. With too many examples, you can be guilty of overkill.

In general, you have four options. You can provide just a few examples, say two or three, and develop each one in great detail. You can provide quite a few examples and develop each one in far less detail. You can provide a moderate number of examples, each developed to a degree somewhere between the other two extremes. Finally, you can have several examples, some highly detailed and some less developed.

As you decide about the number of illustrations and degree of development, keep in mind that whatever number of examples you have, it must be enough to explain and support your generalization adequately; and to whatever degree you develop an illustration, you must have enough detail that your reader appreciates the point it makes.

Your examples can come from a variety of sources, including your own experiences and observations, class readings and lectures, personal reading, and television viewing. Notice how each generalization below is followed by an illustration taken from a different source.

generalization: Too often, young children believe that what they see on television is an accurate representation of reality.

example from personal reading: I recall many years ago reading of a young child who died after jumping from a window and trying to fly like the Superman character he had seen on TV.

generalization: Americans are becoming immune to the plight of the homeless.

example from observation: I watched at least fifty people walk past an obviously sick, homeless man on Federal Street without noticing him.

generalization: Being a salesperson, especially at Christmastime, is difficult.

example from experience: Last Christmas I worked at the jewelry counter of a local department store. Although it is supposed to be a season of goodwill, Christmas made ordinarily pleasant people pushy and demanding. Once, an elderly woman insisted that I bring out every watch in the stockroom just so she could verify that all the styles were on display.

generalization: Many of the early immigrants to this country found life harder here than it was in their homeland.

example from class reading or lecture: My history instructor, for example, explained that many of those who survived the Atlantic crossing spent their lives in sweatshops, working for slave wages.

generalization: People in high-pressure jobs can reduce their risk of heart attack.

example from television viewing: A recent television documentary explained that executives could strengthen their hearts by parking a mile from their office and walking to work with a heavy briefcase.

Some of your examples may be narrations, because a story can be an excellent way to achieve clarity and concreteness. Description, too, can be highly illustrative, so some of your examples may take this form. For example, part of an essay developing the thesis generalization, "Being a salesperson, especially at Christmastime, is difficult," could have a paragraph telling the story of the time the elderly woman demanded to see all the watches in the stockroom. Similarly, an essay developing the thesis generalization, "Many of the early immigrants to this country found life harder here than it was in their homeland," could have a paragraph describing what it was like to work in the sweatshops.

ARRANGING DETAIL

In an illustration essay the thesis can express the generalization and the body paragraphs can present and develop the illustrations of that generalization.

When just a few illustrations are used, each one can be presented and developed in its own body paragraph. If an illustration is an extended example, it may require more than one body paragraph for adequate development. When quite a few illustrations are used and each one gets less extensive development, you can group related examples together in the same body paragraph.

Writers must consider the order of their illustrations. Often, a progressive order is used. If some of your examples are more telling than others, you can save your most compelling example for last in order to build to a big finish. Or you could begin with your second-best example to impress your reader right off with the validity of your generalization. You can also begin with your best example to impress your reader initially, while reserving your second-most-effective example for last to ensure a strong final body paragraph.

Sometimes you can arrange your illustrations in a chronological or spatial order. Say your thesis says the fans at local high school basketball games are rowdy. You could arrange your illustrations chronologically by first giving examples of rowdyism before the game begins, then examples of rowdyism during half-time, and finally examples of rowdyism after the game. You can also sequence your examples in a spatial order. If you are developing the generalization that the playground in the city park was not really designed with children in mind, you could begin at one end of the playground and work your way around, ordering your examples to correspond with this movement through space.

Other logical arrangements are also possible. For example, if some of your examples come from your own, firsthand experience, some from your own observation, and some from the experience of others, you can group together the examples from the same source.

TRYOUT Write out one generalization about education. Then try to discover one example to fit each of the categories listed below. If you are unable to think of an example for a particular category, then try to come up with two for another category. Also, one example may fill more than one category. For example, one example may be a narration from personal experience.

1. Example from personal experience
2. Example from observation
3. Example from personal reading
4. Example from class reading or lecture
5. Example from television viewing
6. Narrative example
7. Descriptive example

PROFESSIONAL ESSAYS

This Is Progress?

Alan L. Otten

Alan Otten uses many examples to point out that one step forward may be two steps back. Because he uses so many illustrations, he does not develop any one in much detail. The essay originally appeared in 1978. As you read, ask yourself if the generalizations and supporting examples still hold true today.

A couple I know checked into one of the new Detroit hotels a few months ago and, in due course, left a 7 A.M. wake-up call. 1

Being an early riser, however, the husband was up long before 7, and decided he'd go down to breakfast and let his wife sleep late. He dialed the hotel switchboard, explained the situation, and said he'd like to cancel the wake-up call. 2

"Sorry, sir," the answer came, "but we can't do that. It's in the computer, and there's no way to get it out now." 3

Consider another story. A while back, a reporter phoned a congressional committee and asked to speak to the staff director. Unfortunately, he was told, the staff director wouldn't be in that morning; there'd been a power failure at his home. Well, the reporter persisted, that was certainly too bad, but just why did a power failure prevent him from coming to work? 4

"He can't get his car out of the garage," the secretary explained. "The garage doors are electrically controlled." 5

As these two anecdotes suggest, this is a column in praise of progress: those wonderful advances in science and technology that leave the world only slightly more snafued than before. 6

The balance sheet will eschew such common complaints as the way the modern office grinds to a halt whenever the copying machine is out of order. Or the computerized magazine subscription lists that take only four times longer than formerly to effect changes of address and which start mailing renewal notices six months before the subscription expires and then continue at weekly intervals. 7

Or the form letters that provide The New Yorker with so many droll end-of-the-column items, like the letter that was sent to the "News Desk, Wall Street Journal," and led off, "Dear Mr. Desk. . . ." Or the new drugs, operations and health regimens that in due time are shown to be more dangerous than the illnesses. 8

Computers bulk centrally in many of the "this is progress?" stories. For instance, a friend recently went to make a deposit at her local bank in upstate New York. The deposit couldn't be accepted, she was informed, "because it's raining too hard." Seems that when the rain gets beyond a certain intensity, the wires transmitting the message from the branch banks to the computer at the main bank in Albany send jumbled signals—and so branch-bank operations have to be suspended temporarily. 9

Every newspaper person knows that each technological advance in the printing process somehow makes news deadlines earlier, rather than later as might logically be assumed. Computers, though, can foul things up in other ways, too. At a recent conference on press coverage of presidential campaigns, many participants suggested that the lengthy background stories prepared early in the campaign by the wire services or such special news services as those of The New York Times and Washington Post might be saved by subscribing papers and then used late in the campaign, when the public was more in the mood to pay attention. 10

"Are you kidding?" demanded a publisher present. "That stuff now all comes in computerized, and it's erased at the end of the day. We don't save any copy anymore." 11

Computers aren't the only villains, to be sure. Everyone has observed bizarre scenes of a dozen people down on hands and knees searching the pavement or the grass or a tennis court for a lost contact lens. The other day, however, 12 a colleague announced she was having trouble seeing out of one eye and was off to the optometrist's. About a half hour later, she was back, giggling. The night before, she had apparently put one contact lens on top of another in the case where she kept an extra lens, and had that morning unwittingly put two lenses in one eye.

During last winter's snow storms, the Amtrak Metroliners frequently had to be removed from service as snow clogged the motors so cleverly mounted underneath the new high-speed trains. (The cars are now beginning to be converted to a different motor-mounting scheme.) A number of high schools in this area have been built with windows that don't open; when the air conditioning fails on a hot spring or fall day, students are given the day off. Last fall, when the nation moved back to standard time, a young friend was appalled to find she was going to have to turn her time-and-date digital wristwatch ahead 30 days and 23 hours. *13*

Still another acquaintance had his car battery go dead while his power windows were rolled down—and then the rains came and poured in while he was parked alongside the highway waiting for help. *14*

Society's rush to credit cards has its convenient aspects—but also unpleasant ones. Just try to check into a hotel announcing that you prefer to pay cash rather than use a credit card. Scorn, suspicion, hostility, un-American, if not downright communistic. *15*

Once upon a time, you could look up at the postmark on a letter and see exactly where and when it had been processed at the post office. *16*

Now, not only does the postmark deny you some or all of this occasionally useful information, but it insists on selling you something instead: "National Guard Month—Gain Skills By Serving" or "Save Energy—Turn Off Lights." *17*

And like most creations of American ingenuity, this, too, has been exported to less fortunate lands. A letter from Belgium the other day carried the exhortatory postmark: *"Prévenez l'Hypertension. Evitez le Sel."** In case your French wasn't up to it, there was a drawing of a salt shaker. *18*

In all likelihood, corrective measures are being developed for many of the problems described above, and helpful correspondents will be writing in to tell me all about it. Yet I remain confident that new examples will come along to fill the gap. After all, that's progress. *19*

Questions on Technique

1. What generalization does Otten illustrate? (Hint: check the thesis.)
2. Some of Otten's examples are more detailed than others. How do you suppose the author determined which ones to develop more extensively?
3. Otten wrote his piece as an article for a large newspaper. Has the author selected his illustrations with his audience in mind? Explain.
4. What is the source of Otten's illustrations?
5. What patterns of development does Otten use for his examples? For each pattern you note, cite one of Otten's illustrations as an example of the pattern.

*"Prevent high blood pressure. Avoid salt."

6. In what kind of order does Otten arrange his examples?
7. What approach does Otten take to his introduction? Why is his introduction so long?
8. What approach does Otten take to his conclusion? Is it effective? Explain.

For Group Discussion or Journal Writing

Develop a list of so-called conveniences or technological advances that have created problems for you. Indicate what the problems are and go on to determine whether or not each convenience or advance is worth the problem it causes.

Darkness at Noon

Harold Krents

Blind from birth, Harold Krents uses examples to educate the reader about the blind in particular and the disabled in general.

Blind from birth, I have never had the opportunity to see myself and have been completely dependent on the image I create in the eye of the observer. To date it has not been narcissistic. 1

There are those who assume that since I can't see, I obviously also cannot hear. Very often people will converse with me at the top of their lungs, enunciating each word very carefully. Conversely, people will also often whisper, assuming that since my eyes don't work, my ears don't either. 2

For example, when I go to the airport and ask the ticket agent for assistance to the plane, he or she will invariably pick up the phone, call a ground hostess and whisper: "Hi, Jane, we've got a 76 here." I have concluded that the word "blind" is not used for one of two reasons: Either they fear that if the dread word is spoken, the ticket agent's retina will immediately detach, or they are reluctant to inform me of my condition of which I may not have been previously aware. 3

On the other hand, others know that of course I can hear, but believe that I can't talk. Often, therefore, when my wife and I go out to dinner, a waiter or waitress will ask Kit if "*he* would like a drink" to which I respond that "indeed *he* would." 4

This point was graphically driven home to me while we were in England. I had been given a year's leave of absence from my Washington law firm to study for a diploma in law degree at Oxford University. During the year I became ill and was hospitalized. Immediately after admission, I was wheeled down to the X-ray room. Just at the door sat an elderly woman—elderly I would judge from the sound of her voice. "What is his name?" the woman asked the orderly who had been wheeling me. 5

"What's your name?" the orderly repeated to me. 6

"Harold Krents," I replied. 7

"Harold Krents," he repeated. 8

"When was he born?" 9

"When were you born?" 10

"November 5, 1944," I responded. 11

"November 5, 1944," the orderly intoned. 12

This procedure continued for approximately five minutes at which point 13
even my saint-like disposition deserted me. "Look," I finally blurted out, "this is absolutely ridiculous. Okay, granted I can't see, but it's got to have become pretty clear to both of you that I don't need an interpreter."

"He says he doesn't need an interpreter," the orderly reported to the 14
woman.

The toughest misconception of all is the view that because I can't see, I can't 15
work. I was turned down by over forty law firms because of my blindness, even though my qualifications included a cum laude degree from Harvard College and a good ranking in my Harvard Law School class.

The attempt to find employment, the continuous frustration of being told 16
that it was impossible for a blind person to practice law, the rejection letters, not based on my lack of ability but rather on my disability, will always remain one of the most disillusioning experiences of my life.

I therefore look forward to the day, with the expectation that it is certain to 17
come, when employers will view their handicapped workers as a little child did me years ago when my family still lived in Scarsdale.

I was playing basketball with my father in our backyard according to proce- 18
dures we had developed. My father would stand beneath the hoop, shout, and I would shoot over his head at the basket attached to our garage. Our next-door neighbor, aged five, wandered over into our yard with a playmate. "He's blind," our neighbor whispered to her friend in a voice that could be heard distinctly by Dad and me. Dad shot and missed; I did the same. Dad hit the rim; I missed entirely; Dad shot and missed the garage entirely. "Which one is blind?" whispered back the little friend.

I would hope that in the near future when a plant manager is touring the fac- 19
tory with the foreman and comes upon a handicapped and nonhandicapped person working together, his comment after watching them work will be, "Which one is disabled?"

Questions on Technique

1. Krents illustrates three misconceptions about blind people. What are these misconceptions?
2. What is the source of Krents's illustrations?
3. In what order does Krents arrange his details?
4. What purpose does the basketball narration serve?
5. What other narration appears in the essay?
6. "Darkness at Noon" originally appeared in *The New York Times*. Are the illustrations suited to the original audience? Explain.

7. What do you judge to be the author's purpose? How do the examples help the author fulfill his purpose?

For Group Discussion or Journal Writing

In the last paragraph of "Darkness at Noon," Krents expresses a hope for the future. How likely do you think it is that his hope will be realized? Explain.

The Honest Repairman—A Vanishing American?

Ken W. Purdy

When you have an item repaired, do you feel that you are being treated fairly? If so, you may change your mind after reading the next selection.

A few weeks ago I took a Minox camera into a New York shop for repairs. The trouble seemed simple enough: I couldn't load it, the film cassette wouldn't go in. The clerk told me it needed cleaning and lubrication, one week, $6.50. When I came back the camera was taken out of a drawer in an elaborately wrapped, stamped, tagged package. I paid the $6.50. It didn't *look* any cleaner than it had been, but I thought the important work had been done on the inside. 1

I bought a cassette of film. It wouldn't go in. Amazement and bafflement were registered by the clerk. He tried to load it. Another clerk tried. Another. No use, it would have to "go back to the shop." Ten days. Right. 2

Next time, when the Minox was taken out of its official-looking wrapping, I realized I was being hustled: when I told the clerk I wanted to *see* if it would take film there was a pregnant pause. I pointed to an open cassette on a nearby shelf. It was "new" and I couldn't use it. . . . I used it anyway. It wouldn't go in, as everybody in the shop had known it would not. 3

I raised the roof. I made a phone call to a famous New York photographer who knew the president of the Minox importing company. Unpleasantness followed, and by next day I could prove that the camera had been nowhere near the repair shop and that it had not even been dusted off, much less cleaned and lubricated. The store returned my $6.50 without a word of argument or defense. The Minox company cleaned, lubricated and practically rebuilt the camera for me without charge, entirely as a courtesy, since the company itself had been in no way involved. But this happy ending came about only because I knew whom to call. Most customers being deliberately cheated are helpless. 4

Unless he's lucky the cheated customer may never find out. I took my daughter's expensive watch, made by an internationally known company, to a shop displaying the company's dealership sign. The watch had been running badly. It needed, the man said, a complete cleaning and adjustment, $20. He was an old-world-craftsman-type, with just a trace of accent, probably fake Swiss, and he looked as trustworthy as your grandmother. When I came back for the watch 5 he said he needed "another three days for checking, just to be sure." I returned, gave him the $20 and took the watch. It stopped dead four days later. Even in my rage, I had to admire the subtlety of his technique. Who could suspect a man who wanted three extra days just to be sure he'd done a great job?

I went to the U.S. headquarters of the company. A woman clerk in the elaborate and luxurious repair department took the watch away, brought it back and told me it needed a complete cleaning and adjustment, $30, ready in 12 weeks. 6

I told her that since the watch had just come from one of its dealerships, I required to know its precise condition. 7

"We don't give out that information," she said. 8

I explained the position more fully: somebody, I said, was a liar and a cheat. After a considerable discussion, and one more trip to consult with the technicians in the back room, she was able to say that the work did in fact need to be done, and that, yes, that indicated pretty clearly that it certainly had not been done by the little old watchmaker with the winning ways. 9

I entered a complaint with an official of the company, but he chose to make no comment. 10

It used to be that occasionally one would find repair work had been badly done. Now it seems to me that more and more one finds it hadn't been done at all. I suspected that a garage was cheating me. I took a car in for gear-box adjustment, but I sealed the gear-box lid. It could be opened easily enough, but it would show. When the car came back, with a bill for over $30, the seal hadn't been broken. Nobody had even looked into the gear-box, much less adjusted anything. I screamed. I refused to pay. I let it come to suit and settled for 50 percent. So, after a great deal of trouble, I came out only half-cheated. 11

Legally to prove a case of non-service, Better Business Bureau officials say, the customer must be expert or sophisticated or lucky or all three. Probably for this reason, and also because often the customer doesn't know he's been victimized, non-service complaints are uncommon. What is *not* uncommon are complaints about incompetent or careless service and repair, or fraudulent guarantees, or "hijacking," the technique of enticing a customer with a promise of a low-cost minor job, then hitting him with expensive, unnecessary work—which may or may not be done at all. 12

"We just don't have enough people to go out and thoroughly investigate nonservice complaints," the Metropolitan New York Better Business Bureau says. "Often it's a case of one man's judgment or opinion. And it's very difficult to get people to testify. One mechanic bills a customer $189 for new transmission parts, let's say. A week later another mechanic, one whom the customer knows and trusts, tells him that no such work has been done. But will he make an affidavit, or testify in court? No, he won't. Almost never. 13

"All we can tell people is to deal with reputable stores and shops, and get written guarantees for work and parts clearly spelled out on the bill. Beware of come-ons, of big bargains. Today it's hard enough to get something for something; you certainly aren't going to get something for nothing." 14

There is no doubt that the standard of morality has dropped sharply in recent years (shoplifting and cheating by customers is booming, too) and there 15 are probably many repairmen who consider themselves honest because they don't do anything worse than persuade a customer to buy something he doesn't need. After all, if the customer actually gets the part or the service he paid for, that's not stealing, is it?

The TV and radio field, which used to be rich ground for swindlers, has 16
been notably cleaned up. Most manufacturers now maintain factory service or use authorized service agencies which are tightly checked and supervised. A service agency with a good company is lucrative, it's well worth having, and smart operators won't risk losing it for the sake of a couple of hundred dollars on the side. If a shop does start to cheat, the word soon gets out. The BBB recently took a Bronx repairman to court when he billed a customer $47.50 on a TV "repair." The set was a plant, in perfect order except for a $7 tube. It was taken straight from the crooked shop to a reputable one, where it was established that $40.50 of the bill was overcharged.

A current gold mine for crooked repairmen is the air-conditioner field. The 17
BBB says that there are no authorized service agencies for air conditioners. A standard ploy begins with a baited offer to recondition your machine for $8.95 or so. The repairman arrives and goes into a well-rehearsed act: your freon is missing, the frattistat valve is completely shot, you could be asphyxiated in your sleep, the conditioner has to go into the shop. The next bulletin is that the bill won't be $8.95, it will be $34.95. You still want the $8.95 special? Well, there's a trucking charge of $7.50 and the conditioner is now all taken apart, it will have to be put together again . . . most people finally authorize the $34.95 overhaul.

Some mechanics find woman customers irresistible targets. Mrs. Anita 18
Lemberg of Brooklyn went to a muffler shop for a while-you-wait replacement. When her car was on the hoist, the mechanic told her a horror story about the condition of her steering system, it was so dangerous she shouldn't drive another foot, and so on. In only two hours, he said, he could "replace all the bushings" and perform other wonders. The bill was $51. Her regular mechanic, doing a lube job a week later, showed her that the grease and grime on her steering system was a year old if it was a minute. She went back to the muffler shop, where she was told that her mechanic was a liar.

An Ellenville, N.Y., woman, Mrs. Marian Talken, had trouble with her 19
clothes dryer. The repairman told her it needed a new drive-shaft and bearings. The bill was $72, and when the original trouble recurred, he wouldn't come back. Another repairman charged $13 to take the dryer apart and show Mrs. Talken that the same old drive-shaft was still in business at the same old spot. He would not, however, be her witness. "I don't want to get involved," he said. "You'll have to settle it yourself."

Doesn't anything *good* ever happen? Well, yes. A few months ago a friend of 20
mine asked a jeweler how much he would charge to fix an old watch. The man said he didn't like to work on anything but brand-new watches. A second watchmaker said, reluctantly, that he'd do it, for around $150. My friend kept shopping around until he got a better price—$7.20—and a prompt, superb job. How? That part was a little tricky: he asked a friendly airline pilot to take it to a shop in London. But even that is not a guaranteed solution. A London jeweler charged me

twice the list price for a wrist-watch crystal three years ago, probably because I had an American accent.

Maybe the answer is to do it yourself, or forget it. 21

Questions on Technique

1. What generalization does Purdy illustrate? Is the generalization implied or stated in a thesis?
2. The first 10 paragraphs function as an introduction. What approach does the author take to this introduction?
3. What method of development does Purdy use for most of his illustrations?
4. What purpose does the example in paragraph 13 serve?
5. What is the topic sentence of paragraph 17? Of paragraph 18?
6. What is the purpose of the example in paragraph 20?
7. In what order does Purdy arrange his illustrations?
8. What approach does Purdy take to his conclusion?

For Group Discussion or Journal Writing

Do you think you are treated fairly by people who repair cars, appliances, jewelry, cameras, and so forth? Explain why you feel as you do. Did reading Purdy's essay influence your view?

STUDENT ESSAYS TO READ AND EVALUATE

The following essays, written by students, are developed with illustrations. All have strengths and weaknesses for you to notice as you read.

The evaluation questions after the essays will guide you through an examination of one student writing so that you can practice forming and supporting critical judgments. This evaluation of student writing will sharpen your critical skill so you are better able to assess your own writing. It will also increase your awareness of what does and does not work in writing.

The Waiting Game

I'd bet that if scientifically analyzed, waiting in line would prove to be a major contribution to stress in human beings. One might think that because most of us are prone to conserve energy whenever possible, this task wouldn't seem so bad. I mean, all we really have to do is stand there and move a little and just stand there some more. But in reality, there is a resistance that keeps us from readily achieving a goal, and any Introduction to Psychology text will tell you that this resistance causes stress. This fact coupled with the amount of time wasted waiting in lines really makes me wonder about the toll it takes on our nervous system. 1

For instance, last summer I found myself waiting in long lines seven times in one day! It all started when I decided to treat my wife and kids (and myself) to a Cleveland Indians baseball game. 2

To start off, we needed gasoline. I suppose because it was Sunday morning and the sun was shining, people were naturally going to be out and about. I was convinced, however, that they all were waiting at the pumps purposely to prevent me from getting an early start! As I waited eight cars back from the pump, I alternately drummed my fingers and checked my watch. My stomach knotted as I realized that instead of arriving comfortably early, I'd be lucky to get a decent parking space at Cleveland stadium. In retrospect, I guess all those people were waiting there because that particular service station was one of the few open. 3

After a twenty-minute wait at the parking area (about a mile from the stadium) as hundreds of cars inched along, we parked, hiked to Gate A and were confronted by about eight hundred anticipants, filing ever so slowly through the metal barriers. As we blended into the stagnant flow, I was reminded of cattle inching forward to the milking parlor. I couldn't believe I was spending good money for this. 4

Once inside, we had to fight the crowds at the souvenir stand. I mean, what's a ball game without a scorecard, pennant, and a souvenir cap! Talk about being milked! Although you couldn't call what I was in a line (it was more like a mob scene), I had to wait eight minutes to spend $20, get three bruises, and very possibly a broken toe. 5

The wait for the hot dogs, cokes, and beer wasn't too bad, but the wait to get rid of the beer (around the fourth inning) at the necessary room was horrible! Another eight minutes shot in less-than-appealing surroundings. 6

All in all, the game itself was really enjoyable. Actually, I suppose I'd do it again any time, but I have to admit I was a bit frazzled when we got home. You see, we had another wait getting out of the parking lot—about twenty minutes. The ride home seemed like a wait also. The kids and I were so anxious we couldn't wait to get back. 7

The total exhaustion I experienced that night and the fact that I still remember more about waiting in line than the final score is an indication that the act of waiting in line is truly a major preoccupation. When we consider how often we wait in lines—renewing driver's licences, buying Big Mac's, going to a movie, etc.—we can see how valuable an alternate solution to waiting in lines could be. Maybe some day I'll work on that solution, and if I'm lucky—well, we'll just have to wait and see. 8

My Dream Car

There was not a cloud in the sky and the sun warmed the early morning air. This was going to be one of the happiest days of my life because I was getting my first car. It was just a tiny two seat Ford EXP, but its maroon paint job shone with an 1 electrifying brilliance. The stereo screamed better than anything I had ever heard, and the car could zip around like a tiny lightning bolt on wheels. My little ball of steel was the best thing I had ever seen—or so I thought. Little did I know that in the months to come my great car would become the most troublesome piece of tin on the road.

All of my troubles began about two months after I had purchased that 2
beastly thing. I was coming home from work, on a September Sunday afternoon, when I noticed that my piece of junk was getting a bit hot. I continued down the road a bit farther; then bang, my car just quit. I pulled off to the side of the road and got out to see what was wrong. There was antifreeze all over the blacktop. I figured that the water pump was broken, and indeed it was. But in addition, the pistons had smashed into the head and mangled the engine like someone crinkling tinfoil. Needless to say, I had to replace the water pump, but more important I had to get a whole new engine. This soaked me for about a thousand dollars, but little did I know that this was only the beginning of many problems.

I noticed my car's next failure about a month after the engine trouble. It was 3
a dreary rain-filled Saturday afternoon, so I decided to go to the gym to work out. I ran to my car and jumped in trying not to get wet. Once inside a strange noise echoed throughout the car. All I could hear was the plop of drops of water splashing onto the passenger side seat. Yes, my car was leaking. A tiny seam in the roof of the car was loose. I didn't know quite what to do, so I ran in the house and got a towel to soak up the water for the drain spout inside my car. The next day I bought some caulking and sealed the leak, but this didn't end my misery. Just two weeks later disaster struck again.

While driving to school, listening to my favorite Journey tape, my stereo 4
seemed to die on the left side of my bucket of bolts, when I hit one of the many craters in the road. Hoping it was just a temporary malfunction, I continued to school just turning up the right speakers to compensate for the lost sound. As you probably have figured out, my stereo did not resume its original capacity. Both the front and back left speakers were blown with no hopes of repair. I didn't have the money to get new speakers because I was still in debt from the engine fiasco, so they have sat in my car waiting to be replaced. After my stereo went on the blink, God decided to give me a reprieve through the rest of the winter, but as soon as spring hit trouble began all over again.

On a Monday morning I filled my car up with gas, and then proceeded 5
to navigate my way through the early morning mayhem on the way to school. During the drive, my gas gauge dropped, fairly quickly, from full, to the half tank marking. Just thinking that the guage was goofed up, not a thought of anything else entered my head. But as my classes came to a close, my mind found itself pondering over my car and what really might be wrong. So when I got to my car, in the parking deck, I started it and looked underneath to see if there was a leak. Well, there it was. A steady stream of gas was flowing onto the cement, like water coming out of a faucet. Yes, something was broken. This time my gas pump had sprung a leak and off to the repair shop it went once again.

The car is a great invention. It saves time, it allows us to travel long distances, it can represent the style of person you are, but it can cause you many headaches and cost you a lot of money. 6

Fishing Woes

Every year I go on a chartered fishing trip. It's usually held on a clear and sunny July afternoon, or at least that is the weather prediction we hope for. After consuming two cups of strong coffee, our venture begins at four A.M. with a three-hour drive to Port Clinton, Ohio. This is where we board "The Sassy Sal," and head out onto Lake Erie. Seven-thirty finds us on course with the captain's eyes glued on the depth finder in search of a school of walleye. Once they're found, the motor is turned off and we begin to fish. This sounds like a great way to spend a Sunday afternoon, huh? Although charter boat fishing is very popular, without a doubt, a few agonizing problems always occur to make each trip a memorable one. Let me explain. 1

One inevitable problem is that the fishing lines get tangled. This usually occurs ten to fifteen seconds after you have dropped your line into the water, and is quickly followed by the cry "I got one!" from the guy on the other side of the boat with whose line you've become entangled, and he almost pulls you overboard trying to reel in his "big one." However, this type of tangle doesn't compare to the twenty-line tangle, which occurs when a guy catches a fish and lets it swim across all the lines on his side of the boat while he is patiently trying to figure out how to operate his new ninety-five dollar spin-cast auto-winder reel. All this can be overcome simply by bringing along a little pair of scissors and while everyone is screaming at this guy, proceed to cut all lines wrapped around your own. It is then wise to take your pole and silently move to the opposite side of the boat while the others are trying to figure out where their lines went. I have also found though that the best way to avoid other problems is to slip the captain a generous tip before you leave the dock. This will assure you the best spot at the bow of the boat next to the cooler of beer. 2

Of course there is always the matter of catching the fish. Yes, this is why we go, but sometimes it's better not to catch any at all. Once you have a fish on your line, you realize you have a coaching staff of nine men, each with his own way of landing the creature. "Reel slower, not so fast," one guy screams in my ear while seven others tell me to "keep the rod tip up." Still another demonstrates for me the correct body motion to use. Once the fish is finally hauled in, you realize no one wants to help you anymore. You're stuck with a seventeen-inch jumping and twisting walleye who would make Mary Lou Retton look like an amateur, followed by the dilemma of how to get your hook out. After several unsuccessful tries and two bloody fingers (yes, they have teeth) you're ready to smash this fish which you've paid fifty dollars for the opportunity to catch. Eventually the hook is removed; relying on your previous generosity, you appeal to the captain for assistance. You breathe a sigh of relief as the fish is laid to rest in the beer cooler. 3

The deed is done! Alas! here comes our second time out expert who feels the need to appraise your catch. He lifts it into the air, sizes it up, and as he minimizes your accomplishment, you watch your fish slip from his grasp and do a two and a half gainer with a one half twist back into the lake.

The final problem one faces occurs half-way through the day, by which time several beers have been consumed. The pitching and rolling motions of the boat activate regurgitation and before you have time to give homage to the porcelain pot, you find yourself hanging over the rail and wishing you were dead. 4

As the sun sets and you head back to port, you shred up your copy of *Field and Stream* and try to remember where the nearest fish market is back home. 5

Ryan

Of all the people I have known, one stands out: my older brother Ryan. Ryan has done everything he could for just about everyone in his life. To say the least, he is a generous person. 1

My twin brother Lloyd and I are very special to Ryan, and he treats us that way. One Christmas, Ryan got everybody what they wanted except Lloyd and me. We had wanted some kind of toy, but what we got instead were football uniforms. Ryan had decided since he made a mistake by not playing football that we wouldn't make the same mistake. 2

Another example of Ryan's generosity occurred on my brother Larry's wedding day. Larry didn't ask Ryan to be in the wedding party. Everyone knew Ryan was upset, but he got over it. To show there were no hard feelings, Ryan gave Larry and his wife a microwave oven for a wedding present. 3

Ryan has always done things for people outside of the family too. For instance, one day while Ryan and I were driving down the road we saw a car with a flat tire parked beside the road. Ryan decided to stop and help out. The driver of the car told Ryan he did not have a spare, and he had an important job interview in half an hour. After hearing this, Ryan thought for a minute and then decided to give the guy his spare tire and address, so the tire could be returned. It never was, but this did not matter to Ryan because he had helped someone in need. 4

Ryan has also given a lot of himself. For instance, for the last six years at the first of every other month he has donated blood to the Red Cross. Also, Ryan does whatever he can for children. Sometimes that means being a big brother to an orphaned child or just saying hello to a lonely child in order to make the kid's day. He also coaches Little League in the summer and Pee Wee football in the fall. Ryan did a lot for me when I was younger. He took me to Pittsburgh Pirates games, the circus, and to the movies. He was always there to take Lloyd and me to basketball practice, no matter what. If Lloyd or I were sick, he called off work to take us to the doctor, since our mother does not drive. 5

I think Ryan gave a little too much to everyone else and left nothing for himself. His ex-wife could not understand why he gave so much to everyone else and hardly anything to her. This is not the truth at all; he did even more for her than 6 any one else. She was jealous of everyone because she wanted him all to herself. When he could not give all of him, she wanted a divorce. After the divorce, Ryan moved to California where he remarried. He and his present wife are houseparents for retarded children.

Everyone who knows Ryan is very fortunate, for he is a person you do not meet every day. He is one in a million, for he tries to live by the golden rule. 7

Becoming a Reliable Critic by Evaluating Writing

This activity gives you additional practice making critical judgments about writing so that when you evaluate your own work, you can do so reliably.

Form a group with two classmates and select one of the previous student essays (or use one your instructor assigns). With your group, prepare a report that notes the chief strengths and weaknesses of the piece. Also decide on the most important revision you would like to see. Be specific. If you say a particular example is not working, explain why and suggest an improvement.

If you like, you can use the following evaluation questions to guide your work.

Evaluation Questions

1. The Introduction
   Does the opening engage your interest? Why or why not?
2. The Thesis
   Does the thesis (stated or implied) make clear what generalization is being presented? What is that generalization?
3. Supporting Details
   Are there enough examples to illustrate the generalization? Evaluate the examples. (Are they adequately detailed, relevant, sufficiently specific, and drawn from the appropriate sources?) Note any points you do not understand.
4. Organization
   What do you think of the order of examples? Evaluate the use of transitions. Does the author use topic sentences?
5. Word Choice and Sentence Effectiveness
   Cite examples of effective words and sentences. Cite examples of words and sentences to revise.
6. The Conclusion
   Does the essay come to a satisfying end? Why or why not?

Essay Topics: Illustration

1. As Purdy does in "The Honest Repairman—A Vanishing American?" (page 189), write an essay that illustrates that the consumer is taken advantage of.
2. Write an essay illustrating that sometimes an automobile can be more trouble than it is worth.

3. Like Otten in "This Is Progress?" (page 184), write an essay illustrating that modern advances bring unexpected problems.
4. Select one modern device (video games, television, computers, washing machines, alarm clocks, microwaves, answering machines, electric blankets, etc.) and write an essay illustrating the problems the device can cause.
5. In "Darkness at Noon" (page 187), Krents illustrates the discrimination he suffers as a result of his disability. Write an essay illustrating how some condition in your life affected you dramatically. You might write about being an only child (oldest child, middle child, etc.), about being the child of divorced parents, about being a member of a minority group, about being tall or short for your age, about being athletic (or musically inclined or artistic), about being the class clown, and so on.
6. Write an essay illustrating that high school did (or did not) adequately prepare you for college.
7. Illustrate the happy times you had with a childhood friend.
8. Illustrate the strengths of your favorite teacher or illustrate the weaknesses of your least favorite one.
9. Select one season of the year and illustrate why you like it (or dislike) it.
10. Illustrate that things do not always go as planned.
11. Illustrate that advertising leads people to view luxuries as necessities.
12. Illustrate that people are at their worst behind the wheel of a car.
13. Illustrate the frustrations (or joys) of college life.
14. Illustrate how some group (homemakers, working women, husbands, police officers, bachelors) is depicted on television.
15. Select a particular situation (such as the first day of school, moving to a new town, losing a job, having a friend move away, etc.) and illustrate the effect it has or had on you.
16. Select a person (or use yourself) and illustrate one of that person's personality traits.
17. Select a person you have been close to or have had many dealings with and illustrate the relationship you have had with that person. You may wish to narrow to one aspect of your relationship.
18. Select a circumstance or situation that makes you feel insecure or frightened or tense. Illustrate times when that circumstance or situation caused the feeling.
19. Illustrate the effect the women's movement has had on television commercials (or magazine ads).
20. Write an essay illustrating the fact that appearances can be deceiving.

Thematic Topics

1. "This Is Progress?" (page 184) points out the drawbacks of some technological advances. Explain what you think life would be like without some technological advance, being sure to note both the advantages and disadvantages.

2. Explain how you think we respond to the disabled and why you think we respond as we do. If you like, you can use some of the information in "Darkness at Noon" (page 187).
3. In "The Honest Repairman—A Vanishing American?" (page 189) Purdy illustrates that consumers are often taken advantage of. In "Ryan" (page 196), the student author tells of a time Ryan was taken advantage of by a motorist he tried to help. Drawing on the information in these essays along with your own experience, observation, and reading, explain why you think people take advantage of each other and how much of a problem this is.

Writing Strategies

Some of the following strategies may help as you experiment to discover your own effective, efficient writing process. Review them, along with the suggestions in Chapters 1 to 3, for alternatives to unsuccessful or inefficient aspects of your process.

Topic Selection

1. Topic selection for an illustration essay amounts to settling on a generalization you can support with examples. One way to arrive at such a generalization is to fill in the blanks in a version of the following sentence: ____________________ is the most ____________________ I know. This will give you something like "Taking a 3-year-old on a long car trip is the trickiest thing I know." You may alter the words in the sentence to get something like "Registration is the biggest hassle I know." With the blanks filled in, you have a topic that can be developed using examples.
2. Another way to arrive at a generalization/topic is to take a common saying and show that it is *not* true. For example, provide illustrations to show that a bird in the hand is *not* worth two in the bush, honesty is *not* the best policy, ignorance is *not* bliss, and so on.

Idea Generation

Answering the questions below may help you discover examples for supporting your thesis.

1. What have I done that illustrates my generalization?
2. What have I seen that illustrates my generalization?
3. What have I heard that illustrates my generalization?
4. What have I read that illustrates my generalization?
5. What have others experienced that illustrates my generalization?
6. What story can I tell to illustrate my generalization?
7. What can I describe that illustrates my generalization?

Outlining

List all the examples you will use and number them in the order they are to appear in your essay. This will give you an informal outline for your body paragraphs.

Reader Response

If you like to secure reader response as part of your revision process, see page 77. In addition, ask your reader to write out the generalization your examples support. Also ask your reader to do the following.

1. Place a checkmark where detail is needed.
2. Place a question mark where something is unclear.
3. Place an exclamation point next to anything particularly strong.

REVISION CHECKLIST

In addition to the checklist on page 80, you can use this checklist to help you revise your illustration essay.

1. What generalization do your examples support?
2. Do your examples provide clarity and concreteness?
3. Are your examples appropriate to your audience and purpose?
4. Have you used enough examples to clarify the generalization, but not so many that you belabor the point? Are your examples developed in sufficient detail? (Remember, the fewer the examples, the more detailed each must be.)
5. Are your examples arranged in a progressive or other suitable order?

CHAPTER 8

Process Analysis

A **process analysis** explains how something is made or done. You encounter process analysis frequently. The directions that explain how to assemble the birthday toy you bought your nephew is a process analysis. The instructions in your biology lab manual explaining how to prepare a slide are also process analysis—so are the explanation for making simple repairs given in the owner's manual of your stereo, the magazine article describing how to land the perfect job, and the directions for preparing a gourmet meal found in the cookbook on the kitchen counter. In short, anything that tells a reader how to do something (such as grow prize-winning roses) or explains how something is made (such as paper) is a process analysis.

PURPOSE

The obvious purpose of a process analysis is to inform a reader about how something is made or done. Often the process analysis is meant to help the reader learn how to make or do something. For example, a process analysis could teach a person how to hang wallpaper and thus avoid paying someone else to do it.

Sometimes the reader already knows how to make or do something. In this case, the purpose can be to make the reader aware of a better or faster way to perform the process. Perhaps your reader already knows how to take an essay examination, but you can describe a process that helps the student budget time better. This would help your reader learn a *better* way to do something.

A process analysis is often written even when the reader will not perform the process. In this case the writer's purpose is to increase the reader's knowledge about how something works or how it is made. For example, if you wrote a description of how computers work or how alligators hunt their prey, your purpose would be to increase your reader's knowledge.

Another reason to write a process analysis is to help your reader appreciate the difficulty, complexity, or beauty of a process. For example, if you think your reader does not appreciate how hard it is to wait on tables, you could describe the process of waiting on tables to heighten your reader's appreciation.

Sometimes the purpose of a process analysis is not to inform but to persuade. You could, for example, describe a process in an effort to convince your reader that it is superior to another way of doing things and should be adopted. This would be the case if you wrote to your campus registrar to describe a registration process that is less troublesome than the current process.

Sometimes the purpose of a process analysis is to entertain, as is the case with the humorous "Loafing Made Easy," on page 208.

To determine your purpose, you can answer these questions.

1. Do I want to describe a process so that my reader can perform it?
2. Do I want to describe a process so that my reader is aware of it?
3. Do I want to describe a process so that my reader will appreciate it more?
4. Do I want to convince my reader that there is a better way to perform a process?
5. Do I want to entertain my reader by showing the humor in a process?

AUDIENCE

Your audience will affect detail selection. For example, if you are explaining how to use a particular word processing program for a reader who understands computer operation, you will not have to explain the computer parts (like *disk drive*) or define many terms (like *format a disk*). However, if your audience is someone who just bought a computer and knows little about it, you should identify the parts and define terms.

The nature of your audience will also affect to what extent you must explain the importance of the process, provide examples, and explain steps.

These questions can help you identify your audience.

1. Who does not know how to perform the process I am describing?
2. Who does not fully understand or appreciate the process?
3. Who should be convinced to perform the process?
4. Who would be entertained by reading about the process?

These questions can help you assess the nature of your audience.

1. Does my reader appreciate the importance of the process?
2. Has my reader had any experience with the process?
3. How interested is my reader in the process?
4. Does my reader need any terms defined?

5. Will any steps in the process prove difficult for my reader to perform or understand?

SELECTING DETAIL

Obviously, the primary detail in a process analysis will be the steps performed in the process. Also, the writer must not omit any steps, or the reader may not be able to understand or perform the process. However, providing the steps alone may not be enough; you may need to explain just *how* the steps are performed. For example, if you are explaining how to discover ideas to include in an essay, do more than note that a writer can try freewriting; also explain how that freewriting is done.

In addition to explaining *how* steps are performed, you may need to explain *why*, particularly if your reader will not appreciate the importance of a step and perhaps skip it. For example, assume you are explaining how to land a perfect job. Also assume that you mention that the reader should send a thank-you note to the personnel director immediately after the interview. If the reader might not appreciate the importance of this step, explain that sending the note impresses the personnel director with your courtesy and follow-through.

Interestingly, sometimes you may find it necessary to explain what is *not* done, especially when your reader might do something unnecessary or incorrect. Assume again that you are explaining how to land the perfect job. You may want to caution your reader *not* to smile too much, for too much smiling can create a frivolous or insincere image.

If a step in the process can prove troublesome, you should point out the possible problem and how to avoid it. For example, when you tell a job applicant to write a thank-you note, you can caution the person to use a business-letter format, which can be found in any handbook.

If your reader must assemble materials to perform the process, be sure to mention everything needed. Also, if your reader needs an understanding of special terms, be sure to provide the definitions. For example, if you are explaining how to make the best-ever chocolate cake, tell your reader early on what ingredients to have on hand. If the cake will be baked in a springform pan, explain what this is if your reader is not likely to know.

Examples and descriptions can also be included in a process analysis to help a reader understand the nature and significance of steps in a process. Thus, you might want to describe a springform pan or give examples of questions to ask during a job interview.

Finally, if your reader does not fully appreciate the importance of performing or understanding the process, include this detail as well. For example, if you are explaining how television advertisements persuade people to buy, you can mention that people should understand this process so that they can recognize attempts to manipulate them.

ARRANGING DETAIL

Chronological order (see page 44) is the most common detail arrangement because most often, a reader needs the steps presented in the order they are performed. At times, however, chronological order is not necessary. For example, if you are explaining how to dress for success, the order of steps may not be significant.

If you are explaining what is *not* done, you should do this near the step the caution is related to. For example, in a cake recipe, you would explain not to overbake at the point you mention baking time. If your process analysis includes several statements of what not to do, you might want to group all the cautions together in their own paragraph.

If you must define a term, do so the first time the term is used. If you explain a troublesome aspect of the process, do so just after presenting the step under consideration. If you explain why a step is performed, do so just before or after your explanation of the step. If necessary materials are listed, group together this information in an early paragraph, perhaps even in the introduction.

The introduction of a process analysis can include a thesis that mentions the process to be explained. In addition, the thesis can note the importance of understanding the process. Here are two examples.

> `Car owners can save a great deal of money if they learn to change their own points and plugs.` (The process is changing points and plugs; understanding the process is important because it can save the reader money.)
>
> `There is only one efficient way to study for a final examination.` (This thesis mentions the process without noting its importance.)

To create interest in your topic, you can explain in the introduction why understanding the process is important (if your thesis does not do this). You can also tell why you are qualified to explain the process, arouse the reader's curiosity about how the process is performed, or combine approaches.

The conclusion can be handled using any of the approaches given for the introduction. However, at times a separate conclusion is unnecessary because the last step in the process provides sufficient closure.

TRYOUT Think of something you do well (shop for bargains, make friends, plan a party, buy used cars, study, baby-sit, and so forth) and assume you will write a process analysis to help your reader learn how to perform the process. Next, list the steps in the process (in the order they are performed if chronological order is important). Review your list of steps and answer these questions:

1. Is it necessary to explain *how* any steps are performed?
2. Is it necessary to explain *why* any steps are performed?

3. Will the reader understand better if I explain something that is *not* done?
4. Are there troublesome aspects that should be explained?
5. Are any materials needed?
6. Should any terms be defined?
7. Is it possible to describe anything?
8. Is it possible to use examples?

PROFESSIONAL ESSAYS

How to Take a Job Interview

Kirby W. Stanat

As a former placement officer at the University of Wisconsin–Milwaukee and a former recruiter, Kirby Stanat knows what he is talking about when he explains how the job interview process works. In addition to providing valuable information, Stanat uses specific diction to keep his process analysis lively and engaging.

To succeed in campus job interviews, you have to know where that recruiter is coming from. The simple answer is that he is coming from corporate headquarters. 1

That may sound obvious, but it is a significant point that too many students do not consider. The recruiter is not a free spirit as he flies from Berkeley to New Haven, from Chapel Hill to Boulder. He's on an invisible leash to the office, and if he is worth his salary, he is mentally in corporate headquarters all the time he's on the road. 2

If you can fix that in your mind—that when you walk into that bare-walled cubicle in the placement center you are walking into a branch office of Sears, Bendix or General Motors—you can avoid a lot of little mistakes and maybe some big ones. 3

If, for example, you assume that because the interview is on campus the recruiter expects you to look and act like a student, you're in for a shock. A student is somebody who drinks beer, wears blue jeans and throws a Frisbee. No recruiter has jobs for student Frisbee whizzes. 4

A cool spring day in late March, Sam Davis, a good recruiter who has been on the college circuit for years, is on my campus talking to candidates. He comes out to the waiting area to meet the student who signed up for an 11 o'clock interview. I'm standing in the doorway of my office taking in the scene. 5

Sam calls the candidate: "Sidney Student." There sits Sidney. He's at a 45 degree angle, his feet are in the aisle, and he's almost lying down. He's wearing well-polished brown shoes, a tasteful pair of brown pants, a light brown shirt, and 6 a good looking tie. Unfortunately, he tops off this well-coordinated outfit with his Joe's Tavern Class A Softball Championship jacket, which has a big woven emblem over the heart.

If that isn't bad enough, in his left hand is a cigarette and in his right hand is a half-eaten apple. 7

When Sam calls his name, the kid is caught off guard. He ditches the cigarette in an ashtray, struggles to his feet, and transfers the apple from the right to the left hand. Apple juice is everywhere, so Sid wipes his hand on the seat of his pants and shakes hands with Sam. 8

Sam, who by now is close to having a stroke, gives me that what-do-I-have-here look and has the young man follow him into the interviewing room. 9

The situation deteriorates even further—into pure Laurel and Hardy. The kid is stuck with the half-eaten apple, doesn't know what to do with it, and obviously is suffering some discomfort. He carries the apple into the interviewing room with him and places it in the ashtray on the desk—right on top of Sam's freshly lit cigarette. 10

The interview lasts five minutes. . . . 11

Let us move in for a closer look at how the campus recruiter operates. 12

Let's say you have a 10 o'clock appointment with the recruiter from the XYZ Corporation. The recruiter gets rid of the candidate in front of you at about 5 minutes to 10, jots down a few notes about what he is going to do with him or her, then picks up your résumé or data sheet (which you have submitted in advance). . . . 13

Although the recruiter is still in the interview room and you are still in the lobby, your interview is under way. You're on. The recruiter will look over your sheet pretty carefully before he goes out to call you. He develops a mental picture of you. 14

He thinks, "I'm going to enjoy talking with this kid," or "This one's going to be a turkey." The recruiter has already begun to make a screening decision about you. 15

His first impression of you, from reading the sheet, could come from your grade point. It could come from misspelled words. It could come from poor erasures or from the fact that necessary information is missing. By the time the recruiter has finished reading your sheet, you've already hit the plus or minus column. 16

Let's assume the recruiter got a fairly good impression from your sheet. 17

Now the recruiter goes out to the lobby to meet you. He almost shuffles along, and his mind is somewhere else. Then he calls your name, and at that instant he visibly clicks into gear. He just went to work. 18

As he calls your name he looks quickly around the room, waiting for somebody to move. If you are sitting on the middle of your back, with a book open and a cigarette going, and if you have to rebuild yourself to stand up, the interest will run right out of the recruiter's face. You, not the recruiter, made the appointment for 10 o'clock, and the recruiter expects to see a young professional come popping out of that chair like today is a good day and you're anxious to meet him. 19

At this point, the recruiter does something rude. He doesn't walk across the 20 room to meet you halfway. He waits for you to come to him. Something very important is happening. He wants to see you move. He wants to get an impression about your posture, your stride, and your briskness.

If you slouch over to him, sidewinderlike, he is not going to be impressed. He'll figure you would probably slouch your way through your workdays. He wants you to come at him with lots of good things going for you. If you watch the recruiter's eyes, you can see the inspection. He glances quickly at shoes, pants, coat, shirt; dress, blouse, hose—the whole works. 21

After introducing himself, the recruiter will probably say, "Okay, please follow me," and he'll lead you into his interviewing room. 22

When you get to the room, you may find that the recruiter will open the door and gesture you in—with him blocking part of the doorway. There's enough room for you to get past him, but it's a near thing. 23

As you scrape past, he gives you a closeup inspection. He looks at your hair; if it's greasy, that will bother him. He looks at your collar; if it's dirty, that will bother him. He looks at your shoulders; if they're covered with dandruff, that will bother him. If you're a man, he looks at your chin. If you didn't get a close shave, that will irritate him. If you're a woman, he checks your makeup. If it's too heavy, he won't like it. 24

Then he smells you. An amazing number of people smell bad. Occasionally a recruiter meets a student who smells like a canal horse. That student can expect an interview of about four or five minutes. 25

Next the recruiter inspects the back side of you. He checks your hair (is it combed in front but not in back?), he checks your heels (are they run down?), your pants (are they baggy?), your slip (is it showing?), your stockings (do they have runs?). 26

Then he invites you to sit down. 27

At this point, I submit, the recruiter's decision on you is 75 to 80 percent made. 28

Think about it. The recruiter has read your résumé. He knows who you are and where you are from. He knows your marital status, your major and your grade point. And he knows what you have done with your summers. He has inspected you, exchanged greetings with you and smelled you. There is very little additional hard information that he must gather on you. From now on it's mostly body chemistry. 29

Many recruiters have argued strenuously with me that they don't make such hasty decisions. So I tried an experiment. I told several recruiters that I would hang around in the hall outside the interview room when they took candidates in. 30

I told them that as soon as they had definitely decided not to recommend (to department managers in their companies) the candidate they were interviewing, they should snap their fingers loud enough for me to hear. It went like this. 31

First candidate: 38 seconds after the candidate sat down: Snap! 32

Second candidate: 1 minute, 42 seconds: Snap! 33

Third candidate: 45 seconds: Snap! 34

One recruiter was particularly adamant, insisting that he didn't rush to judgment on candidates. I asked him to participate in the snapping experiment. He 35 went out in the lobby, picked up his first candidate of the day, and headed for an interview room.

As he passed me in the hall, he glared at me. And his fingers went "Snap!" 36

Questions on Technique

1. For what purpose do you think Stanat wrote his process analysis? Who is his intended audience?
2. Paragraphs 5–11 form a narration. What purpose does that narration serve? What other paragraphs form a narration?
3. In which paragraphs does Stanat use examples to illustrate aspects of the process?
4. In which paragraphs does the author do the following:
   a. Explain what *not* to do?
   b. Explain *why* a step is performed?
   c. Explain *how* to perform a step?
5. Stanat explains the behavior of both the interviewer and the student-applicant. Is this dual perspective on the interview process a good idea? Explain.
6. Stanat explains how the campus recruiter works. Write out a list of the steps in that process.
7. Stanat's simple, specific diction contributes to the essay's engaging, lively quality. Cite three examples of simple, specific diction.

For Group Discussion or Journal Writing

Consider the following questions: What, if anything, did you learn about the interview process as a result of reading "How to Take a Job Interview"? Did you find anything surprising about the interviewer's procedures? As you think back over job interviews you have had in the past, can you recall the interviewer following any of the procedures described in the essay? If so, which ones?

Loafing Made Easy

Sam Negri

Sam Negri's humorous explanation of how to loaf first appeared in The New York Times. *The piece is very amusing, but effective humor usually has a kernel of truth at its core. Ask yourself what truth Negri builds his humor around.*

The fabled season of the sun is upon us and it is once again time to hook our thumbs in our suspenders and talk about America's most treasured art form, loafing. 1

The purest form of loafing is practiced in Arizona, where summertime temperatures will often exceed 110 degrees. If we regard the Arizona loafer as a nat- 2 ural resource, as I've been doing for the last eight years, we will see that the art form has applications that go far beyond the business of surviving in hot weather.

When I came to Arizona, I was a mediocre loafer, displaying a definite need for a degree of mental reconditioning. I'd moved here from Connecticut, where people relax by putting aside their copy of Gray's "Anatomy" and picking up a novel by Dostoevsky. In Arizona, this is referred to as insanity. 3

Here is a better method: 4

To begin with, shut the damper on your fireplace, if you have one, and turn on your air-conditioner, if you have one. Otherwise, hang a wet sheet in the window and pray for a breeze. 5

Now you are ready to memorize a handful of important and useful phrases. Try these: "I don't know"; "I don't care"; "no"; and the old standby, "well . . ." 6

These phrases are extremely valuable when your jaws are sagging like deflated bicycle tubes and your mind has turned to wax. 7

For example, it is 106 degrees in the shade and your son comes racing in the house, shouting, "Hey, you seen those long-handled pliers anywhere?" With a minimum of effort you are free to say, "no." 8

His anger may mount and he'll insist: "But you were using them yesterday! Where'd you leave 'em?" 9

If you haven't passed out from the strain of this conversation, you can then reply, "I don't know." 10

"But I need those pliers to fix my skateboard," he will cry. Then you break out the ultimate weapon in the loafer's lexicon. Without any inflection whatsoever, you declare, "Well . . ." 11

You can now get back to some serious loafing, which means that you will try to prove that Benjamin Franklin was correct when he observed: "It is hard for an empty sack to stand upright." In short, empty your mind. Learn to ask questions like these: "Mail come yet?" and "Anything doin'?" The responses to these questions usually involve one word, and often they aren't debilitating. 12

There are a few additional rules to keep in mind for successful loafing. 13

First, never loaf near a pool or a lake because you might be tempted to go for a swim. Swimming frequently leaves a body feeling refreshed and may lead to a desire to do something. 14

Second, under no circumstances should you allow anyone to coax you into a camping trip in the mountains. Mountains tend to be lush, green and cool, and next thing you know you'll be wanting to split logs for a fire, go for a hike, or pump up your Coleman stove. Resist. "Patience is a necessary ingredient of genius," said Disraeli. If you want to be a fine loafer you have to make enemies. 15

Of course, it is impossible to get by in life if you don't do something, even in the summer. Household jobs are the easiest for a loafer to contend with, if he is selective and deliberate. 16

One satisfying and undemanding job involves a ball of twine. Find a ball of twine that a cat has unraveled so badly that you can't find the end. Get scissors and slowly cut it into small pieces, scrunch it into a smaller ball, and throw it away. Now look at all the extra space you have in your junk drawer. 17

Another relatively simple and useful job for summertime loafing centers on 18 light bulbs. Limp through your house or apartment, removing the light bulbs from every lamp. Coat the very bottom of each bulb with petroleum jelly and put it back in the lampsocket. This will clean some of the crud off the contact point and solve the problems with flickering lightbulbs. For variety you can take the bulb that was in a living-room lamp and put it in a bedroom lamp. It helps to sigh and gaze wistfully at the base of the lightbulb as you are performing this function.

Last, if you have a dog, sit in your most comfortable chair and stare at your dog's eyes for five or 10 minutes. Every so often, mutter something incomprehensible. Your dog is certain to understand, and your family will not come near you for the rest of the afternoon. 19

Questions on Technique

1. What is the thesis of "Loafing Made Easy"? Does the thesis present just the process or the process and its significance?
2. A four-paragraph introduction precedes the explanation of the process. What purposes do these four paragraphs serve?
3. What do you judge to be the writer's purpose?
4. This essay first appeared in *The New York Times.* How does Negri address the needs of his audience?
5. Although used to achieve comic ends, Negri employs some standard process analysis techniques. For example, he explains what *not* to do. In which paragraph does he do this, and what purpose does it serve?
6. Negri also uses illustrations for comic effect. Which paragraphs include illustrations, and how do they contribute to the humor?
7. Which part of the essay relies heavily on chronological order? Why is chronological order less significant later in the essay?
8. Negri moves the reader smoothly from step to step with transitions. Cite three sentences with transitions that ease the reader into a new step or rule.
9. What approach does Negri take to his conclusion?

For Group Discussion or Journal Writing

Negri's piece is lighthearted, but there is a serious side to loafing. Recreation and relaxation are important to a balanced life. Consider the role and importance of loafing. Also consider whether people know how to loaf effectively. If you like, you can limit your consideration to loafing and the college student.

A Delicate Operation

Roy C. Selby, Jr.

Because the following process analysis describes brain surgery, it is obviously not meant to teach the reader how to perform a process. It does, however, help the reader appreciate the complexity—and even the beauty—of a very dramatic undertaking.

In the autumn of 1973 a woman in her early fifties noticed, upon closing one eye while reading, that she was unable to see clearly. Her eyesight grew slowly worse. Changing her eyeglasses did not help. She saw an ophthalmologist, who found that her vision was seriously impaired in both eyes. She then saw a neurologist, who confirmed the finding and obtained X rays of the skull and an EMI scan—a photograph of the patient's head. The latter revealed a tumor growing between the optic nerves at the base of the brain. The woman was admitted to the hospital by a neurosurgeon. 1

Further diagnosis, based on angiography, a detailed X-ray study of the circulatory system, showed the tumor to be about two inches in diameter and supplied by many small blood vessels. It rested beneath the brain, just above the pituitary gland, stretching the optic nerves to either side and intimately close to the major blood vessels supplying the brain. Removing it would pose many technical problems. Probably benign and slow-growing, it may have been present for several years. If left alone it would continue to grow and produce blindness and might become impossible to remove completely. Removing it, however, might not improve the patient's vision and could make it worse. A major blood vessel could be damaged, causing a stroke. Damage to the undersurface of the brain could cause impairment of memory and changes in mood and personality. The hypothalamus, a most important structure of the brain, could be injured, causing coma, high fever, bleeding from the stomach, and death. 2

The neurosurgeon met with the patient and her husband and discussed the various possibilities. The common decision was to operate. 3

The patient's hair was shampooed for two nights before surgery. She was given a cortisonelike drug to reduce the risk of damage to the brain during surgery. Five units of blood were cross-matched, as a contingency against hemorrhage. At 1:00 P.M. the operation began. After the patient was anesthetized her hair was completely clipped and shaved from the scalp. Her head was prepped with an organic iodine solution for ten minutes. Drapes were placed over her, leaving exposed only the forehead and crown of the skull. All the routine instruments were brought up—the electrocautery used to coagulate areas of bleeding, bipolar coagulation forceps to arrest bleeding from individual blood vessels without damaging adjacent tissues, and small suction tubes to remove blood and cerebrospinal fluid from the head, thus giving the surgeon a better view of the tumor and surrounding areas. 4

A curved incision was made behind the hairline so it would be concealed when the hair grew back. It extended almost from ear to ear. Plastic clips were applied to the cut edges of the scalp to arrest bleeding. The scalp was folded back to the level of the eyebrows. Incisions were made in the muscle of the right temple, and three sets of holes were drilled near the temple and the top of the head because the tumor had to be approached from directly in front. The drill, powered by nitrogen, was replaced with a fluted steel blade, and the holes were connected. The incised piece of skull was pried loose and held out of the way by a large sponge. 5

Beneath the bone is a yellowish leatherlike membrane, the dura, that sur- 6 rounds the brain. Down the middle of the head the dura carries a large vein, but in the area near the nose the vein is small. At that point the vein and dura were cut, and clips made of tantalum, a hard metal, were applied to arrest and prevent bleeding. Sutures were put into the dura and tied to the scalp to keep the dura open and retracted. A malleable silver retractor, resembling the blade of a butter knife, was inserted between the brain and skull. The anesthesiologist began to administer a drug to relax the brain by removing some of its water, making it easier for the surgeon to manipulate the retractor, hold the brain back, and see the tumor. The nerve tracts for smell were cut on both sides to provide additional room. The tumor was seen approximately two-and-one-half inches behind the base of the nose. It was pink in color. On touching it, it proved to be very fibrous and tough. A special retractor was attached to the skull, enabling the other retractor blades to be held automatically and freeing the surgeon's hands. With further displacement of the frontal lobes of the brain, the tumor could be seen better, but no normal structures—the carotid arteries, their branches, and the optic nerves—were visible. The tumor obscured them.

A surgical microscope was placed above the wound. The surgeon had 7
selected the lenses and focal length prior to the operation. Looking through the microscope, he could see some of the small vessels supplying the tumor and he coagulated them. He incised the tumor to attempt to remove its core and thus collapse it, but the substance of the tumor was too firm to be removed in this fashion. He then began to slowly dissect the tumor from the adjacent brain tissue and from where he believed the normal structures to be.

Using small squares of cotton, he began to separate the tumor from very 8
loose fibrous bands connecting it to the brain and to the right side of the part of the skull where the pituitary gland lies. The right optic nerve and carotid artery came into view, both displaced considerably to the right. The optic nerve had a normal appearance. He protected these structures with cotton compresses placed between them and the tumor. He began to raise the tumor from the skull and slowly to reach the point of its origin and attachment—just in front of the pituitary gland and medial to the left optic nerve, which still could not be seen. The small blood vessels entering the tumor were cauterized. The upper portion of the tumor was gradually separated from the brain, and the branches of the carotid arteries and the branches to the tumor were coagulated. The tumor was slowly and gently lifted from its bed, and for the first time the left carotid artery and optic nerve could be seen. Part of the tumor adhered to this nerve. The bulk of the tumor was amputated, leaving a small bit attached to the nerve. Very slowly and carefully the tumor fragment was resected.

The tumor now removed, a most impressive sight came into view—the 9
pituitary gland and its stalk of attachment to the hypothalamus, the hypothalamus itself, and the brainstem, which conveys nerve impulses between the body and the brain. As far as could be determined, no damage had been done to these structures or other vital centers, but the left optic nerve, from chronic pressure of the tumor, appeared gray and thin. Probably it would not completely recover its function.

After making certain there was no bleeding, the surgeon closed the wounds and placed wire mesh over the holes in the skull to prevent dimpling of the scalp over the points that had been drilled. A gauze dressing was applied to the patient's head. She was awakened and sent to the recovery room. 10

Even with the microscope, damage might still have occurred to the cerebral cortex and hypothalamus. It would require at least a day to be reasonably certain there was none, and about seventy-two hours to monitor for the major postoperative dangers—swelling of the brain and blood clots forming over the surface of the brain. The surgeon explained this to the patient's husband, and both of them waited anxiously. The operation had required seven hours. A glass of orange juice had given the surgeon some additional energy during the closure of the wound. Though exhausted, he could not fall asleep until after two in the morning, momentarily expecting a call from the nurse in the intensive care unit announcing deterioration of the patient's condition. 11

At 8:00 A.M. the surgeon saw the patient in the intensive care unit. She was alert, oriented, and showed no sign of additional damage to the optic nerves or the brain. She appeared to be in better shape than the surgeon or her husband. 12

Questions on Technique

1. The thesis of "A Delicate Operation" is implied rather than stated. What is the thesis? Where is it most strongly suggested?
2. The introduction is the first three paragraphs. What approach do these paragraphs take?
3. Who would you judge to be Selby's intended audience? What is his purpose?
4. In what order are the details arranged?
5. Selby frequently defines medical terms. Cite three terms that he defines. Why does he provide these definitions?
6. In which paragraphs does Selby explain why steps are performed? How do these explanations help Selby fulfill his purpose?
7. In which paragraph does Selby explain how a step is performed? How does this explanation help Selby fulfill his purpose?
8. Paragraph 6 includes description. What purpose does this description serve?
9. In which two paragraphs does Selby note troublesome aspects of the process? What does this contribute?
10. What approach does the author take to the conclusion?

For Group Discussion or Journal Writing

Selby's process analysis describes brain surgery. However, it also gives us some knowledge of the neurosurgeon. Use the clues in the essay to construct a sketch of the neurosurgeon's personality.

STUDENT ESSAYS TO READ AND EVALUATE

Some of the following student essays are better than others, but each has strengths and weaknesses. The evaluation activity after the readings will help you identify these strengths and weaknesses. Doing so will teach you to better judge the effective and ineffective features of your own drafts, and it will increase your knowledge of what does and does not work in writing.

Horse Sense

Some people think a horse is just another dumb animal, but they are wrong. Horses are very smart, and their intelligence is clearly shown when you try to break them. If you break horses, you will find that each has an instinctive bag of tricks to try to get you off his back. He'll do this by matching his wits against yours. 1

The battle of wits will begin the moment you step into the horse's stall. You don't realize it, but he's always watching you. Even if he isn't looking straight at you but pretending to be interested in the wall straight ahead of him, he's watching you out of the corner of his eye. 2

If you have to walk behind the horse, be careful! If he's in a good mood, you might only get a well-aimed, stinging slap in the face by his tail. If the horse is ornery, you could end up becoming the target of two muscular, hard-kicking hind legs. 3

The horse knows exactly where your feet are. One well-maneuvered sidestep from the horse and you could suddenly find your foot anchored to the floor of the stall. As you yell, glad that there is a cushion of straw on the floor, and struggle to push him off of your foot, he'll glance at you, pretending to wonder what all the ruckus is about. 4

When you're ready to put the saddle on him, you'll notice his belly suddenly becomes extended. He does this to keep you from pulling the cinch as tightly as needed to keep the saddle securely on his back. He does this hoping that while you're on his back riding, you'll suddenly find yourself sitting on the ground, watching him trot away with a loose saddle bouncing under his belly. From about fifteen yards away, the horse will stop, turn his head toward you, and let out a shrill whinny, which is his way of laughing at you. To prevent this embarrassing event, you have to be sure that the cinch is tight. 5

After the saddle is on properly, you're ready to get on his back to try and stay in the saddle. Since the horse is not broken, your first ride will be the first of many battles with him to find out which one of you is going to be the boss. Before you get on him, he's going to try to intimidate you by snorting loudly, pawing at the ground, and rolling his eyes. As you get your foot in the stirrup, he'll turn his head toward your leg and try and leave a temporary tattoo of the imprint of his teeth on your calf. As soon as you're seated in the saddle, he'll start rearing up on his hind legs. Reaching higher and higher towards the sky with his front hoofs, it'll 6 feel as if you and the horse might topple over backwards onto the hard ground behind you. Beginning to buck, he'll leap forward and upward suddenly, trying to dislodge you from the saddle. After minutes of this bone-jarring ride, he'll spring straight up into the air, landing stiff legged, making it feel as if you've just stoved your whole body.

After resting for just seconds, the horse takes off in a dead run with his ears back against his head. You can see that his destination is a grove of trees with low-hanging branches. You realize that if you don't duck your head lower than the horse's, the grabbing fingers of the branches will snatch you off the horse and leave you lying in a heap on the ground. The horse will also swerve as close to a tree as possible, trying to batter your leg against the trunk. By lifting your leg onto the horse's back, you safely make it past the horse's intended target and through the tree grove, scratched and bruised but still in one piece. You wonder, "How did this horse make it through unscathed?" 7

A horse can also stop and turn on a dime and will use this ability to try to dismount you. He'll run straight for a fence and while you're deciding if this horse can clear the three loosely stranded, rusted barbed wires, you brace yourself for the jump. Instead, the horse digs its hoofs into the ground and stops suddenly, as if he had just slammed into a brick wall. As you're thrown forward, your arms wrap around the horse's neck involuntarily, your head is thrown between his ears, and your legs are tossed up into the air. 8

As you regain your seat, you glance to the left and right, hoping that nobody saw you in that ridiculous-looking acrobatic position. The horse takes off again. Ahead you see a five-foot-wide stream. As you approach the swiftly moving water, you wonder if the horse will run through the current or jump it. Now you're also prepared for his quick-stop trick. Being only feet from the obstacle, the horse suddenly makes a lightning-quick 90-degree right turn in one quick, jolting motion. This move leaves you dangling from the horse's left side by one leg with a hand grasping the saddle horn. At this point, you decide it's time for a reprieve and take the horse back to the weather-beaten barn. 9

As you leave your spirited, four-legged companion stomping and munching grain in his stall, you shuffle across the straw-covered floor and sink into a pile of loose hay. Before a horse is broken, it's just a natural instinct for him to use any means to get you off his back. 10

Homemade Pizza

When I smell the unmistakable scent of the spicy, pungent sauce bubbling on the stove, I know there is only one thing that can possibly fill the void in my stomach—my mother's homemade pizza. 1

The most difficult and frustrating episode of the process is fighting with the dough on the pizza pans. My mother begins by retrieving six well-used pizza pans from the overcrowded cupboard. A little oil rubbed over each pan by well experienced hands makes the pans so slippery they are difficult to handle. With a keen 2 eye, she then divides the dough into six precision-cut pieces. Now the real battle begins. It's woman against the yeast dough. She rolls the soft and slippery dough and pulls it out to the border of the pan. As she releases it, it snaps back into a little circle like a rubber band. Again and again she gently pulls, pushes, and rolls the dough back into its position. After several tries it finally ceases to retreat to the middle of the pan. By the time she has won the battle, she looks as though she hasn't the strength to continue. However, another smell of the fine aroma of the sauce revives her.

After spreading a tiny portion of oil onto the defeated dough, she begins the 3
addition of all the ingredients that really make a fantastic pizza. As she spoons the red, bubbling sauce onto the shiny dough, I can distinctly smell the onion bits, oregano, garlic salt, and the salt and pepper that the sauce contained. The once-white dough is now painted a bright red. With her hand she crumbles the dark brown chunks of the cooked ground sausage and sprinkles it evenly over the six pizzas. Next comes the main item. The little, round, coarse pieces of pepperoni accurately sliced the right thickness bring out all the flavor of the heavy spices. With a careful touch, she tops it off with long, smooth slices of mozzarella cheese that taste as mild as they feel.

The oven is hot and she steps back a few steps to survey her fine sculptures. 4
Carefully, so as not to destroy them, she inserts two of the pizzas into the oven. With an eager eye, she peers through the glass oven door. The crusts turn to a golden, nut brown, the sausage browns even darker, and the thin strips of cheese melt and cover the entire surface as though they were hot lava flowing over rough ground.

After what seems like eternity, the entire family gathers to gobble up every 5
last crumb. When it is all over, I sit back and release a belch of satisfaction and realize the great taste was well worth the wait.

Brownnosing Your Way to Academic Success

This is for those misguided souls who are going through school the hard way, by 1
studying. Listen up all you drudges because you're working too hard. And where does it get you? Lonely Saturday nights in the library. Sunday afternoons sweating over biology notes. Hours upon hours pouring over thick philosophy texts. Wise up, scholars; there's an easier way to earn that degree. With the proper effort and guidance, you too can brownnose your way to academic success.

The key to successful brownnosing is subtle technique. A successful 2
brownnose is not the sniveling, apple-polishing, boot-licking, fawning sort. No indeed. The expert brownnose has finesse. He drops by Professor Boredom's office just before class to announce with just the right amount of awe that the last lecture really inspired him and would he mind recommending additional reading? An experienced brownnose will linger a moment after Dr. Confusion's

class to mention that this is the first time he has ever understood quantum physics.

One of the most skilled brownnoses it has been my pleasure to know came up with this brilliant ploy. He wrote a letter to the dean singing the praises of his history teacher, a prof long known for giving impossible exams guaranteed to flunk two-thirds of the class. Well, aspiring brownnoses, take heed. My friend who knew about as much history as my 4-year-old nephew earned a respectable C in his history class. 3

So, if you're still going for your degree the hard way, consider the rewards of brownnosing. You too can party hearty and still keep from flunking out. Just learn the art of brownnosing. 4

A Disc Jockey's Work

Most people see the disc jockey as someone who simply plays music. To them, the disc jockey's job is easy. This attitude could be expected from someone who has not actually had the chance to experience the job. A closer examination will reveal that a lot of work goes on before, during, and after the show. 1

The process begins when the disc jockey accepts a "booking." That is, someone calls to inquire about his/her services, and the disc jockey accepts the proposal. In order for this to happen, the disc jockey must have one of two things. The disc jockey should have a well-established reputation and/or have spent time and money advertising. 2

The disc jockey and the interested party reach a mutual agreement. They discuss and settle issues such as a date, time, location, amount of money involved, and the length of the show. Some issues are the responsibility of the interested party, while others such as length of the show and the fee depend more on the disc jockey. An acceptable show length is usually four hours, and the fee can range from \$100–\$400. This depends on the disc jockey's reputation and the type of party or special occasion. Weddings, for example, are generally more expensive. 3

The date finally arrives and the disc jockey meets with the client at least thirty minutes before the show. This is when final payments and other details are dealt with. Sometimes a deposit is required in advance to hold a date, but usually an oral agreement is sufficient. 4

At this point the real work begins. In the next thirty minutes the disc jockey has to unload all of the necessary equipment from the van or truck, and move it inside. This can be a difficult task when you take into account that some stereo components can weigh in excess of seventy pounds. These components are large, cumbersome, and bulky. It may be necessary to make ten or more trips to unload them all. 5

When all of the equipment is moved inside, the disc jockey begins to get it ready for playing. In some cases the disc jockey has to connect twenty or 6 more wires and plugs. Each wire has a specific place to go, and can be color and number coded accordingly. Making the wrong connection could send an electrical surge through the system. This could cause a short circuit and destroy the entire system, causing hundreds of dollars worth of damage. With so many different wires and possible connections, to the untrained eye, the system looks like the complicated pieces of a jigsaw puzzle. The disc jockey quickly makes sense of the tangled mess of wires and connects each one to its proper place within minutes.

After a careful final check of the entire system, it is time for the show to 7
begin. The first hour is extremely important. The disc jockey has to measure the crowd's tastes and preferences, or their likes and dislikes. This is done by taking requests and by playing a wide variety of different musical selections. After this first hour the disc jockey should know what the audience wants to hear, and choose the right mixture of music accordingly. Upbeat dance songs, slow romantic ballads, country, and top forty pop rock can all be incorporated into the show.

Often, finding the music is difficult. While one song is playing, the disc 8
jockey is rapidly searching for the next selection to be played. Since the average length of a song is four to five minutes, the disc jockey has only this long to find that selection and get ready to introduce it. The disc jockey is constantly busy searching for records, and while this is going on he/she must also take additional requests and dedications. This confusion can last for three or more hours, and can be extremely stressful since you can not please everyone all of the time.

As the fourth and final hour draws to a close, the disc jockey chooses the 9
final song of the evening. A slow ballad begins to play as the disc jockey announces to the crowd that this will be the last dance of the evening. The once large and noisy crowd has dwindled to only a few remaining couples, who now find their way to the dance floor one final time. As the song slowly fades, the disc jockey says in a deep, mellow voice, "Good night ladies and gentlemen, I've had a wonderful time here this evening and I hope you did too. Thank you for coming—goodnight."

Some stragglers continue to dance despite the lack of music. Others sit 10
around and talk, and for just a second the disc jockey feels an overwhelming sense of satisfaction. The work, however, is still not done. Now the disc jockey must disassemble and reload all of the equipment that was unloaded just over four and a half hours ago. This does not require as much skill or preparation as setting up does, but it is still time-consuming. After all, this equipment is delicate and expensive, and must be handled carefully.

While the party-goers are home in bed the disc jockey is still hard at work 11
putting equipment into storage. This work often takes the disc jockey into the early hours of the morning. The disc jockey's work is not easy, and it's not glamorous. It is a lot of work that can be exhausting, both physically and mentally, but for someone who loves music and entertaining, the sense of personal satisfaction after the show is well worth the aggravation.

Becoming a Reliable Critic by Evaluating Writing

This activity gives you experience determining the successful and unsuccessful features of writing so you can better decide what changes to make in your own drafts.

Break into groups of three. Select one of the previous student essays (or use one your instructor assigns). As a group choose the strongest features of the essay and the features most in need of revision. Then prepare a group report that explains the essay's chief strengths and weaknesses. Be sure the report notes the specific kinds of changes needed. For example, do not just say that more detail is needed in paragraph 3; state that paragraph 3 should explain how the step is performed. When your report is complete, present it to the rest of the class. (The following evaluation questions can be used to guide you through your assessment of the essay.)

Evaluation Questions

1. The Introduction
   Does the introduction engage your interest? Why or why not?
2. The Thesis
   Does the thesis (stated or implied) mention the process and its significance?
3. Supporting Details
   Does the essay include all the necessary steps in the process? Where necessary, does the essay explain how steps are performed, why steps are performed, and what is *not* done? Are troublesome aspects of the process explained? Does the essay list needed materials and explain unfamiliar terms? Are any examples or description needed? Is there anything you do not understand?
4. Organization
   Do all the body paragraphs have topic sentences? If not, is this a problem? Are there any relevance problems?
5. Word Choice and Sentence Effectiveness
   Cite examples of effective word choice. Cite examples of word choice to revise. Are transitions needed? Where? Note any places where sentence variety is needed.

Essay Topics: Process Analysis

1. Describe a process you perform well so that someone else can perform it. You can describe how to change the oil in a car, how to train for an athletic competition, how to build a campfire, how to serve a tennis ball, how to buy a used car, how to plant a garden—anything you have had successful experience with. (see the Tryout on page 204 for ideas.)
2. As Negri does in "Loafing Made Easy," write a process analysis for comic effect. Possibilities include how to avoid working, how to make a

rotten impression on a first date, how to fail an exam, how to waste time, and how to annoy a professor.

3. As Selby does in "A Delicate Operation," describe a process to increase the reader's appreciation. Possibilities include how to write a poem, how to design clothing, how to raise show dogs, how to design scenery for a play, how legislation is passed in Congress, and how plants manufacture oxygen.
4. Help your reader give up a bad habit you have overcome by writing about how to quit smoking, how to lose weight, how to stop procrastinating, etc.
5. Write about any of these processes to help first-year students at your college:

   a. How to register
   b. How to select a major
   c. How to select an adviser
   d. How to find and check out a book from the campus library
   e. How to study for an exam
   f. How to meet people
   g. How to live with a roommate

6. Think of something that you know how to make, and describe the process so that someone else can make it.
7. Some miscellaneous topics that might appeal to you are

   a. How to survive adolescence
   b. How to buy the perfect gift
   c. How to plan the perfect party
   d. How to make the perfect pizza (or some other food)
   e. How to buy the right running shoes or camping equipment
   f. How to choose the right college
   g. How to catch a bass or train a dog
   h. How to form a band

8. Describe a process that can save a life (CPR, first aid, etc.).

Thematic Topics

1. Stanat describes the interview process in "How to Take a Job Interview" (page 205). Tell about an experience you had applying or interviewing for a job. Your essay should teach something about how the job applicant should or should not behave.
2. In "Brownnosing Your Way to Academic Success" (page 216), the student author describes the behavior of one campus type, the brownnoser. Pick another campus type and tell what that person is like. If you wish, you can make this essay humorous.

3. Explain how much of the interview process that Stanat describes in "How to Take an Interview" (page 205) is applicable to Harold Krents in "Darkness at Noon" (page 187). Does Krents deserve special consideration by the interviewer? Explain and support your view.

Writing Strategies

In addition to the strategies you learned in Chapters 1 to 3, the following suggestions may help you as you write your process analysis.

Topic Selection

1. Think of your past experiences and activities. They may suggest processes you can describe. If you were involved in athletics, perhaps you can describe how to coach Little League, how to block a tackle, how to shoot a foul shot, or how to prepare mentally for a game. If you were a scout, maybe you can explain how to prepare for a hike or how to survive in the wilderness. If you baby-sat, maybe you can explain how to sit for very young children, and so forth.
2. Think of what you have learned in your classes. Maybe as a result of what you have learned you can explain how to teach reading, how to prepare a slide to view under a microscope, how the Depression started, and so forth.

Generating and Ordering Ideas

1. List every step in the process in the order it is performed.
2. For each step you have listed, answer the following questions:

    a. Should I explain how the step is performed?
    b. Should I explain why the step is performed?
    c. Should I explain something that is *not* done?
    d. Should I explain a troublesome aspect of the step?
    e. Should I define a term?
    f. Should I describe something?
    g. Should I illustrate something?

Reader Response

If you like to secure reader response as part of your revision process, see page 77. In addition, give your draft to a reader and ask that person if there are any aspects of the process that are hard to follow.

REVISION CHECKLIST

In addition to the checklist on page 80, you can use this checklist to help you revise your process analysis.

1. Does your thesis mention the process and the significance of the process? If not, should it?
2. Will your reader know why it is important to understand the process and/or why you are qualified to describe the process?
3. Have you mentioned all the steps in the process and how they are performed?
4. Where necessary, have you explained why steps are performed and noted what is not done?
5. Have you defined unfamiliar terms and, if necessary, given a list of items needed?
6. Have you explained troublesome aspects of the process?

CHAPTER 9

Comparison-Contrast

When we **compare** and **contrast,** we place two or more things side by side to point out and examine their similarities and differences.

One way to develop a thesis for a comparison-contrast essay is to state the subjects you are considering and indicate whether you are comparing or contrasting, or doing both. Below are three possible thesis statements developed this way.

1. `I expected college to be vastly different from high school, but I soon discovered they are not much different at all.` (This thesis indicates that high school and college will be compared.)
2. `After a month in my own apartment, I realized that living on my own was not what I imagined it to be.` (The thesis states that the reality of and the author's expectation for living alone will be contrasted.)
3. `The book and movie versions of` *`The Firm`* `are alike in many ways, but they differ significantly as well.` (The thesis states that the book and movie versions of *The Firm* will be compared and contrasted.)

SELECTING SUBJECTS

You should give careful thought to topic selection. For one thing, the items compared or contrasted must have enough in common to warrant their side-by-side consideration. Usually this means that the subjects must belong to the same category. For example, you can sensibly compare or contrast a Villager with a Voyager because both of these belong to the same category—minivans. You can compare or contrast two jobs, two teachers, two forms of government, two ways to study, two kinds of dates, two ways to celebrate Christmas, two cities you have lived in, and so on. These comparisons and contrasts are possible and sensible because the items viewed next to each other share enough features to make their comparison or contrast logical and meaningful. It would be silly, however, to compare learning to use a personal computer and learning to roller skate. Even if you could manage some corresponding statements about both of these activities, the comparison would be strained, probably more clever than valid, and the contrasts would be so obvious, they go without saying. As a result, the essay would serve no useful purpose.

PURPOSE

A comparison-contrast essay can serve a variety of purposes. Sometimes it clarifies the unknown by placing it next to something more familiar to determine in what ways the two are alike and in what ways they are different. For example, an essay comparing and contrasting rugby (less understood) with football (well known) could serve this purpose. Once the lesser-known rugby is explained in light of how it is like and unlike the better-known football, rugby can be better understood.

Sometimes the purpose of a comparison-contrast is to lend a fresh insight into something familiar. This can be achieved when similarities are drawn between things typically viewed as dissimilar or when differences are noted in things usually seen as comparable. Love and hate, for example, are usually seen as opposites, but an essay that explains their similarities by pointing out that both emotions are highly motivating, potentially self-destructive, and sometimes irrational can lead to new awarenesses about these familiar feelings.

A comparison-contrast can sometimes serve to bring things into sharper focus. For example, while we may understand what Catholicism and Protestantism are, an essay comparing and contrasting their basic tenets may lead to a clearer understanding of each religion.

Finally, a comparison-contrast essay can serve a persuasive purpose because when the features of one thing are compared or contrasted with the features of another, it is possible to judge which one is superior. For example, the platforms of two mayoral candidates can be compared and contrasted to determine which candidate would make the better mayor.

Your purpose will influence the details you select to develop your essay. Say, for example, that you decide to note the differences between dating practices today and those of 30 years ago. If your purpose is to demonstrate that women are more assertive now, you might note that they can take the initiative today but that 30 years ago they seldom asked men out or picked up bar tabs. If your purpose is to argue that dating was easier 30 years ago, you might mention that relationships were simpler before the sexual revolution. If you wish to clarify how prescribed codes of conduct have relaxed and blurred, you might explain the expected ways men and women behaved on a date 30 years ago and then explain the less predictable ways they behave now.

To determine your purpose, you can ask these questions.

1. Do I want to clarify the nature of one unfamiliar subject by placing it next to another, more familiar subject?
2. Do I want to lend a fresh insight into one subject by placing it next to another?
3. Do I want to bring one or both of my subjects into sharper focus?
4. Do I want to show that one of my subjects is superior to the other?

AUDIENCE

Like purpose, audience will affect detail selection. How much your reader knows about your subjects, how your reader feels about your subjects, and how strong these feelings are—these influence the details you choose. For example, let's return to the essay that contrasts dating practices today with those of 30 years ago, and let's say your purpose is to convince the reader that dating was more fun 30 years ago. If your reader is a feminist, you will not note that 30 years ago men and women had more prescribed roles and hence were more certain how to act. However, if your reader is a teenager who finds the sexual revolution frightening, you might note that there was less sexual pressure for teens who dated 30 years ago.

To determine your audience, you can ask yourself these questions.

1. Who could learn something by reading my essay?
2. Who could be influenced to share my point of view?
3. Who does not currently know much about one of my subjects?
4. Who would enjoy reading my essay?

Once you have targeted your audience, you can determine the nature of that audience by answering these questions.

1. How much does my reader know about my subjects?
2. How much interest does my reader have in my subjects?
3. How does my reader feel about my subjects?
4. How strongly does my reader feel about my subjects?

SELECTING DETAIL

Comparison and contrast detail can include the patterns of development discussed so far in this book: description, narration, process analysis, and illustration. Comparing cars can involve you in a description of interiors and options. Comparing ways to celebrate Christmas can involve you in narrations of two different Christmas celebrations you were part of. Contrasting teachers can involve you in illustrations of the methods of each. Contrasting study techniques can involve explaining how each one works. Combining all or some of these methods within the same essay is also possible.

Regardless of your patterns of development, work to maintain balance among the points you discuss. This means that any point you discuss for one subject should also be mentioned for the other. Let's say, for example, you are comparing your family life before your parents divorced with your family life after they divorced, for the purpose of explaining that children can be better off if their parents end an unhappy marriage. If you describe mealtime before the divorce as a time of squabbling that made you tense and afraid, then you should say something about what mealtime was like after the divorce.

This need for balance does not require you to treat a point with exactly the same degree of development for each subject. You may, for example, describe extensively the mealtime squabbling that occurred before the divorce to give your reader a clear picture of its nature and effect on you. Then you can note the peaceful nature of meals after the divorce in just two or three sentences. Similarly, you may find that either the comparison or the contrast is more detailed, or that one of the subjects gets more development than the other. This is fine. As long as everything treated is developed *adequately,* it need not be developed *equally.*

As you select your detail, avoid comparisons and contrasts that are so obvious they do not need to be mentioned. If, for example, you were comparing two cars, it would be silly to note that they both have engines.

ARRANGING DETAIL

Comparison-contrast must be carefully organized, or your points will be disconnected and confusing. One logical arrangement is **subject by subject**. With this organization, you make all your points about your first subject, and then you go on to make all your points about your second subject. Say, for example, that you are comparing and contrasting living in a residence hall with living at home. To organize using a subject-by-subject pattern, first provide all your details about living in one place (in one or more paragraphs), and then provide all your details about living in the other place (in one or more paragraphs). The outline could look like this:

```
Preliminary thesis: Both living in a residence hall and living
at home have advantages and disadvantages.

 I. Living in a residence hall
    A. No privacy
    B. Poor climate for studying
    C. Uncomfortable living space
    D. Considerable freedom
II. Living at home
    A. More privacy
    B. Good climate for studying
    C. Comfortable living space
    D. Little freedom
```

Note the balance in the outline. The points discussed for the first subject (privacy, climate for studying, living space, and freedom) are also discussed for the second. You need not develop each point equally, but you should treat the same points for each subject. Otherwise, you will not have a comparison-contrast but an assortment of details on two subjects—an assortment that does not hang together in any way.

The subject-by-subject organization generally works best for an essay that is not long, complex, or developed with a great many points. Otherwise, the reader working through your points on the second subject must keep too many points about the first subject in mind.

Longer, more complex essays can be organized following the **point-by-point** arrangement. With this pattern you make a point about your first subject and then treat the corresponding point about your second subject. Then you treat the next point about your first subject and follow it with the corresponding point about your second subject. You continue in this alternating fashion until all your points have been presented and developed. Say, for example, that you are contrasting your high school history teacher with your college history teacher. Assume that you plan to discuss the way each presents material, the way each interacts with students, and the way each tests students' knowledge. An outline for your essay could look like this:

Preliminary thesis: My high school history teacher and my college history teacher differ in their presentation of material, their interaction with students, and their tests of student knowledge.

I. Presentation of material
   A. High school teacher
      1. Gave long, boring lectures
      2. Had no class participation
   B. College teacher
      1. Gives brief, stimulating lectures
      2. Has a great deal of class participation

II. Interaction with students
   A. High school teacher
      1. Was standoffish
      2. Acted superior to students
   B. College teacher
      1. Interacts with students often
      2. Acts as though students are her equal

III. Tests of student knowledge
   A. High school teacher
      1. Gave only two tests each term
      2. Gave objective tests
      3. Asked trick questions
   B. College teacher
      1. Gives four tests each term
      2. Gives essay tests
      3. Never asks trick questions

You can tell from the outline that balance is important in point-by-point development. You must treat the same points for both subjects, although you need not give the same degree of development to each point for each subject.

For essays that show both similarities and differences, a third method of organization is possible. You can first discuss all the similarities between your subjects and then go on to discuss all the differences, or you can reverse this order. Say you wanted to show how Las Vegas and Atlantic City compare and contrast as vacation spots. An outline that deals first with similarities and then with differences could look like this.

```
Preliminary thesis: Although Atlantic City has some things in
common with its big sister, Las Vegas, the East Coast gambling
town is not the vacation site Las Vegas is.

 I. Similarities
    A. Both have gambling.
    B. Both have top-level entertainment.
    C. Both have high-class hotels.
II. Differences
    A. Gambling is different.
       1. There are more casinos in Vegas.
       2. There is cheaper gambling available in Vegas.
       3. Gambling is available 24 hours a day, 7 days a week
          in Vegas.
    B. Top-level entertainment is different.
       1. There are more big-name entertainers in Vegas.
       2. There is more free entertainment in Vegas.
    C. The high-class hotels are different.
       1. There are more hotels in Vegas.
       2. There is greater variety of accommodations in
          Vegas.
       3. There are lower room rates available in Vegas.
```

In the above outline, first the similarities are noted, using a point-by-point development, and then the differences are cited, again using a point-by-point pattern. However, the similarities can be developed with a point-by-point pattern and the differences with a subject-by-subject pattern. With this organization the outline would look like this.

```
 I. Similarities
    A. Gambling
    B. Top-level entertainment
    C. High-class hotels
II. Differences
    A. Atlantic City
       1. Gambling
       2. Entertainment
       3. Hotels
```

```
B. Las Vegas
   1. Gambling
   2. Entertainment
   3. Hotels
```

Although the same aspects (gambling, entertainment, hotels) are discussed for the similarities and for the differences, this balance is not necessary. You can discuss some features of similarity between both subjects and then go on to discuss different features of contrast. Whether you discuss the similarities first or the differences first depends on which you want to emphasize more. Points treated second get the greater emphasis because the closer to the end, the more emphatic the position.

You have no doubt gathered that the arrangement of details for a comparison-contrast requires careful planning. Even if you do not ordinarily outline, you may want to do so for a comparison-contrast paper. Without an outline it can be tricky to arrange details logically while achieving the necessary balance.

TRYOUT To gain experience identifying and organizing comparison-contrast, try this: assume that you will write a comparison-contrast essay about your current writing process and the one you used at some point in the past (perhaps before this term began). Make one list of all the similarities you can think of and one list of all the differences. Review your lists and decide whether you will treat similarities, differences, or both. Finally, write an outline for a possible organization of your ideas, using a subject-by-subject pattern, a point-by-point pattern, or some combination of these.

PROFESSIONAL ESSAYS

A Fable for Tomorrow

Rachel Carson

Rachel Carson is considered one of the forerunners of environmentalism. Her book Silent Spring *(1962) made the general public aware of the effects of chemical weed and insect killers. "A Fable for Tomorrow," which is an excerpt from* Silent Spring, *uses contrast to warn of the dangers of chemical pesticides.*

There was once a town in the heart of America where all life seemed to live in harmony with its surroundings. The town lay in the midst of a checkerboard of prosperous farms, with fields of grain and hillsides of orchards where, in spring, white clouds of bloom drifted above the green fields. In autumn, oak and maple and birch set up a blaze of color that flamed and flickered across a backdrop of pines. 1

Then foxes barked in the hills and deer silently crossed the fields, half hidden in the mists of the fall mornings.

Along the roads, laurel, viburnum and alder, great ferns and wildflowers delighted the traveler's eye through much of the year. Even in winter the roadsides were places of beauty, where countless birds came to feed on the berries and on the seed heads of the dried weeds rising above the snow. The countryside was, in fact, famous for the abundance and variety of its bird life, and when the flood of migrants was pouring through in spring and fall people traveled from great distances to observe them. Others came to fish the streams, which flowed clear and cold out of the hills and contained shady pools where trout lay. So it had been from the days many years ago when the first settlers raised their houses, sank their wells, and built their barns. 2

Then a strange blight crept over the area and everything began to change. Some evil spell had settled on the community: mysterious maladies swept the flocks of chickens; the cattle and sheep sickened and died. Everywhere was a shadow of death. The farmers spoke of much illness among their families. In the town the doctors had become more and more puzzled by new kinds of sickness appearing among their patients. There had been several sudden and unexplained deaths not only among adults but even among children, who would be stricken suddenly while at play and die within a few hours. 3

There was a strange stillness. The birds, for example—where had they gone? Many people spoke of them, puzzled and disturbed. The feeding stations in the backyards were deserted. The few birds seen anywhere were moribund; they trembled violently and could not fly. It was a spring without voices. On the mornings that had once throbbed with the dawn chorus of robins, catbirds, doves, jays, wrens, and scores of other bird voices there was now no sound; only silence lay over the fields and woods and marsh. 4

On the farms the hens brooded, but no chicks hatched. The farmers complained that they were unable to raise any pigs—the litters were small and the young survived only a few days. The apple trees were coming into bloom but no bees droned among the blossoms, so there was no pollination and there would be no fruit. 5

The roadsides, once so attractive, were now lined with browned and withered vegetation as though swept by fire. These, too, were silent, deserted by all living things. Even the streams were now lifeless. Anglers no longer visited them, for all the fish had died. 6

In the gutters under the eaves and between the shingles of the roofs, a white granular powder still showed a few patches; some weeks before it had fallen like snow upon the roofs and the lawns, the fields and streams. 7

No witchcraft, no enemy action had silenced the rebirth of new life in the stricken world. The people had done it themselves. 8

This town does not actually exist, but it might easily have a thousand counterparts in America or elsewhere in the world. I know of no community that has experienced all the misfortunes I describe. Yet every one of these disasters has actually happened somewhere, and many real communities have already suffered 9 a substantial number of them. A grim specter has crept upon us almost unnoticed, and this imagined tragedy may easily become a stark reality we all shall know.

Questions on Technique

1. Is Carson comparing, contrasting, or doing both?
2. What are the subjects placed next to each other in Carson's essay?
3. What pattern does Carson use for the arrangement of her details?
4. Is the treatment of both subjects balanced? Explain.
5. Carson develops her discussion of the town after the blight in greater detail than she does her discussion of the town before the blight. Is this a problem? What effect does this have on the reader?
6. "A Fable for Tomorrow" is a contrast piece with some narration and description. How does the narration function? The description?
7. How does Carson effect the transition from her first subject to her second?
8. What is the purpose of Carson's essay? That is, what point does her contrast make?
9. Where in the essay does Carson make her point known?
10. Carson does not use a formal introduction. Is this a problem? Why or why not?
11. What kind of conclusion does Carson use? Is it effective? Explain.

For Group Discussion or Journal Writing

Chemicals are still widely used in agriculture to destroy weeds, kill insects, encourage growth, and preserve food. Consider how safe you feel eating food treated with these chemicals. In many areas, food grown without chemicals is available, but it costs considerably more money. Would you pay more for this food? Explain.

Columbus and the Moon

Tom Wolfe

Journalist Tom Wolfe has written several books, including The Right Stuff *(1979), which earned the American Book Award. In "Columbus and the Moon," which originally appeared in the* New York Times, *Wolfe compares space exploration with the explorations of Columbus.*

The National Aeronautics and Space Administration's moon landing 10 years ago *1*
today was a Government project, but then so was Columbus's voyage to America in 1492. The Government, in Columbus's case, was the Spanish Court of Ferdi-

nand and Isabella. Spain was engaged in a sea race with Portugal in much the same way that the United States would be caught up in a space race with the Soviet Union four and a half centuries later.

The race in 1492 was to create the first shipping lane to Asia. The Portuguese expeditions had always sailed east, around the southern tip of Africa. Columbus decided to head due west, across open ocean, a scheme that was feasible only thanks to a recent invention—the magnetic ship's compass. Until then ships had stayed close to the great land masses even for the longest voyages. Likewise, it was only thanks to an invention of the 1940's and early 1950's, the high-speed electronic computer, that NASA would even consider propelling astronauts out of the Earth's orbit and toward the moon. 2

Both NASA and Columbus made not one but a series of voyages. NASA landed men on six different parts of the moon. Columbus made four voyages to different parts of what he remained convinced was the east coast of Asia. As a result both NASA and Columbus had to keep coming back to the Government with their hands out, pleading for refinancing. In each case the reply of the Government became, after a few years: "This is all very impressive, but what earthly good is it to anyone back home?" 3

Columbus was reduced to making the most desperate claims. When he first reached land in 1492 at San Salvador, off Cuba, he expected to find gold, or at least spices. The Arawak Indians were awed by the strangers and their ships, which they believed had descended from the sky, and they presented them with their most prized possessions, live parrots and balls of cotton. Columbus soon set them digging for gold, which didn't exist. So he brought back reports of fabulous riches in the form of manpower; which is to say, slaves. He was not speaking of the Arawaks, however. With the exception of criminals and prisoners of war, he was supposed to civilize all natives and convert them to Christianity. He was talking about the Carib Indians, who were cannibals and therefore qualified as criminals. The Caribs would fight down to the last unbroken bone rather than endure captivity, and few ever survived the voyages back to Spain. By the end of Columbus's second voyage, in 1496, the Government was becoming testy. A great deal of wealth was going into voyages to Asia, and very little was coming back. Columbus made his men swear to return to Spain saying that they had not only reached the Asian mainland, they had heard Japanese spoken. 4

Likewise by the early 1970's, it was clear that the moon was in economic terms pretty much what it looked like from Earth, a gray rock. NASA, in the quest for appropriations, was reduced to publicizing the "spinoffs" of the space program. These included Teflon-coated frying pans, a ballpoint pen that would write in a weightless environment, and a computerized biosensor system that would enable doctors to treat heart patients without making house calls. On the whole, not a giant step for mankind. 5

In 1493, after his first voyage, Columbus had ridden through Barcelona at the side of King Ferdinand in the position once occupied by Ferdinand's late son, Juan. By 1500, the bad-mouthing of Columbus had reached the point where he was put in chains at the conclusion of his third voyage and returned to Spain in 6 disgrace. NASA suffered no such ignominy, of course, but by July 20, 1974, the fifth anniversary of the landing of Apollo 11, things were grim enough. The public had become gloriously bored by space exploration. The fifth anniversary celebration consisted mainly of about 200 souls, mostly NASA people, sitting on folding chairs underneath a camp meeting canopy on the marble prairie outside the old Smithsonian Air Museum in Washington listening to speeches by Neil Armstrong, Michael Collins, and Buzz Aldrin and watching the caloric waves ripple.

Extraordinary rumors had begun to circulate about the astronauts. The 7
most lurid said that trips to the moon, and even into earth orbit, had so traumatized the men, they had fallen victim to religious and spiritualist manias or plain madness. (Of the total 73 astronauts chosen, one, Aldrin, is known to have suffered from depression, rooted, as his own memoir makes clear, in matters that had nothing to do with space flight. Two teamed up in an evangelical organization, and one set up a foundation for the scientific study of psychic phenomena—interests the three of them had developed long before they flew in space.) The NASA budget, meanwhile, had been reduced to the lightbill level.

Columbus died in 1509, nearly broke and stripped of most of his honors as 8
Spain's Admiral of the Ocean, a title he preferred. It was only later that history began to look upon him not as an adventurer who had tried and failed to bring home gold—but as a man with a supernatural sense of destiny, whose true glory was his willingness to plunge into the unknown, including the remotest parts of the universe he could hope to reach.

NASA still lives, albeit in reduced circumstances, and whether or not history 9
will treat NASA like the admiral is hard to say.

The idea that the exploration of the rest of the universe is its own reward is 10
not very popular, and NASA is forced to keep talking about things such as bigger communications satellites that will enable live television transmission of European soccer games at a fraction of the current cost. Such notions as "building a bridge to the stars for mankind" do not light up the sky today—but may yet.

Questions on Technique

1. What subjects does Wolfe bring together in his essay? Are these subjects compared, contrasted, or both?
2. In what pattern does Wolfe arrange his details—subject-by-subject or point-by-point?
3. What do you judge to be the purpose of Wolfe's comparison?
4. Wolfe's comparison has balance for the most part, but one point is made about Columbus that is not made about NASA. What is that point? Why is the corresponding point not made about NASA?
5. Although Wolfe does not compare the value of Columbus's voyages across time and NASA's worth in the future, a comparison can be drawn by the reader. What is it?
6. Which paragraphs include illustration?
7. What approach does Wolfe take to his conclusion?

For Group Discussion or Journal Writing

The journalist usually presents unadorned facts in straightforward fashion. Wolfe, however, is known for a personal style that includes emotion, description, evaluation of facts, and judgments. For example, in paragraph 4, Wolfe says, "Columbus was reduced to making the most desperate claims," rather than "Columbus lied about his discoveries." Cite several similar examples of this style. What do you think it contributes?

Neat People vs. Sloppy People

Suzanne Britt

Columnist, English teacher, textbook author, and essayist, Suzanne Britt here uses contrast to entertain her reader. However, as is often the case with humor, some serious points are made as well.

I've finally figured out the difference between neat people and sloppy people. The distinction is, as always, moral. Neat people are lazier and meaner than sloppy people. 1

Sloppy people, you see, are not really sloppy. Their sloppiness is merely the unfortunate consequence of their extreme moral rectitude. Sloppy people carry in their mind's eye a heavenly vision, a precise plan, that is so stupendous, so perfect, it can't be achieved in this world or the next. 2

Sloppy people live in Never-Never Land. Someday is their métier. Someday they are planning to alphabetize all their books and set up home catalogs. Someday they will go through their wardrobes and mark certain items for tentative mending and certain items for passing on to relatives of similar shape and size. Someday sloppy people will make family scrapbooks into which they will put newspaper clippings, postcards, locks of hair, and the dried corsage from their senior prom. Someday they will file everything on the surface of their desks, including the cash receipts from coffee purchases at the snack shop. Someday they will sit down and read all the back issues of *The New Yorker*. 3

For all these noble reasons and more, sloppy people never get neat. They aim too high and wide. They save everything, planning someday to file, order, and straighten out the world. But while these ambitious plans take clearer and clearer shape in their heads, the books spill from the shelves onto the floor, the clothes pile up in the hamper and closet, the family mementos accumulate in every drawer, the surface of the desk is buried under mounds of paper and the unread magazines threaten to reach the ceiling. 4

Sloppy people can't bear to part with anything. They give loving attention to every detail. When sloppy people say they're going to tackle the surface of the desk, they really mean it. Not a paper will go unturned; not a rubber band will go unboxed. Four hours or two weeks into the excavation, the desk looks exactly the same, primarily because the sloppy person is meticulously creating new piles of papers with new headings and scrupulously stopping to read all the 5 old book catalogs before he throws them away. A neat person would just bulldoze the desk.

Neat people are bums and clods at heart. They have cavalier attitudes toward possessions, including family heirlooms. Everything is just another dust-catcher to them. If anything collects dust, it's got to go and that's that. Neat people will toy with the idea of throwing the children out of the house just to cut down on the clutter. 6

Neat people don't care about process. They like results. What they want to do is get the whole thing over with so they can sit down and watch the rasslin' on TV. Neat people operate on two unvarying principles: Never handle any item twice, and throw everything away. 7

The only thing messy in a neat person's house is the trash can. The minute something comes to a neat person's hand, he will look at it, try to decide if it has immediate use and, finding none, throw it in the trash. 8

Neat people are especially vicious with mail. They never go through their mail unless they are standing directly over a trash can. If the trash can is beside the mailbox, even better. All ads, catalogs, pleas for charitable contributions, church bulletins and money-saving coupons go straight into the trash can without being opened. All letters from home, postcards from Europe, bills and paychecks are opened, immediately responded to, then dropped in the trash can. Neat people keep their receipts only for tax purposes. That's it. No sentimental salvaging of birthday cards or the last letter a dying relative ever wrote. Into the trash it goes. 9

Neat people place neatness above everything, even economics. They are incredibly wasteful. Neat people throw away several toys every time they walk through the den. I knew a neat person once who threw away a perfectly good dish drainer because it had mold on it. The drainer was too much trouble to wash. And neat people sell their furniture when they move. They will sell a La-Z-Boy recliner while you are reclining in it. 10

Neat people are no good to borrow from. Neat people buy everything in expensive little single portions. They get their flour and sugar in two-pound bags. They wouldn't consider clipping a coupon, saving a leftover, reusing plastic nondairy whipped cream containers or rinsing off tin foil and draping it over the unmoldy dish drainer. You can never borrow a neat person's newspaper to see what's playing at the movies. Neat people have the paper all wadded up and in the trash by 7:05 A.M. 11

Neat people cut a clean swath through the organic as well as the inorganic world. People, animals, and things are all one to them. They are so insensitive. After they've finished with the pantry, the medicine cabinet, and the attic, they will throw out the red geranium (too many leaves), sell the dog (too many fleas), and send the children off to boarding school (too many scuffmarks on the hardwood floors). 12

Questions on Technique

1. Which sentence acts as Britt's thesis, indicating the subjects to be placed side by side and letting us know that those subjects will be contrasted? What are the subjects, and what words indicate that contrast will occur?

2. Does Britt develop her contrast with a subject-by-subject or point-by-point pattern?
3. Britt uses topic sentences to indicate the focus of her body paragraphs. What are those topic sentences?
4. Which paragraphs develop points with examples?
5. Britt does not always treat the same points about both of her subjects. Is the lack of balance a problem? Explain.
6. Why do you think that Britt provides more detail about neat people than about sloppy people? Is it a problem that the two subjects are not treated in equal detail? Explain.
7. Britt does not write a formal conclusion. How does she end the essay? Is the technique effective?

For Group Discussion or Journal Writing

Like many humorists, Britt uses exaggeration for humorous effect. Cite three examples of exaggeration and explain why they are humorous. Also like many humorists, Britt speaks some truth. What elements of truth do you see in the essay? Cite at least two examples. Would the essay have been as effective if either the exaggeration or the truth had been omitted? Explain.

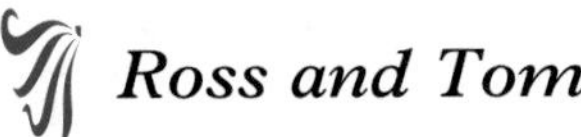

Ross and Tom

John Leggett

Two successful authors die, disillusioned, and writer-editor John Leggett wants to know why. Leggett compares and contrasts the two authors and discovers, among other things, the force of the "dark side of achievement."

Taking my life is inconceivable to me. I shall lose it soon enough. To abandon even one of my allotted minutes might be to miss some important or funny thing, perhaps even the point. 1

Also—and there is a connection—I am ambitious. I have been bred to "getting ahead," to the belief that if I fall behind, shame and starvation will catch me, but if I achieve something I will be looked after, admired and loved in perpetuity. Long ago I accepted these as the rules of the game. I only quarrel with them when the score is running against me. 2

Sometime during World War II I decided to have my achievement as a writer. It took me five years and a fat swatch of rejection slips to find out how hard that was and, in frustration, to take a job with a book publisher. 3

Thus it was in Houghton Mifflin's warren overlooking Boston Common that I learned about a dark side of achievement—how, a few years earlier, two young novelists, just my age and no more promising in background, had been published so successfully that their first books made them rich and famous. Then, at the peak of their acclaim, they died. 4

The first, Ross Lockridge, took his own life, locking his new garage doors 5
behind his new Kaiser and asphyxiating himself. The second, Thomas Heggen, drowned in his bathwater—an accident, it was claimed, but it was the accident of a desperate man.

Tom and Ross were similar in that neither had any previous notoriety and 6
they came from obscure, middle-class, Midwest backgrounds. Yet as men they could not have been more different.

Ross was an oak of prudence and industry. He rarely drank and he never 7
smoked. He excelled at everything he did. He had married his hometown sweetheart, was proudly faithful to her and produced four fine children. After a sampling of success on both coasts he had gone home to the Indiana of his parents and childhood friends.

Tom Heggen had a taste for low life. He had been divorced, had no children 8
and shared bachelor quarters in New York with an ex-actor and screenwriter, Dorothy Parker's estranged husband, Alan Campbell. Tom was a drinker and a pill addict. He turned up regularly at the fashionable restaurant "21," usually bringing along a new girl, a dancer or an actress.

After the success of their first novels, neither Ross nor Tom had been able 9
to start a new book. At the time of their deaths neither had written anything in months.

What had happened to them? There were grumblings that some villainy of 10
Houghton Mifflin's had done Ross Lockridge in, that in publishing his huge novel, *Raintree County,* the firm had exploited him, somehow threatened both his income and his privacy. (There had been a quarrel and Ross had made unpleasant accusations.)

Could it have been fatigue—had the two novelists written themselves out, 11
found they had nothing more to say? Or was it disappointment: had the finished book—or in Heggen's case the dramatic version of *Mister Roberts* which was then playing on Broadway—fallen short of some original notion of perfection? There are always spoilers. *Raintree County*'s first reviews had called it a masterpiece and compared its author to Thomas Wolfe, but these were followed by some contemptuous ones, and there had been a denouncement by a Jesuit priest which struck at Ross's own self-doubts.

Still, none of these sounded as likely an explanation as that of the bitch-god- 12
dess herself—the writer spoiled by success, his need to write smothered in a surfeit of reward. Clearly there is something disillusioning in attainment. Many writers (such as J. D. Salinger and James Gould Cozzens, among others) drift into unproductivity after a big, popular success, just as the very productive ones such as Henry James are often those who pursue, yet never quite attain, an enthusiastic public embrace.

There is still another area for conjecture. Suppose that Tom Heggen's and 13
Ross Lockridge's final act was not one of surrender at all, but defiance. Perhaps success had brought them to some promontory from which they could see the whole of their path and from there they had made this appalling comment about it. What could so disillusion them about that view? I needed to know. If they were rejecting their own incentives, they were, so far as I knew, rejecting mine.

Searching for an entryway to their spirits, I drew a professional comparison. Lockridge was a Vesuvius. When he was at work, twenty or thirty pages spewed from his typewriter each day, some on their way to the wastebasket, others to be revised, endlessly before they were satisfactory, but always expanding. Progress toward a desired shape was by laying on more material. 14

Heggen was the reverse, a distiller. The molding was a prelude to writing and was done in his head. He would sit by the hour, staring out a window, so that a passerby would think him daydreaming. But then he would turn to his typewriter and strike a flawless passage, each word and inflection so precisely chosen there was no need for revision. 15

But in spite of this difference in the way they worked, Ross and Tom appeared to be equally single-minded about writing, each compelled to it with a force that dwarfed the other elements of his life. Thus the common experience preceding their deaths, of wanting to write again and not being able to, is significant. The being able to—the energy—is the essential part of incentive and I had the impression they had lost that, knew they had lost it and knew that without it they were useless men. 16

What *is* a writer's incentive? That he has a gift for expression in words can be taken for granted; but I suspect that gift doesn't contribute half so much to motivation as social failure. I know that my own feelings of inadequacy and shyness were first routed when, in the third grade, my piece on tadpoles appeared in the school paper, and I suspect that only a man who doubts the persuasiveness of his tongue and fists would sit alone dirtying good paper when he could be in company. 17

Wanting to write fiction has even more elaborate roots and these reach not just into a writer's present reveries but back into his childhood. When he is read to, when he is sick and is brought an adventure book with his medicine, a child gets a first set of furnishings for his dream world. When he graduates to adult novels his debt to fiction is increased by a more utilitarian, though still romantic, vision of himself and a way to behave. If he chooses wisely and is lucky in the library he can find dream enough to sustain him for a lifetime. 18

But the path of a writer is too lonely and discouraging for any kind of propulsion but the hugest. In an essay on Willa Cather, Leon Edel notes that for her novel about an ambitious opera singer, *The Song of the Lark,* she chose the epigraph "It was a wondrous lovely storm that drove me," and that this was not only appropriate for Thea, the heroine, but for the author. 19

"It was a wondrous, lovely storm that drove Willa Cather," he says, "and what she cared for above all was the storm. With success achieved . . . she felt depressed. She didn't know what to do with success; or rather, she seems to have experienced a despair altogether out of proportion to the actual circumstances of her achievement . . . Success, by the very testimony of the tales she wrote, created for Willa Cather a deep despair and even a wish for death . . ." 20

Willa Cather's experience of depression in achievement makes a striking parallel with Ross's and Tom's. And I cannot find a better description for the kind of force a novelist wants to contain than "the wondrous lovely storm." It is vague, yet so evocative of the emotion and energy that can bring forth a significant 21 book—wondrous in its mysterious origin and awesome power, lovely because it is not terrifying at all, but blissful, as though it is love itself.

When I first looked into Tom Heggen's and Ross Lockridge's lives, seeking some clues to their deaths, I found myself in barren country. Neither had the nature for casual confessions nor the kind of apprenticeships which called for public self-examinations. An even bigger difficulty lay with those who had known them best. They suffered from having been present at, yet unable to prevent, a tragedy. Understandably the families were wary of talking about the darker, human parts of the natures and experiences of the two writers. 22

Still, inconsequential, even irrelevant details about them intrigued me. Instead of flagging, my interest grew. Occasionally I felt I might be guilty of dancing on their graves, a jig for my own compensating survival. But what most absorbed me was self-discovery. 23

Ross, Tom and I grew up to the same music, worshiping the same idols, suffering from the same inhibitions. It was remarkably easy for me to slip into their adolescent skins. As an adult and a writer, I could recognize in those highs of self-certainty, in those plunging lows of self-doubt, my own emotional weather. Finally, in each of their natures—one black, reckless; the other a marching band of virtues—I saw two halves of my own. 24

Questions on Technique

1. Which paragraph presents Leggett's thesis? What words indicate that the subjects will be both compared and contrasted?
2. Which paragraphs point out similarities between Ross and Tom?
3. Why do you think Leggett compares Ross and Tom to Willa Cather?
4. Which paragraphs point out differences?
5. Leggett does not treat all the similarities together and all the differences together. Instead, he alternates his discussion of similarites and differences. How does he help the reader follow this organizational plan?
6. What do you judge to be Leggett's purpose for his comparison-contrast?

For Group Discussion or Journal Writing

What do you think Leggett means when he refers to "a dark side of achievement" (paragraph 4)? Try to cite one or two examples that illustrate the phrase.

STUDENT ESSAYS TO READ AND EVALUATE

Each of the following comparison-contrast essays written by students has strengths and areas that could be improved with revision. Thus, each essay can teach something about techniques to try and strategies to avoid. Furthermore, evaluating the essays will sharpen your critical abilities and make you a more reliable judge of your own writing. The evaluation activity after the essays will help you draw conclusions about the pieces.

The Human and the Superhuman: Two Very Different Heroes

In the late 1930s a small company in the fledging comic book business decided to create something new and different for the public: the superhero. Two of the first characters to be created were opposites of one another. One had the powers of a god while the other was only a man, yet Superman and Batman were the mythic creations that set the stage for all who followed. *1*

Superman was created in 1938 by two imaginative young men named Jerry Siegel and Joe Schuster. They wanted to create a character that was immensely powerful. What emerged was someone "faster than a speeding bullet, more powerful than a locomotive, and able to leap tall buildings in a single bound." The powers that Superman possessed brought about much reader interest. The story of the sole survivor of a doomed planet coming to earth to battle the forces of evil contained the idealism people wanted during those post-Depression days. Although times have changed, the public still enjoys a bit of idealism once in a while, and Superman provides it. *2*

Unlike Superman, Batman was not created for idealistic purposes, but rather for vengeance. While Superman was flying far above society, Batman was stalking the seedy underside of Gotham, preying on the criminal element. Bob Kane created Batman in 1939 with the human element in mind. The public enjoyed the idea of having a hero as human as they. Also the concept of revenge associated with the murder of Batman's parents struck a chord with the public's conscience. This troubled hero has become more popular than Superman in recent years because the rise in crime that is prevalent in society today has been documented within the Batman books. With urban society becoming increasingly violent, Batman's methods in combating crime have changed accordingly. The Batman is not an idealistic role model, but rather a warrior fighting a never-ending battle. *3*

The major differences between Superman and Batman revolve around the former's benevolence and the latter's malevolence. Superman acts with restraint and exudes a noble, benevolent attitude. Criminals do not fear Superman because of his personality, but rather they fear his power. Batman, on the other hand, strikes fear into the criminal element with his methods and obvious modus operandi: the dark, threatening bat. Criminals are afraid of Batman simply because they don't know what he will do if he apprehends them. This psychological factor is employed by the Batman because of his vulnerability. Fear makes the criminal sloppy, and that sloppiness makes it much easier for the Batman to apprehend him. Because of Superman's obvious invincibility, he does not bother with such tactics. Also, because of Batman's methods, he is not much of a team player. He would much rather work alone than with a group of his fellow costumed heroes. Superman, however, enjoys working with, and sometimes leading, his fellow superheroes. He is a group player. The different personalities of these characters can be compared to day and night. *4*

Superman and Batman have both survived for over 50 years. The reason for 5
their longevity can be simply explained. Each was a pioneer character in the comic book medium. Superman showed readers that a man could fly. Batman showed them that being human isn't all that bad. The influence of each character on American culture will help both heroes survive at least another 50 years.

Like Mother Like Daughter

My mother died of cancer when I was 19 years old. She suffered a slow, painful 1
death, and the final five years of her life were devastating to me. Having been the youngest of her four children, it was I who remained at home to do the housekeeping chores, plan and prepare meals, and just give her care and support when necessary. I felt resentful that my teenage years were marred by that feeling of being trapped at home. On the other hand, I never questioned the fact that it was my responsibility to be there when she needed me. The feelings of sadness, guilt, and denial completely overshadowed any fond, happy memories I had for my mother during the years I was growing up and she was healthy. It was not until seven years following her death that my attitude toward my mother changed.

By this time I was married and the mother of two sons. I was hosting a fam- 2
ily reunion—my brother and his family came from California, and my two sisters and their families arrived from New York and New Jersey. There were fourteen of us living together at my house for two whole weeks, and although chaos prevailed, I loved being together.

To prevent the children from becoming bored, we kept busy picnicking, 3
swimming, playing tennis, and visiting relatives. Then one evening, my brother and I were alone. We were reminiscing about the fact that I was only 6 years old when he left home for college and that he never really knew me. He looked at me and said, "I want you to know that you are more like Mom than Ruth and Rose will ever be." He pointed out that I was functioning as a mother and a homemaker exactly as she did. It was like opening a door to my past, and the more we talked, the more I realized that my mother gave me more love and direction than I could ever give back.

I began to remember the lessons I learned. She was the daughter of Italian 4
immigrants and had a total preoccupation with food. I was constantly at her side licking cake batter, rolling pie dough, stirring spaghetti sauce. When family or company visited, we seldom sat in her immaculate parlor; she ordered everyone to sit at the old chrome kitchen table while she perked fresh, steaming coffee. How remarkable that our friends today seem to gather in the kitchen rather than the family room. Could it be that I lead them there?

To my mother, food was the symbol of life. We were healthy to her because 5
we were fat! I too push food in front of my family; if company arrives, I head for the refrigerator. How I envy my skinny friends who can fast all day while I have to eat breakfast by 8:30.

My mother taught me respect for food. I can still hear her preach, "Eat, eat . . . think of those poor children in India who don't have food!" How ironic that I have repeated those same words to my sons as they rush from the table with plates half-full. To this day, I cannot bear to see food wasted. 6

Thrift was a profound lesson that I learned. She managed my father's paycheck from the mill better than any banker. She took me to sales and clearances and taught me to bargain-hunt. How remarkable that I rarely pay full retail price for clothing or merchandise today. 7

Finally, the most important trait my mother shared with me was a warmth and loyalty to family. Her only job in life was to keep house and care for her family. And even though I am pursuing an education and career now, I will never regret staying home with my family when they were babies and young children. Although my children never knew their grandmother, I have kept her memory alive without being consciously aware that I did. 8

Running the Distance

My daughters, Laura and Jennifer, ran with the Columbiana High School Cross Country Team. Although they both had determination and devotion, their training techniques, running styles, and attitudes toward spectators were quite different. 1

During training, Laura developed a vigorous stretching routine which she used before each meet. She made adjustments in her running position to help increase her speed, such as leaning forward when running uphill. Since she wore out easily, she went to bed earlier and watched her diet. She ate balanced meals and believed that a steak dinner was the best meal to have the evening before a meet. 2

Laura's running style was a pleasure to watch. Her short frame seemed to be made for running. She looked like a thoroughbred horse gracefully running the course. Her legs stretched out as she made strong, even strides. She paced herself so she could, at just the right moment, begin to speed up for her big sprint to the finish. Since she never seemed to sweat, she appeared to still have energy after crossing the finish line. 3

Laura thrived on the spectators' cheers. The encouragement she received from the crowd motivated her to try harder. She always wanted people positioned along the course to cheer for her and to give her instructions. The coach would run back and forth across the course to give her tips during the race. Her best running time was when the entire boy's team went from point to point along the course and cheered for her from start to finish. 4

Jennifer's approach to running was totally different. While she was training, her stretching routine was kept at the bare minimum, and she made few adjustments in her running position. She never went to bed early. When she was hungry, her stomach came before her runner's diet. For example, when a county meet 5 was delayed because of rain, she filled her empty stomach with greasy french fries. Spaghetti was her ideal meal the night before a meet.

Since Jennifer had runner's knee, her running style was far from graceful. Her entire body seemed to be fighting her determination to run. The agonizing pain of each step could be seen in her distorted face. She wore a sweat band around her head to keep the perspiration from streaming into her eyes. With each stride of her long, slender legs, her feet appeared to plop heavily to the ground. Jennifer's speed only varied slightly during a race. Although she was never able to sprint, it was evident that she gave all she had to the race. After she crossed the finish line, her body would collapse to the ground in gruelling pain. When describing her running, her younger brother Kurt jokingly commented, "When Jennifer runs, she looks like a dog with two legs. And those two legs have cement blocks on them." 6

Since the cheering spectators interfered with Jennifer's concentration, she preferred to run without onlookers. She made me aware of this preference at her first cross-country meet. As she ran past me, I cheered, "Come on Jennifer!" While still running, she turned and looked at me with glaring eyes. She snapped, "You get out here and try it!" After the meet, she informed me that I could continue to come to the meets if I promised never to cheer for her. 7

Although their training techniques, running styles, and attitudes toward spectators differed, each daughter received awards and trophies for her efforts. Along with acknowledgments for devotion, Laura was recognized for her speed and Jennifer for her determination. 8

The Reality Trip of Soap Operas

Imagine a place where the economy is good, people are rich, and the sun always shines. There are beautifully landscaped mansions where the richer of the rich live and penthouses where expensive works of art decorate the walls where the less fortunate live. Everyone is friends with everyone, but they are all out to get someone. The people of this place are immortal; they can get stabbed, blown up, shot, and buried alive, but they are always ready to take on more punishment on the next day's episode. The people who do die always come back two months down the road. Well, if you can imagine this place, welcome to the fantasy world of soap operas. 1

The family structure of soap operas isn't even close to the reality of the real world. Soaps contain whole families; by that I mean a mother, father, 2.5 children, and a dog. There are hardly ever any divorces, and if there are, the mother and father are still friends. The soap opera families have butlers and maids to wait on them anytime of the day. At dinner the whole family sits down to eat together. They say grace, and then get served dinner by the hired hands. 2

Now let's take a trip to reality. In one home there is the mother and 2.5 children; in another there is the father and the dog if he's lucky. The divorce rate is 3 approximately 51 percent, and the mother and father never get along. The only person who could afford a butler or maid in this economy is Ross Perot. At dinner, the members of the real life family prepare their own meal, they never say grace, and the only time anybody gets served is after they're asked, "Hi, welcome to McDonalds. My name is Kim. How can I help you?"

Another unrealistic feature is the way soap operas portray death. A widow just gets home from burying her husband and finds his watch on the living room endtable. There is only complete silence. She cries, "This is John's watch. He was buried with it on!" Then the faint sound of music can be heard in the background while the announcer in a deep voice tells you, "Tune in Monday to see if John is still alive, or if somebody is playing a cruel joke." Nobody ever dies in soaps; even if you witness the person take a last breath on an operating table and the doctors try to save him, you can bet that two months down the road that that person will come back to the show. 4

In the land of today, a grieving widow who finds her husband's watch on the endtable is going to do one of two things. She will either sell the watch for the dough, or she will sue the funeral home for not following her instructions. 5

Another irritating part of the soap opera is the "long-lost relative syndrome." That is when a man is hanging from a skyscraper by one hand and is pleading for mercy to the person who pushed him off the building. 6

"Help me, please!" 7

"Why should I?" 8

(The stunning sound of the orchestra can be heard.) 9

"Because I'm your father!" 10

"How can that be?" In disbelief, "My father died when I was two years old." 11

"I left your mother," the hanging man screams, "and she told you I died." 12

The person starts to pull the father up but looses the grip. The father screams as he plummets to an unruly death. Don't worry, he isn't dead. Remember, they never are. He will show up on next week's show, and everybody will live happily ever after. 13

Time to wake up and smell the coffee. If a man was hanging from a skyscraper and screamed to the person who pushed him that he was that person's father, that person would most likely laugh in the man's face and then step on his fingers to make him fall. It's true folks, there are psychos out there who would do that. Isn't reality scary? 14

Becoming a Reliable Critic by Evaluating Writing

With some classmates, form a group and select one of the previous student essays to evaluate (or use one your instructor assigns). Designate a recorder to take down the group's conclusions and a spokesperson to report those conclusions to the class. If you like, you can use the following evaluation questions to help you assess the essay's chief strengths and weaknesses.

Evaluation Questions

1. The Thesis
   Does the thesis, stated or implied, note the subjects and whether comparison, contrast, or both will occur? Is there a logical basis for comparing or contrasting the subjects?
2. The Introduction
   What do you think of the opening? Does it engage your interest?
3. Supporting Details
   Note any points you do not understand, any that are not relevant, or any that require additional support. Are the same points discussed for both subjects?
4. Organization
   How is the detail arranged? Is this the best organization to use? Evaluate the use of transitions and topic sentences to help the reader move from subject to subject and point to point.
5. The Conclusion
   Does the essay come to a satisfying end? Explain.
6. Overview
   What do you like best about the essay? What is the single most important revision the author should make?

Essay Topics: Comparison-Contrast

1. Write an essay that compares and/or contrasts two books, television shows, or movies that have similar themes.
2. Contrast the styles of two athletes who play the same sport.
3. Select two entertainers, movies, television shows, or songs and use comparison and/or contrast to reveal how they reflect the values of two different groups of people or the climates of two periods of time. For example, contrast *Leave It to Beaver* and *The Simpsons* to show that the former reflects the fifties and the latter reflects the nineties.
4. A fable is a story, written in a simple style, with a moral or lesson. Write a fable in the style of Carson's "A Fable for Tomorrow" in which you compare and/or contrast life as it is today with life as it would be if population growth continued unchecked, if the unemployment rate continued to climb, or if some other problem continued unresolved. Begin your fable, as Carson does, with "There was once." Be sure some moral or lesson is apparent.
5. Compare and/or contrast life as it is today with life as it would be without some modern fact of life, such as the car, the telephone, antibiotics, professional or collegiate football, airplanes, computers, alarm clocks, etc. Be careful not to dwell on the obvious.
6. Compare and/or contrast the way you view something or someone now with the way you did when you were a child.

7. Compare and/or contrast two magazine ads or two television commercials for the same kind of product (wine, cigarettes, cars, jeans, cold remedies, etc.).
8. Like Suzanne Britt (see page 234), compare and/or contrast neat people and sloppy people. However, use humor to show the superiority of neat people.
9. Compare and/or contrast two celebrations of the same holiday (Halloween, Thanksgiving, New Year's Eve, etc.).
10. Compare and/or contrast the way men and women approach a particular situation (shopping, dating, friendship, cleaning, etc.).
11. Compare and/or contrast two people you enjoy who have very different outlooks on life. Try to determine why both people appeal to you.
12. Compare and/or contrast two ways to do something difficult (diet, quit smoking, save money, raise your grades, offer criticism, etc.).
13. Compare and/or contrast two people you admire for their success.
14. Compare and/or contrast the way some group of people (working women, teachers, doctors, fathers, police officers, children, etc.) is depicted on television with the way that group is in reality.
15. Compare and/or contrast two restaurants.
16. Compare and/or contrast two vacations you have had. Be sure to find a focus. You cannot discuss everything about both vacations.
17. Compare and/or contrast two cities you have spent time in. Be sure to find a focus; you cannot discuss everything about both cities.
18. Compare and/or contrast the way you thought something would be with the way it actually turned out to be.
19. Compare and/or contrast what advertisements say about some products with the way these products actually are and the way they actually perform. For example, does using a certain toothpaste really guarantee white teeth and romance?
20. Compare and/or contrast the way problems are solved on soap operas with the way they are solved in real life. (Or compare and/or contrast some other feature of soap operas with the same feature in real life.)

Thematic Topics

1. In "A Fable for Tomorrow" (page 229), Rachel Carson points out that we are destroying our environment. "Fable" first appeared in Carson's *Silent Spring* in 1962. Do you think our treatment of the environment has improved since the essay was written? Cite specific examples to support your view.
2. In "Columbus and the Moon" (page 231), Tom Wolfe writes about space exploration. Do you think the money spent on the space program should go elsewhere? Why or why not?
3. Explain what it means to be a writer for someone about to enter a freshman writing course. Draw on your own experience and any one or more of the following essays for details: "Ross and Tom" (page 236), "How I

Wrote 'Fat Chance' " (page 88), "The Watcher at the Gates" (page 86) and "What Is Writer's Block?" (page 283).

Writing Strategies

As you write your comparison-contrast essay and experiment to improve your writing process, you may find some of the following strategies helpful. In addition, you may wish to try some of the techniques described in Chapters 1 to 3.

Topic Selection

Consider discussing the similarities between two things generally thought of as different or the contrasts between two things generally viewed as similar. For example, an essay noting the differences between getting a degree and getting an education could clarify the real essence of education, despite the fact that "getting a degree" is commonly equated with "getting an education." Similarly, an essay discussing the similarities between eccentricity and genius, two very different states in many ways, could foster greater understanding of one or both of these. Be sure your comparisons or contrasts are valid and useful. While it is possible to compare studying for an exam with preparing for war, this would have little use beyond an exercise in ingenuity.

Idea Generation

1. List writing can be particularly helpful for generating ideas. Make two lists, one with every similarity you can think of, and the second with every difference. At this point, write everything that occurs to you without evaluating the worth of anything.
2. When you have completed your lists, circle each comparison that you find particularly meaningful or interesting, and do the same for the contrasts.
3. If you are not certain whether to treat similarities or differences, or both, consider the ideas in your lists. However, do not think that if you have circled more similarities than differences that it is obviously similarities you should deal with. Take some time to consider whether the differences lead to the more significant conclusion.

Outlining

Even if you do not customarily outline, you may find that outlining makes organizing comparison-contrast easier. You may even want to outline your draft *after* it is written to check for balance.

Reader Response

If you like to secure reader response before revising, see page 77. In addition, ask your reader to place a checkmark any place where the movement from subject to subject or point to point seems abrupt. (Consider adding transitions and topic sentences here.) Also ask your reader to place a checkmark any place where an idea is unclear.

REVISION CHECKLIST

In addition to the checklist on page 80, you can use this checklist for revising your comparison-contrast.

1. Is there a logical basis for comparing or contrasting your subjects? Is it clear what your subjects are?
2. Does your comparison-contrast do one of the following?
   a. Clarify something unknown or not well understood
   b. Lead to a fresh insight or a new way of viewing something
   c. Bring one or both of the subjects into sharper focus
   d. Show that one subject is better than the other
3. Does your thesis present the subjects and indicate whether you are comparing, contrasting, or both?
4. Have you discussed the same points for both subjects?
5. Have you used a point-by-point or subject-by-subject pattern to best advantage?
6. Have you used transitions and topic sentences to help your reader move from point to point and subject to subject?

CHAPTER 10

Cause-and-Effect Analysis

A cause-and-effect analysis examines why an event or action occurred (the causes) or what resulted from the event or action (the effects), or both. We engage in cause-and-effect analysis regularly because it helps us make sense of the world. For example, cause-and-effect analysis can help us understand the past if we identify the causes of the stock market crash in 1929 and go on to determine how that event affected our country and its people. Cause-and-effect analysis can also help us look to the future. For example, we might predict the effects of the current air pollution rate on the quality of life 20 years from now.

PURPOSE AND AUDIENCE

A cause-and-effect analysis can inform. For example, to inform your reader, you could explain what causes leaves to change color in autumn, or you could explain the effects of divorce on teenagers.

A cause-and-effect analysis can also persuade. For example, you could explain the causes of teenage alcoholism to persuade your reader to address those causes, or you could explain the effects of too much television to convince parents to limit their children's viewing time.

A cause-and-effect analysis can even let the writer share. For example, if you write about how your parents' divorce affected you, your purpose could be to share your feelings and experiences. Similarly, if you write about what caused you to join the band, your purpose might also be to share feelings and experiences.

To establish a purpose for your cause-and-effect analysis, you can answer these questions.

1. Can I inform my reader of something?
2. Can I persuade my reader to think or act a certain way?
3. Can I share my feelings or experiences with a reader?

To identify an audience for your cause-and-effect analysis, answer these questions.

1. Who would be interested in my cause-and-effect analysis?
2. Who could learn something from my cause-and-effect analysis?
3. Who could the cause-and-effect analysis persuade to think or act a certain way?
4. Who would I like to share my feelings or experiences with?

SELECTING DETAIL

When you select detail for a cause-and-effect analysis, remember to identify *underlying* causes and effects. For example, if you are examining the causes of the high divorce rate, you might note the increase in two-career marriages. This would be an obvious cause. However, a closer examination of this cause would reveal underlying causes. Two-career marriages mean less clearly defined roles, less clearly defined divisions of labor, added job-related stress, and increased competition between partners. If you are discussing effects, then you should be on the lookout for underlying effects. For example, say you are examining the effects of being the youngest child in a family. One obvious effect is that the youngest is considered "the baby." Look beyond that obvious effect, and you can discover underlying effects: The youngest can come to view himself or herself as the baby and hence less capable, less mature, and less strong; the youngest, viewed as a baby, may not be taken seriously by other family members.

Many cause-and-effect relationships are part of causal chains. A **causal chain** occurs when a cause leads to an effect and that effect becomes a cause which leads to another effect and that effect becomes a cause leading to another effect, and so on. To understand causal chains, consider the effects of raising the cost of a stamp.

First the government raises the price of a postage stamp. What is the effect? Once the cost of the stamp goes up, it costs more to mail a letter. That is the first effect. This effect becomes a cause: it causes business expenses to rise for companies. What is the effect of this cause? The cost of doing business increases. This effect becomes a cause: it causes companies to raise the prices on their goods and services. What is the effect? Consumers cannot afford the increase, so they buy less. This effect becomes a cause: it causes the economy to slow down. Causal chains like this one are often part of a cause-and-effect analysis.

One way to develop detail for a cause-and-effect analysis is to think of each cause and effect as a generalization to support with adequate detail (see page 42 on supporting generalizations). Sometimes an illustration will do this. For example, say you are explaining the effects of moving to a new town when you were in seventh grade, and one of those effects was that you felt like an outsider. You could illustrate this point with the example of the time no one wanted to sit with you at lunch.

You can also use description. For example, if you are discussing the effects of dumping industrial waste into rivers, you can describe the appearance of a river that has had industrial waste dumped into it.

Narration can also appear in a cause-and-effect analysis. Say you are explaining why more women than men suffer from math anxiety, and you note that females are often told that they are not as good at math as males. To support this point, you can tell the story of the time your seventh-grade guidance counselor told you not to take algebra because you were a girl.

Another way to support a cause or effect generalization is with process analysis. For example, assume you are explaining the long-term effects of using pesticides, and you mention that pesticides work their way into the food chain. To support this point, you could describe the process whereby the pesticide goes from soil to plant to animal to human.

Sometimes explaining why or how something is a cause or effect is necessary. For example, assume that you state that one effect of divorce on young children is to make them feel responsible for the breakup of their parents' marriage. You should go on to explain why: young children think that if they had behaved better, their parents would not have fought as much and would have stayed married.

Sometimes a cause-and-effect analysis must explain that something is *not* a cause or effect. For example, say you are explaining the causes of math anxiety among women. If many people believe women are genetically incapable of excelling in math and you know this is not the case, then you should note this fact. You may also go on to explain *why* this is not true: No studies to date have proved that anyone is genetically good or bad at mathematics.

When you are generating ideas for a cause-and-effect analysis, remember that something that happens before an event cannot always be taken as the cause of that event. Thus, if you wash the car and then it rains, you cannot assume that washing a car causes rain.

ARRANGING DETAIL

The detail for a cause-and-effect analysis can be arranged a number of ways. Often a progressive order is used. In this case, the most significant or obvious causes or effects are given first, and the writer works progressively to the least significant or obvious causes or effects. You can also move from the least significant or obvious to the most significant or obvious.

A chronological arrangement is possible if the causes or effects occur in a particular time order. If you are reproducing causal chains, a chronological order is likely since one cause will lead to effects and other causes that occur in a particular time sequence. When reproducing causal chains, get the sequence of causes and effects in the correct order.

Sometimes you will group causes and effects in particular categories. For example, say you are explaining what causes high school students to drop out of school. You could group together all the causes related to home life, then group together all the causes related to peer pressure, and then group together all the causes related to academic environment.

The introduction of a cause-and-effect analysis can be handled in any of the ways described in Chapter 2. Another approach is to explain why understanding the cause-and-effect relationship is important. For example, if you want to provide reasons for adolescent drug abuse, your introduction could note that understanding the reasons for the problem is an important first step toward solving the problem.

If your essay will treat the causes of a problem, your introduction can provide a summary of the chief effects. For example, say you will explain why fewer people are entering the teaching profession. Your introduction can note some of the chief effects of this phenomenon: fewer qualified teachers, a decline in the quality of education, and larger class sizes. Similarly, if your essay will explain the effects of something, your introduction can note the chief causes. For example, if your essay will discuss the effects of increased tuition fees at your school, your introduction can briefly explain the causes of the increase: lower enrollment generating less income, higher operating costs, an expensive building program.

A suitable thesis for a cause-and-effect analysis can indicate the relationship to be analyzed. It can also note whether causes or effects, or both, will be treated. Here are some examples.

> `If we are to solve the problem of teenage drug abuse, we must first understand what leads teenagers to take drugs.` (This thesis notes that the essay will analyze the causes of drug use among teenagers.)
>
> `Not everyone realizes the subtle yet devastating effects unemployment has on a person's self-image.` (This thesis notes that the essay will analyze the effects of unemployment on self-image.)
>
> `The reasons Congress is cutting aid to the homeless are clear, but the effects of this action are less well understood.` (This thesis notes that the essay will treat both the causes and effects of cuts in aid to the homeless.)

The conclusion of a cause-and-effect analysis can be handled in any of the ways described in Chapter 2. Often a cause-and-effect analysis ends with a conclusion drawn from the cause-and-effect relationship. For example, if your essay has shown what the causes of teenage drug abuse are, your essay could end with a conclusion drawn about the best way to combat the problem. A summary can also be an effective way to end. If the cause-and-effect relationship is complex, with several causal chains, your reader may appreciate a final reminder.

TRYOUT To gain experience discovering causes and effects, try this. Pick an important decision you made sometime in your life (quitting the football team, choosing a college, joining the army, moving away from home, and so forth). Make one list of everything that caused you to make your decision. Then make a second list of all the effects of your decision. Finally, try to identify one causal chain and list every cause and effect in that chain.

PROFESSIONAL ESSAYS

Why Marriages Fail

Anne Roiphe

Novelist Anne Roiphe wrote "Why Marriages Fail" for Family Weekly *magazine. Her examination of what causes marriages to fail also speaks to ways couples can save their marriages.*

These days so many marriages end in divorce that our most sacred vows no longer ring with truth. "Happily ever after" and "Till death do us part" are expressions that seem on the way to becoming obsolete. Why has it become so hard for couples to stay together? What goes wrong? What has happened to us that close to one-half of all marriages are destined for the divorce courts? How could we have created a society in which 42 percent of our children will grow up in single-parent homes? If statistics could only measure loneliness, regret, pain, loss of self-confidence and fear of the future, the numbers would be beyond quantifying. 1

Even though each broken marriage is unique, we can still find the common perils, the common causes for marital despair. Each marriage has crisis points and each marriage tests endurance, the capacity for both intimacy and change. Outside pressures such as job loss, illness, infertility, trouble with a child, care of aging parents and all the other plagues of life hit marriage the way hurricanes blast our shores. Some marriages survive these storms and others don't. Marriages fail, however, not simply because of the outside weather but because the inner climate becomes too hot or too cold, too turbulent or too stupefying. 2

When we look at how we choose our partners and what expectations exist at the tender beginnings of romance, some of the reasons for disaster become quite clear. We all select with unconscious accuracy a mate who will recreate with us the emotional patterns of our first homes. Dr. Carl A. Whitaker, a marital therapist and emeritus professor of psychiatry at the University of Wisconsin, explains, "From early childhood on, each of us carried models for marriage, femininity, masculinity, motherhood, fatherhood and all the other family roles." Each of us falls in love with a mate who has qualities of our parents, who will help us redis- 3 cover both the psychological happiness and miseries of our past lives. We may think we have found a man unlike Dad, but then he turns to drink or drugs, or loses his job over and over again or sits silently in front of the T.V. just the way Dad did. A man may choose a woman who doesn't like kids just like his mother or who gambles away the family savings just like his mother. Or he may choose a slender wife who seems unlike his obese mother but then turns out to have other addictions that destroy their mutual happiness.

A man and a woman bring to their marriage bed a blended concoction of conscious and unconscious memories of their parents' lives together. The human way is to compulsively repeat and recreate the patterns of the past. Sigmund Freud so well described the unhappy design that many of us get trapped in: the unmet needs of childhood, the angry feelings left over from frustrations of long ago, the limits of trust and the recurrence of old fears. Once an individual senses this entrapment, there may follow a yearning to escape, and the result could be a broken, splintered marriage. 4

Of course people can overcome the habits and attitudes that developed in childhood. We all have hidden strengths and amazing capacities for growth and creative change. Change, however, requires work—observing your part in a rotten pattern, bringing difficulties out into the open—and work runs counter to the basic myth of marriage: "When I wed this person all my problems will be over. I will have achieved success and I will become the center of life for this other person and this person will be my center, and we will mean everything to each other forever." This myth, which every marriage relies on, is soon exposed. The coming of children, the pulls and tugs of their demands on affection and time, place a considerable strain on that basic myth of meaning everything to each other, of merging together and solving all of life's problems. 5

Concern and tension about money take each partner away from the other. Obligations to demanding parents or still-depended-upon parents create further strain. Couples today must also deal with all the cultural changes brought on in recent years by the women's movement and the sexual revolution. The altering of roles and the shifting of responsibilities have been extremely trying for many marriages. 6

These and other realities of life erode the visions of marital bliss the way sandstorms eat at rock and the ocean nibbles away at the dunes. Those euphoric, grand feelings that accompany romantic love are really self-delusions, self-hypnotic dreams that enable us to forge a relationship. Real life, failure at work, disappointments, exhaustion, bad smells, bad colds and hard times all puncture the dream and leave us stranded with our mate, with our childhood patterns pushing us this way and that, with our unfulfilled expectations. 7

The struggle to survive in marriage requires adaptability, flexibility, genuine love and kindness and an imagination strong enough to feel what the other is feeling. Many marriages fall apart because either partner cannot imagine what the other wants or cannot communicate what he or she needs or feels. Anger builds until it erupts into a volcanic burst that buries the marriage in ash. 8

It is not hard to see, therefore, how essential communication is for a good marriage. A man and a woman must be able to tell each other how they feel and 9 why they feel the way they do; otherwise they will impose on each other roles and actions that lead to further unhappiness. In some cases, the communication patterns of childhood—of not talking, of talking too much, of not listening, of distrust and anger, of withdrawal—spill into the marriage and prevent a healthy exchange of thoughts and feelings. The answer is to set up new patterns of communication and intimacy.

At the same time, however, we must see each other as individuals. "To achieve a balance between separateness and closeness is one of the major psychological tasks of all human beings at every stage of life," says Dr. Stuart Bartle, a psychiatrist at the New York University Medical Center. *10*

If we sense from our mate a need for too much intimacy, we tend to push him or her away, fearing that we may lose our identities in the merging of marriage. One partner may suffocate the other partner in a childlike dependency. *11*

A good marriage means growing as a couple but also growing as individuals. This isn't easy. Richard gives up his interest in carpentry because his wife, Helen, is jealous of the time he spends away from her. Karen quits her choir group because her husband dislikes the friends she makes there. Each pair clings to each other and are angry with each other as life closes in on them. This kind of marital balance is easily thrown as one or the other pulls away and divorce follows. *12*

Sometimes people pretend that a new partner will solve the old problems. Most often extramarital sex destroys a marriage because it allows an artificial split between the good and the bad—the good is projected on the new partner and the bad is dumped on the head of the old. Dishonesty, hiding and cheating create walls between men and women. Infidelity is just a symptom of trouble. It is a symbolic complaint, a weapon of revenge, as well as an unraveler of closeness. Infidelity is often that proverbial last straw that sinks the camel to the ground. *13*

All right—marriage has always been difficult. Why then are we seeing so many divorces at this time? Yes, our modern social fabric is thin, and yes the permissiveness of society has created unrealistic expectations and thrown the family into chaos. But divorce is so common because people today are unwilling to exercise the self-discipline that marriage requires. They expect easy joy, like the entertainment on TV, the thrill of a good party. *14*

Marriage takes some kind of sacrifice, not dreadful self-sacrifice of the soul, but some level of compromise. Some of one's fantasies, some of one's legitimate desires have to be given up for the value of the marriage itself. "While all marital partners feel shackled at times it is they who really choose to make the marital ties into confining chains or supporting bonds," says Dr. Whitaker. Marriage requires sexual, financial and emotional discipline. A man and a woman cannot follow every impulse, cannot allow themselves to stop growing or changing. *15*

Divorce is not an evil act. Sometimes it provides salvation for people who have grown hopelessly apart or were frozen in patterns of pain or mutual unhappiness. Divorce can be, despite its initial devastation, like the first cut of the surgeon's knife, a step toward new health and a good life. On the other hand, if the partners can stay past the breaking up of the romantic myths into the develop- *16* ment of real love and intimacy, they have achieved a work as amazing as the greatest cathedrals of the world. Marriages that do not fail but improve, that persist despite imperfections, are not only rare these days but offer a wondrous shelter in which the face of our mutual humanity can safely show itself.

Questions on Technique

1. What are the two earliest clues that Roiphe will examine causes?
2. Which sentence is Roiphe's thesis? What words indicate that the author will discuss causes?
3. Which paragraphs begin with topic sentences that present a cause to be examined?
4. Which two paragraphs support a cause-and-effect generalization with examples?
5. How does Roiphe use process analysis to examine a cause of marital failure?
6. In which paragraphs does Roiphe explain *why* something is a cause? Is this detail important to developing the thesis? Explain.
7. In paragraph 13, Roiphe offers infidelity as an *obvious* cause of marital failure. Does she also offer an *underlying* cause? Explain.
8. Roiphe's essay concludes on a positive note. She says that divorce can be healthy and that marriages that survive are a "wondrous shelter." Why do you think she ends in such an upbeat way?
9. Roiphe's original audience was the readers of *Family Weekly* magazine. For what purpose do you think she wrote her essay for this audience?

For Group Discussion or Journal Writing

Study paragraph 14 and consider to what extent you agree or disagree with Roiphe's explanation for the current increase in the divorce rate.

It Is Time to Stop Playing Indians

Arlene B. Hirschfelder

Arlene Hirschfelder, a staff member of the Association on American Indian Affairs and a longtime advocate of Native American rights, examines the detrimental effects of using Indian symbols for merchandising, holiday images, and sports mascots.

It is predictable. At Halloween, thousands of children trick-or-treat in Indian costumes. At Thanksgiving, thousands of children parade in school pageants wearing plastic headdresses and pseudobuckskin clothing. Thousands of card shops stock Thanksgiving greeting cards with images of cartoon animals wearing feathered headbands. Thousands of teachers and librarians trim bulletin boards with Anglo- 1 featured, feathered Indian boys and girls. Thousands of gift shops load their shelves with Indian figurines and jewelry.

Fall and winter are also the seasons when hundreds of thousands of sports fans root for professional, college and public school teams with names that summon up Indians—"Braves," "Redskins," "Chiefs." (In New York State, one out of eight junior and senior high school teams call themselves "Indians," "Tomahawks" and the like.) War-whooping team mascots are imprinted on school uniforms, postcards, notebooks, tote bags and car floor mats. 2

All of this seems innocuous: why make a fuss about it? Because these trappings and holiday symbols offend tens of thousands of other Americans—the Native American people. Because these invented images prevent millions of us from understanding the authentic Indian America, both long ago and today. Because this image-making prevents Indians from being a relevant part of the nation's social fabric. 3

Halloween costumes mask the reality of high mortality rates, high diabetes rates, high unemployment rates. They hide low average life spans, low per capita incomes and low educational levels. Plastic war bonnets and ersatz buckskin deprive people from knowing the complexity of Native American heritage—that Indians belong to hundreds of nations that have intricate social organizations, governments, languages, religions and sacred rituals, ancient stories, unique arts and music forms. 4

Thanksgiving school units and plays mask history. They do not tell how Europeans mistreated Wampanoags and other East Coast Indian peoples during the 17th century. Social studies units don't mention that, to many Indians, Thanksgiving is a day of mourning, the beginning of broken promises, land theft, near extinction of their religions and languages at the hands of invading Europeans. 5

Athletic team nicknames and mascots disguise real people. Warpainted, buckskin-clad, feathered characters keep the fictitious Indian circulating on decals, pennants and team clothing. Toy companies mask Indian identity and trivialize sacred beliefs by manufacturing Indian costumes and headdresses, peace pipes and trick-arrow-through-the-head gags that equate Indianness with playtime. Indian figures equipped with arrows, guns and tomahawks give youngsters the harmful message that Indians favor mayhem. Many Indian people can tell about children screaming in fear after being introduced to them. 6

It is time to consider how these images impede the efforts of Indian parents and communities to raise their children with positive information about their heritage. It is time to get rid of stereotypes that, whether deliberately or inadvertently, denigrate Indian cultures and people. 7

It is time to bury the Halloween costumes, trick arrows, bulletin-board pinups, headdresses and mascots. It has been done before. In the 1970s, after student protests, Marquette University dropped its "Willie Wampum," Stanford University retired its mascot, "Prince Lightfoot," and Eastern Michigan University and Florida State modified their savage-looking mascots to reduce criticism. 8

It is time to stop playing Indians. It is time to abolish Indian images that sell merchandise. It is time to stop offending Indian people whose lives are all too often filled with economic deprivation, powerlessness, discrimination and gross injustice. This time next year, let's find more appropriate symbols for the holiday and sports seasons. 9

Questions on Technique

1. For what purpose do you think Hirschfelder wrote "It Is Time to Stop Playing Indians"?
2. Hirschfelder examines the effects of "playing Indian." Why didn't she look at the causes of this behavior?
3. Which paragraph embodies the thesis of the essay?
4. Which paragraphs include examples? What purpose do these examples serve?
5. Paragraphs 4–7 cite the effects of using Indian images for athletic teams and holiday celebrations. Many effects are given, but none is developed in much detail. Why? Is the original audience a factor? Explain. (The essay first appeared in the Los Angeles *Times*.)
6. What is the effect of opening each of the last three paragraphs with "It is time"?

For Group Discussion or Journal Writing

Hirschfelder hopes that we can find "more appropriate symbols for the holiday and sports seasons" (paragraph 9). Make a list of possible symbols for each of the following: Halloween, Thanksgiving, a baseball or football team. Explain why the symbols are appropriate.

When Bright Girls Decide That Math Is "A Waste of Time"

Susan Jacoby

"When Bright Girls Decide That Math Is 'A Waste of Time'" first appeared in the New York Times *in 1983. In the essay, Susan Jacoby examines both the causes and effects of the tendency of females to avoid math and science courses.*

Susannah, a 16-year-old who has always been an A student in every subject from algebra to English, recently informed her parents that she intended to drop physics and calculus in her senior year of high school and replace them with a drama seminar and a work-study program. She expects a major in art or history in college, she explained, and "any more science or math will just be a waste of my time." 1

Her parents were neither concerned by nor opposed to her decision. "Fine, dear," they said. Their daughter is, after all, an outstanding student. What does it matter if, at age 16, she has taken a step that may limit her understanding of both machines and the natural world for the rest of her life? 2

This kind of decision, in which girls turn away from studies that would give them a sure footing in the world of science and technology, is a self-inflicted female disability that is, regrettably, almost as common today as it was when I was in high school. If Susannah had announced that she had decided to stop taking English in her senior year, her mother and father would have been horrified. I also think they would have been a good deal less sanguine about her decision if she were a boy. 3

In saying that scientific and mathematical ignorance is a self-inflicted female wound, I do not, obviously, mean that cultural expectations play no role in the process. But the world does not conspire to deprive modern women of access to science as it did in the 1930's, when Rosalyn S. Yalow, the Nobel Prize–winning physicist, graduated from Hunter College and was advised to go to work as a secretary because no graduate school would admit her to its physics department. The current generation of adolescent girls—and their parents, bred on old expectations about women's interests—are active conspirators in limiting their own intellectual development. 4

It is true that the proportion of young women in science-related graduate and professional schools, most notably medical schools, has increased significantly in the past decade. It is also true that so few women were studying advanced science and mathematics before the early 1970's that the percentage increase in female enrollment does not yet translate into large numbers of women actually working in science. 5

The real problem is that so many girls eliminate themselves from any serious possibility of studying science as a result of decisions made during the vulnerable period of midadolescence, when they are most likely to be influenced—on both conscious and subconscious levels—by the traditional belief that math and science are "masculine" subjects. 6

During the teen-age years the well-documented phenomenon of "math anxiety" strikes girls who never had any problem handling numbers during earlier schooling. Some men, too, experience this syndrome—a form of panic, akin to a phobia, at any task involving numbers—but women constitute the overwhelming majority of sufferers. The onset of acute math anxiety during the teen-age years is, as Stalin was fond of saying, "not by accident." 7

In adolescence girls begin to fear that they will be unattractive to boys if they are typed as "brains." Science and math epitomize unfeminine braininess in a way that, say, foreign languages do not. High-school girls who pursue an advanced interest in science and math (unless they are students at special institutions like the Bronx High School of Science where everyone is a brain) usually find that they are greatly outnumbered by boys in their classes. They are, therefore, intruding on male turf at a time when their sexual confidence, as well as that of the boys, is most fragile. 8

A 1981 assessment of female achievement in mathematics, based on research conducted under a National Institute for Education grant, found significant differences in the mathematical achievements of 9th and 12th graders. At age 13 girls were equal to or slightly better than boys in tests involving algebra, problem solving and spatial ability; four years later the boys had outstripped the girls. 9

It is not mysterious that some very bright high-school girls suddenly decide that math is "too hard" and "a waste of time." In my experience, self-sabotage of mathematical and scientific ability is often a conscious process. I remember deliberately pretending to be puzzled by geometry problems in my sophomore year in high school. A male teacher called me in after class and said, in a baffled tone, "I don't see how you can be having so much trouble when you got straight A's last year in my algebra class." 10

The decision to avoid advanced biology, chemistry, physics and calculus in high school automatically restricts academic and professional choices that ought to be wide open to anyone beginning college. At all coeducational universities women are overwhelmingly concentrated in the fine arts, social sciences and traditionally female departments like education. Courses leading to degrees in science- and technology-related fields are filled mainly by men. 11

In my generation, the practical consequences of mathematical and scientific illiteracy are visible in the large number of special programs to help professional women overcome the anxiety they feel when they are promoted into jobs that require them to handle statistics. 12

The consequences of this syndrome should not, however, be viewed in narrowly professional terms. Competence in science and math does not mean one is going to become a scientist or mathematician any more than competence in writing English means one is going to become a professional writer. Scientific and mathematical illiteracy—which has been cited in several recent critiques by panels studying American education from kindergarten through college—produces an incalculably impoverished vision of human experience. 13

Scientific illiteracy is not, of course, the exclusive province of women. In certain intellectual circles it has become fashionable to proclaim a willed, aggressive ignorance about science and technology. Some female writers specialize in ominous, uninformed diatribes against genetic research as a plot to remove control of childbearing from women, while some well-known men of letters proudly announce that they understand absolutely nothing about computers, or, for that matter, about electricity. This lack of understanding is nothing in which women or men ought to take pride. 14

Failure to comprehend either computers or chromosomes leads to a terrible sense of helplessness, because the profound impact of science on everyday life is evident even to those who insist they don't, won't, can't understand why the changes are taking place. At this stage of history women are more prone to such feelings of helplessness than men because the culture judges their ignorance less harshly and because women themselves acquiesce in that indulgence. 15

Since there is ample evidence of such feelings in adolescence, it is up to parents to see that their daughters do not accede to the old stereotypes about "mas- 16 culine" and "feminine" knowledge. Unless we want our daughters to share our intellectual handicaps, we had better tell them no, they can't stop taking mathematics and science at the ripe old age of 16.

Questions on Technique

1. What paragraphs form Jacoby's introduction? What is the thesis of the essay?
2. The introduction includes narration and illustration. What does each of these patterns of development contribute?
3. Does the essay treat causes or effects, or both?
4. What does Jacoby offer as the *obvious* cause of females' turning from math and science? What does she offer as the *underlying* causes?
5. Where does the explanation of effects begin? What does the author present as the effects of females' avoiding math and science?
6. What approach does Jacoby take to the conclusion?
7. Who do you judge to be the intended audience? What is Jacoby's purpose?

For Group Discussion or Journal Writing

A number of high schools with both male and female students are experimenting with same-sex math and science classes. One purpose of these classes is to give girls an opportunity to be "brainy" without concern for the boys in the class. Explain what you think of this arrangement and why you think as you do.

STUDENT ESSAYS TO READ AND EVALUATE

The following cause-and-effect analyses were written by students. They are of varying quality, but all have strengths and weaknesses. As you read these essays, identify their chief strong and weak points. This will help you become a reliable judge of writing so you can better decide how to revise. An evaluation exercise follows the student essays.

Athletes on Drugs: It's Not So Hard to Understand

On June 17, 1986, Len Bias, a basketball star from the University of Maryland, was the second pick in the National Basketball Association amateur draft. Bias had everything going for him; he was a 22-year-old kid about to become a millionaire and superstar. He was on top of the world (or so it seemed). Forty hours later Len Bias was dead—from an overdose of drugs. The Len Bias story is tragic, but it is just one of the many cases that have surfaced recently. Just 8 days following the Bias tragedy, Cleveland Browns all-pro safety Don Rogers, then 23, 1 died of a drug overdose. Steve Howe, once a dazzling pitcher in the early 1980s, now finds himself out of baseball because of his drug problems. And the list goes on. Why? Why are professional athletes, people who have money, success, fame, and power, destroying their lives with drugs?

To most people the life of professional athletes is filled with glamour. All they see are the sports cars, the million-dollar contracts, and the adoring fans. People do not realize the mental anguish that is involved with being a professional athlete. The loneliness, the fear of failure, and the insecurities of their jobs are just a few of the pressures that athletes have to deal with every day. In some sports, such as baseball, basketball, and hockey, the teams play five to seven games a week, so the athletes must travel to two or three different cities. This constant travel has an adverse effect on athletes' ability to cope with daily pressures. They begin to miss family and friends, often becoming lonely and depressed. As an alternative to this depression, they turn to drugs. 2

In most cases, professional athletes of today have been the best in their sports since childhood. They have won honors and awards for their talents all through their lives. They have seldom been failures, and fear of becoming one is their worst nightmare. The athletes are surrounded by family, friends, and coaches who tell them they are the best. These people attempt to make the athletes feel flawless, incapable of making a mistake. Therefore, when players do have a bad day, they not only let themselves down but those people too. Again, in order to deal with the pressure, drugs become a solution. 3

For most of today's professional athletes, sports is all they know. Many do not have a college education, and, more than likely, without sports they would not have a career. Athletes must remain above the competition to keep their jobs. In some cases, when the God-given ability is not enough, the player uses drugs for improvement. Athletes have found that some drugs, such as amphetamines, can increase their physical abilities. These drugs help the athlete to perform better, therefore giving her or him a greater chance of success. For example, steroids have almost become a norm in some sports. Bodybuilders and football players have discovered that these drugs speed up the development of strength and muscles. In professional football, large numbers of offensive and defensive linemen claim to have used steroids at least once in their careers. Those professional athletes who refuse to use amphetamines and steroids are no doubt at a disadvantage. 4

In today's sports athletes are bigger, stronger, and faster; therefore, more injuries are occurring. Injuries are part of the game, and all players have suffered at least one in their careers. The most discomforting fact about injuries for professional athletes of today is not the pain but the drugs that are used to ease their discomfort. In many cases, coaches and trainers strongly encourage the use of such drugs. In the high-priced world of sports, time is money. Athletes cannot afford to sit out and allow their injuries to heal properly. They often turn to drugs to help speed up the healing process. Often these drugs are illegal; sometimes they are more dangerous than the injury itself, but for the athlete the use of the drug appears to be the only choice. Without the drugs, the players face the loss of thousands of dollars as well as their livelihoods. 5

The professional athlete has to deal with a great deal of pressure. As the mental struggles begin to mount and the aches and pains begin to multiply, the athlete becomes more susceptible to drug use. Drug use should never be accepted, but in the case of the professional athlete, condemning the problem will not solve it. The fans, owners, and especially the players themselves must reexamine the pressures and stop the drug problem before it destroys more people's lives. 6

Small but Mighty

"Adam Ant! Adam Ant!" I can still hear it echo through my head, a name that has plagued me my entire life. Ever since my youth, I was the smallest kid in class, and I couldn't do anything about it. I was born a midget. Well, maybe I wasn't a midget, but sometimes I felt like I was. 1

My height problem began even before I can remember. When I was four years old, I was able to enter kindergarten. My parents, being unsure of enrolling me because of my age, had taken me to a psychologist to get her opinion. I was scholastically ready for school. I could tie my shoes, I could recite the alphabet, I could distinguish the colors; I knew all the things I would learn in kindergarten. I also would have been a year and a half younger than all the others. Because of my height and age, the psychologist did not advise that I go. She was afraid my abilities would deteriorate if I was teased about my size. I didn't start until the next year. 2

In grade school, everyone was small, but I, of course, was the smallest. Back then I didn't worry much about it. If someone did tease me, I was told not to let it bother me because I would grow as I got older. I grew, but not as much as I expected to. Anyway, I was a normal kid. I played games, made fun of girls, and did all the usual stuff kids do. I was pretty popular in school, and I had a lot of friends, too. No one really made a big deal about my height because none of them were towering giants either. It wasn't until the fourth or fifth grade that my height really began to bother me. 3

I started to feel insecure about myself the first year I played football. I was on the pee-wees. Go figure! It was my coach who labeled me with the infamous name "Adam Ant." At first I laughed and paid no attention; it wasn't until the other kids started calling me it that I became bothered. I tried not to show that it bothered me. I just played a little harder. I decided that I would be the best no matter how small I was. I became a starter. That made me feel good. I also played baseball. Along with me came the name. I worked hard and made the All-Stars. I wanted to show everyone that I was not handicapped. 4

My height kept me from doing things that I liked. For instance, I didn't try out for the basketball team. I was only a freshman, a small freshman. I felt very insecure about myself, so I skipped it. 5

I was in the seventh grade when I tried to do something about my size. I knew that I couldn't make myself taller, so I decided to make myself bigger. 6

Bulkier, that is. A couple of friends and I began weight training. I was surprised at the amount of weight I could lift. At first, I wasn't very serious, but I was excited. It was something new to me.

After a couple of months, I could feel myself getting stronger and growing bigger. Other people also noticed. I'd hear things like, "Wow! You look huge" and "What's your mom feeding you?" This really helped build my confidence. No one talked about my height anymore. In fact, my height is kind of a blessing. Because I have a small frame, the muscle builds up more and I look like a monster. 7

I now realize that I was dubbed "Adam Ant" not only because of my height, but because I performed activities that were considered out of reach. 8

Modern Technology Solves a Family Dilemma

The gentle ring of the telephone was a welcome sound in my home. I would casually walk to the phone and cheerfully answer each call. As I picked up the receiver, I would curiously wonder who was calling. Thoughtful friends called with invitations to delightful gatherings or with news of some importance; that was ten years ago. 1

In the years that followed, my life changed considerably. I purchased a home and became the mother of three children. A ringing telephone was now a blaring noise that echoed off the screams of children. The phone ringing and a baby crying brought the condition to near dangerous decibel levels. 2

Getting to the telephone was no easy feat. An obstacle course was now in existence between myself and the receiver. After the children came home from school, I resembled an athlete at a track meet when I attempted to answer the phone. The first ring of the phone would signal the beginning of the event. The cheering crowd would then begin to holler, "Hurry, Mom, get the phone!" Hurdling over lunch boxes, toys and children, I would reach the phone just as it stopped ringing. 3

As the children grew older, their reaction time improved. The sound of the phone ringing would occasionally cause a stampede. From all corners of the house the race would begin to see who could successfully tackle the phone. My phone has survived what most quarterbacks could not endure. 4

My phone lines were now held hostage by telephone solicitors. They telephoned day and night concerned with the condition of my roof, windows, and doors. To their list of concerns they also added my childrens's needs. My children will not grow up illiterate if I purchase books, magazines, or speed reading courses that are guaranteed to teach the average baby to read in days. 5

Friends who telephoned were now greeted with a busy signal. In frustration, the telephone receiver was laid to rest on the kitchen counter. There it would remain for the better part of the day. It became apparent, after missing several important phone calls, that this problem needed a better solution. 6

Fortunately, technology had already discovered a solution to this problem. Its inventor is unknown to me, yet I am sure we have shared many of the same problems. The recent purchase of an answering machine has returned my home to the relaxed atmosphere it once knew. Calmly, my family sits and listens to the phone ring. In the background a faint voice can be heard saying, "We are unable to answer the phone. Please leave your message after the beep." 7

Friends at Work

You may have had experience with or heard statements about the disadvantages of having friends who suddenly become coworkers. Trust me; what you heard is correct. 1

Last spring I worked at a small but heavily trafficked truck stop. My boss decided to hire some new employees to increase the efficiency of the afternoon shift, so I recommended my friend Robert. Dreading the process of taking in numerous applications and granting endless interviews, my boss agreed to hire Robert. I was sure Robert was a good choice, so I was not anticipating any problems. 2

The first day with Robert started out smoothly. I discovered that he was a very hard worker and that he possessed the strength to unload delivery trucks and scrub the fuel islands, which I was unable to do. I knew the boss would be pleased. When the time arrived for Robert to work at the cashier's counter, however, his incompetency in that area overwhelmed me. At first, a few difficulties were to be expected until he became familiar with the routines. As the weeks passed, though, his progress was minimal, and I found myself answering his same questions over and over again. I stressed firmly but politely that he would have to concentrate harder and to interrupt my own customer relations less often. His efforts thereafter were admirable, but the more Robert worked on his own, the more mistakes he made; the situation was going out of control. 3

Robert was fired after the boss realized his incompatibility with the job. I felt sorry for Robert, but because of his mistakes (and the mistake of hiring him at all), I knew it would take awhile for me to redeem myself in the eyes of my employer. After all, I persuaded him to have the utmost confidence in Robert. 4

The opportunity to redeem myself came a few weeks later after more attempts to find competent help failed. I then discovered that my friend Joyce, who was presently working at a truck stop, would consider leaving her position for the higher-paying job on my shift. I convinced the supervisor that she would be much better for the job than Robert was since she was already familiar with truck stop procedures. To my surprise, my boss decided to take another chance with my recommendation. 5

Joyce and I worked well together and had fun doing our jobs. Our problems, however, started when we learned that the assistant manager was leaving and his position would be filled using one of the five cashiers. I assumed that I would be 6 considered because of my seniority over the others and my unblemished work record. To my extreme shock and dismay, I learned from Joyce that she was appointed to the job. "That's great," I muttered sarcastically. Apparently, she had developed a "relationship" with one of the regional supervisors, who requested the store manager to give her the promotion. I could not believe she accepted it—she knew that promotions were always granted on the basis of seniority. She certainly did not exhibit any special skills above and beyond mine, except of course with the regional supervisor.

When I confronted my boss about the unfair situation, he seemed not to be 7
concerned and figured that I would "get over it." He did not even satisfy me with an explanation of how the decision was made. I had difficulty understanding such callous disregard for my abilities and feelings. The following day, my letter of resignation was delivered.

The causes are not always the same, but the effects usually are: friends who 8
work together do not stay friends for long. I regret the strain on the friendships I had with two people, and I regret having to give up my job. But I should have known better.

Becoming a Reliable Critic by Evaluating Writing

Form a group and select one of the previous student essays (or use one your instructor assigns). Designate a recorder to take down the group's findings and a spokesperson to report those findings to the class. Then study the essay to identify its chief strengths and weaknesses. If you like, you can use the following evaluation questions to guide your work.

Evaluation Questions

1. The Thesis
   What is the thesis? If it does not indicate whether causes and/or effects will be discussed, should it?
2. The Introduction
   Does the introduction engage your interest? Why or why not?
3. Supporting Details
   Note any points you do not understand, any points that are not relevant, and any points that need more development. Is there a faithful reproduction of causal chains? If necessary, does the author explain something that is *not* a cause or effect? If necessary, does the author explain why or how something is a cause or effect?
4. Organization
   Are all the details in an easy-to-follow, logical order? Evaluate the use of transitions and topic sentences.
5. The Conclusion
   Does the essay come to a satisfying end? Explain.

6. Sentence Effectiveness and Word Choice
   Note any places where sentence variety is needed. Note any places where the author should revise to eliminate wordiness or clichés. Is the diction simple, yet specific?
7. Overview
   What do you like best about the essay? What is the single most important revision the author should make?

Essay Topics: Cause-and-Effect Analysis

1. Anne Roiphe (page 253) explains why marriages fail. Write an essay that explains why students fail.
2. If you avoided math and science in the way described by Susan Jacoby (page 258), consider the causes and effects of your avoidance. Or consider the causes and effects of avoiding some other subject.
3. Think back to your earlier school days and recall a traumatic event (not making the baseball team, losing a class election, breaking up with a girlfriend or boyfriend, failing a course, and so forth). Write an essay that analyzes the causes and/or effects of this event.
4. Analyze the effects of some recent innovation or invention such as the VCR, the compact disc player, the word processor, or video games.
5. Analyze the effects of a divorce on you or someone you know.
6. Analyze the effects of your association with a religious group, sorority or fraternity, ethnic group, theater group, or some other organization.
7. Analyze the causes and effects of a long-term friendship.
8. Identify a problem on your campus (inadequate housing, crowded classes, outdated requirements, high tuition, etc.) and analyze its causes and/or effects.
9. Explain why some college students drop out of school.
10. Analyze the causes and/or effects of a fear you have now or in the past.
11. Analyze the causes and/or effects of one of your bad habits.
12. Explain the effects college has had on your life.
13. Analyze the effects of television portrayals of some group (women, police officers, fathers, teenagers, doctors, etc.).
14. Explain the causes or effects of either racial or religious prejudice.
15. Explain how someone other than a family member (a teacher, scout leader, coach, neighbor, friend, etc.) has influenced your life.
16. Explain the long-term effects of a childhood experience.
17. If you or a family member has been unemployed, explain the effects of this unemployment.
18. Where we grow up has an enormous effect on who and what we become. How did where you grew up (big city, small town, farm, poor neighborhood, affluent suburb, etc.) affect you?
19. Explain how the way we dress affects how people perceive us.
20. Explain how television influences our view of the world.

Thematic Topics

1. Susan Jacoby wrote "When Bright Girls Decide That Math 'Is a Waste of Time' " (page 258) in 1983. Discuss to what extent things have or have not changed for girls since that time. Support your points with specific examples.
2. The student author of "Athletes on Drugs: It's Not So Hard to Understand" (page 261) explains why athletes turn to drugs. What do you think can be done to solve the problem? Describe a specific plan to address the issues in the student's essay and any other you find pertinent.
3. Drawing on your own ideas and those in "Athletes on Drugs: It's Not So Hard to Understand" (page 261), "Friends" (page 173), and "Why Drug Testing Is Needed" (page 321), explain what would be gained and what would be lost if we tested high school and college students for drug use.

Writing Strategies

In addition to the suggestions in Chapters 1 to 3, some of the following strategies may help with your cause-and-effect analysis.

Topic Selection

1. Think of something you do particularly well or particularly badly (run track, do math, make friends, play the piano, paint, etc.). Then consider why you do the thing well or badly and how your ability or lack of it has affected you.
2. Identify something about your personality, environment, or circumstances, and assess how this factor has affected you. You could analyze the effects of poverty, shyness, a large family, moving, and so forth.

Idea Generation

1. To generate ideas, list every cause and/or effect you can think of. Do not censor yourself; write down everything that occurs to you.
2. To get at underlying causes and effects, ask *why?* and *then what?* after every cause and effect in your list. For example, if you listed difficulty making friends as an effect of shyness, ask *then what?* and you may get the answer "I was lonely." This answer could be an underlying effect of your shyness. If you listed strong legs as a reason for your success at running track, ask *why?* and you may get the answer "I lifted weights to increase leg strength." This would give you an underlying cause. Asking *then what?* will also help you discover causal chains.
3. Ask yourself why an understanding of the cause-and-effect relationship is important. The answer to this question can appear in your introduction or conclusion.

Reader Response

If you like to secure reader response when revising, see page 77. In addition, have your reader ask *why?* and *then what?* after all your causes and effects. If doing so leads your reader to any underlying causes or effects you should discuss, have that person note them on the draft.

REVISION CHECKLIST

In addition to the checklist on page 80, you can use this checklist for revising your cause-and-effect analysis.

1. Is it clear what cause-and-effect relationship will be analyzed and whether causes, effects, or both will be examined?
2. Have you included underlying causes and/or effects?
3. Have you reproduced causal chains?
4. As necessary, have you explained what is *not* a cause or effect?
5. As necessary, have you supported cause-and-effect generalizations with illustration, description, narration, and process analysis?
6. As necessary, have you shown why or how something is a cause or effect?

CHAPTER 11

Definition

To discover what a word means, you go to the dictionary. However, sometimes the dictionary is not enough. Sure, you can check a dictionary to learn the meaning of a word like *fun,* but what's fun to you may not be fun to someone else, and so the full meaning of that word will vary among individuals to an extent. Some words symbolize abstractions, the subtleties of which cannot all be taken in by an inch or so of space in a dictionary. What, for example, does *justice* mean? Certainly it is a concept with complexities far beyond its neat dictionary definition. In addition, some words have meanings so complex that a dictionary definition can only hit the high points, leaving quite a bit unexplained. *Democracy* is such a word. Not only is its meaning complex, but it varies greatly according to which country's democracy is referred to.

Thus, dictionary definitions can tell us much, but when it comes to the controversial, abstract, or complex, something more may be needed. This something can be an extended definition. An **extended definition** goes beyond the concise, formal definition in a dictionary to explore the *nature* of something, including the aspects, significances, nuances, or complexities that are not part of what a dictionary takes in.

PURPOSE

Many concepts—ones like *wisdom, courage, freedom, hate,* and so on—are multifaceted and difficult to grapple with. In fact, people do not always agree on what these concepts mean. An extended definition of such a term can provide clarification.

A second purpose of an extended definition can be to bring to the reader's attention something that is taken for granted. For example, an extended definition of a *free press* can lead the reader to a fresh appreciation of something so much a part of daily life that it is undervalued.

Another purpose of an extended definition can be to bring the reader to a sharper awareness of something familiar but only vaguely understood. An essay defining the *microchip* might serve this purpose. An extended definition can also explain the meaning and nature of something not at all understood by the reader, say, a *token economy*. You can even inform the reader of something new by defining the commonplace. An extended definition of *senior citizen* might lead to a new knowledge of what it means to grow old in this country. Sometimes definition makes a statement about some issue that goes beyond the subject defined. For example, an essay that defines *rock music* can also comment on the orientation, values, and thinking of young people. That is, because musical preferences among youth are often an index to the prevailing needs and attitudes of young people, a definition of one makes significant statements about the other.

Thus, an extended definition can clarify, inform, or increase awareness of the nature of something. It can force a study of something taken for granted or only casually understood, and it can provide fresh appreciation for the commonplace. It can even make statements that have significance to issues beyond the idea or thing being defined. To determine your purpose, you can answer the following:

1. Do I want to clarify the nature of a familiar subject?
2. Do I want my reader to become more aware of something taken for granted?
3. Do I want my reader to better understand an unfamiliar subject?
4. Do I want to give my reader a fresh outlook on my subject?
5. Do I want to make a statement about an issue that goes beyond (but is related to) the subject defined?
6. Do I want my reader to appreciate my subject more?

Your purpose will influence your detail. Let's say you decide to define *fear* to give your reader a fresh outlook on this feeling by helping him or her see that fear is really a positive emotion. You might note that fear is adaptive because it ensures our survival. You might also note instances when we would endanger ourselves needlessly were it not for fear. However, a different purpose would mean different detail. If you want your definition to show that fear keeps us from realizing our potential, you might include detail that relates lack of achievement to fear of failure and fear of taking risks.

AUDIENCE

Because your reader affects detail selection, you should answer questions like these.

1. How much does my reader know about my subject?
2. Does my reader feel as I do about my subject?

3. How much interest does my reader have in my subject?
4. How receptive to my point of view will my reader be?

To see how audience affects detail selection, assume that you are writing an essay defining *teenager* and your purpose is to make your reader aware of how difficult the teen years are. If your reader is 25 and likely to remember adolescence, you will have to explain less than if your audience is much further removed from those years and needs to be reminded of a few things. Similarly, if your audience is a neighbor who has been expressing concern over "what the youth in this country have come to," you may want to explain why teenagers behave as they do in order to address and discharge your reader's negative feelings. However, if your audience is a teenager, there will be no ill will to overcome, so you might instead include detail to reassure the teen that he or she is not alone in the struggle.

To target a specific audience, you can answer the following questions.

1. With whom would I like to share my view?
2. Who would be influenced by my essay?
3. Who sees my subject differently than I do?
4. Who does not fully understand my subject?
5. Who takes my subject for granted?
6. Who would enjoy reading my definition?

SELECTING DETAIL

An extended definition can include any of the patterns of development discussed in this book. If you are defining *Christmas spirit,* you could tell a story that reveals what Christmas spirit is, or you could compare and contrast Christmas spirit with the feelings people get on other holidays in order to clarify the nature of the spirit. You could provide a number of examples to illustrate the nature of Christmas spirit, or you could describe how it makes people feel and what it makes people do. You can also combine two or more patterns.

Sometimes, you may want to explain what your subject is *not.* For example, if you are defining *freedom,* you may want to say that freedom is *not* doing anything you want, it is *not* a privilege, and it is *not* necessarily guaranteed to everyone. From here you could go on to explain what freedom *is.* This technique can be useful when you wish to make important distinctions or dispel common misunderstandings.

When you select your detail, avoid stating the obvious. For example, if you are defining *Christmas spirit* and you state that it is a mood that occurs at Christmastime, you run the risk of insulting your reader, who does not need to be reminded of such an obvious point. Also, although you are writing a definition, avoid the style found in dictionaries. It lacks the vitality essential to a good essay. If you write that "Christmas spirit is that seasonal mood of ebullience and feeling of goodwill and generosity characteristic of and emanating from the yearly celebration of the birth of Jesus," you will not hold your reader's interest.

ARRANGING DETAIL

You can indicate in the thesis what you are defining and what point can be drawn from the definition. Such a thesis might be "Christmas spirit is not what it used to be" or "Christmas spirit is a natural high."

If your body paragraphs are developed with other patterns of development, follow the organization principles that govern these techniques. Otherwise, a progressive arrangement is frequently effective, perhaps beginning and ending with your strongest points.

Interesting introductions can be crafted in a variety of ways. You can explain what many people believe your subject means if you plan to show it means something else, or you can explain why it is important to arrive at a definition of your subject. Often an anecdote about your subject can pave the way for a definition of that subject. It can also be interesting to explain what your subject used to mean if your essay will go on to show how that meaning has changed. Usually, however, you should avoid including a dictionary definition in your introduction. Your reader will know, at least approximately, how your subject is defined in Webster's, and so a formal definition will probably annoy or bore your audience.

The conclusion of an extended definition often elaborates on the significance of the definition—the points to be drawn from it. This approach is particularly effective when the thesis is only a broad statement of the writer's point of view (as are the two sample theses about Christmas spirit given at the beginning of this discussion of detail arrangement).

TRYOUT

To gain experience developing detail for an extended definition, try this: Select a concept (freedom, justice, good taste, sportsmanship, etc.), object (compact disc, microchip, etc.), person (a good teacher, a friend, etc.), or movement (environmentalism, feminism, etc.) to define. Come up with four points to help define the word you choose by answering the following questions:

1. What is the most distinguishing characteristic of my subject? The second-most distinguishing characteristic?
2. What story can I tell to help define my subject?
3. What features of my subject can I describe?
4. What examples would help define my subject?
5. What can I compare my subject to? What can I contrast it with?
6. What is my subject *not?*

PROFESSIONAL ESSAYS

Spanglish Spoken Here

Janice Castro, with Dan Cook and Cristina Garcia

"Spanglish Spoken Here" first appeared in Time *magazine in 1988. The essay helps the reader understand the growing effect Spanish is having on English by defining the hybrid dialect, Spanglish.*

In Manhattan a first-grader greets her visiting grandparents, happily exclaiming, "Come here, *siéntate!*" Her bemused grandfather, who does not speak Spanish, nevertheless knows she is asking him to sit down. A Miami personnel officer understands what a job applicant means when he says, *"Quiero un* part time." Nor do drivers miss a beat reading a billboard alongside a Los Angeles street advertising CERVEZA—SIX-PACK! 1

This free-form blend of Spanish and English, known as Spanglish, is common linguistic currency wherever concentrations of Hispanic Americans are found in the U.S. In Los Angeles, where 55% of the city's 3 million inhabitants speak Spanish, Spanglish is as much a part of daily life as sunglasses. Unlike the broken-English efforts of earlier immigrants from Europe, Asia and other regions, Spanglish has become a widely accepted conversational mode used casually—even playfully—by Spanish-speaking immigrants and native-born Americans alike. 2

Consisting of one part Hispanicized English, one part Americanized Spanish and more than a little fractured syntax, Spanglish is a bit like a Robin Williams comedy routine: a crackling line of cross-cultural patter straight from the melting pot. Often it enters Anglo homes and families through the children, who pick it up at school or at play with their young Hispanic contemporaries. In other cases, it comes from watching TV; many an Anglo child watching *Sesame Street* has learned *uno dos tres* almost as quickly as one two three. 3

Spanglish takes a variety of forms, from the Southern California Anglos who bid farewell with the utterly silly *"hasta la* bye-bye" to the Cuban-American drivers in Miami who *parquean* their *carros.* Some Spanglish sentences are mostly Spanish, with a quick detour for an English word or two. A Latino friend may cut short a conversation by glancing at his watch and excusing himself with the explanation that he must *"ir al* supermarket." 4

Many of the English words transplanted in this way are simply handier than their Spanish counterparts. No matter how distasteful the subject, for example, it is still easier to say "income tax" than *impuesto sobre la renta.* At the same time, many Spanish-speaking immigrants have adopted such terms as VCR, microwave and dishwasher for what they view as largely American phenomena. Still other English words convey a cultural context that is not implicit in the Spanish. A friend who invites you to *lonche* most likely has in mind the brisk American cus- 5 tom of "doing lunch" rather than the languorous afternoon break traditionally implied by *almuerzo.*

Mainstream Americans exposed to similar hybrids of German, Chinese or 6
Hindi might be mystified. But even Anglos who speak little or no Spanish are somewhat familiar with Spanglish. Living among them, for one thing, are 19 million Hispanics. In addition, more American high school and university students sign up for Spanish than for any other foreign language.

Only in the past ten years, though, has Spanglish begun to turn into a 7
national slang. Its popularity has grown with the explosive increases in U.S. immigration from Latin American countries. English has increasingly collided with Spanish in retail stores, offices and classrooms, in pop music and on street corners. Anglos whose ancestors picked up such Spanish words as *rancho, bronco, tornado* and *incommunicado,* for instance, now freely use such Spanish words as *gracias, bueno,* amigo *and por favor.*

Among Latinos, Spanglish conversations often flow easily from Spanish into 8
several sentences of English and back.

Spanglish is a sort of code for Latinos: the speakers know Spanish, but their 9
hybrid language reflects the American culture in which they live. Many lean to shorter, clipped phrases in place of the longer, more graceful expressions their parents used. Says Leonel de la Cuesta, an assistant professor of modern languages at Florida International University in Miami: "In the U.S., time is money, and that is showing up in Spanglish as an economy of language." Conversational examples: *taipiar* (type) and *winshi-wiper* (windshield wiper) replace *escribir a máquina* and *limpiaparabrisas.*

Major advertisers, eager to tap the estimated $134 billion in spending power 10
wielded by Spanish-speaking Americans, have ventured into Spanglish to promote their products. In some cases, attempts to sprinkle Spanish through commercials have produced embarrassing gaffes. A Braniff airlines ad that sought to tell Spanish-speaking audiences they could settle back *en* (in) luxuriant *cuero* (leather) seats, for example, inadvertently said they could fly without clothes *(encuero).* A fractured translation of the Miller Lite slogan told readers the beer was "Filling, and less delicious." Similar blunders are often made by Anglos trying to impress Spanish-speaking pals. But if Latinos are amused by mangled Spanglish, they also recognize these goofs as a sort of friendly acceptance. As they might put it, *no problema.*

Questions on Technique

1. Which sentence forms the thesis because it indicates what will be defined?
2. The authors use several patterns of development to create their definition. Cite an example of a paragraph that includes each of these patterns: illustration, comparison-contrast, and cause-and-effect analysis.
3. Where do the authors indicate why an understanding of the definition is important? What is that importance?

4. "Spanglish Spoken Here" is a lively essay, partly because of the specific yet simple diction. For example, the authors refer to Spanglish as "a crackling line of cross-cultural patter" (paragraph 3). Cite three other examples of specific, simple word choice.
5. This essay first appeared in *Time* magazine. How do the authors meet the needs of their readers?
6. For what purpose do you think the authors wrote "Spanglish Spoken Here"?
7. What approach do the authors take to their conclusion?

For Group Discussion or Journal Writing

Discuss whether or not you enjoyed "Spanglish Spoken Here." Develop a list of reasons for why you did or did not like the essay.

Appetite

Laurie Lee

British author Laurie Lee has done it all. He has written poems, plays, children's books, scripts, travel books, and his autobiography. The following selection from one of his longer works says as much about anticipation as it does about appetite.

One of the major pleasures in life is appetite, and one of our major duties should be to preserve it. Appetite is the keenness of living; it is one of the senses that tells you that you are still curious to exist, that you still have an edge on your longings and want to bite into the world and taste its multitudinous flavours and juices. *1*

By appetite, of course, I don't mean just the lust for food, but any condition of unsatisfied desire, any burning in the blood that proves you want more than you've got, and that you haven't yet used up your life. Wilde said he felt sorry for those who never got their heart's desire, but sorrier still for those who did. I got mine once only, and it nearly killed me, and I've always preferred wanting to having since. *2*

For appetite, to me, is that state of wanting, which keeps one's expectations alive. I remember learning this lesson long ago as a child, when treats and orgies were few, and when I discovered that the greatest pitch of happiness was not in actually eating a toffee but in gazing at it beforehand. True, the first bite was delicious, but once the toffee was gone one was left with nothing, neither toffee nor lust. Besides, the whole toffeeness of toffees was imperceptibly diminished by the gross act of having eaten it. No, the best was in wanting it, in sitting and looking at it, when one tasted an inexhaustible treasure-house of flavours. *3*

So, for me, one of the keenest pleasures of appetite remains in the wanting, not the satisfaction. In wanting a peach, or a whisky, or a particular texture or sound, or to be with a particular friend. For in this condition, of course, I know that the object of desire is always at its most flawlessly perfect. Which is why I *4* would carry the preservation of appetite to the extent of deliberate fasting, simply because I think that appetite is too good to lose, too precious to be bludgeoned into insensibility by satiation and over-doing it.

For that matter, I don't really want three square meals a day—I want one 5
huge, delicious, orgiastic, table-groaning blow-out, say every four days, and then not be sure where the next one is coming from. A day of fasting is not for me just a puritanical device for denying oneself a pleasure, but rather a way of anticipating a rarer moment of supreme indulgence.

Fasting is an act of homage to the majesty of appetite. So I think we should 6
arrange to give up our pleasures regularly—our food, our friends, our lovers—in order to preserve their intensity, and the moment of coming back to them. For this is the moment that renews and refreshes both oneself and the thing one loves. Sailors and travellers enjoyed this once, and so did hunters, I suppose. Part of the weariness of modern life may be that we live too much on top of each other, and are entertained and fed too regularly. Once we were separated by hunger both from our food and families, and then we learned to value both. The men went off hunting, and the dogs went with them; the women and children waved goodbye. The cave was empty of men for days on end: nobody ate, or knew what to do. The women crouched by the fire, the wet smoke in their eyes; the children wailed; everybody was hungry. Then one night there were shouts and the barking of dogs from the hills, and the men came back loaded with meat. This was the great reunion, and everybody gorged themselves silly, and appetite came into its own; the long-awaited meal became a feast to remember and an almost sacred celebration of life. Now we go off to the office and come home in the evenings to cheap chicken and frozen peas. Very nice, but too much of it, too easy and regular, served up without effort or wanting. We eat, we are lucky, our faces are shining with fat, but we don't know the pleasure of being hungry any more.

Too much of anything—too much music, entertainment, happy snacks, or 7
time spent with one's friends, creates a kind of impotence of living by which one can no longer hear, or taste, or see, or love, or remember. Life is short and precious, and appetite is one of its guardians, and loss of appetite is a sort of death. So if we are to enjoy this short life we should respect the divinity of appetite, and keep it eager and not too much blunted.

It is a long time now since I knew that acute moment of bliss that comes 8
from putting parched lips to a cup of cold water. The springs are still there to be enjoyed—all one needs is the original thirst.

Questions on Technique

1. What is the thesis of "Appetite"?
2. What do you judge to be the purpose of Lee's definition?
3. In what paragraphs does the author use examples to illustrate the subject's distinguishing characteristics?
4. In what paragraph does Lee explain the importance of the topic?
5. What elements of cause-and-effect analysis appear in the essay?
6. In what paragraph does the author explain what the subject is *not?*

7. What do you judge to be the significance of Lee's definition? Where is this significance presented?
8. What approach does the author take to the conclusion?

For Group Discussion or Journal Writing

In paragraph 6, Lee says, "We eat, we are lucky, our faces are shining with fat, but we don't know the pleasure of being hungry any more." Explain what you think Lee means and go on to cite examples to illustrate his view.

The Egalitarian Error

Margaret Mead and Rhoda Metraux

Margaret Mead and Rhoda Metraux, respected anthropologists who worked extensively in the field, published both scholarly and popular works. The following definition of an important concept works to dispel common misunderstandings.

Almost all Americans want to be democratic, but many Americans are confused about what, exactly, democracy means. How do you know when someone is acting in a democratic—or an undemocratic—way? Recently several groups have spoken out with particular bitterness against the kind of democracy that means equal opportunity for all, regardless of race or national origin. They act as if all human beings did not belong to one species, as if some races of mankind were inferior to others in their capacity to learn what members of other races know and have invented. Other extremists attack religious groups—Jews or Catholics—or deny the right of an individual to be an agnostic. One reason that these extremists, who explicitly do not want to be democratic, can get a hearing even though their views run counter to the Constitution and our traditional values is that the people who *do* want to be democratic are frequently so muddled. 1

For many Americans, democratic behavior necessitates an outright denial of any significant differences among human beings. In their eyes it is undemocratic for anyone to refer, in the presence of any other person, to differences in skin color, manners or religious beliefs. Whatever one's private thoughts may be, it is necessary to act as if everyone were exactly alike. 2

Behavior of this kind developed partly as a reaction to those who discriminated against or actively abused members of other groups. But it is artificial, often hypocritical behavior, nonetheless, and it dulls and flattens human relationships. If two people can't talk easily and comfortably but must forever guard against some slip of the tongue, some admission of what is in both persons' minds, they are likely to talk as little as possible. This embarrassment about differences reaches a final absurdity when a Methodist feels that he cannot take a guest on a tour of his garden because he might have to identify a wild plant with a blue flower, called the wandering Jew, or when a white lecturer feels he ought not to mention the name of Conrad's beautiful story *The Nigger of the "Narcissus."* But it is no less absurd when 3 well-meaning people, speaking of the physically handicapped, tell prospective employers: "They don't want special consideration. Ask as much of them as you do of everyone else, and fire them if they don't give satisfaction!"

Another version of false democracy is the need to deny the existence of per- 4
sonal advantages. Inherited wealth, famous parents, a first-class mind, a rare voice, a beautiful face, an exceptional physical skill—any advantage has to be minimized or denied. Continually watched and measured, the man or woman who is rich or talented or well educated is likely to be called "undemocratic" whenever he does anything out of the ordinary—more or less of something than others do. If he wants acceptance, the person with a "superior" attribute, like the person with an "inferior" attribute, often feels obliged to take on a protective disguise, to act as if he were just like everybody else. One denies difference; the other minimizes it. And both believe, as they conform to these false standards, that they act in the name of democracy.

For many Americans, a related source of confusion is success. As a people 5
we Americans greatly prize success. And in our eyes success all too often means simply outdoing other people by virtue of achievement judged by some single scale—income or honors or headlines or trophies—and coming out at "the top." Only one person, as we see it, can be the best—can get the highest grades, be voted the most attractive girl or the boy most likely to succeed. Though we often rejoice in the success of people far removed from ourselves—in another profession, another community, or endowed with a talent that we do not covet—we tend to regard the success of people close at hand, within our own small group, as a threat. We fail to realize that there are many kinds of success, including the kind of success that lies within a person. We do not realize, for example, that there could be in the same class one hundred boys and girls—each of them a "success" in a different kind of way. Individuality is again lost in a refusal to recognize and cherish the differences among people.

The attitude that measures success by a single yardstick and isolates the one 6
winner and the kind of "democracy" that denies or minimizes differences among people are both deeply destructive. Imagine for a moment a family with two sons, one of whom is brilliant, attractive and athletic while the other is dull, unattractive and clumsy. Both boys attend the same high school. In the interest of the slower boy, the parents would want the school to set equally low standards for everyone. Lessons should be easy; no one should be forced to study dead languages or advanced mathematics in order to graduate. Athletics should be noncompetitive; every boy should have a chance to enjoy playing games. Everyone should be invited to all the parties. As for special attention to gifted children, this is not fair to the other children. An all-around education should be geared to the average normal child.

But in the interest of the other boy, these same parents would have quite 7
opposite goals. After all, we need highly trained people; the school should do the most it can for its best students. Funds should be made available for advanced classes and special teachers, for the best possible coach, the best athletic equipment. Young people should be allowed to choose friends on their own level. The aim of education should be to produce top-flight students.

This is an extreme example, but it illustrates the completely incompatible aims that can arise in this kind of "democracy." Must our country shut its eyes to the needs of either its gifted or its less gifted sons? It would be a good deal more sensible to admit, as some schools do today, that children differ widely from one another, that all successes cannot be ranged on one single scale, that there is room in a real democracy to help each child find his own level and develop to his fullest potential. *8*

Moving now to a wider scene, before World War I Americans thought of themselves as occupying a unique place in the world—and there was no question in most minds that this country was a "success." True, Europeans might look down on us for our lack of culture, but with a few notable, local exceptions, we simply refused to compete on European terms. There was no country in the world remotely like the one we were building. But since World War II we have felt the impact of a country whose size and strength and emphasis on national achievement more closely parallel our own. Today we are ahead of Russia, or Russia is ahead of us. Nothing else matters. Instead of valuing and developing the extraordinary assets and potential of our country for their own sake, we are involved in a simple set of competitions for wealth and power and dominance. *9*

These are expensive and dangerous attitudes. When democracy ceases to be a cherished way of life and becomes instead the name of one team, we are using the word democracy to describe behavior that places us and all other men in jeopardy. *10*

Individually, nationally and, today, internationally, the misreading of the phrase "all men are created equal," exacts a heavy price. The attitudes that follow from our misconceptions may be compatible with life in a country where land and rank and prestige are severely limited and the roads to success are few. But they are inappropriate in a land as rich, as filled with opportunities as our own. They are the price we pay for being less democratic than we claim to be. *11*

"All men are created equal" does not mean that all men are the same. What it does mean is that each should be accorded full respect and full rights as a unique human being—full respect for his humanity *and* for his differences from other people. *12*

Questions on Technique

1. What is the purpose of the authors' definition? Where in the essay do Mead and Metraux present their purpose?
2. Which sentence is the thesis of the essay?
3. What technique do Mead and Metraux rely on most heavily to develop their definition? Why is this technique a logical choice?
4. What other methods of development do the authors use, and where in the essay are these found?
5. In which paragraphs do the authors explain the significance of their definition?
6. What approach do Mead and Metraux take to their introduction?
7. What approach do Mead and Metraux take to their conclusion?

For Group Discussion or Journal Writing

Many schools group children in classes according to their ability so that all the bright students are together, all the average students are together, and so forth. What do you think Margaret Mead and Rhoda Metraux would think of such grouping? What do you think of it? Is it "democratic"? Explain.

STUDENT ESSAYS TO READ AND EVALUATE

The extended definitions that follow were written by students. Some are stronger than others, but each has something to recommend it. As you study the essays, you will improve your ability to assess strengths and weaknesses so that you can better judge your own writing. In addition, you will learn successful techniques to incorporate into your own work and unsuccessful techniques to avoid. Following the student writings, is a formal evaluation exercise to work on.

Tacky Hits Home

Because my own family is overrun with tackiness, I have become an authority on 1 the subject. There is no tackiness, regardless of how subtle, that I cannot recognize and become instantly repulsed by. First, tacky is Aunt Sonya in polyester pants. I find myself cringing at the sight of her fat dimples poking through the tight, scratchy material. Even worse, most of her pants are purchased in an array of carnival colors that include blinding aqua, iridescent lime, and resonant red. Because these shades are so difficult to match, most of her shirts (which may look nice with other pants) also appear tacky because of the clashing colors.

Tacky is also Aunt Sonya's daughter Betsy wearing bulky sweat socks with 2 dress shoes. The very thought of her cramming those thick socks into those delicate shoes irritates me.

Tackiness is not limited to the women in my family. Uncle Harold, Aunt 3 Sonya's husband, tucks his pants into his cowboy boots. Those who have never heard of *GQ* may find this appealing, but I find it appalling. Then there is Uncle Sammy, who is stuck in a clothing time warp wearing his favorite sky-blue leisure suit. To compound the offense, he combines this relic with a flashy disco shirt and white fake leather shoes.

The most tacky male award goes to my Uncle Earl, who belongs to that 4 intriguing breed of men who find it impossible to purchase clothing that fits properly. I lose my appetite when I see Uncle Earl hunched over the counter with his derrier protruding out over his jeans for all to see. As if that weren't bad enough, he insists on wearing his favorite tee-shirts that have stupid sayings such as "six-pack attack" on the front of them.

In the field of home decorating, it is my Aunt Sue and Uncle Mort who win 5 the tackiness-of-the-year award. In their front yard, they have these stupid Dutch kids kissing. They must have been at it a long time because the paint on their lips has peeled off. In the center of the back yard is a rusted swing set, with no swings attached. The inside of the house is even worse. Tacky is definitely Aunt Sue and Uncle Mort's kitchen: plastic mustard and ketchup bottles sit on the dinette, dried yellow and red gorp clinging to the sides; the cat's litter box is in the corner, and that mangy feline roams the kitchen counters at will.

Although I grew up with tackiness, I am sure anyone can recognize it. Pink flamingos in the front yard, bowling trophies on the mantle, plastic daisies on the kitchen table, parents diapering babies in public, people smoking on elevators, teenagers singing out loud the songs they hear on their headphones—tackiness is everywhere. There really ought to be a law against bad taste. 6

What It Means to Be a Friend

Although I feel that it is not extremely difficult for two people to begin establishing a relationship, maintaining that relationship may not be quite as easy. Undoubtedly, we all have our faults and flaws, our marks of imperfection, and as two people come to know more about one another, these flaws become more and more evident. It is the degree of emphasis placed on these flaws that determines whether or not a relationship blossoms into a true friendship. If a person is truly your friend, then even after he has come to know a lot about you, he will still care very much for you. A true friend is fun to be with, trustworthy, and reliable. 1

As I vividly recollect the past, I can recall the attempts that a certain young fellow and I made at establishing a true friendship. We tried to be courteous, respectful, and even witty. Yet our efforts were made in vain because we could never overlook one another's faults. I viewed him as being boisterous and cocky, and he often told me that I was extremely stubborn. Our relationship never really developed, for we constantly focused on the negative aspects of one another's characters. Eventually, we lost hope, and the relationship sort of faded out. 2

For some time after this experience, I didn't really try to make any new friends. Then one day, I met a certain individual, and after a while, he and I began associating on a regular basis. Fortunately, we were able to accept those flaws that we had detected, and we focused on the better characteristics we had also spotted. As a result of our efforts, our relationship grew stronger, and it developed into what I feel is truly a friendship. 3

As far as my true friend is concerned, I would have to say that he is a guy with whom I have been able to share fun times. We've gone to ball games, to parks, and to movies. We've enjoyed playing basketball and football. We've shared countless jelly donuts, bags of potato chips, and candy bars. Over the years, we have really enjoyed one another's company. 4

In addition to being a joy to be around, my friend is also someone whom I have come to trust. We could have never grown as close as we are had we not shared secrets, and we would have never shared secrets had we not trusted one another. Now in the early stages of our relationship, we were both tentative about 5 relaying too much information about ourselves. However, gradually, we became more open, and we began sharing some of those deeper, inner feelings. For instance, once I was scared to go to school because I knew that this big, hulking fellow wanted to beat me up; yet, the only one to whom I was able to admit fear was my true friend. Somehow, I knew that he wouldn't brand me a coward, and just being able to tell someone what I was undergoing did wonders for my ego. Because he could be trusted, I could tell him that I was afraid, and I could rest assured that no one else would know of my fear. Because of trust, we were able to open up and thus come closer to one another.

Perhaps that which best exemplifies my true friend is his being available in times of need. Once, I was really in dire need of assistance. As I recall, I was playing football up the street from where I live. Suddenly, this band of ten-speed-bike-riding desperadoes came roaring up the street. Overcome with fright, I desperately sought to flee from the scene because I immediately remembered angering the forerunner of the gang the day before. Now, since they were rambling up the street and I lived down the street, my chances of getting home didn't look very good. Meanwhile, the other guys who were playing football had the luxury of living nearby, and they promptly ran home. However, my true friend remained, and though he also could have run home like the others, he first grabbed hold of me, and then together, we ran to his house. No doubt he saved me from considerable bodily injury, and my folks from outrageous hospital bills. For his act of valor, I will always be indebted, as I am for the times when I have needed someone to talk to, to console me, to encourage me, and to advise me, and he has been there. 6

As I recollect the various experiences that our relationship has undergone, I must say that my friend and I have come to know one another very well, and I believe that we have come to care about each other very much. To me, he has truly been fun to be with, trustworthy, and reliable, and I hope and pray that to some degree, I have been the same to him. 7

What Is Writer's Block?

I have writer's block. For the last two days I have sat at this table, staring at a blank piece of paper. My mother calls to ask what I'm doing, and I say I'm writing. She asks me what, and I say nothing, for I have writer's block. "Well, write something," she replies. Something? Obviously, she does not understand writer's block. 1

Writer's block is pacing. Up and down in front of the table with pen in hand. Wearing a ragged trail in an otherwise okay carpet. Pacing. Palms sweating. Knowing you have a deadline that is creeping up on you like a fairy tale troll, following behind, and steadily getting closer and closer with each tick of the clock. 2

Writer's block is trying. Sitting down ready and willing to work. Picking up a freshly sharpened pencil and advancing on a clean crisp piece of paper only to have a sense of emptiness come over you. The pencil falters above the paper, and the words stubbornly refuse to leave their hiding places in the recesses of my 3 mind. Now the sweaty hand forces the pencil down onto the paper. Write something. Doodles. Lots and lots of doodles. Squiggly little lines. Bold black circles. Delicate little spider webs. Angry dots! Names . . . Julie . . . Mike . . . John . . . Jimmy. Why won't the words come? What are they afraid of? Try, make those sweaty palms produce. Deadlines.

Writer's block is doubting myself, being convinced I can't write. It is waiting, waiting for the block to recede. It is starting, stopping, starting over, stopping again. 4

Writer's block is anticipation. I know they will come, if I can just be patient a few more minutes. I can feel them; the words are there. As soon as they're ready, they will come spilling out, tumbling all over each other, mixing letters and vowels in their rush to be heard. Then the pencil will have to restrain them and take them one by one and put them in their proper order. 5

Until that time, I can only see a dam. I can feel the force of the words straining behind it. I can see them bouncing off the tall, unyielding walls. Occasionally, one or two escape through the overflow. Open those floodgates, and let them flow. 6

The Final Stage

She has white hair, cloudy eyes, and a mind that wanders. Her voice crackles when she speaks. Her teeth are gone, for they were pulled many years ago. She's deaf. Her shoulders are stooped, her back hunched. She has brittle bones, wrinkled skin, and gnarled hands. She no longer recognizes her bowel urges. Her legs are weak. She's skinny. Because she dressed herself, her dress is on backward. She wears two pair of underwear and no shoes. She's not hungry. She never is. Fits of depression and crying jags are a usual occurrence. She is moody. She's confused and disoriented. Some days she is mean and nasty, uttering cruel words and spouting prejudices. She's disheveled and messy. She's tired. She's alone. She needs love, kindness, and patience. She is old. 1

This shell of a person used to be a productive human being. She was a mother, sister, wife, and daughter. She has lived, loved, and dealt with tragedy in her lifetime, and now she is walking her final miles. She remains in her own world completely dependent upon others for her care and personal safety. 2

This need for care and supervision leads her to a nursing home, where she will spend her remaining days enclosed in a building with very little mental stimulation. Consequently, she will become more confused and disoriented. Once in a while a family member may come to visit, send a card, or send some flowers. Rarer still, someone will come to take her out for the day. 3

Abandoned and alone, she loses sight of what little reality she has left. Loneliness and fear will be magnified as the darkness of night engulfs her, which in turn will set off a series of unfounded fears. As she cries out from her bed, she will accept little in the way of comfort and reassurance, for she is sure in her mind that the nurse or aide is there to harm her. 4

For many people, this is the final stage. Healthy limbs will atrophy. Intelli- 5
gent minds will no longer function. A nimble step will become a shuffle. This is the final stage of life. This is old age.

Becoming a Reliable Critic by Evaluating Writing

Form a group and select one of the previous student essays, or use one your instructor assigns. Take three sheets of paper; label one sheet *Introduction,* label one sheet *Body,* and label one sheet *Conclusion.* Go back through the essay and on the appropriate sheets record what you agree are the strengths and weaknesses. Also record an explanation for why each noted feature is strong or weak. You need not record *every* strength and weakness—just the major ones. If group members disagree, note this disagreement on your sheet. You may wish to refer to some or all of the evaluation questions that follow.

Evaluation Questions

1. The Thesis
   What is the thesis? Is it a clear indication of what is being defined?
2. The Introduction
   Does the introduction engage your interest? Why or why not?
3. Supporting Details
   Note any points you do not understand, any points that are not relevant, and any points that need more development. Has the author avoided a dictionary style definition and statements of the obvious? Is the reason for the definition clear?
4. Organization
   Are all the details in a logical order? Evaluate the use of transitions and topic sentences.
5. The Conclusion
   Does the essay come to a satisfying end? Explain.
6. Sentence Effectiveness and Word Choice
   Note any places where sentence variety is needed, where wordiness is a problem, or where clichés are a problem. Is the diction simple and specific?
7. Overview
   What do you like best about the essay? What is the single most important revision the author should make?

Essay Topics: Definition

1. Define a *freshman* (or senior or some other campus type, such as a jock, fraternity guy/sorority gal, egghead, etc.).
2. Define *male chauvinism* (or *male liberation* or *feminism*).
3. Define *frustration* or *excitement.*
4. Define *friendship.*
5. Define *anticipation* (or *dread*).

6. Define *maturity.*
7. Define *adolescence.*
8. Define *defeat* or *success.*
9. Define a *good parent.*
10. Define *satisfaction* or *greed.*
11. Define a *bureaucrat.*
12. Define the nature of a *superhero* or *hero* (Wonder Woman, Superman, Rambo, John Wayne, etc.).
13. Define *education.*
14. Define *inner strength.*
15. Define the current trend in popular music.
16. Define *Christmas spirit.*
17. Define *patriotism.*
18. Define an ethnic term (*chutzpah, gringo,* etc.) that is not generally understood in all its connotations.
19. Define *ambition* or *class.*
20. Define the nature of a *successful (popular,* not necessarily *good) television show.*
21. Define *jealousy* or *sportsmanship.*
22. Define *hospitality.*
23. Define *runner's high.*
24. Define *cynicism.*
25. Define *writer's block.*

Thematic Topics

1. According to Margaret Mead and Rhoda Metraux (page 278), what is the "egalitarian error"? To what extent do you think this error exists in society today? What are the effects of the error?
2. In "Appetite" (page 276), Laurie Lee argues that anticipation is better than satisfaction. Write an essay that argues that the opposite is true.
3. Explain the views of democracy in "The Egalitarian Error" (page 278) and "Democracy" (page 357), being sure to point out any similarities and differences in the views. Then go on to explain your own view of democracy, drawing on ideas in these essays and your own thinking.

Writing Strategies

In addition to the strategies noted in Chapters 1 to 3, the following suggestions may help you write your definition and experiment to improve your writing process.

Topic Selection

1. Leaf through the pages of a dictionary and consider the various entries. Make a list of words you might like to define and then choose one subject from this list.

2. If you have difficulty settling on a topic, consider your own experience. What moods or emotions have you known lately? Depression, anger, surprise, love—these can all be defined using narrations and illustrations from your own life. Also, think of people you have observed recently. Coaches, teachers, salespeople, doctors—these can be defined on the basis of your own observation.

Idea Generation

Letter writing can be a productive idea-generation technique (see page 20). Write a letter to someone you are comfortable with, and begin the letter in this way: "I'd like to explain what ____________________ means to me."

Reader Response

If you like to secure reader response during revision, consult page 77. In addition, ask your reader to note any distinguishing characteristics of your subject that you neglected to mention. Also, ask your reader to write out the significance of your definition so that you can check to be sure this point is clear.

REVISION CHECKLIST

In addition to the checklist on page 80, you can use this checklist for revising your extended definition.

1. Does your definition do one of the following?
   a. Clarify a complex subject
   b. Create appreciation for or a fresh awareness of something taken for granted
   c. Inform about something not understood
   d. Provide a new understanding of a familiar subject
   e. Make a statement about an issue related to the subject defined
2. If your definition includes other patterns of development, have you conformed to the conventions for handling those patterns?
4. Have you explained the distinguishing characteristics of your subject?
5. When appropriate, have you explained what your subject is *not?*
6. Have you avoided dictionary-style definitions and statements of the obvious?
7. Is the significance of your definition clearly stated or strongly implied?

CHAPTER 12

Classification

Classification, which is a way of ordering items and information, involves grouping things according to their characteristics. We encounter classification all the time. The yellow pages group businesses by type; libraries shelve books according to subject; your college catalog explains degree requirements according to school and major; *TV Guide* lists programs according to the day of the week and time of day; classified ads list job vacancies under headings such as *secretarial, sales,* and *medical;* and textbooks arrange information according to topics.

Without classification, life would be enormously difficult. To appreciate this, imagine a library without a classification system. If you wanted to read a mystery, you would have to scan the shelves until you got lucky and ran across an appropriate book. Fortunately, libraries have classification systems that allow you to go quickly to the area where all the mysteries are shelved. Shopping, too, would be daunting. Imagine taking your list to a grocery store that shelved items randomly, instead of grouping canned goods together, produce together, dairy products together, and so forth.

PURPOSE

People often classify because ordering information makes for easier study. In biology, for example, grouping animals into classifications such as mammals, birds, reptiles, and amphibians allows scientists to study animal life more efficiently. You, too, may classify in order to facilitate the examination of information or items. For example, if you wanted to determine the best bicycle to buy, you could classify the available models (racing, touring, dirt bikes, etc.) according to their chief characteristics (price, frame design, tire size, etc.) to make a careful study of the chief features of bicycles.

Classification is also a way to clarify similarities and differences. For example, if you classified diet programs, you would discover how these programs are similar and different. Such information could help you decide which program is the best for you. In addition, such a classification could point out which features are shared by successful programs. Knowing this information can help you predict the chances of success for any program you encounter.

Another purpose for classification can be to bring the reader to a fresh way of viewing something. For example, television programs are usually classified as dramas, situation comedies, game shows, soap operas, variety shows, and so forth. However, an essay that classifies programs according to how they portray women can lead the reader to a greater awareness of how television influences our perception of women.

Classification can also help readers understand something they may not be familiar with. For example, you could classify Eastern religions to inform a reader who knows little about Eastern beliefs.

Classification can also persuade. For example, to persuade the reader that telephone solicitors should be treated with more respect, you could classify them according to why they take the job. One group could include those who are unprepared for other work (high school dropouts, the unskilled, those with low intelligence, etc.); one group could include those who are housebound (mothers who have no one to care for their children, those with no transportation, etc.); another group could include those who are physically unable to perform other work (the disabled, the elderly, etc.).

Finally, classification can entertain. You could, for example, write an amusing piece that classifies colds according to how they affect people. One category could humorously describe how the runny head cold affects people; another category could humorously describe how the stuffed-head variety affects people; another category could humorously describe how the cold accompanied by a hacking cough affects people.

To determine your purpose, you can ask yourself these questions.

1. Do I want to clarify by showing how elements are alike and different?
2. Do I want to bring the reader to a fresh way of viewing something?
3. Do I want to persuade the reader to think or act a particular way?
4. Do I want to entertain the reader?

AUDIENCE

Audience is an important consideration in classification because your reader will affect your detail selection. For example, let's say you are classifying home computers. If your reader knows little about computers, you may have to define terms like *byte;* however, if your reader currently uses a computer, such a definition may not be necessary. Similarly, how extensively you use examples may depend on your reader. For instance, if you are classifying video games for a parent who has never played them, you may need to give many examples of each type; however, if your reader is a teenager who plays the games often and is knowledgeable about them, fewer examples will be called for.

Your audience's feelings also influence detail selection. Assume that you wish to convince your reader to treat telephone solicitors with more respect and that to do so you will classify solicitors according to the reasons they take the job. If your reader has been annoyed by frequent interruptions from telephone solicitors, you will have to work harder than you would if your reader has not been annoyed. For the annoyed reader, you could take pains to describe the difficult circumstances that prompt solicitors to take the job.

To determine your audience, you can ask these questions.

1. Who could learn something from my classification?
2. Who could be brought to a fresh appreciation of what I am classifying?
3. Who could be persuaded to think or act a particular way?
4. Who would enjoy reading my classification?

You can establish the nature of your audience with these questions.

1. How much does my reader know about the elements I am classifying?
2. What strong feelings does my reader have?
3. How much interest does my reader have in what I am classifying?
4. What information does my reader need to appreciate and accept my classification?

DISCOVERING A PRINCIPLE OF CLASSIFICATION

To be meaningful, a classification must group elements according to some principle. This principle provides the logic for the classification. Consider, for example, a classification of teachers. One group could be those who lecture, one group could be those who use a question-and-answer format, and one group could be those who guide student discussion. The principle of classification in this case is instructional methods.

Of course, most elements can be classified according to more than one principle. Teachers, for example, could also be classified according to degree of interest in students, levels of formality, testing techniques, amount of skill, and so forth. The principle of classification used, in large measure, depends on your audience and your purpose. For example, if your audience is teachers, it would be silly to classify according to testing techniques because teachers are already aware of these techniques. However, if you believe teachers are not sufficiently aware of how levels of formality affect students, you might classify this way. Your purpose could be informational (to let teachers know how students are affected by varying degrees of formality and informality); or your purpose could be persuasive (to persuade teachers to be more informal because informality engages student interest and relaxes students).

Always be sure that your principle of classification is a useful one for your audience. Say, for example, that you are classifying movies recently released on videocassette. Obviously this can be done several ways: according to genre (comedy, drama, science fiction, etc.), according to critical response, according to rating (G, PG, PG-13, NC-17, R), according to theme, and so forth. However, if your audience consists of parents trying to decide which movies are suitable for 5- to 8-year-olds, some of these classifications are not useful. One useful way to classify would be according to the amount of violence in the movies and the nature of that violence.

Finally, be sure your principle of classification allows at least three groupings. If you have only two groupings, you are probably writing a comparison-contrast essay.

SELECTING DETAIL

When you classify, you place elements in groups according to your principle of classification. Your supporting detail can indicate what the groups are, what elements are in each group, and what the characteristics of the elements are. Assume, for example, that you are classifying aerobics classes according to the amount of impact they have on the joints. Your supporting detail would note your categories (perhaps high impact, moderate impact, and low impact). Your detail would also note which classes (perhaps dance aerobics, step aerobics, and yoga aerobics) fall into each category. Finally, your detail would describe the relevant aspects of the classes in each category (perhaps kind of movements, speed of movements, number of repetitions). In other words, your detail will arrange items in groups and explain what the elements in the group are like.

When you explain what the elements in the group are like, you may rely heavily on explanation, illustration, description, and narration. For example, let's say you are writing a humorous classification of baby-sitters. You could *explain* that the nervous sitter does not let the children eat anything for fear they will choke. You could *illustrate* what the inattentive sitter is like by citing the example of the sitter who talked on the phone while the child wandered through the neighborhood. You could *describe* the appearance of the slovenly teenage sitter, and you could *narrate* the story about the time the cleanliness nut washed the children and the walls.

Finally, do not feel you must develop each grouping in equal detail, for some groupings may need more explanation than others. As long as all groupings are explained *adequately,* they need not be explained *equally.*

ARRANGING DETAIL

The introduction of a classification can be handled a number of ways. You can, for example, explain the value of the classification. If you are classifying movies recently released on videocassettes and your audience consists of parents, you can explain that the classification is important because it helps parents choose suitable movies for their youngsters. Your introduction can also explain why you are capable of establishing the classification. For example, if you are classifying cookbooks, you can explain that you have been a cookbook collector and gourmet cook for many years. This approach gives your classification credibility because you establish yourself as knowledgeable. Another approach is to explain how you discovered the classification. If you are classifying baseball coaches, you might note that you arrived at your classification after years of observing your children's coaches.

A suitable thesis can be shaped by stating what you are grouping and your principle of classification. Here are two examples.

> `Commercial weight-loss programs can be distinguished by the kind of positive and negative reinforcement they provide.` (This thesis states that commercial weight-loss programs will be grouped; the principle of classification is the positive and negative reinforcement provided.)
>
> `Some students classify teachers according to whether they are hard or easy, but a better way to classify them is according to their teaching techniques.` (This thesis notes that teachers will be classified; the principle of classification is teaching techniques.)

Another way to shape a thesis is to state your topic and provide words that indicate you will classify (without mentioning the principle of classification). Here is an example.

> `After working as a waitress for five years, I have concluded that four kinds of people eat out regularly.` (Here, the topic is people who eat out regularly; the words *four kinds* indicate that classification will occur.)

Another approach is to state your groupings in your thesis.

> `White lies can be harmless, embarrassing, or hurtful.`

In your body paragraphs, topic sentences can introduce each grouping as it is presented. For example, the following topic sentences could appear in a classification of white lies.

> `Most white lies are harmless.`
>
> `At times, white lies prove embarrassing to the teller.`
>
> `Unfortunately, a small percentage of white lies are hurtful.`

After the topic sentence that presents the grouping, you can provide the supporting details that give the characteristics of the elements in the group.

Groups can sometimes be arranged in a progressive order. For example, in the classification of white lies, the groupings can be arranged according to how serious the consequences of the lies are. You can discuss the harmless lies first, then the embarrassing lies, then the hurtful ones.

Sometimes groups can be arranged in chronological order. For example, if you are classifying ways to discipline children, you can do so according to the age of the child.

Many times you can present your groupings in a random order because no organizational pattern is apparent or called for. However, if you discuss the same characteristics for each grouping, use the same order each time. For example, if you classify salespeople and discuss personality, technique, and willingness to help for each group, you should present these aspects in the same order each time.

TRYOUT

To gain experience identifying a principle of classification and shaping a thesis, do the following.

1. Identify a principle of classification for each of these subjects: friends, teachers, students.
2. Write three thesis statements, one for each subject and principle of classification you identified. Each thesis should include words that indicate you are classifying or words that present the principle of classification.

PROFESSIONAL ESSAYS

The Ways of Meeting Oppression

Martin Luther King, Jr.

Martin Luther King, Jr., who won the Nobel Peace Prize in 1964, was the most prominent civil rights leader of the 1950s and 1960s. In the following essay, taken from his book Stride Toward Freedom, *King classifies responses to oppression and evaluates the effectiveness of those responses.*

Oppressed people deal with their oppression in three characteristic ways. One way is acquiescence: the oppressed resign themselves to their doom. They tacitly adjust themselves to oppression, and thereby become conditioned to it. In every movement toward freedom some of the oppressed prefer to remain oppressed. Almost 2800 years ago Moses set out to lead the children of Israel from the slavery of Egypt to the freedom of the promised land. He soon discovered that slaves do not always welcome their deliverers. They become accustomed to being slaves. They would rather bear those ills they have, as Shakespeare pointed out, than flee 1 to others that they know not of. They prefer the "fleshpots of Egypt" to the ordeals of emancipation.

There is such a thing as the freedom of exhaustion. Some people are so 2
worn down by the yoke of oppression that they give up. A few years ago in the slum areas of Atlanta, a Negro guitarist used to sing almost daily: "Been down so long that down don't bother me." This is the type of negative freedom and resignation that often engulfs the life of the oppressed.

But this is not the way out. To accept passively an unjust system is to coop- 3
erate with that system; thereby the oppressed become as evil as the oppressor. Noncooperation with evil is as much a moral obligation as is cooperation with good. The oppressed must never allow the conscience of the oppressor to slumber. Religion reminds every man that he is his brother's keeper. To accept injustice or segregation passively is to say to the oppressor that his actions are morally right. It is a way of allowing his conscience to fall asleep. At this moment the oppressed fails to be his brother's keeper. So acquiescence—while often the easier way—is not the moral way. It is the way of the coward. The Negro cannot win the respect of his oppressor by acquiescing; he merely increases the oppressor's arrogance and contempt. Acquiescence is interpreted as proof of the Negro's inferiority. The Negro cannot win the respect of the white people of the South or the peoples of the world if he is willing to sell the future of his children for his personal and immediate comfort and safety.

A second way that oppressed people sometimes deal with oppression is to 4
resort to physical violence and corroding hatred. Violence often brings about momentary results. Nations have frequently won their independence in battle. But in spite of temporary victories, violence never brings permanent peace. It solves no social problem; it merely creates new and more complicated ones.

Violence as a way of achieving racial justice is both impractical and immoral. 5
It is impractical because it is a descending spiral ending in destruction for all. The old law of an eye for an eye leaves everybody blind. It is immoral because it seeks to humiliate the opponent rather than win his understanding; it seeks to annihilate rather than to convert. Violence is immoral because it thrives on hatred rather than love. It destroys community and makes brotherhood impossible. It leaves society in monologue rather than dialogue. Violence ends by defeating itself. It creates bitterness in the survivors and brutality in the destroyers. A voice echoes through time saying to every potential Peter, "Put up your sword."* History is cluttered with the wreckage of nations that failed to follow this command.

If the American Negro and other victims of oppression succumb to the 6
temptation of using violence in the struggle for freedom, future generations will be the recipients of a desolate night of bitterness, and our chief legacy to them will be an endless reign of meaningless chaos. Violence is not the way.

The third way open to oppressed people in their quest for freedom is the 7
way of nonviolent resistance. Like the synthesis in Hegelian philosophy, the principle of nonviolent resistance seeks to reconcile the truths of two opposites—the

*The apostle Peter had drawn his sword to defend Christ from arrest. The voice was Christ's, who surrendered himself for trial and crucifixion (John 18:11).

acquiescence and violence—while avoiding the extremes and immoralities of both. The nonviolent resister agrees with the person who acquiesces that one should not be physically aggressive toward his opponent; but he balances the equation by agreeing with the person of violence that evil must be resisted. He avoids the nonresistance of the former and the violent resistance of the latter. With nonviolent resistance, no individual or group need submit to any wrong, nor need anyone resort to violence in order to right a wrong.

It seems to me that this is the method that must guide the actions of the 8
Negro in the present crisis in race relations. Through nonviolent resistance the Negro will be able to rise to the noble height of opposing the unjust system while loving the perpetrators of the system. The Negro must work passionately and unrelentingly for full stature as a citizen, but he must not use inferior methods to gain it. He must never come to terms with falsehood, malice, hate, or destruction.

Nonviolent resistance makes it possible for the Negro to remain in the South 9
and struggle for his rights. The Negro's problem will not be solved by running away. He cannot listen to the glib suggestion of those who would urge him to migrate en masse to other sections of the country. By grasping his great opportunity in the South he can make a lasting contribution to the moral strength of the nation and set a sublime example of courage for generations yet unborn.

By nonviolent resistance, the Negro can also enlist all men of good will in his 10
struggle for equality. The problem is not a purely racial one, with Negroes set against whites. In the end, it is not a struggle between people at all, but a tension between justice and injustice. Nonviolent resistance is not aimed against oppressors but against oppression. Under its banner consciences, not racial groups, are enlisted.

Questions on Technique

1. Which sentence is the thesis of "The Ways of Meeting Oppression"?
2. King's groupings are presented in topic sentences. List those topic sentences.
3. What is King's principle of classification?
4. In what kind of order does King present his groupings?
5. What purpose does the cause and effect analysis in paragraphs 5–6 serve? What purpose does the cause and effect analysis in paragraphs 8–10 serve?
6. What definition occurs in paragraph 7? What purpose does that definition serve?
7. Which paragraphs include examples? What purpose do those examples serve?
8. What is the purpose of King's classification? How do you know?

For Group Discussion or Journal Writing

Martin Luther King, Jr., believed that nonviolent resistance was superior to violence because "violence never brings permanent peace" (paragraph 4). Are there ever times when violence is the best solution? Explain, using examples if possible.

What, Me? Showing Off?

Judith Viorst

Judith Viorst is a poet and essayist who frequently contributes to popular magazines like Redbook, *in which "What, Me? Showing Off?" first appeared. In the essay, Viorst classifies showoffs. She concludes that we all show off at times, but we must forgive each other for the lapse.*

We're at the Biedermans' annual blast, and over at the far end of the living room an intense young woman with blazing eyes and a throbbing voice is decrying poverty, war, injustice and human suffering. Indeed, she expresses such anguish at the anguish of mankind that attention quickly shifts from the moral issues she is expounding to how very, very, very deeply she cares about them. *1*

She's showing off. *2*

Down at the other end of the room an insistently scholarly fellow has just used *angst, hubris,* Kierkegaard and *epistemology* in the same sentence. Meanwhile our resident expert in wine meditatively sips, then pushes away, a glass of unacceptable Beaujolais. *3*

They're showing off. *4*

And then there's us, complaining about how tired we are today because we went to work, rushed back to see our son's school play, shopped at the market and hurried home in order to cook gourmet, and then needlepointed another diningroom chair. *5*

And what we also are doing is showing off. *6*

Indeed everyone, I would like to propose, has some sort of need to show off. No one's completely immune. Not you. And not I. And although we've been taught that it's bad to boast, that it's trashy to toot our own horn, that nice people don't strut their stuff, seek attention or name-drop, there are times when showing off may be forgivable and maybe even acceptable. *7*

But first let's take a look at showing off that *is* obnoxious, that's *not* acceptable, that's *never* nice. Like showoffs motivated by a fierce, I'm-gonna-blow-you-away competitiveness. And like narcissistic showoffs who are willing to do anything to be—and stay—the center of attention. *8*

Competitive showoffs want to be the best of every bunch. Competitive showoffs must outshine all others. Whatever is being discussed, they have more—expertise or money or even aggravation—and better—periodontists or children or marriages or recipes for pesto—and deeper—love of animals or concern for human suffering or orgasms. Competitive showoffs are people who reside in a permanent state of sibling rivalry, insisting on playing Hertz to everyone else's Avis. *9*

(You're finishing a story, for instance, about the sweet little card that your five-year-old recently made for your birthday when the CSO interrupts to relate how *her* daughter not only made her a sweet little card, but also brought her breakfast in bed and saved her allowance for months and months in order to buy her—obviously much more beloved—mother a beautiful scarf for her birthday. *Grrr.*) *10*

Narcissistic showoffs, however, don't bother to compete because they don't 11
even notice there's anyone there to compete with. They talk nonstop, they brag, they dance, they sometimes quote Homer in Greek, and they'll even go stand on their head if attention should flag. Narcissistic showoffs want to be the star while everyone else is the audience. And yes, they are often adorable and charming and amusing—but only until around the age of six.

(I've actually seen an NSO get up and leave the room when the conversa- 12
tion shifted from his accomplishments. "What's the matter?" I asked when I found him standing on the terrace, brooding darkly. "Oh, I don't know," he replied, "but all of a sudden the talk started getting so superficial." *Aagh!*)

Another group of showoffs—much more sympathetic types—are showoffs 13
who are basically insecure. And while there is no easy way to distinguish the insecure from the narcissists and competitors, you may figure out which are which by whether you have the urge to reassure or to strangle them.

Insecure showoffs show off because, as one close friend explained, "How 14
will they know that I'm good unless I tell them about it?" And whatever the message—I'm smart, I'm a fine human being, I'm this incredibly passionate lover—showoffs have many different techniques for telling about it.

Take smart, for example. 15

A person can show off explicitly by using flashy words, like the hubris- 16
Kierkegaard fellow I mentioned before.

Or a person can show off implicitly, by saying not a word and just wearing 17
a low-cut dress with her Phi Beta Kappa key gleaming softly in the cleavage.

A person can show off satirically, by mocking showing off: "My name is Bill 18
Sawyer," one young man announces to every new acquaintance, "and I'm bright bright bright bright bright bright bright."

Or a person can show off complainingly: "I'm sorry my daughter takes after 19
me. Men are just so frightened of smart women."

Another way showoffs show off about smart is to drop a Very Smart 20
Name—if this brain is my friend, goes the message, I must be a brain too. And indeed, a popular showing-off ploy—whether you're showing off smartness or anything else—is to name-drop a glittery name in the hope of acquiring some gilt by association.

The theory seems to be that Presidents, movie stars, Walter Cronkite and 21
Princess Di could be friends, if they chose, with anyone in the world, and that if these luminaries have selected plain old Stanley Stone to be friends with, Stanley Stone must be one hell of a guy. (Needless to say, old Stanley Stone might also be a very dreary fellow, but if Walt and Di don't mind him, why should I?)

Though no one that I know hangs out with Presidents and movie stars, they 22
do (I too!) sometimes drop famous names.

As in: "I go to John Travolta's dermatologist." 23

Or: "I own the exact same sweater that Jackie Onassis wore in a newspaper 24
photograph last week."

Or: "My uncle once repaired a roof for Sandra Day O'Connor." 25

Or: "My cousin's neighbor's sister-in-law has a child who is Robert Red- 26
ford's son's best friend."

We're claiming we've got gilt—though by a very indirect association. And I think that when we do, we're showing off. 27

Sometimes showoffs ask for cheers to which they're not entitled. Sometimes showoffs earn the praise they seek. And sometimes folks achieve great things and nonetheless do not show off about it. 28

Now *that's* impressive. 29

Indeed, when we discover that the quiet mother of four with whom we've been talking intimately all evening has recently been elected to the state senate—*and she never even mentioned it!*—we are filled with admiration, with astonishment, with awe. 30

What self-restraint! 31

For we know damn well—*I* certainly know—that if we'd been that lucky lady, we'd have worked our triumph into the conversation. As a matter of fact, I'll lay my cards right on the table and confess that the first time some poems of mine were published, I not only worked my triumph into every conversation for months and months, but I also called almost every human being I'd ever known to proclaim the glad tidings both local and long distance. Furthermore—let me really confess if a stranger happened to stop me on the street and all he wanted to know was the time or directions, I tried to detain him long enough to enlighten him with the news that the person to whom he was speaking was a Real Live Genuine Honest-to-God Published Poet. 32

Fortunately for everyone, I eventually—it took me awhile—calmed down. 33

Now, I don't intend to defend myself—I was showing off, I was bragging and I wasn't the slightest bit shy or self-restrained, but a golden, glowing, glorious thing had happened in my life and I had an overwhelming need to exult. Exulting, however (as I intend to argue farther on), may be a permissible form of showing off. 34

Exulting is what my child does when he comes home with an *A* on his history paper ("Julius Caesar was 50," it began, "and his good looks was pretty much demolished") and wants to read me the entire masterpiece while I murmur appreciative comments at frequent intervals. 35

Exulting is what my husband does when he cooks me one of his cheese-and-scallion omelets and practically does a tap dance as he carries it from the kitchen stove to the table, setting it before me with the purely objective assessment that this may be the greatest omelet ever created. 36

Exulting is what my mother did when she took her first grandson to visit all her friends, and announced as she walked into the room, "Is he gorgeous? Is that a gorgeous baby? Is that the most gorgeous baby you ever saw?" 37

And exulting is what that mother of four would have done if she'd smiled and said, "Don't call me 'Marge' any more. Call me 'Senator.' " 38

Exulting is shamelessly shouting our talents or triumphs to the world. It's saying: I'm taking a bow and I'd like to hear clapping. And I think if we don't overdo it (stopping strangers to say you've been published is overdoing it), and I think if we know when to quit ("Enough about me. Let's talk about you. So what do you think about me?" does not count as quitting), and I think if we don't get 39 addicted (i.e., crave a praise-fix for every poem or *A* or omelet), and I think if we're able to walk off the stage (and clap and cheer while others take their bows), then I think we're allowed, from time to time, to exult.

Though showing off can range from very gross to very subtle, and though the point of showing off is sometimes nasty, sometimes needy, sometimes nice, showoffs always run the risk of being thought immodest, of being harshly viewed as . . . well . . . showoffs. And so for folks who want applause without relinquishing their sense of modesty, the trick is keeping quiet and allowing someone else to show off *for* you. 40

And I've seen a lot of marriages where wives show off for husbands and where husbands, in return, show off for wives. Where Joan, for instance, mentions Dick's promotion and his running time in the marathon. And where Dick, for instance, mentions all the paintings Joanie sold at her last art show. And where both of them lean back with self-effacing shrugs and smiles and never once show off about themselves. 41

Friends also may show off for friends, and parents for their children, though letting parents toot our horns is risky. Consider, for example, this sad tale of Elliott, who was a fearless and feisty public-interest lawyer: 42

"My son," his proud mother explained to his friends, "has always been independent." (Her son blushed modestly.) 43

"My son," his proud mother continued, "was the kind of person who always knew his own mind." (Her son blushed modestly.) 44

"My son," his proud mother went on, "was never afraid. He never kowtowed to those in authority." (Her son blushed modestly.) 45

"My son," his proud mother concluded, "was so independent and stubborn and unafraid of authority that we couldn't get him toilet-trained—he wet his pants till he was well past four." (Her son . . .) 46

But showing off is always a risk, whether we do it ourselves or whether somebody else is doing it for us. And perhaps we ought to consider the words Lord Chesterfield wrote to his sons: "Modesty is the only sure bait when you angle for praise." 47

And yes, of course he's right, we know he's right, he must be right. But sometimes it's so hard to be restrained. For no matter what we do, we always have a lapse or two. So let's try to forgive each other for showing off. 48

Questions on Technique

1. Viorst's introduction is long; it runs eight paragraphs. What approach does she take to her introduction, and why is it so long?
2. What is the thesis of the essay? Which words indicate that classification will occur?
3. What is the principle of classification?
4. In what order are the categories arranged?
5. What are the primary patterns of development in the essay? What purpose do these patterns of development serve?

6. "What, Me? Showing Off?" originally appeared in *Redbook*. Which paragraph seems directly aimed at a female audience? Can a male audience appreciate this essay?
7. What do you judge to be Viorst's purpose?
8. What approach does the author take to the conclusion?

For Group Discussion or Journal Writing

The accomplishments of people who "hide their light under a bushel" often go unnoticed. These people may be underappreciated, particularly in a work environment. Should such people show off more? If so, how? If not, why not?

The Plot Against People

Russell Baker

Newspaper columnist Russell Baker won the Pulitzer Prize in 1979 for distinguished commentary. "The Plot Against People" is an entertaining classification that achieves its humor through a mock scientific tone.

Inanimate objects are classified scientifically into three major categories—those that break down, those that get lost, and those that don't work. *1*

The goal of all inanimate objects is to resist man and ultimately to defeat him, and the three major classifications are based on the method each object uses to achieve its purpose. As a general rule, any object capable of breaking down at the moment when it is most needed will do so. The automobile is typical of the category. *2*

With the cunning peculiar to its breed, the automobile never breaks down while entering a filling station which has a large staff of idle mechanics. It waits until it reaches a downtown intersection in the middle of the rush hour, or until it is fully loaded with family and luggage on the Ohio Turnpike. Thus it creates maximum inconvenience, frustration, and irritability, thereby reducing its owner's lifespan. *3*

Washing machines, garbage disposals, lawn mowers, furnaces, TV sets, tape recorders, slide projectors—all are in league with the automobile to take their turn at breaking down whenever life threatens to flow smoothly for their enemies. *4*

Many inanimate objects, of course, find it extremely difficult to break down. Pliers, for example, and gloves and keys are almost totally incapable of breaking down. Therefore, they have had to evolve a different technique for resisting man. *5*

They get lost. Science has still not solved the mystery of how they do it, and no man has ever caught one of them in the act. The most plausible theory is that they have developed a secret method of locomotion which they are able to conceal from human eyes. *6*

It is not uncommon for a pair of pliers to climb all the way from the cellar to the attic in its single-minded determination to raise its owner's blood pressure. Keys have been known to burrow three feet under mattresses. Women's purses, despite their great weight, frequently travel through six or seven rooms to find hiding space under a couch. 7

Scientists have been struck by the fact that things that break down virtually never get lost, while things that get lost hardly ever break down. A furnace, for example, will invariably break down at the depth of the first winter cold wave, but it will never get lost. A woman's purse hardly ever breaks down; it almost invariably chooses to get lost. 8

Some persons believe this constitutes evidence that inanimate objects are not entirely hostile to man. After all, they point out, a furnace could infuriate a man even more thoroughly by getting lost than by breaking down, just as a glove could upset him far more by breaking down than by getting lost. 9

Not everyone agrees, however, that this indicates a conciliatory attitude. Many say it merely proves that furnaces, gloves, and pliers are incredibly stupid. 10

The third class of objects—those that don't work—is the most curious of all. These include such objects as barometers, car clocks, cigarette lighters, flashlights and toy-train locomotives. It is inaccurate, of course, to say that they *never* work. They work once, usually for the first few hours after being brought home, and then quit. Thereafter, they never work again. 11

In fact, it is widely assumed that they are built for the purpose of not working. Some people have reached advanced ages without ever seeing some of these objects—barometers, for example—in working order. 12

Science is utterly baffled by the entire category. There are many theories about it. The most interesting holds that the things that don't work have attained the highest state possible for an inanimate object, the state to which things that break down and things that get lost can still only aspire. 13

They have truly defeated man by conditioning him never to expect anything of them. When his cigarette lighter won't light or his flashlight fails to illuminate, it does not raise his blood pressure. Objects that don't work have given man the only peace he receives from inanimate society. 14

Questions on Technique

1. Baker's thesis states what will be classified and the groupings. Write out the thesis, underline what will be classified, and bracket the groupings.
2. Is opening with the thesis an effective technique in this essay? Explain.
3. The first topic sentence is in an unusual place. Where is that topic sentence? Would you recommend a different placement for the topic sentence? Explain.
4. What topic sentence introduces the second grouping? The third grouping?
5. What is Baker's principle of classification?
6. In what order does Baker arrange his groupings?

7. For what purpose does Baker present his classification? Who is his intended audience?
8. What techniques contribute to the humor of the classification?
9. For what purpose does Baker use illustration?

For Group Discussion or Journal Writing

Explain the significance of the title of Baker's essay and why you think he used that title. Then compose an alternate title and explain whether or not you like it as well as Baker's and why.

STUDENT ESSAYS TO READ AND EVALUATE

The classification essays that follow were written by students. Each has strengths and aspects that could be improved with revision. As you study these essays, you will improve your ability to assess strengths and weaknesses so that you can better judge and revise your own work. Following the student writings is a formal evaluation exercise to work on.

My Search for Operator Ideal

When I started college, I began to use the telephone a lot, often requiring operator assistance to place long distance, collect calls. Three types of operators have handled my calls frequently: Phone-A-Stone, Dial-A-Smile, and Converse-With-A-Hearse. 1

Phone-A-Stone is the operator who is always very unfriendly. She acts as if she has somewhere better to be or someone she would rather talk to. In fact, talking to her is like conversing with one of the Undead. When she mumbles, "May I help you?" in her monotone rasp, I can tell that what she really means is, "Why are you bothering me while I'm in the middle of filing my nails?" I envision Phone-A-Stone slouching in her chair with a cigarette dangling from the corner of her mouth. She is bored with her job and not particularly fond of people. 2

The second type of operator is Dial-A-Smile. This woman sounds as though there is nothing she would rather do than answer phones all day. When I'm done telling Dial-A-Smile how she can assist me, she chirps brightly, "Thank you for using AT&T!" Dial-A-Smile is twenty years old, still living with her parents. Her father calls her Princess, and her dog Fluffy sleeps in her bed. She took the job as an operator because she "likes to work with people." 3

The last type of operator I have encountered is Converse-With-A-Hearse. This type obviously views her job as an opportunity to nap. When she finally connects with my line (after a minimum of twelve rings), she murmurs, " 'lo?" over the cracking of her joints as she stretches. She can't resist a yawn in the middle of 4 the necessary, "The initial period is over, Ma'am; please signal when through." Perhaps Converse-With-A-Hearse took the night shift at AT&T because she needs the money to continue going to cosmetology school during the day.

Isn't there an operator out there who is easy to deal with? Someone to whom 5
I don't have to repeat my name for a collect call because she was yawning or giggling or grumbling the first time I said it? Somebody business-like and efficient? Believe me, if I encounter such a person, I'll be sure to send her name to *Ripley's Believe It or Not.*

They're Off and Running

Waterford Park is a rather remote horse-racing track wedged between the moun- 1
tains of West Virginia. I go there often, not so much to test my luck as to observe the fascinating people.

Upon entering Waterford Park, a person first encounters a sign that reads, 2
"Lucky Louie's Daily Selections." Beneath the sign sits the founder, selling his "winners" for 1 dollar. A portly man, Louie is usually dressed in an outlandish plaid sports jacket accessorized with a shirt and tie bearing the remains of his meals for the past week. A smoking cigar clenched between decayed teeth juts from his mouth, emitting a stench that keeps his clientele on the move. Every so often in his sandpaper voice Louie emits a garbled announcement: "Get your winners here!"

Another character frequently seen at Waterford Park is the inebriated bum. 3
He looks like he stumbled down from his moonshine still in the mountains to gamble his last 2 bucks. Clothed in a pair of grimy overalls and a stained jacket of indeterminate color, the sot can usually be found sleeping it off in a sheltered area of the grandstand, his nip bottle in one hand and his tattered ticket in the other. More often than not the bum loses, and when he does, he begins staggering around cursing the ponies for his rotten luck.

Of course there are those who have worries other than money: the flamboy- 4
ant and well-heeled. They have their own club on the premises, known as the Cap and Whip. As the grandstand crowd eat their sausage sandwiches and guzzle their beer, this elite group dines on filet mignon and Asti Spumante served at their reserved tables. Protected from the elements, they sit back for a night of racing. There is no need for them to challenge the betting lines, since they have their own courtesy betting service. They lavishly toss two or three hundred dollars into the hands of the club steward who places the bets for them. Beautifully tailored three-piece suits and designer evening gowns are the standard attire of these affluent people. The air around them is heavy with the scent of Giorgio perfume and the aroma of Cuban cigars.

The hustlers, the sots, and the privileged can be viewed on any given 5
evening at Waterford Park. By 7 P.M., they are all in their places as the familiar cry echoes over the track: "They're off and running!"

A Matter of Attitude

At first jeans were nothing more than work pants, something durable and functional for laborers to labor in. Then jeans became a status symbol. People paid ridiculous prices just to sport names like Calvin Klein, Jordache, and Gloria Vanderbilt on their backsides. Now, there is a wide range of jeans styles to suit a wide range of tastes, body shapes, and budgets. However, it is possible to classify jeans according to the attitude the wearer wants to reflect to the world. 1

Most people who want to present a relaxed image are found wearing faded or stone-washed denim. These jeans look worn even when new. When teamed with tennis shoes and a sweatshirt bearing a college name (as they commonly are), these jeans announce to the world that the wearer is laid back, totally relaxed, and cool. A person in faded or stone-washed jeans can go anywhere from a football game to a party feeling comfortable. 2

Baggy jeans are the most versatile. They can be sloppy one moment (announcing to the world that the wearer doesn't care about a thing at the moment), or they can be teamed with penny loafers and a crew neck sweater (to state that the wearer is neat, pressed, and in control). If you get up in the morning, and it's raining, your hair is frizzed, and you feel like an 18 wheeler ran over your face during the night, you probably realize that it is not going to be your best day. The perfect solution is to slide on a pair of baggies with the oldest shirt in your closet. Then you will be letting people know not to expect great things. On the other hand, if you feel on top of it all and you want to dress up but those tight pants don't look right with your penny loafers and argyle socks, just march to your closet and throw on those baggies, roll a cuff in the bottom, and slip on a great looking sweater. 3

Finally, acid-washed jeans are worn by those who want to be noticed. The colors are usually bright red, green, or purple. These jeans are usually worn with shirts equally bright. The outfit tells the world you are confident and ready for anything. Acid-washed jeans beg the world to sit up and take notice. 4

Gone are the days when jeans made a simple statement like "I'm on my way to work" or "I have status." Now jeans reflect a range of attitudes. 5

Horror Movies

Horror movies started out harmless enough, but they have developed over the years into stomach-turning trash. 1

The first popular horror movies were the mass destruction movies. These include *The Blob, Invasion of the Body Snatchers,* and the classic *War of the Worlds.* In these movies the human race is threatened with destruction by odd creatures, usually from another planet. The early mass destruction movies are the least gory of the horror flicks. There is no graphic violence, murder, or mutilation. The camera cuts away at the moment someone is done in, and eerie music hints at the 2 mayhem that occurs. The early mass destruction movies give an audience plenty of frightening moments without turning anyone's stomach. They are harmless fun for those who like a good scare.

The supernatural thrillers came next. These movies tend to be very scary 3
and even more nauseating. They deal with the satanic and the occult, and vampires and evil spirits are often reeking havoc on unsuspecting, average human beings. In *The Exorcist* a young girl was possessed by the devil who caused her to vomit green gorp, spin her head in a full circle, and otherwise disgust the audience. *The Omen* and *Rosemary's Baby* fit into this class of movies that causes knee-clanking fear while souring the stomach.

The worst group of horror movies is undoubtedly the psychopath chop 'em 4
up group. These movies, unlike many of the supernatural thrillers, have weak plots. They rely solely on gore to keep the audience interested. Take, for example, the movie series *Friday the Thirteenth.* In these, indestructible Jason uses an ice pick and an axe to attack his victims. The violence is graphic; blood flies everywhere. *The Texas Chainsaw Massacre, Halloween,* and *Nightmare on Elm Street*—all of these depict mutilation, murder, and mayhem vividly and in detail. Strangely, these movies should be the most disturbing, but audiences love them, returning for sequel after sequel. What does this say about us? Why do the simple, scary mass destruction movies no longer provide sufficient thrills? Perhaps the answers to these questions are even scarier than the movies.

Becoming a Reliable Critic by Evaluating Writing

Form a group with two classmates and select one of the previous student essays (or use one your instructor assigns). Prepare a report that notes the chief strengths of the essay and the revisions you would like to see. If you like, you can use the following evaluation questions to guide your work.

Evaluation Questions

1. The Thesis
   What is the thesis? Is it clear what is being classified and what the principle of classification is?
2. The Introduction
   Does the introduction engage your interest? Why or why not?
3. Supporting Details
   Note any elements omitted from a grouping and any place where the characteristics of a grouping are unclear. Also note anything that is not relevant or that is inadequately developed.
4. Organization
   Are there at least three groupings? Are the groupings placed in a logical order? Evaluate how effectively the author moves from grouping to grouping.

5. The Conclusion
   Does the essay come to a satisfying end? Explain.
6. Sentence Effectiveness and Word Choice
   Note any places where sentence variety is needed, where wordiness is a problem, or where clichés are a problem. Cite any inappropriate word choice.
7. Overview
   What do you like best about the essay? What is the single most important revision the author should make?

Essay Topics: Classification

1. In "The Ways of Meeting Oppression" (page 293), Martin Luther King, Jr., classifies the ways to deal with oppression and notes which of the ways is best. In similar fashion, write an essay that classifies the ways to deal with one of the following: sexual harrassment, sex discrimination, stress, depression, or peer pressure. Be sure to note which way is the best.
2. Viorst classifies showoffs in "What, Me? Showing Off?" (page 296). Do you agree with her classification? If not, write one of your own.
3. Like Baker, in "The Plot Against People" (page 300), write a humorous classification of inanimate objects. Perhaps you can classify Christmas gifts, wedding presents, or kitchen gadgets.
4. Classify any of the following people according to types:
   a. College students or professors
   b. Disc jockeys
   c. Football coaches
   d. Automobile drivers
   e. Salespeople
   f. Roommates
   g. Game show hosts
   h. Talk show hosts
   i. Baby-sitters
   j. Blind dates
   k. Bosses
   l. Table servers
5. Classify your friends
6. Classify the types of radio stations.
7. Classify kinds of lies.
8. Classify types of cigarette advertisements (or advertisements for another product such as shampoo, deodorant, beer, pain relievers, etc.).
9. Classify the fads of the last ten years.
10. Classify study techniques.
11. Classify test-taking strategies.
12. Classify outlooks on life.

13. Classify types of horror movies.
14. Classify types of situation comedies.
15. Classify ways to procrastinate (make this one humorous).
16. Classify the kinds of stress a college student experiences.
17. Classify types of pizza (your purpose should be to entertain).
18. Classify kinds of courage.
19. Classify types of practical jokes.
20. Classify types of baseball pitches.
21. Classify the styles of professional basketball players.
22. Classify the types of roller coasters.
23. Classify the types of home computers.

Thematic Topics

1. Cite one or more examples of oppression that you have experienced or observed and explain how that oppression could be addressed using the nonviolent resistance that Martin Luther King, Jr., advocates in "The Ways of Meeting Oppression" (page 293).
2. Although Judith Viorst classifies showoffs in "What, Me? Showing Off?" (page 296), she also speaks to the causes and effects of showing off. Pick some behavior (bullying, being a workaholic, being competitive, telling dirty jokes, and so forth), and explain its causes and effects.
3. Dick Gregory (see "Shame," page 165) and Harold Krents (see "Darkness at Noon," page 187) suffer humiliation and oppression, as do Native Americans (see "It's Time to Stop Playing Indians," page 256). Explain which of the ways of meeting oppression (see "The Ways of Meeting Oppression") the essays note have been used to deal with the oppression. Evaluate the success of these methods and comment on whether other methods would be more successful.

Writing Strategies

In addition to the strategies described in Chapters 1 to 3, the following suggestions may help as you work to improve your writing process.

Idea Generation

1. Write every element that can be grouped on a separate index card. On the back of each card list all the characteristics of the element.
2. To discover a principle of classification, study the characteristics on the back of the index cards, and then make a list of every possible principle of classification.
3. Once you have your principle, select the index cards with the elements that will appear in your classification. You are not likely to use every card, every element, and every characteristic.

Organization

1. Place the index cards in piles to correspond to the groupings in your classification.
2. As an alternative, make columns on a sheet of paper, one column for each grouping. Label each grouping at the top of its column and list the elements of each group in the appropriate column. Also list the characteristics of the elements in the group.
3. As another alternative, construct a formal outline. Because outlines are themselves forms of classification, they can be particularly helpful in planning a classification essay.

Reader Response

If you like to secure reader response during revision, consult page 77. In addition, ask your reader to write out your principle of classification and the significance of the classification to be sure these points are clear.

REVISION CHECKLIST

In addition to the checklist on page 80, you can use this checklist when you revise your classification.

1. Does your classification group elements according to some principle?
2. Does your classification serve one of these purposes?
   a. Order information to make for easier study
   b. Clarify by identifying how elements are alike and different
   c. Bring the reader to a fresh way of viewing something
   d. Persuade the reader to think or act a particular way
   e. Entertain the reader
3. Does your thesis do one of the following?
   a. State what is being grouped and the principle of classification
   b. State the topic and include words that indicate that classification will occur
   c. State what the groupings are
4. Have you presented the groupings in topic sentences?
5. If the same characteristics are discussed for each grouping, are they arranged in parallel order?
6. Is the value of the classification clear?

CHAPTER 13

Argumentation-Persuasion

Argumentation and persuasion are everywhere—a friend tries to talk you into skipping a class and catching an afternoon movie; a politician delivers a speech to win your vote; a newspaper editor writes an editorial to convince you of the dangers of the national debt; an advertising executive creates an ad to make you believe that the surest path to popularity is using the right deodorant soap.

Sometimes people use cool logic and sound reasoning to convince—that's **argumentation**. Sometimes they appeal to our emotions—that's **persuasion**. Most often, however, argumentation and persuasion are combined to sway us to specific lines of thought or courses of action. For example, to convince you to help the homeless, I could appeal to your intellect by explaining that helping the homeless reduces crime, and I could appeal to your emotions by describing the abominable living conditions of the homeless.

TOPIC SELECTION

A topic for argumentation-persuasion must be debatable; it must have at least two sides to it. It would serve no purpose, for example, to write an essay arguing that everyone needs some relaxation. No one would disagree with you. It *would* be purposeful, however, to argue that places of business should have recreation areas to allow employees to relax during lunch and break periods. Similarly, it would be pointless to write a persuasive essay on a matter of individual taste. To argue that it is more pleasant to listen to Mozart than Bach makes little sense because the issue is strictly a matter of personal preference.

As a student writer, you may want to avoid some of the standard topics. Most instructors are weary of reading about abortion, capital punishment, legalizing drugs, lowering the drinking age, and the like. Unless you can find a fresh approach to topics like these, avoid them.

One reason so many papers have been written on these standard topics may be that students feel that to be significant, their essays must be on topics of major importance. Yet this is not so. Many smaller-scale issues matter, and can be written about. Campus issues, work matters, and community concerns suggest topics. You *can,* however, write on matters of larger concern; just try to select something fresh. For example, a paper arguing that the elderly should be cared for at home rather than in institutions is significant yet not overworked. At the same time, you can also treat something of narrower concern. You could, for example, argue that your school should offer a major in hospital administration.

AUDIENCE AND PURPOSE

You might think that establishing audience and determining purpose are simple: the purpose is to convince the reader, and the reader is someone who disagrees. However, that is only part of the picture. Let's consider audience first.

Certainly your audience will be someone who disagrees with you to some extent, for why bother trying to convince someone who already agrees with you? However, it is important to establish how great the disagreement is. Let's say you are writing an essay in opposition to dispensing birth control in schools. If your audience is a member of Planned Parenthood, you will need to be far more persuasive than if your reader is someone who believes something closer to what you do.

When considering audience, you must determine how much your reader knows about your issue. Let's say you are writing in support of the legislative veto. If your audience is knowledgeable about the workings of the federal government, you can supply less background information than if your reader has only limited knowledge in this area.

Your purpose also deserves careful consideration. Sure, you want to convince your reader to see things just as you do, but that may be an unreasonable expectation. If you favor gun control and are writing to a member of the National Rifle Association, it would be realistic to set your purpose as convincing the reader we need stricter enforcement of existing laws. It might be unrealistic to expect you can convince your reader that handguns should be banned.

Sometimes a particular audience is so opposed to your view that the best you can hope for is that the reader will consider your points and agree that they have some merit. For example, if you are writing to the president of the local teachers' union about the hardships of teachers' strikes, you cannot expect your reader to come out against such strikes. However, if you present a good enough case, your reader can come to understand something he or she never realized before, and become more sympathetic to your view. Perhaps this new understanding will influence the reader's thinking and actions in the future.

To decide on your audience, you can ask these questions.

1. Who disagrees with me?
2. Of those who disagree, who might be influenced by my writing?

3. Of those who might be influenced, who has the power to act in accordance with my point of view?

After answering the third question, you will have your audience. Then you can answer the following questions to arrive at your purpose.

1. What can I reasonably expect my audience to think or do after reading my essay?
2. Of these things, which are the most important to me?

DETAIL

Above all, argumentative detail must be firmly rooted in reason. If a thoughtful reader is to adopt your view, that person must see the wisdom of your stand. This means that you must provide a carefully thought out argument—one that presents well-reasoned points in support of your view. Think of yourself as a lawyer presenting facts, examples, and evidence to a jury to persuade that body to recognize the validity of your case.

However, as any successful attorney knows, sound logic and compelling facts are not all that influence a person. Emotion, too, plays a role. After all, when we make up our minds about something, how we *feel* about the issue can determine our decision along with what we *think* about it. For this reason, a writer may include persuasive detail to move the reader's emotions. This is why the writer of a toothpaste ad may emphasize fewer cavities *and* a brighter smile. Our intellect makes us understand the virtue of fewer cavities, but our emotional desire to be attractive makes us want a bright smile.

Still, a writer must be careful with emotional appeals. They should be used sparingly and with restraint. You can call upon the reader's patriotism to earn support for defense spending, but it is unfair, inflammatory, and illogical to whip up emotions by saying that anyone who does not support the spending is un-American. Use emotional appeals only to enhance your logical argument.

Argumentation-persuasion draws on the patterns of development you have learned so far. Narration, description, illustration, comparison and contrast, cause-and-effect analysis, definition, classification—one or more of these may appear in your essay. Say, for example, that you wish to convince your reader to vote for Chris Politician. You might *narrate* an episode that reveals Politician's integrity. You might also *describe* the various personality traits that identify Politician as the best candidate, or you might *illustrate* Politician's strengths with several examples. You could *compare and contrast* Politician with one or more of the other candidates. You could explain the *effects* of electing Politician. You could even *define* what a good public official is and then show how Politician fits this definition.

Another effective technique is to consider what would happen if your view were adopted (or what would happen if it were *not* adopted). You could say, for example, that if Politician were elected, a bigger budget would be allotted to the safety forces so that police and fire protection would improve. Or you could explain something negative that would happen if Politician were *not* elected: police and fire protection would continue at substandard levels.

RAISING AND COUNTERING OBJECTIONS

No matter what stand you take on an issue, some intelligent, reasonable people will disagree with you. If you ignore their opposing views, you will weaken your position because you will not come across as someone who has weighed all sides of the issue before drawing conclusions. However, if you acknowledge and come to terms with the most significant arguments on the other side, you help incline your reader toward your position because it appears more carefully thought out. Furthermore, even if you ignore the opposition's points, your reader will have them in mind. To be convincing, then, you must deal with the chief objections head-on to dispel some of your reader's disagreement. The process of acknowledging and coming to terms with opposing views is called raising and countering objections.

Raising and countering objections is a two-part operation. First you state the opposition's point; this is **raising the objection**. Then you make the point less compelling by introducing a point of your own; this is **countering the objection**.

Let's return to the paper written to convince a reader to vote for Chris Politician and examine how raising and countering objections works. Your first step is to identify your reader's most compelling objections to your view. Let's say they are these.

1. Politician lacks experience in city government.
2. Politician's proposed safety forces budget is inflationary.
3. Politician's health problems will undermine her effectiveness.

After identifying the chief objections, you must find a way to soften their force. You can do this in one of two ways: by offering an equally compelling point of your own to balance out the opposition or by showing that the opposition's point is untrue. Here are some examples.

<u>Offering an Equally Compelling Point</u>

Some people claim that Politician's lack of experience in municipal government will make her a poor city manager. *(objection raised)* However, while she has not had actual experience in city government, 10 years as president of City Bank have provided Politician with all the managerial skills any mayor could need. Furthermore, our current mayor, who came to the job with five years of experience on City Council, has mismanaged everything from Street Department funds to the city's public relations efforts. Thus, experience in city government does not guarantee success. *(objection countered)*

Although some contend that the increased safety forces budget that Politician supports is inflationary, *(objection raised)* the fact remains that without adequate police and fire protection, we will not attract new industry to our area. *(objection countered)*

<u>Showing That the Opposition's Point Is Untrue</u>

Some of Politician's detractors say that she is not well enough to do the job. *(objection raised)* However, Politician's physical examination last month shows her to be in perfect health and any discussion to the contrary is based on rumor and falsehood. *(objection countered)*

As the above examples show, an objection is sometimes countered in a single sentence and sometimes countered in several sentences. If an objection is particularly compelling, you may need to devote one or more paragraphs to the counter. Usually, you need not raise and counter every objection to your view. You should, however, identify your reader's most important objections and deal with those.

SELECTING DETAIL

As you decide on persuasive detail, assess your audience carefully. How much does your reader know about your subject? Should you provide background information on the issue and lots of explanation for each point? How receptive will your audience be to your stand? Some audiences are harder to persuade than others. For example, it would be easier to convince a principal that candy machines should be taken out of schools than it would be to convince the students. How much are you asking of your audience? It would be easier to convince people to donate $5 to the leukemia drive than it would be to get them to donate $50 to the Save the Caribou Fund. How knowledgeable your audience is, how inclined toward your view, and how difficult the desired response—these will affect your detail.

You will also have to decide which objections to raise and counter. For the most part, you can base this decision on which objections will be the most compelling and most likely to interfere with acceptance of your view. Let's return to persuading a reader that candy machines should be removed from schools. If your audience is the principal, one objection could be that students would be angry about the removal and perhaps create problems. This objection could be countered with an explanation that annoyance would soon pass as students grew accustomed to not having the machines around.

If, however, your audience is the students themselves, a likely objection could be that removing the machines would eliminate one of the few pleasures of school. Because this audience would not be appeased by being told they would get used to it, another approach to the counter is necessary. You could, for example, suggest that the money usually fed into the machines could be donated to finance a class trip. This stands a better chance of winning your audience over to your view. Thus, persuasive writers must select carefully the objections to raise, and they must counter them with equal care.

Detail for argumentation-persuasion can come from a variety of sources. It can be based on what you have learned from your own experience and observation or from your reading, television viewing, and class lectures. You might even develop support as a result of talking to people knowledgeable about your subject. If some of your support comes from library research, however, check with your instructor. He or she may want you to document these sources according to the conventions discussed in Chapter 15.

USING INDUCTION AND DEDUCTION

To convince a reader, the reasoning in your argumentation-persuasive essay must be flawless. For this reason, you should understand the two most common patterns of reasoning: induction and deduction.

Induction is a movement from specific evidence to a general conclusion, like this.

specific evidence: The number of adolescent suicide attempts is increasing.

specific evidence: In the last year, the local high school has reported four attempted suicides.

specific evidence: Guidance counselors in the middle school and high school are counseling more students for depression than ever before.

specific evidence: Today's high school students are under a great deal of stress.

conclusion: Our high school should institute a suicide prevention program.

Inductive reasoning allows you to argue your case by showing how specific evidence (facts, statistics, cases, examples, etc.) lead to the point you want to convince your reader of. Thus, if you wanted to convince your reader that the local high school should institute a suicide prevention program, you could do so by stating and explaining each piece of evidence that—by way of induction—leads to your conclusion that the program is a good idea.

To avoid faulty inductive reasoning, you must be sure that your conclusion is based on sufficient evidence. Thus, you cannot conclude that today's teens are suicidal based on the fact that there are four attempted suicides in one high school.

A second reasoning pattern is **deduction**, which involves moving from a generalization (known as a **major premise**) to a specific case (known as a **minor premise**) and on to a conclusion. Deduction works like this.

generalization (major premise): `Our city has a serious unemployment problem.`

specific case (minor premise): `A proposed federal prison would create 500 new jobs.`

conclusion: `If the new federal prison is built in our city, we could put 500 people to work.`

Deductive reasoning can help you organize the argument for your stand on an issue. Let's say you want to convince your reader that your city should compete for the new federal prison. You can support your view, in part, by reproducing your deductive reasoning: the city needs jobs, and the prison will provide them.

To argue well, however, you must avoid the illogical conclusions that result from inaccurate or sweeping generalizations. Notice the problems with the following deductive reasoning.

generalization (major premise): `All students cheat at one time or another.`

specific case (minor premise): `Lee is a student.`

conclusion: `Lee cheats.`

This conclusion is illogical because the first generalization is inaccurate—all students do not cheat.

generalization (major premise): `Foreign cars are better made than American cars.`

generalization (minor premise): `My car was made in Germany.`

conclusion: `My car is better made than American cars.`

This conclusion is illogical because the first generalization is sweeping—many foreign cars are not better made than American cars.

AVOIDING LOGICAL FALLACIES

Errors in reasoning, called **logical fallacies,** will weaken your case. If they are serious or frequent enough, your reader will reject your position outright. When you read about induction and deduction, you learned about three types of faulty logic: basing a conclusion on insufficient evidence, using sweeping generalizations, and using inaccurate generalizations. In addition, you should guard against the following logical fallacies.

1. Do not attack an idea on the basis of the people associated with that idea.

example: `Only liberals oppose balancing the federal budget, and we all know the mess they've gotten this country into.`

explanation: The groups of people who do or do not champion an idea or course of action have nothing to do with the validity of that idea or action.

2. Avoid name calling.

example: `The president of this college is an idiot if he thinks students will sit still for another tuition increase.`

explanation: It is legitimate to criticize what people do or think, but it is unfair to attack the personalities of the people themselves.

3. Do not defend or attack an idea or action on the grounds that people have always believed that idea or performed that action.

example: `Children have always learned to read in first grade, so why should we begin teaching them any earlier now?`

explanation: Everything believed and done in the past and present is not always for the best. Perhaps new research in education indicates children are capable of reading before the first grade.

4. Avoid illogical comparisons.

example: `The voters in this city have not passed a school levy for seven years. They will never vote for a teacher to become our next senator.`

explanation: How voters feel about school levies has nothing to do with how they feel about a political candidate who happens to be a teacher. The comparison is not logical.

5. Do not assume that what is true for one person will be true for everybody.

example: `When I was a child, my parents spanked me regularly, and I turned out just fine. Clearly, there is no harm in spanking as a form of punishment.`

explanation: It does not hold that because one person suffered no ill effects from spanking, no one will suffer ill effects from spanking.

6. Do not assume that a debatable point is the truth, or you will be guilty of begging the question.

example: `Unnecessary programs like shop and home economics should be eliminated to balance the new school budget.`

explanation: The importance of shop and home economics is debatable, so you cannot assume they are unnecessary and argue from there. You must first prove they are unnecessary.

7. Avoid drawing a conclusion that does not follow from the evidence. This is called a **non sequitur.**

example: `Feminism is a potent social force in the United States. No wonder our divorce rate is so high.`

explanation: Many factors contribute to the divorce rate; no logical reason establishes feminism as the sole cause or even one cause.

8. Do not present only two options when more than two exist. This is the **either/or fallacy.**

example: `Either you support the strike, or you are opposed to organized labor.`

explanation: The sentence ignores other possibilities, such as opposing the strike but believing the union's demands should be met, and opposing the strike but calling for further negotiations.

9. Avoid bandwagon appeals that argue that everyone believes something so the reader should too.

example: All the professors I spoke to in the political science department favor the trade agreement with Japan, so it must be a good idea.

explanation: The issue should be argued on the merits of the trade agreement, not on the basis of who favors it.

10. Do not assume that an event that precedes another event is the cause of that event. This is called a **post hoc fallacy.**

example: After the freshman class read Catcher in the Rye, the number of teen pregnancies increased. The book causes promiscuity.

explanation: Although the pregnancies followed reading the book, other factors may have caused the increase in pregnancy rate.

11. Do not digress from the matter at hand by introducing a distraction (called a **red herring**).

example: We should not spend more money on AIDS research because so many AIDS victims chose to put themselves at risk.

explanation: The behavior of some people who contract AIDS is not the issue but a distraction (a red herring) meant to direct the reader's attention away from the issue—whether or not more money should be spent on AIDS research.

ARRANGING DETAIL

A progressive order from the least to the most compelling points is effective because the potency of your argument gradually builds. An effective alternative is to begin with your second-strongest point and then build from your least to most compelling reasons. This arrangement allows you to begin and end powerfully, creating strong initial and final impressions.

Often the reasons that support a view have a relationship to each other that dictates a certain arrangement. For example, one supporting argument may be the result of or grow out of another. When this is the case, you must arrange details so that the relationship between them is clear.

You must also decide where to raise and counter objections. Usually the most effective way is to raise and counter objections at the points where the objections logically emerge. For example, say you are arguing that children should not be allowed to play with toy guns, and you explain that violent play leads to violent behavior. In that paragraph (or in a paragraph immediately after) you can raise and counter the objection that gun play can vent violent tendencies harmlessly and thus reduce violent behavior.

Another way to handle objections to your view is to raise them all in your introduction or in your first body paragraphs. The rest of the essay can be devoted to an extensive countering of the objections. This arrangement is most useful when your stand is unpopular, with many objections to it. Then you can make your point by showing how the prevailing beliefs are mistaken. Such an approach would work if you were taking the unpopular stand that military service should be mandatory for all 18-year-olds. For this argument, you could first cite all the reasons people are opposed to this and then go on to show why these reasons are not good ones.

When you are arranging your persuasive detail, remember that you need a clear statement of the issue and your stand on the issue. Typically, this is the thesis statement in your introduction. The rest of your introduction can provide necessary background, explain why the issue is important, trace the history of the issue, or raise and counter objections.

TRYOUT

To gain experience raising and countering objections, try this. First pick one of the following to be your issue and stand.

1. High school seniors should be required to pass a proficiency test in order to graduate.
2. High school seniors should not be required to pass a proficiency test in order to graduate.

Assume that your audience will be the members of your local school board. With that audience in mind, write out two possible objections to your stand and explain how you can counter those objections.

PROFESSIONAL ESSAYS

Indian Bones

Clara Spotted Elk

Clara Spotted Elk is a consultant to the government on Native American affairs. Her essay "Indian Bones" first appeared in the New York Times *in 1989.*

Millions of American Indians lived in this country when Columbus first landed on our shores. After the western expansion, only about 250,000 Indians survived. What happened to the remains of those people who were decimated by the advance of the white man? Many are gathering dust in American museums. 1

In 1985, I and some Northern Cheyenne chiefs visited the attic of the Smithsonian's Natural History Museum in Washington to review the inventory of 2 their Cheyenne collection. After a chance inquiry, a curator pulled out a drawer in one of the scores of cabinets that line the attic. There were the jumbled bones of an Indian. "A Kiowa," he said.

Subsequently, we found that 18,500 Indian remains—some consisting of a 3
handful of bones, but mostly full skeletons—are unceremoniously stored in the Smithsonian's nooks and crannies. Other museums, individuals and Federal agencies such as the National Park Service also collect the bones of Indian warriors, women and children. Some are on display as roadside tourist attractions. It is estimated that another *600,000* Indian remains are secreted away in locations across the country.

The museum community and forensic scientists vigorously defend these 4
grisly collections. With few exceptions, they refuse to return remains to the tribes that wish to rebury them, even when grave robbing has been documented. They want to maintain adequate numbers of "specimens" for analysis and say they are dedicated to "the permanent curation of Indian skeletal remains."

Indian people are tired of being "specimens." The Northern Cheyenne 5
word for ourselves is "tsistsistas"—human beings. Like people the world over, one of our greatest responsibilities is the proper care of the dead.

We are outraged that our religious views are not accepted by the scientific 6
community and that the graves of our ancestors are desecrated. Many tribes are willing to accommodate some degree of study for a limited period of time—provided that it would help Indian people or mankind in general. But how many "specimens" are needed? We will not accept grave robbing and the continued boarding of our ancestors' remains.

Would this nefarious collecting be tolerated if it were discovered that it 7
affected other ethnic groups? (Incidentally, the Smithsonian also collects skeletons of blacks.) What would happen if the Smithsonian had 18,500 Holocaust victims in the attic? There would be a tremendous outcry in this country. Why is there no outcry about the Indian collections?

Indians are not exotic creatures for study. We are human beings who prac- 8
tice living religions. Our religion should be placed not only on a par with science when it comes to determining the disposition of our ancestors but on a par with every other religion practiced in this country.

To that end, Sen. Daniel K. Inouye will soon reintroduce the "Bones Bill" 9
to aid Indians in retrieving the remains of their ancestors from museums. As in the past, the "Bones Bill" will most likely be staunchly resisted by the collectors of Indian skeletons—armed with slick lobbyists, lots of money and cloaked in the mystique of science.

Scientists have attempted to defuse this issue by characterizing their oppo- 10
nents as radical Indians, out of touch with their culture and with little appreciation of science. Armed only with a moral obligation to our ancestors, the Indians who support the bill have few resources and little money.

But, in my view, the issue should concern all Americans—for it raises very 11
disturbing questions. American Indians want only to reclaim and rebury their dead. Is this too much to ask?

Questions on Technique

1. Write out a sentence that expresses the issue and Clara Spotted Elk's stand on the issue. Which sentence in the essay comes closest to expressing that thesis?
2. Clara Spotted Elk chooses words for their emotional impact. For example, in paragraph 1, she uses "decimated" to emphasize that Native Americans were victimized by whites on a huge scale. Cite three other examples of word choice with similar emotional impact.
3. What elements of emotional appeal appear in the essay in addition to the emotional language? Is the emotional appeal restrained? Does the author rely more on emotional appeal or logic? Explain.
4. Which paragraphs include narration? How does that narration help the author convince the reader?
5. In which paragraphs does the author raise and counter objections? What are the objections and how are they countered?
6. Do you find the comparison to Holocaust victims in paragraph 7 convincing? Why or why not? Do you find the reference in paragraph 7 to collecting the skeletons of blacks convincing? Why or why not?
7. A **rhetorical question** does not require an answer. Do you think the rhetorical question in the last paragraph makes an effective closing? Explain.
8. "Indian Bones" first appeared in *The New York Times*. Is the argumentation geared to the original audience? Explain.

For Group Discussion or Journal Writing

Compose a one- to two-page dialogue between Clara Spotted Elk and a museum official wherein the official argues for the museum to retain its Indian bones and Spotted Elk argues for their return for ceremonial burial.

Why Drug Testing Is Needed

American Society for Industrial Security

The American Society for Industrial Security is a professional organization of people involved in the public and private security business. In the following selection, the organization presents and defends its position on drug testing in the workplace.

The illicit drug trade in America has fast become a $110 billion annual business.[1] *1* According to the Research Triangle Institute, a North Carolina-based research organization, drug abuse cost the US economy $60 billion in 1983, nearly a 30 percent increase from the more than $47 billion estimated for 1980.[2]

No one seriously disputes that drug abuse in the workplace is a serious and *2* growing problem for both public and private employers. Increasingly, the problem continues to contribute to the high rate of employee absenteeism, rising health care costs, a high rate of accidents, and the low productivity of our work force. It has been aptly called an American tragedy.

As a result, ASIS—and its Standing Committee on Substance Abuse—is in favor of drug testing efforts by both business and government. We believe a comprehensive drug testing program puts drug abusers on notice that they will be held strictly accountable for their actions. 3

There Is Basis for Concern

Let there be no doubt that drug abuse in the workplace carries a heavy price tag for our society—one that translates not only into dollars but also into pain and suffering for innocent members of the public. The following are some examples of that price tag: 4

• Since 1975, more than fifty train accidents have been attributed to drug-impaired employees. In these mishaps, more than eighty people were injured, thirty-seven lost their lives, and property valued at more than $34 million was destroyed.[3] 5

• In 1979, a Conrail employee, while under the influence of drugs, lost control of his locomotive and crashed into the rear of another train. Two people lost their lives and damages exceeded $400,000.[4] The same scenario repeated itself only recently. 6

• A recent study by the US Department of Justice found that more than 50 percent of all persons arrested in New York and Washington, DC, for serious crimes were found to be using one or more illegal drugs. Cocaine seemed to be the drug of choice among those who were arrested.[5] 7

• Cocaine, once the drug of the rich and famous, now has a clientele of more than 4 million regulars, reaching from the assembly line to the boardroom of many of our major corporations.[6] 8

• Employees who use drugs are at least three times as likely to be involved in an accident, seven times as likely to be the target of garnishment proceedings, and often function at only 65 percent of their work potential.[7] 9

Presently, some 20 percent of all federal agencies and more than 25 percent of all Fortune 500 companies conduct some type of drug screening or testing program.[8] The utility, petroleum, and chemical industries—the first private employers to use drug testing—are now being joined by a multitude of other industries, including state and local governments, in screening or testing their employees for drugs. 10

Because of the sensitive nature of their work, airlines and railroads are also turning to drug testing programs as a way of filtering out employees who pose a danger to the public. Recently, they were joined by such corporate giants as AT&T, IBM, and DuPont. Drug testing, like going through metal detectors at today's airports, has become an unfortunate necessity. 11

ASIS views drug testing, when properly and lawfully applied, as a positive step towards combating drug abuse both at the workplace and in our society at large. ASIS also thinks that ultimately it is the public who stands to gain. 12

ASIS is cognizant that, if abused, drug testing can prove detrimental. But, in those few cases involving abuses, the courts have demonstrated both a willingness and an ability to intervene. 13

ASIS is also cognizant that drug testing by itself cannot rid the workplace or our society of drugs. Rather, it must be carried out in conjunction with educational and related programs, for our growing dependence on drugs poses a direct long-term threat to our society. 14

Need for Drug Prevention Programs

For drug testing to prove both meaningful and useful, it must be conducted in conjunction with educational, counseling, and treatment programs. Among other things, we recommend the following: 15

• *An active antidrug program.* Employers should establish clear, comprehensive, and well-documented policies concerning the use, possession, and sale of drugs at the workplace. The antidrug program should be publicized and include sanctions. It should encompass all strata of the work force. 16

• *Judicious use of screening and testing.* Both federal and local courts have upheld the validity of drug testing provided it is carried out at the preemployment stage; conducted for cause; or, within certain confines, conducted at random. 17

The courts have also made it amply clear they will allow drug testing where it is not discriminatory or abusive, has been published well in advance, is not used as a subterfuge to discourage union activities, is not clearly in violation of public policy, and is in compliance with any collective bargaining agreement or other contractual arrangement between an employer and his or her employees. 18

• *Use of employee assistance programs.* Attempts to rehabilitate otherwise good employees make both economic and political sense. Not only can it prove time-consuming to recruit, hire, and train a new employee, it can also prove costly in terms of dollars. Counseling and treatment can go a long way in helping employees who are addicted to drugs—provided employees also want to help themselves. A concerted effort should be made to assist them. 19

• *Education and training.* The ultimate goal should be to obtain a work environment that is 100 percent drug-free. In addition to the aforementioned programs, this goal can be achieved through a continuous educational process involving films, free literature, training seminars, community involvement, counseling, incentives, etc. Keeping in mind that a drug-free workplace is a healthier and happier environment, a continuing drug education program results in better morale as well as financial benefits. 20

Conclusion

A drug-free workplace, though ideal, should be the goal of every business and government agency in America. However, drug testing is only one of several steps that must be taken to achieve this objective. When incorporated into a comprehensive antidrug effort, drug testing can go a long way in combating drug abuse at the workplace. 21

Notes

1. "The Plague Among Us," *Newsweek,* June 16, 1986, p. 15.
2. "Battling the Enemy Within," *Time,* March 17, 1986, p. 53.

3. "Battling the Enemy Within," p. 53.
4. "Battling the Enemy Within," p. 53.
5. "Wide Drug Use Found in People Held in Crimes," *New York Times,* June 4, 1986, p. 1.
6. "The Plague Among Us," p. 15.
7. "Drug Abuse in the Workplace," *DEA/Registrant Facts,* 1985, p. 6.
8. Nell Henderson. "Drug-Testing Industry Flourishes," *Washington Business,* June 30, 1986, p. 1.

Questions on Technique

1. The issue and stand are presented in a thesis. What is that thesis?
2. The first three paragraphs form the introduction. What approach is taken to that introduction?
3. Which paragraphs are developed with examples? What purpose do these examples serve?
4. What element of emotional appeal appears in the examples?
5. In which paragraphs are objections raised and countered?
6. Which paragraph provides the reason for the author's view?
7. What is the purpose of mentioning AT&T, IBM, and DuPont in paragraph 11?
8. What is the purpose of suggesting that drug testing be combined with the program described in paragraphs 16 to 20?
9. Who do you judge to be the intended audience for this essay?
10. What approach is taken to the conclusion?

For Group Discussion or Journal Writing

In paragraphs 13 and 14, two arguments against drug testing in the workplace are presented. What other objections might people have to the position advanced by ASIS? Should these objections have been raised and countered? Why or why not?

Parents Also Have Rights

Ronnie Gunnerson

Ronnie Gunnerson argues that parents, not the pregnant teenager, should be legally empowered to decide the fate of the teen's unborn child. Her essay first appeared in Newsweek*'s "My Turn" column.*

"What's a parent to do?" is the punch line to many a joke on the perils of raising children. But what a parent does when a teenager gets pregnant is far from a joke: it's a soul-searching, heart-wrenching condition with responses as diverse as the families affected. 1

In an era besotted with concern for both the emotional and social welfare of teenage mothers and their babies, anger seems to be forbidden. Yet how many 2 parents can deny anger when circumstances over which they have no control force them into untenable situations?

And untenable they are. What I discovered after my 16-year-old stepdaughter became pregnant shocked me. Parents have no rights. We could neither demand she give the baby up for adoption, nor insist on an abortion. The choice belongs to the teenage mother, who is still a child herself and far from capable of understanding the lifelong ramifications of whatever choice she makes. 3

At the same time, homes for unwed mothers, at least the two we checked in Los Angeles, where we live, will house the teenager at no cost to the family, but they will not admit her unless her parents sign a statement agreeing to pick up both her and her baby from a designated maternity hospital. Parents may sit out the pregnancy if they so desire, but when all is said and done, they're stuck with both mother and baby whether they like it or not. 4

In essence, then, the pregnant teenager can choose whether or not to have her baby and whether or not to keep it. The parents, who have the legal responsibility for both the teenage mother and her child, have no say in the matter. The costs of a teenage pregnancy are high; yes, the teenager's life is forever changed by her untimely pregnancy and childbirth. But life is forever changed for the rest of her family as well, and I am tired of the do-gooders who haven't walked a yard, let alone a mile, in my shoes shouting their sympathy for the "victimized" teen. 5

What about the victimized parents? Are we supposed to accept the popular notion that we failed this child and that therefore we are to blame for her lack of either scruples or responsibility? Not when we spend endless hours and thousands of dollars in therapy trying to help a girl whose behavior has been rebellious since the age of 13. Not when we have heart-to-heart talks until the wee hours of the morning which we learn are the butt of jokes between her and her friends. And not when we continually trust her only to think afterward that she's repeatedly lied to us about everything there is to lie about. 6

Yes, the teenager is a victim—a victim of illusions fostered by a society that gives her the right to decide whether or not to have an illegitimate baby, no matter what her parents say. Many believe it is feelings of rejection that motivate girls to have babies; they want human beings of their own to love and be loved by. I wouldn't disagree, but another motive may be at work as well: the ultimate rebellion. Parents are forced to cope with feelings more devastating than adolescent confusion. And I'm not talking about the superficial, what-will-the-Joneses-think attitudes. I mean gut-gripping questions that undermine brutally the self-confidence it can take adults years to develop. 7

We can all write off to immaturity mistakes made in adolescence. To what do we attribute our perceived parental failures at 40 or 50? Even as I proclaim our innocence in my stepdaughter's folly, I will carry to my grave, as I know my husband will, the nagging fear that we could have prevented it *if only* we'd been *better* parents. 8

And I will carry forevermore the sad realization that I'm not the compassionate person I'd tried so hard to be and actually thought I was. My reaction to my stepdaughter's pregnancy horrified me. I was consumed with hatred and 9 anger. Any concern I felt for her was overridden by the feeling that I'd been had. I'd befriended this child, housed her and counseled her for years, and what did I get in return? Not knowing her whereabouts that culminated in her getting pregnant with a boy we didn't even know. At first I felt like a fool. When I discovered how blatantly society's rules favor the rule breaker, I felt like a raving maniac.

Resentment and rage: It took more hours of counseling for me to accept my anger than it did for my stepdaughter to deal with her pregnancy. But then, she had the support of a teenage subculture that reveres motherhood among its own and a news-media culture that fusses and frets over adolescent mothers. Few ears were willing to hear what my husband and I were feeling. While I can't speak for my husband, I can say that today, a year after the baby's birth, he still turns to ice when his daughter is around. Smitten as he is with his first grandchild, he hasn't forgotten that the joy of the boy's birth was overshadowed by resentment and rage. 10

Fortunately, my stepdaughter recently married a young man who loves her son as his own, although he is not the father. Together, the three of them are a family who, like many a young family, are struggling to make ends meet. Neither my stepdaughter nor her husband has yet finished high school, but they are not a drain on society as many teenage parents are. She and her husband seem to be honest, hard workers, and I really think they will make it. Their story will have a happy ending. 11

My stepdaughter says she can't even understand the person she used to be, and I believe her. Unfortunately, the minds of adults are not quite as malleable as those of constantly changing adolescents. My husband and I haven't forgotten—and I'm not sure we've forgiven—either our daughter or ourselves. We're still writing the ending to our own story, and I believe it's time for society to write an ending of its own. If a pregnant teenager's parents are ultimately responsible for the teenager and her baby, then give those parents the right to decide whether or not the teenager keeps her baby. Taking the decision away from the teen mother would eliminate her power over her parents and could give pause to her reckless pursuit of the "in" thing. 12

Questions on Technique

1. The most direct statement of Gunnerson's issue and stand does not appear in the introduction but in the conclusion. What sentence provides this statement?
2. What approach does Gunnerson take to her introduction?
3. What purpose do paragraphs 2 and 3 serve?
4. Does Gunnerson rely more heavily on emotional appeal or logical argument?
5. "Parents Also Have Rights" first appeared in *Newsweek.* Is the strong emotional appeal in the essay likely to move the author's intended audience? Explain.

6. In what paragraphs does Gunnerson raise and counter objections? How does she counter each objection?
7. What are Gunnerson's reasons for believing parents should decide the fate of their teenager's baby?
8. Does the fact that Gunnerson's stepdaughter ultimately married and made a life for herself (although a difficult one) detract from the author's argument? Explain.
9. Where does Gunnerson speculate about what would happen if her view were adopted?
10. What approach does Gunnerson take to her conclusion?

For Group Discussion or Journal Writing

Ronnie Gunnerson admits to feeling angry about her step-daughter's pregnancy and its effect on the family. Consider to what extent Gunnerson's anger adds to or detracts from the convincingness of her essay.

STUDENT ESSAYS TO READ AND EVALUATE

The argumentation-persuasion essays that follow were written by students. Some are more effective than others, but each has strengths and weaknesses. Reading and evaluating these essays will make you a more knowing judge of your own writing. Also, by studying what others have done, you can discover successful techniques to incorporate into your own writing and less successful techniques to avoid.

The Old Ball Game

"For it's one, two, three strikes you're out at the old ball game." A catchy tune if you happen to be singing it, agonizing reality if you happen to be 6 or 7 years old and playing in an organized baseball league. Six- and seven-year-old children are simply not emotionally ready, and therefore should simply not be permitted, to play on an organized baseball team. 1

Consider this not-so-uncommon scene: The pitch is made. The bat and ball connect, and the grounder heads toward the 3 1/2-foot-tall first baseman. He opens his glove. He just has to pick up the ball, tag first base, and the runner will be out. He misses the ball. Hurriedly trying to retrieve it, the first baseman's attempt is futile, and the runner is safe. The manager, the father of one of the boys, stops the game, walks out halfway toward the first baseman, and yells, "What are you doing, Michael? You should have had that ball. Now settle down." There's nothing like public humiliation to damage a tender psyche. 2

Some people argue that just as much, if not more, yelling goes on during 3 backyard neighborhood games. This is true, but the yelling there goes back and forth among the kids. In the organized leagues, the manager yells at, and sometimes even humiliates, his players. The player, of course, is not permitted to respond, and thus frustration and feelings of inadequacy can build. He can only try to cope with these feelings that have been heaped on him, which can be quite an emotional struggle for a child so young.

Even major league baseball players make mistakes on the field; can a 6- or 7-year-old player be expected to be any better? If a player misses the ball, no one feels worse than he does. Instead, why not praise the good plays made by the kids and ignore the mistakes? Unfortunately, this doesn't seem to be what happens in many cases. 4

I believe the goal of organized sports is for the children involved to have fun. Unfortunately, this frequently does not happen. Too much emphasis is placed on winning by both the managers and the parents. This inevitably leads to feelings of disappointment and failure in the children. Imagine being 6 years old and up to bat. One hit is all you need to win the ball game. This would create a lot of pressure for many adults. It is simply too much pressure for 6- and 7-year-olds. The pitch is made and you're out. Some might say that children must learn to deal with disappointment and failure. I also believe this is true, but certainly not at such a young age. 5

It has been said that organized sports are a good source of discipline. However, children should be learning discipline in the home, as well as in school. Further sources of discipline are unnecessary. 6

To me, there is nothing more heartbreaking than watching a 6- or 7-year-old baseball player crying because he just struck out, he missed the ball, or he just got yelled at by his manager. I guess I'm old-fashioned—I prefer games that make children laugh and leave them smiling. 7

Ban Those Traps

American history reveals that one of the keys to survival in this country has been trapping such animals as beaver, otter, muskrat, mink, fox, coyote, bear, mountain lion, rabbit, and raccoon for their meat and hides. There is no longer a need for the meat of these animals, however, because humans have developed easier ways of getting food. Yet they remain victims of trappers because of the value of their pelts. Today trapping supports very few people, and most of those who do derive income from it have other sources of income. This fact alone should discourage trapping, but there are other, stronger reasons which should encourage action to prohibit it: The techniques of trapping animals are cruel; trapping can lead to the extinction of animal species; and above all, there is no longer a need to trap because modern technology has introduced better ways to secure food and pelts. 1

Trapping is death by torture for the animals who are its victims, for they are 2 strangled, drowned, or starved to death, depending on the trapping device used. There are two types of steel traps which are commonly used. The Conibear trap is set in the water and grabs the animal behind the ears, cutting off the circulation. Sometimes this causes the animal to die instantly, but frequently it causes the animal to fall and drown. The leg-hold trap clamps down on the victim's leg or paw with bone-crushing force, causing painful entrapment. A victim may be left in the trap for days before the trapper arrives to release and kill it. The pain suffered by the animal is so intense that many times, although the trapper finds the animal still alive, it has gnawed its trapped leg or paw, broken its teeth from gnawing on the trap, or frozen its tongue to the cold steel trap. Often the animal is dead from loss of blood, gangrene, infection, or internal bleeding. If the victim was "fortunate" enough to escape, it managed to do so only by gnawing off the leg or paw, which then made the animal easy prey for predators. A third kind of trap, the snare, consists of a rope which is tied in a hangman's noose and cast over a tree or branch with a piece of bait attached. The bait is placed over a concealed hole in the ground. When the animal approaches the bait, it falls into the hole and is caught by the rope and consequently hanged. Other traps, such as the deadfall or pitfall, lure the animal with bait and then kill it by either striking it with a log or rock or forcing it to fall on sharp sticks. In every case, trapped animals are victims of cruel treatment because they cannot defend themselves as they would in natural conditions.

All of this suffering and destruction serves no real need. Modern technology 3
meets the demands of fashion with human-made and ranch-grown furs. We now have human-made furs that look and feel like the real thing, but are better. They are moth-proof, they need no cold storage, and they do not crack with age. In addition, many people now breed and raise fur-bearing animals on ranches specifically for the use of their pelts. These animals are fed and cared for properly, and they are killed humanely.

Trapping, therefore, should be outlawed. It is cruel, it can cause extinction 4
of valuable species, and it is unnecessary because modern technology has replaced the need for it with pelts of better quality which are acquired much more easily and humanely. Although trappers claim that their hobby provides a fantastic experience because it allows them to enjoy the solitude and beauty of the wilderness, they are really contributing to the destruction in that wilderness. That destruction must be stopped.

Bilingual Education: Breaking Down the Barriers

When young Hispanic-Americans enter an elementary school classroom for the 1
first time, they face numerous psychological and educational barriers. Immediately, they will recognize that the language spoken by the teacher and classmates is completely unfamiliar. While other students are laughing and conversing with one another, they are forced to sit quietly, alienated from the mainstream.

Undoubtedly, this leads to feelings of isolation for many Hispanic-American children, and this is certainly detrimental to the learning process. The sad truth about this situation is that America, which prides itself on being "the land of equal opportunity" is not providing the programs necessary for these children to excel.

Children learn their native language in the context of a caring family. Within this context, they communicate with those they love and respect. However, once they get to school, the native language may be neglected, and this creates problems. 2

First, children who know only Spanish feel inadequate and second-class. These feelings are likely to stay with the children creating numerous psychological problems. The loss of self-esteem may never be made up, so even when English is finally learned, these students feel worthless or at best second-rate. 3

Second, Spanish-speaking students may not learn to read quickly or well enough. Learning to read is a difficult enough task to accomplish without having to learn a new language at the same time. Yet, many Hispanic-American students are forced to do both simultaneously. The result is impaired progress. 4

The obvious solution is bilingual instruction for elementary students. Bilingual education, which employs the child's native language for instruction, speeds learning and helps children feel good about their ability and their culture. Eventually, when English is learned, instruction can occur in English, but until then only bilingual education will break down the barriers many Hispanic-American students encounter in the classroom. 5

Equality? "Yeah, You Bet!"

For many years the man held dominant in all aspects of society. The man worked, while the woman stayed home to raise the children. The man also handled the finances and provided a means of transportation. Today, women work, handle finances, and drive themselves around. The women's movement has now reached total equality. So, one question arises. Why must male drivers, under 25 years of age, pay more for auto insurance? An average male of that age group pays at least 300 dollars more a year than a female, in the same age bracket. If equality is the issue, then the gender clause should be dropped from insurance policies. 1

Today, parents cringe when their children turn sweet sixteen and get their driving permit. Females' parents are faced with a five or six hundred dollar increase in coverage costs, while a sixteen-year-old male's parents are faced with an increase of eight or nine hundred dollars. People assume that the rate difference is due to the fact that male teenagers are more reckless and get into more accidents. However, we had an insurance agent visit our drivers' education class in high school. The agent showed us his personal records. His statistics showed 2 that his clientele, male as well as female, each drove the same amount. His figures also showed that females caused just as many accidents as males.

In another class of mine, physics, we took an accident analysis. Among thirty-five students, there were twelve reported accidents. Each of these twelve accidents was the student's fault. Nine of the accidents were caused by females. That only leaves three left for the males. Five of the nine accidents were caused by one girl. In the five accidents, this girl totaled four cars. After these five accidents, resulting in four total losses, her insurance went up considerably. But with the increase, her coverage cost was just barely the same amount that I started out paying. Is it fair that I paid as much as she did when I had no accidents whatsoever? Statistics of that sort are never discussed by the insurance companies though. 3

In the past men not only drove more often, but the vehicles were built differently. It was not uncommon to buy a car in the 1960s that did not boast much less than 300 horsepower. If not built that way at the factory, men could easily modify these motors for such results. Mainly the teenage guys were the ones to make modifications on their vehicles to increase speed and power. Besides increasing speed and power, they also increased the number of accidents. Obviously they were faced with increased rates because of such accidents. Today's cars are built altogether differently than the cars built in the 1960s. The cars being built today must meet tough emission standards. Each one must also meet a minimum miles-per-gallon ratio. So bigger motors took a back seat to smaller motors that are more fuel efficient. Today's cars are also very hard to modify without the proper schooling. Cars are now mainly fuel injected, instead of the old carburated. With the change in today's cars, why is there still a difference in rates of insurance? 4

In March of 1989, the Pennsylvania Department of Transportation, along with the Bureau of Motor Vehicles, lowered men's insurance rates a small amount. They also raised women's rates to try and bridge the gender gap. The difference was lessened, but not all the way. At least a small bit was accomplished while striving for equality. 5

The gender clause for auto insurance policies should be eliminated completely. Rates should start out even, unless the individual is being insured on a sport or high-performance vehicle or a recreational vehicle. Women now drive as often as men. Women are also involved in just as many accidents. Men between the ages of sixteen and twenty-five are definitely being discriminated against. 6

Becoming a Reliable Critic by Evaluating Writing

Form a group and select one of the previous student essays or use one your instructor assigns. Study the essay to identify its chief strengths and weaknesses. Have a recorder note these and a spokesperson report them to the rest of the class. If you like, you can use the following evaluation questions to guide your study.

Evaluation Questions

1. The Thesis
   What is the thesis? What does it present as the issue and the writer's stand on the issue? Is the issue debatable?
2. The Introduction
   Does the introduction engage your interest? Why or why not?
3. Supporting Details
   Note any details that are unclear or irrelevant. Note any logical fallacies or unrestrained appeals to emotion. Evaluate the raising and countering of objections. How convincing is the essay? Why?
4. Organization
   Are the details placed in a progressive or other logical order? Evaluate the use of transitions and topic sentences.
5. The Conclusion
   Does the essay come to a satisfying end? Why or why not?
6. Sentence Effectiveness and Word Choice
   Note any problems with word choice or sentence variety.
7. Overview
   What do you like best about the essay? What is the single most important revision the author should make?

Essay Topics: Argumentation-Persuasion

1. In "Indian Bones" (page 319), Clara Spotted Elk argues that museums should turn Indian remains over to Native Americans for proper, ceremonial burial. Write an essay arguing the opposite—that museums should keep the bones for study and preservation.
2. In response to "Why Drug Testing Is Needed" (page 321), write an essay entitled, "Why Drug Testing Is Not Needed." Raise and counter some of the arguments put forth by the American Society for Industrial Security in calling for drug testing (or counter all the arguments if you prefer).
3. Argue against the point of view reflected in "Parents Also Have Rights" (page 324). That is, argue that unwed teens, not their parents, should decide the fate of their babies.
4. Taking the view opposite that of the student who wrote "The Old Ball Game" (page 327), defend organized baseball leagues for 6- and 7-year-olds.
5. Taking the view opposite that of the student who wrote "Bilingual Education: Breaking Down the Barriers" (page 329), argue against bilingual education.
6. Write an essay for or against allowing advertising in television programming aimed at children.
7. Write an essay advocating some specific change at your college or where you work.

8. Write a letter to the brother or sister of one of your friends in order to persuade that person to attend (or not to attend) your college.
9. Defend or attack the following proposition: Professional athletes should be paid salaries equal to those of teachers.
10. Defend or attack the following proposition: In order to graduate from high school, students should have to pass a proficiency examination.
11. If you had the power to draft one piece of legislation that would improve the quality of life in this country, what would it be? Write an essay that explains the legislation and argues for its passage.
12. Defend or attack the practice of awarding athletes scholarships so they can play college ball.
13. Argue for or against tax credits for those who send their children to private schools.
14. Argue for or against a mandatory retirement age.
15. Pick one invention or technological advance and argue that it has done more harm than good.
16. Argue for or against the open-admissions policy of many colleges.
17. Argue for or against a law to regulate the amount of violence on television.

Thematic Topics

1. Paragraph 14 of "Why Drug Testing Is Needed" (page 321) says that "drug testing by itself cannot rid the workplace or our society of drugs. . . . It must be carried out in conjunction with educational and related programs. . . ." Design one program to address our drug problem and explain how that program will help solve the problem. The program can be for the general public, workers, students, athletes, the military, or whatever segment of society you want to target.
2. "Parents Also Have Rights" (page 324) was written in 1987. However, teenage pregnancy remains a serious problem. Explain why you think the problem exists. As an alternative, explain what you think can be done to solve the problem.
3. Using the information in "Indian Bones" (page 319) and "It's Time to Stop Playing Indians" (page 256), along with evidence from your television and movie viewing, explain how some people view and treat Native Americans. Then go on to explain how you think Native Americans should respond to this treatment, perhaps drawing on "The Ways of Meeting Oppression" (page 293) for ideas.

Writing Strategies

The following strategies, along with those in Chapters 1 to 3, may include some procedures you would like to try as you work to improve your writing process.

Topic Selection

1. Review the editorial pages and letters to the editor in your campus and community newspapers. They will present controversial issues that can serve as topics.
2. Fill in the blank in the following sentence: I think it is unfair that ____________________. If, for example, you complete the sentence to get "I think it is unfair that students cannot go on strike," you can write an essay arguing that students should be permitted to strike.
3. Other fill-in-the-blank sentences that can lead to a topic include
   a. I have always been angry that ____________________. (Argue for a change in what angers you.)
   b. The worst feature of this university is ____________________. (Argue for a change that would improve the feature.)
   c. If I had the power, I would ____________________. (Argue for the advisability of what you would do.)
   d. I disagree with people who believe ____________________. (Show why these people are wrong and support your view.)

Idea Generation

1. To generate ideas to support your view, answer the following questions.
   a. Why is my issue important?
   b. What would happen if my view were adopted?
   c. What would happen if my view were not adopted?
   d. What are the two strongest objections to my view?
   e. How can these objections be countered?
2. To help generate ideas *and* determine methods of development, answer these questions.
   a. What story can I tell to support my view?
   b. Is there anything I can describe to support my view?
   c. What examples can I provide to support my view?
   d. Are there any comparisons I can make to support my view?
   e. Are there any contrasts I can draw to support my view?
   f. Do any aspects of my topic require definition? classification?
   g. Do any cause-and-effect relationships support my view?
3. List every reason you can think of to support your stand. Do not evaluate the strength of these reasons; just get down everything that occurs to you. When you can think of no more reasons, take a second sheet and list every reason you can think of to oppose your view. This second list will be a source of ideas for raising and countering objections. Next to each opposition point, jot down a few words to remind you of how the objection can be countered.

Establishing Audience and Purpose

Here is a chart of audience and purpose and some ways these can function together.

If your audience . . .	*. . . a possible purpose is:*
1. is well informed and strongly opposed to your view,	1. to lessen the opposition by convincing the audience that some of your points are valid and worth consideration.
2. is poorly informed and opposed to your view,	2. to inform the audience and to change the audience's view.
3. would find it difficult to perform the desired action,	3. to convince the audience that it is worth the sacrifice or to convince the audience to do some part of what is desired.
4. would not find it difficult to perform the desired action,	4. to convince the audience to perform the action.
5. has no interest one way or the other in the issue,	5. to arouse interest and persuade the audience to your view.

Reader Response

If you like to secure reader response during revision, consult page 77. In addition, ask your reader to note any important objections you failed to raise and counter. Also ask your reader to note any convincing points you failed to include.

REVISION CHECKLIST

In addition to the checklist on page 80, you can use this checklist when you revise your argumentation-persuasion.

1. Is your issue debatable and not a matter of taste?
2. Does your thesis note the issue and your stand?
3. Have you avoided logical fallacies?
4. Are your emotional appeals properly restrained?
5. Have you raised and countered compelling objections?
6. Where appropriate, have you speculated about what would happen if your view were (or were not) adopted?
7. Have you provided and explained all the reasons for your view?

CHAPTER 14

Writing in Response to Reading

Throughout college, you will write in response to reading. In fact, writing in response to reading is the single most important way scholars, including student scholars, communicate with one another. One person writes something he or she thinks is significant, and someone else reacts by writing a response, which may prompt yet another person to write a reaction. All these written responses make up scholarly journals, newsletters, books, student newspapers, theses, and dissertations—the means by which teachers and other scholars communicate with one another.

As a college student, you are a part of this community of writers—this group of people who read and react in writing to share ideas, inform others of developments, and argue points of view. In addition, writing in response to reading is an important part of your college life because it helps you grapple with the ideas of others and shape your reactions to those ideas. In short, writing in response to reading is one way you learn.

This chapter will help you become more comfortable writing in response to reading so you can take your place in the ongoing written exchange and so you can use writing as a means of learning.

AUDIENCE AND PURPOSE

Sometimes your instructors will require you to summarize an author's main points to be sure you have read and comprehended important material. At other times, they will ask you to analyze and evaluate an author's view and determine your sense of its worth. On still other occasions, you will be asked to express your personal reactions to a piece and share the associations and feelings the writing strikes within you. Although you most often will be writing as a student for a teacher, make no mistake—you are part of the exchange of views and information that is at the heart of the academic community.

When you write in response to reading, you may do so to share, to inform, or to persuade. For example, after reading "School Is Bad for Children" later in this chapter, you may be moved to share some of your early school experiences, to inform your reader about how paired learning works, or to persuade your reader that compulsory attendance laws should be abolished. The writing assignments in this chapter will give you experience writing in response to reading for a variety of purposes.

Your audience for an essay written in response to reading is likely to be a member of the academic community. Often, your reader is your classroom teacher. However, a suitable audience can also be your classmates, a member of the administration, readers of the campus newspaper, members of a professional organization (such as the American Psychological Association or the National Council of Teachers of English), or anyone with a professional or scholarly interest in your subject. Whoever your audience is, remember to assess the needs of your reader and to address those needs.

SELECTING DETAIL

Everything you have learned about supporting detail in this book applies when you are writing in response to reading. Your detail must be adequate (see page 42), relevant (see page 44), and suited to your audience and purpose (see pages 25 and 24).

When you write in response to reading, you may find yourself combining patterns of development. For example, let's say you are responding to "School Is Bad for Children," on page 338 by explaining the advantages of collaborative learning. You might define collaborative learning, describe collaborative learning procedures, include examples of successful collaborative learning activities you have engaged in, and then explain the effects of collaborative learning—all this would have you combining definition, process analysis, illustration, and cause-and-effect analysis.

In addition to combining methods of development, you are likely to find yourself paraphrasing and quoting from the reading you are responding to. (Paraphrasing and quoting are discussed on page 376 and page 378.) For example, let's return again to a response to "School Is Bad for Children." This time, assume that you wish to disagree with the author and argue that we should not abolish compulsory school attendance laws. To do this, you can bring up the author's points by paraphrasing and quoting them and then go on to counter those points with your own ideas. For an example of how this is done, see the student essay "Compulsory School Attendance Laws Make Sense," on page 344.

Detail for your essay can come from your own experience and observation, as well as from material you have learned in your classes and from books and articles in the library. If you borrow material from books and articles, however, remember to document these borrowings according to the conventions described in Chapter 15.

MARKING A TEXT

When writing in response to reading, you can discover topics and ideas to develop topics by using the idea-generation techniques in Chapter 1. In addition, an excellent form of idea generation (and an excellent way to improve reading comprehension) is to mark the text as you read.

To mark the text as you read, do the following.

1. Underline the thesis if it is stated.
2. Underline the main points (often given in topic sentences). Avoid underlining subpoints, or the page will be cluttered with underlining.
3. In the margins, write your responses to the reading, including areas of agreement and disagreement, personal associations the text evokes, questions that arise, and so forth. Your marginal notations can include jottings like these: "yes," "I disagree," "reminds me of Dale," "I don't get this," and so forth.
4. Also in the margins, evaluate what you are reading. Note whether you find something untrue, biased, fair, unproven, unclear, interesting, unsupported, angry, surprising, sarcastic, or dated. You can write things like "unclear"; "not true where I live"; "Where's the proof?"; "good example"; "seems strange"; "sounds great"; and "not true anymore."
5. Place an asterisk (*) next to words, phrases, or sentences that you find particularly appealing.
6. Place a question mark next to anything you do not understand, including words to look up in the dictionary.

Marking a text helps you become more involved with your reading. In addition, the marginal notes can supply writing topics and ideas for developing topics. Below is an example of how a reader can mark a text. Following the marked text, there are sample student response essays for you to study.

School Is Bad for Children

John Holt

John Holt (1923–1985) was a teacher and writer who gained notoriety in the 60s and 70s for advocating that children control their own learning. His most famous book is How Children Fail *(1964).*

Almost every child, on the first day he sets foot in a school building, is smarter, more curious, less afraid of what he doesn't know, better at finding and figuring things out, more confident, resourceful, persistent and independent than he will ever be again in his schooling—or, unless he is very unusual and very lucky, for the rest of his life. Already, by paying close attention to and interacting with the world and people around him, and 1 without any school-type formal instruction, he has done a task far more difficult, complicated and abstract than anything he will be asked to do in school, or than any of his teachers has done for years. He has solved the mystery of language. He has discovered it—babies don't even know that language exists—and he has found out how it works and learned to use it. He has done it by exploring, by experimenting, by developing his own model of the grammar of language, by trying it out and seeing whether it works, by gradually changing it and refining it until it does work. And while he has been doing this, he has been learning other things as well, including many of the "concepts" that the schools think only they can teach him, and many that are more complicated than the ones they do try to teach him.

In he comes, this curious, patient, determined, energetic, skillful 2
learner. We sit him down at a desk, and what do we teach him? Many things. First, that learning is separate from living. "You come to school to learn," we tell him, as if the child hadn't been learning before, as if living were out there and learning were in here, and there were no connection between the two. Secondly, that he cannot be trusted to learn and is no good at it. Everything we teach about reading, a task far simpler than many that the child has already mastered, says to him, "If we don't make you read, you won't, and if you don't do it exactly the way we tell you, you can't." In short, he comes to feel that learning is a passive process, something that someone else does *to* you, instead of something you do for yourself.

sexist; what about females?

In a great many other ways he learns that he is worthless, untrustwor- 3
thy, fit only to take other people's orders, a blank sheet for other people to write on. Oh, we make a lot of nice noises in school about respect for the child and individual differences, and the like. But our acts, as opposed to our talk, say to the child, "Your experience, your concerns, your curiosities, your needs, what you know, what you want, what you wonder about, what you hope for, what you fear, what you like and dislike, what you are good at or not so good at—all this is of not the slightest importance, it counts for nothing. What counts here, and the only thing that counts, is what we know, what we think is important, what we want you to do, think and be." The child soon learns not to ask questions—the teacher isn't there to satisfy his curiosity. Having learned to hide his curiosity, he later learns to be ashamed of it. Given no chance to find out who he is—and to develop that person, whoever it is—he soon comes to accept the adults' evaluation of him.

Yes! I've seen this happen many times.

School becomes a game.

Yes, just do the minimum to get by.

He learns many other things. He learns that to be wrong, uncertain, 4
confused, is a crime. Right Answers are what the school wants, and he learns countless strategies for prying these answers out of the teacher, for conning her into thinking he knows what he doesn't know. He learns to dodge, bluff, fake, cheat. He learns to be lazy. Before he came to school, he would work for hours on end, on his own, with no thought of reward, at the business of making sense of the world and gaining competence in it. In school he learns, like every buck private, how to goldbrick, how not to work when the sergeant isn't looking, how to know when he is looking, how to make him think you are working even when he is looking. He learns that in real life you

don't do anything unless you are bribed, bullied or conned into doing it, that nothing is worth doing for its own sake, or that if it is, you can't do it in school. He learns to be bored, to work with a small part of his mind, to escape from the reality around him into daydreams and fantasies—but not like the fantasies of his preschool years, in which he played a very active part.

This guy really hates teachers.

5 The child comes to school curious about other people, particularly other children, and the school teaches him to be indifferent. The most interesting thing in the classroom—often the only interesting thing in it—is the other children, but he has to act as if these other children, all about him, only a few feet away, are not really there. He cannot interact with them, talk with them, smile at them. In many schools he can't talk to other children in the halls between classes; in more than a few, and some of these in stylish suburbs, he can't even talk to them at lunch. Splendid training for a world in which, when you're not studying the other person to figure out how to do him in, you pay no attention to him.

Nice sarcasm.

6 In fact, he learns how to live without paying attention to anything going on around him. You might say that school is a long lesson in how to turn yourself off, which may be one reason why so many young people, seeking the awareness of the world and responsiveness to it they had when they were little, think they can only find it in drugs. Aside from being boring, the school is almost always ugly, cold, inhuman—even the most stylish, glass-windowed, $20-a-square-foot schools.

I disagree here.

7 And so, in this dull and ugly place, where nobody ever says anything very truthful, where everybody is playing a kind of role, as in a charade, where the teachers are no more free to respond honestly to the students than the students are free to respond to the teachers or each other, where the air practically vibrates with suspicion and anxiety, the child learns to live in a daze, saving his energies for those small parts of his life that are too trivial for the adults to bother with, and thus remain his. It is a rare child who can come through his schooling with much left of his curiosity, his independence or his sense of his own dignity, competence and worth.

No! Lots of kids thrive in this environment.

8 So much for criticism. What do we need to do? Many things. Some are easy—we can do them right away. Some are hard, and may take some time. Take a hard one first. We should abolish compulsory school attendance. At the very least we should modify it, perhaps by giving children every year a large number of authorized absences. Our compulsory school-attendance laws once served a humane and useful purpose. They protected children's right to some schooling, against those adults who would otherwise have denied it to them in order to exploit their labor, in farm, store, mine or factory. Today the laws help nobody, not the schools, not the teachers, not the children. To keep kids in school who would rather not be there costs the schools an enormous amount of time and trouble—to say nothing of what it costs to repair the damage that these angry and resentful prisoners do every time they get a chance. Every teacher knows that any kid in class who, for whatever reason, would rather not be there not only doesn't learn anything

No way!

Kids still need protection.

Jobs aren't that plentiful.

himself but makes it a great deal tougher for anyone else. As for protecting the children from exploitation, the chief and indeed only exploiters of children these days *are* the schools. Kids caught in the college rush more often than not work 70 hours or more a week, most of it on paper busywork. For kids who aren't going to college, school is just a useless time waster, preventing them from earning some money or doing some useful work, or even doing some true learning.

get real!

9 Objections. "If kids didn't have to go to school, they'd all be out in the streets." No, they wouldn't. In the first place, even if schools stayed just the way they are, children would spend at least some time there because that's where they'd be likely to find friends; it's a natural meeting place for children. In the second place, schools wouldn't stay the way they are, they'd get better, because we would have to start making them what they ought to be right now—places where children would *want* to be. In the third place, those children who did not want to go to school could find, particularly if we stirred up our brains and gave them a little help, other things to do—the things many children now do during their summers and holidays.

I agree.

We need something like this in 8th grade & it was great.

10 There's something easier we could do. We need to get kids out of the school buildings, give them a chance to learn about the world at first hand. It is a very recent idea, and a crazy one, that the way to teach our young people about the world they live in is to take them out of it and shut them up in brick boxes. Fortunately, educators are beginning to realize this. In Philadelphia and Portland, Oreg., to pick only two places I happen to have heard about, plans are being drawn up for public schools that won't have any school buildings at all, that will take the students out into the city and help them to use it and its people as a learning resource. In other words, students, perhaps in groups, perhaps independently, will go to libraries, museums, exhibits, courtrooms, legislatures, radio and TV stations, meetings, businesses and laboratories to learn about their world and society at first hand. A small private school in Washington is already doing this. It makes sense. We need more of it.

A good way for high school kids to learn about careers.

Nice!

11 As we help children get out into the world, to do their learning there, we can get more of the world into the schools. Aside from their parents, most children never have any close contact with any adults except people whose sole business is children. No wonder they have no idea what adult life or work is like. We need to bring a lot more people who are *not* full-time teachers into the schools, and into contact with the children. In New York City, under the Teachers and Writers Collaborative, real writers, working writers—novelists, poets, playwrights—come into the schools, read their work, and talk to the children about the problems of their craft. The children eat it up. In another school I know of, a practicing attorney from a nearby city comes in every month or so and talks to several classes about the law. Not the law as it is in books but as he sees it and encounters it in his cases, his problems, his work. And the children love it. [It is real, grown-up, true, not *My Weekly Reader*,] not "social studies," not lies and baloney.

I hate group work. Someone always takes over.

Something easier yet. Let children work together, help each other, learn from each other and each other's mistakes. We now know, from the experience of many schools, both rich-suburban and poor-city, that children are often the best teachers of other children. What is more important, we know that when a fifth- or sixth-grader who has been having trouble with reading starts helping a first-grader, his own reading sharply improves. A number of schools are beginning to use what some call Paired Learning. This means that you let children form partnerships with other children, do their work, even including their tests, together, and share whatever marks or results this work gets—just like grownups in the real world. It seems to work. 12

Take tests together? Is this fair?

Let the children learn to judge their own work. A child learning to talk does not learn by being corrected all the time—if corrected too much, he will stop talking. *He* compares, a thousand times a day, the difference between language as he uses it and as those around him use it. Bit by bit, he makes the necessary changes to make his language like other people's. In the same way, kids learning to do all the other things they learn without adult teachers—to walk, run, climb, whistle, ride a bike, skate, play games, jump rope—compare their own performance with what more skilled people do, and slowly make the needed changes. But in school we never give a child a chance to detect his mistakes, let alone correct them. We do it all for him. We act as if we thought he would never notice a mistake unless it was pointed out to him, or correct it unless he was made to. Soon he becomes dependent on the expert. We should let him do it himself. Let him figure out, with the help of other children if he wants it, what this word says, what is the answer to that problem, whether this is a good way of saying or doing this or that. If right answers are involved, as in some math or science, give him the answer book, let him correct his own papers. Why should we teachers waste time on such donkey work? Our job should be to help the kid when he tells us that he can't find a way to get the right answer. Let's get rid of all this nonsense of grades, exams, marks. We don't know now, and we never will know, how to measure what another person knows or understands. We certainly can't find out by asking him questions. All we find out is what he doesn't know—which is what most tests are for, anyway. Throw it all out, and let the child learn what every educated person must someday learn, how to measure his own understanding, how to know what he knows or does not know. 13

Yes! Yes! Yes! In college too.

We could also abolish the fixed, required curriculum. People remember only what is interesting and useful to them, what helps them make sense of the world, or helps them get along in it. All else they quickly forget, if they ever learn it at all. The idea of a "body of knowledge," to be picked up in school and used for the rest of one's life, is nonsense in a world as complicated and rapidly changing as ours. Anyway, the most important questions and problems of our time are not *in* the curriculum, not even in the hotshot universities, let alone the schools. 14

Children want, more than they want anything else, and even after 15
years of miseducation, to make sense of the world, themselves, and other human beings. Let them get at this job, with our help if they ask for it, in the way that makes most sense to them.

Student Response Essay 1: Sharing Personal Reactions and Associations

The following student essay is an example of a piece that shares personal reactions and associations. After reading "School Is Bad for Children," the student was moved to draw on her own school experiences to bear out Holt's point that in school a child "learns that he is worthless, untrustworthy, fit only to take other people's orders." To make her point, the student combines illustration, narration, and cause-and-effect analysis.

School Was Bad for Me

I share John Holt's view that school harms children. My own negative experiences 1
in elementary school have haunted me over the years and affected the way I present myself to my college professors. In fact, it has taken two years of college life for me to really feel comfortable talking to my instructors, largely because of my early school experiences with teachers.

Holt says that a child in school "learns that he is worthless, untrustworthy, 2
fit only to take other people's orders," and I couldn't agree more. I can remember walking into Crestview Elementary School on the first day of first grade, anxious, nervous, and very shy. The first thing the teacher did was go over all the rules and procedures for the class: we were not allowed to speak without raising our hands; we could only get a drink when we went to the lav and we could only go to the lav once in the morning and once in the afternoon; both of our feet had to be on the floor at all times; and we had to respect the rights of others (that was a big one, but I was never sure what it meant). Of course, the teacher was careful to point out that any infraction of the class rules would be swiftly and severely punished. From that moment, I was terrified that I would break a rule. To be sure that I didn't, I didn't do anything. I didn't speak, I didn't ask questions, and I didn't participate in any way. From the start, I knew that she was the general and I was the soldier trying to get through basic training without getting into any trouble. I was so intimidated that when any child broke a rule, I shook in sympathy. When Tommy's spelling words weren't written neatly enough and he had to do them over, my stomach ached. When Erica's math paper had messy erasure smudges and she was accused of having a messy mind, I smarted with humiliation. I was always sure I would be the next to break a rule.

I made it through first grade by keeping my mouth shut, but second grade 3 proved more troublesome. My coping strategy failed me almost at once. Soon into the year, the teacher asked a question, but rather than call on someone whose hand was waving wildly in the air, she called on me. I instantly panicked. The words stuck in my throat and my lips froze. I couldn't utter a sound. "What's the matter; has the cat got your tongue?" the teacher cleverly asked. I've never forgotten the humiliation of that moment.

Although I have had positive experiences with teachers over the years, that initial put-down made me hesitant to speak out in class by voicing an opinion or asking a question. Even in college, I could not at first participate in class or ask a question when I did not understand. Yes, as Holt points out, I felt worthless and fit only to take orders. That's what I learned in school. 4

Student Response Essay 2: Evaluating an Author's Ideas

The following student essay responds to reading by evaluating an author's ideas. The student argues that Holt is wrong—abolishing compulsory education would be a mistake. To make his point, he cites ideas in Holt's essay and refutes them, and he also draws on examples from his personal experience.

Compulsory School Attendance Laws Make Sense

In "School Is Bad for Children," John Holt says, "We should abolish compulsory school attendance." He believes that only those who want to go to school should attend and that children should be allowed unauthorized absences. I disagree with Holt completely. School is *not* bad for children. On the contrary, children need to be educated, and for that to happen, children need to be in school. Compulsory attendance laws, therefore, should not be abolished. 1

Holt claims that at one time mandatory attendance laws made sense because children needed to be protected from adults who would keep them out of school and send them to work. Sad to say, children still need the protection the laws afford, for exploitive and abusive adults still exist and children still need protection from them. Without the law, plenty of parents would force their children into the workforce and worse. For children born into poverty and abusive homes, education may be the only way to a better life. If compulsory attendance laws did not exist, then these children would lose their tickets out of difficult situations. 2

Even if children do not need protection from adults, they must be required to attend school to improve their situations. Holt says that "for kids who aren't going to college, school is just a useless time waster, preventing them from earning some money." Sure, they can earn money doing minimum wage jobs that do not require a diploma. But how can people support themselves as well as a family earning a little more than four dollars an hour? An education is more important than a low-paying job at an early age because a person must have a chance at a 3 better job in the future. I know of one person who dropped out of school, and today he is on welfare trying to support three children. He is twenty-six and has little to look forward to. Furthermore, his children are already at a disadvantage because their needs cannot be met, and they cannot enjoy the benefits that many of us had when we were young. Fortunately, these children will be required to go to school, so they may find a way out of their poverty.

Holt also blames compulsory attendance for the problems that exist in schools today. Those who don't want to be in school, says Holt, make things difficult for those who do. Perhaps, but the solution is not to let young people leave school. Instead, the solution is to find ways to make these people *want* to be in school. We need to do whatever it takes to attract the most talented people into teaching so all students can be motivated to stay in school and learn. 4

Some might think that Holt's suggestion that students be given unauthorized absences makes sense. But here too I see problems. How is a teacher supposed to maintain continuity with a steady stream of students coming and going? The teacher would spend more time repeating lessons to bring students up to date than teaching necessary material. 5

Mandatory attendance should not be abolished. Students need to be in school to receive the education they need to make a satisfactory life for themselves. Doing away with compulsory attendance laws would do more harm than any Holt sees with the existing laws. 6

Essay Topics: Writing in Response to "School Is Bad for Children"

1. In addition to criticizing schools, Holt offers suggestions for improvement. Write an essay explaining what change or changes should be instituted to improve the public school system in your area. Your audience will be the local school board, and your purpose will be to convince the board to implement the change you suggest.
2. Holt says, "We should abolish compulsory school attendance." Do you agree? Write an essay arguing for or against Holt's view. Be sure to speak to the points Holt offers to support his view as well as to the objections he counters. Your audience is your classmates, and your purpose is to convince them of the wisdom of your stand.
3. Holt says that in school, children learn that "to be wrong, uncertain, confused, is a crime." Did you learn this in school? If so, write an essay narrating specific events that taught you this. Your audience is your classroom teacher, and your purpose is to share a portion of your past.
4. Do you share Holt's view that students are dishonest, that they learn "to dodge, bluff, fake, cheat"? If so, explain how this happens and what can be done about it. Your audience is the local PTA, and your purpose is to describe a serious problem and suggest a solution.
5. What event in your previous schooling had the greatest impact on you? Describe the event and tell how it affected you and why you believe it affected you the way it did. Your purpose is to share, and your audience is your teacher and classmates.

6. Holt is a believer in paired learning, which is today referred to as **collaborative learning.** In the library, find some books and articles that discuss collaborative learning. Read about this technique, and then write an essay advocating or denouncing its use as a classroom practice. Your audience consists of members of the National Education Association, and your purpose is to convince your readers to use (or not to use) collaborative learning in their classrooms. (Review the conventions for handling library research in Chapter 15.)

ESSAYS TO READ AND RESPOND TO

The rest of this chapter contains previously published essays, each of which is followed by a selection of topics that will give you experience writing in response to reading.

Values and Violence in Sports Today

Brenda Jo Bredemeier and David L. Shields

Brenda Jo Bredemeier is a professor of sport psychology and David L. Shields is a physical education researcher. In the following essay, the authors examine the ethics of violence and aggression in athletics.

To be good in sports, you have to be bad. Or so many athletes, coaches and sports fans believe. Heavyweight champion Larry Holmes, for example, revealed a key to his success during a *60 Minutes* interview with Morley Safer: Before he enters the ring, he said, "I have to change, I have to leave the goodness out and bring all the bad in, like Dr. Jekyll and Mr. Hyde." 1

Even sports fan Ronald Reagan suggested that normally inappropriate ways of thinking and acting are acceptable in sports. When he was governor of California, he reportedly told a college team during a pep talk that in football, "you can feel a clean hatred for your opponent. It is a clean hatred since it's only symbolic in a jersey." 2

Does success today really depend on how well an athlete or team has mastered the art of aggression? The question is usually answered more by ideology than by evidence. But there is a more fundamental question that needs to be asked: Is it really OK to be bad in sports? In particular, is aggression an acceptable tactic on the playing field? If it is morally unacceptable, the debate about its utility misses the mark. 3

It seems odd to ask whether being bad is all right. But in contact sports particularly, acts of aggression are seldom condemned, usually condoned and often praised. Sport is a "world within a world" with its own unique conventions and moral understandings. 4

5 Lyle and Glenn Blackwood of the Miami Dolphins are nicknamed "the bruise brothers." Their motto—"We don't want to hurt you, just make you hurt"—aptly expresses the ambiguity many people feel about sport aggression. To reduce such ambiguity, many athletes appeal to game rules, informal agreements or personal convictions to decide the legitimacy of aggressive acts. As one collegiate basketball player told us in an interview: "It's OK to try to hurt somebody if it is legal and during the game. If the guy doesn't expect it, it's a cheap shot. That's no good. You can be aggressive and do minor damage without really hurting him and still accomplish your goal."

6 As social scientists, we are interested in the moral meaning athletes and fans attach to aggression. Do sport participants think about aggression in moral terms? Does the maturity of athletes' moral reasoning influence their aggressive behavior? What are the unique characteristics of sport morality and how does this "game reasoning" influence the perceived legitimacy of aggression?

7 Most recommendations for reducing sport aggression have focused on rules and penalties against fighting, beanballs, slugging and other forms of violence. We believe, however, that reducing athletic aggression requires the transformation of both external sports structures such as rules and penalties and internal reasoning structures. To reduce aggression, we must first understand the meaning athletes attach to it.

8 By aggression, we mean acts that are intended to inflict pain or injury. Robust, physically forceful play not meant to harm another player is better termed assertion. Unfortunately, this distinction is often blurred on the mat, the ice and the Astroturf.

9 We believe that aggression is more than a convention; it is a moral issue and can be investigated as such. If this is true, there should be an inverse relationship between the maturity of athletes' moral reasoning and their acceptance of aggression. Our research suggests that this relationship exists. The higher their level of moral reasoning, the less aggression athletes practice and condone.

10 Establishing a link between moral reasoning and sport aggression is only the first step in understanding it. It is still not clear why many people find everyday aggression objectionable but have few moral qualms when they or others hurl a beanball at a batter. We can develop a more complete portrait of athletic aggression by exploring the unique patterns of moral reasoning that sport encourages.

11 Some social scientists have noted a curious fact that athletes and fans take for granted. Sport is set apart both cognitively and emotionally from the everyday world. Anthropologist Don Handelman, for example, has observed that play "requires a radical transformation in cognition and perception." Sociologist Erving Goffman has described play activities as enclosed within a unique "social membrane" or conceptual "frame."

12 In a 1983 interview, Ron Rivera, then a linebacker with the University of California at Berkeley and now with the Chicago Bears, described the personality transformation he undergoes on the field. The off-field Ron, he said, is soft-spoken, considerate and friendly. When asked to describe the on-field Ron, he replied, "He's totally opposite from me. . . . He's a madman. . . . No matter what happens, he hits people. He's a guy with no regard for the human body." Elabo-

rating further, Rivera revealed, "I'm mean and nasty then. . . . I'm so rotten. I have a total disrespect for the guy I'm going to hit."

Does this personality transformation include a fundamental change in moral reasoning? To explore this possibility, we designed a study to see whether the same people would use similar levels of moral reasoning in response to hypothetical dilemmas set in sport-specific and daily life contexts. One "sport dilemma," for example, centered on Tom, a football player who is told by his coach to injure an opponent to help Tom's team win. One of the "daily life" dilemmas hinged on whether a person should keep his promise to deliver some money to a rich man or use it to help his hungry kin. 13

We presented four dilemmas to 120 high school and college athletes and nonathletes and asked them to reason about the best way to resolve each dilemma. Most of the students clearly perceived a difference between morality in sport and in everyday life. One comment by a high school female basketball player exemplified this perspective: "In sports, it's hard to tell right from wrong sometimes; you have to use game sense." Both athletes and nonathletes used lower-level egocentric moral reasoning when thinking about dilemmas in sport than when addressing moral issues in other contexts. 14

These and other findings suggest that moral norms which prescribe equal consideration of all people are often suspended during competition in favor of a more egocentric moral perspective. One male college basketball player explained the difference this way: "In sports you can do what you want. In life it's more restricted. It's harder to make decisions in life because there are so many people to think about, different people to worry about. In sports you're free to think about yourself." 15

This theme was echoed by many others who referred to sport as a field where each person or team seeks personal triumph and where opponents need not be given equal consideration. 16

There are several reasons sports may elicit an egocentric style of game reasoning. The very nature of competition requires that self-interest be temporarily adopted while the athlete strives to win. In everyday life, such preoccupation with self almost inevitably leads to moral failings. But in sport, participants are freed to concentrate on self-interest by a carefully balanced rule structure that equalizes opportunity. Players are guarded against the moral defaults of others by protective rules and by officials who impose sanctions for violations. Moral responsibility is thus transferred from the shoulders of players to those of officials, the enforcers of the rules, and to coaches, whom the players learn to see as responsible for all decisions. 17

If the nature of competition encourages egocentricity, the "set aside" character of sport helps to justify it. Sport consists of artificial goals that are achieved through arbitrarily defined skills and procedures. Although running across a line or shooting a ball through a hoop is all-important in the immediate game context, neither has significant consequences outside sports. This lack of any "real world" meaning to sport actions helps make egocentric reasoning seem legitimate. 18

Not all sport goals, of course, lack real-world implications. In boxing, for 19 example, where the goal involves damage to another person, serious injury or even death is possible. Another exception is professional sports, and even some collegiate and high school sports, where winners may receive prizes, bigger paychecks, more perks or expanded educational and professional opportunities. The moral implications of harm as a sport goal (boxing) and extrinsic rewards contingent on sport performance (in professional and quasiprofessional sports) still need to be investigated.

The dynamic of competition, the structural protection provided by officials and rules and the relatively inconsequential implications of sport intentions combine to release sport participants from the usual demands of morality. But game-specific moral understandings do not completely replace everyday morality. Just as sport exists in a unique space and time within the everyday world, so game reasoning is a form of "bracketed morality." The transformed morality that occurs in sport does not take the place of everyday morality; rather, it is embedded in the broader, more encompassing morality of daily life. 20

Because of this, most athletes limit the degree of sport aggression they accept as legitimate in line with their general understanding of the rights of others. Coordinating these two sets of standards is not easy. Consider, for example, how one athlete reasoned about the football dilemma in which Tom is told to injure his opponent: 21

"If Tom looks at it as a game, it's OK to hurt the guy—to try to take him out of the game. But if he looks at the halfback as a person, and tries to hurt him, it's not OK." Asked, "How do you decide which to go by?" the athlete explained, "When you're on the field, then the game is football. Before and after, you deal with people morally." 22

This man recognized that aggression can be viewed from two contrasting viewpoints but eliminated his ambivalence by subordinating everyday morality to game reasoning. For him, an opponent is a player, not a person. This objectification of opponents reduces an athlete's sense of personal responsibility for competitors. 23

Among some of the other athletes we interviewed, accountability was alleviated by simply "not thinking about it." As one athlete stated succinctly, "In sports you don't think about those things [hurting others]; mostly you don't think about other people, you just think about winning." 24

Most athletes, however, tried to coordinate game and everyday morality by distinguishing between legitimate and illegitimate aggression. As one man explained: "Some [aggressive acts] are not acceptable. The game is a game. You go out to win, but there's a line—limitations—there are rules. . . . You try to dominate the other player, but you don't want to make him leave the game." 25

Another athlete put it this way: "Tom shouldn't try to hurt him. He should just hit him real hard, stun him, make him lose his wind, make sure he's too scared to run the ball again." 26

Players use a complex moral logic in attempts to coordinate the goal of winning with the need to respect limits to egocentricity. Some athletes identify the rules as the final arbiter of legitimacy, but most appeal to less formal criteria. 27

Themes such as intimidation, domination, fairness and retribution are continuously woven into participants' fabric of thought, providing a changing picture of what constitutes legitimate action.

Shifting expectations, created by the fast-paced and emotionally charged 28
action, can readily lead to perceived violations or "cheap shots." Cheap shots, of course, are in the eye, or ribs, of the beholder. As a college basketball player explained, physical contact may be interpreted by athletes as either assertive or aggressive, depending on their perception of intent: "I've played with guys who try to hurt you. They use all kinds of cheap shots, especially elbows in the face and neck. But that's different than trying to maintain position or letting a guy know you're there. An elbow can be for intimidation or it can be for hurting. I just use elbows in the regular course of the game."

Given the complex and variable conditions of sport, it is not surprising that 29
among the athletes we interviewed there was not a clear consensus about the line between legitimate and illegitimate aggression. Generally, we found that the more mature the athletes' moral reasoning, the less aggression they accepted as legitimate—both for the fictitious character Tom in the hypothetical football dilemma and for themselves as they reasoned about personal aggression.

Yet even the more morally mature athletes often accepted minor forms of 30
aggression as legitimate game strategy. In fact, such minor aggression was sometimes viewed as a positive, enhancing aspect of the game. As a high school player explained: "Football is a rough game and if it weren't for rules people would get hurt real bad—even killed. Some people just want to hurt other people real bad." Asked, "Should the present rules be changed to reduce football injuries?" he replied, "No. Nobody will want to play if the rules get so uptight that you can't hit hard."

Moral research inevitably leads beyond descriptions about what people do 31
to questions about what people ought to do. Perhaps most athletes accept some aggression as "part of the game," but should they? Should any degree of aggression be considered legitimate?

Based on what we have learned about game reasoning, we believe two crite- 32
ria can be employed to distinguish morally mature athletes' judgments of aggression which they may perceive as legitimate from aggression which certainly is not. First, any act intended to inflict an injury that is likely to have negative consequences for the recipient once the game has ended is illegitimate. The legitimacy of game reasoning depends partly on the irrelevance of sport action to everyday life. Consequently, inflicting such "game-transcending" injuries as a broken leg or a concussion cannot be morally justified.

Second, game reasoning is also legitimated because it occurs within a situa- 33
tion that is defined by a set of rules that limit the relevant procedures and skills which can be used during the game. Therefore, any act is illegitimate if it occurs apart from the strategic employment of game-relevant skills, even if such an act is intended to cause only minor injury or mild discomfort. Such behavior impinges upon the protective structure that releases participants from their normal moral obligations.

The implications of our research on athletes' game reasoning may extend to other spheres of life. If game reasoning is distinct from the morality of general life, are there other context-specific moralities, such as business reasoning or political reasoning? Perhaps the list could be extended indefinitely. While every context raises unique moral issues, however, we agree with most moral-development theorists that the fundamental structure of moral reasoning remains relatively stable in nearly all situations. 34

Sport is employed frequently as a metaphor for other endeavors, and game language is often utilized in discussions of such diverse topics as business, politics and war. A recent book by Thomas Whisler of the University of Chicago, *Rules of the Game,* has little to do with sport and everything to do with corporate boardrooms. 35

The borrowing of sport images and language may reflect a tendency to transplant game morality from its native soil to foreign gardens. If this is the case, game reasoning has social implications that extend far beyond the limited world of sport. Game morality is legitimated by protections within the sport structure, but most other contexts lack such safeguards. If game reasoning leads to manipulation to gain job advancement, for example, are adequate laws available and enforced to guarantee equal opportunity? Can the dirty tricks of politics be legitimated as if they were just a game? Does game reasoning encourage a view that nuclear war is winnable, propelling us toward the "game to end all games"? And if it does, who consents to play these games? 36

Essay Topics: Writing in Response to "Values and Violence in Sports Today"

1. Bredemeier and Shields say that many people believe that "to be good in sports, you have to be bad." Explain the meaning of this quotation, and go on to agree or disagree with it. Draw your supporting details from the essay and your own experience with sports, either as a player or spectator. Your audience is the parents of student athletes, and your purpose is to inform them of the nature of athletic competition.
2. Do you agree that "sport is a 'world within a world' with its own unique conventions and moral understandings"? Write an argumentation-persuasion essay arguing your point of view. Draw your supporting details from the essay and your own experience with sports, either as a player or spectator. Your audience is your classroom teacher.
3. Assume that you are one of the starting five on a scholastic basketball team playing in the finals of an important championship. At the start of the fourth quarter, your team is behind by 12 points, and your point guard has twisted an ankle and is on the bench. Your coach sends you in as a replacement with orders to "take out" the other team's star shooter. You don't have to injure the player seriously, just be sure the person hurts enough to be returned to the bench for a few minutes so that your team can take the lead. Write an essay explaining whether you will follow

the coach's orders and why or why not. Also explain the effects of your decision on you and your teammates. Your audience consists of student athletes, and your purpose is to convince them that your course of action is the correct one.

4. Think back over your own experiences with athletics (either as a player or a spectator) and write an essay that cites specific examples of violence in sports. Explain whether this violence was justifiable. Your audience is your classmates, and your purpose is to share your experiences and convince your reader that violence is (or is not) justifiable in sports.
5. When does aggression in sports go too far? Write a set of guidelines explaining how much aggression is acceptable in high school football or basketball. Your audience consists of high school coaches, athletic directors, and players. Your purpose is to convince your audience to adopt your guidelines.
6. The violence among spectators at athletic events is becoming a greater concern. In the library, research violence among spectators and write an essay that describes the nature and extent of this violence and recommends a solution to the problem. Consider limiting yourself to discussion of violence among fans of a particular sport such as soccer, baseball, or football. Your audience will be the readers of *Psychology Today,* and your purpose will be to inform them of the extent of the violence and convince them of the wisdom of your proposal for curtailing it.

Born Beautiful: Confessions of a Naturally Gorgeous Girl

Ellen Paige

Is life easier for the beautiful people of the world? Ellen Paige, a staff writer for a national women's magazine, seems to think so.

My blind date is trudging up the four flights to my New York apartment. I'm waiting, in suspense. Will he be a little like William Hurt? Have a touch of Tom Hanks' winsomeness? When there's one flight to go, I can't wait any longer. I poke my head out the door and over the bannister to check him out. Not bad—except that he looks like his best friend just died. 1

Until he glances up and sees me. In a second his brow relaxes, his eyes brighten, a wave of visible relief sweeps across his face. He grins and bounds up the last few steps. Why is this man suddenly so cheerful? I already know the reason: it's because I'm pretty. And does this little scene make me feel great? Well, yes. But I'm used to it. 2

I've been pretty most of my life, except for a few awkward phases. I know this because people tell me—both directly and in more subtle ways (like the way my blind date's face did). Sometimes when I look in the mirror, I can see what they mean; other times—as with every woman who has her good and bad days—I can't. 3

But even when I can't, there's no denying the effect of my good looks; it wraps around me like a cocoon, my magic charm. Being beautiful can keep pain at bay.

It's like this: I've made a stupid mistake at work and am feeling embarrassed 4 and worthless—or my ego has been bruised by a particularly bad fight with my boyfriend. So I put on something I think I look great in and head for the door. Outside, what happens usually cheers me up: men turn and react appreciatively as I walk by. I don't mean they catcall or harass me (although no woman on earth can successfully escape that kind of attention). And I'm not talking about the chorus of whistles you get from construction workers or truck drivers. I mean that nice-looking men, well-dressed, carrying briefcases—men I might want to go out with—check me out in a way I think is flattering. Women also look at me, but in a different, more investigative way. They eye me, taking in everything as if they're gathering details, maybe shopping for a new look for themselves.

Sure, I'd probably feel even better if my boss told me how smart I was or if 5 my boyfriend showed up on my doorstep apologetic and holding roses. But who can count on that happening? What I can count on are the turned heads, the appreciative glances, the "hey, beautiful." And that goes a long way toward making me feel good.

Shallow, you say? Dating success shouldn't depend on how pretty someone 6 is; a setback at work shouldn't be soothed by skin-deep compliments. Maybe not, but it's also undeniable: looks count. If you were hoping to hear that being beautiful isn't all it's cracked up to be, I'm going to disappoint. It *is* what it's cracked up to be—and more.

By now you're probably wondering what I look like. Most of what I know 7 about my looks comes from other people, who tell me I'm the earthy, natural type. But I do know my features are small and even, my brown eyes and hair are a good match, I'm tall and fit, and I can look sexy and sophisticated when I want. I wasn't the type of child adults cooed over; my parents let me know they were proud of my looks, partly because all parents do, but mainly to instill confidence. For the most part, though, beauty was not a big deal in my family. There was some sibling rivalry between my younger sister and me that we now know stemmed from the disparity in our looks—she kept her baby fat well into her teens and I didn't. 8

I suppose she was right to be jealous of my looks, because in school, beauty was definitely a big deal. Being cute had a lot to do with the number of friends I had. My popularity certainly wasn't due to my outgoing personality (I was and am very shy) or my academic record (unremarkable). Girls, I could tell, admired my looks, but it was the boys who first let me know they thought I was good-looking, usually by threatening to pummel my little brother after school if he didn't dish the latest dirt on me. (Unfortunately he always complied, which accounts for how the entire fifth grade knew when I got my first bra.) As I got older, the boys got braver and started to say things—not compliments exactly, but as close to them as adolescents ever get. Sometimes it was flattering, and I liked it. But other times it was unsettling.

I'm at the beach. I'm thirteen and an "older" man (actually a boy of about 9 eighteen) is talking to me while I wait in line for ice cream. He asks me how old I am. When I tell him, he stops cold, steps back and stares at my skimpy bikini, and says one word: "Wow." The way he utters that word—slowly, solemnly—is a revelation, both frightening and enlightening. I realize then that beauty bestows power.

I was just starting to get wise to what my looks could mean to me when I headed to high school. That's where I got an advanced degree in "pretty politics." Once, in the restroom, I overheard someone say about me, "She's pretty and she knows it." Translated, that meant I was vain, conceited, stuck-up. Nice girls, you see, weren't supposed to know they were pretty. I got the message. I learned to deny what was as obvious as the nose, and every other feature, on my face. The way to be liked—and being liked is paramount to a teenager—was to be pretty and *not* know it. So I tried hard to get voted Best Personality; I always won Best-Looking instead. 10

In high school there were no secrets. Our reputations as freshmen followed us to senior year. When I went to college, though, to a university the size of a small city, I faded into the crowd. I no longer stood out because of the way I looked. In fact, there were many girls in my dorm, not to mention on the whole campus, who were more than my equals in the looks department. Instead of feeling inferior, I was less self-conscious about my appearance. The pressure was off, and that let me relax enough to start enjoying my looks. When someone told me I was attractive, I felt as though I'd earned the compliment. "Pretty" was no longer just a label that showed my high-school status. 11

Once during the summer between my sophomore and junior years, I ran into a guy I knew from high school. He was surprised to hear I was studying biology at a prestigious university. "You never seemed like the type," he said. Maybe I should have been offended, but instead I just laughed; I *was* the type, and always had been. But college had freed me from my looks. 12

Now that I'm on my own, out of school and working in New York, it's become clearer exactly what being attractive can do for me. It doesn't guarantee glamour, excitement, or adventure, or that I'll marry Mr. Right. But it does make some good things come my way—and make life more comfortable. 13

For one thing, people notice me: a waiter at a nearby café gives me delicious whole-wheat rolls for free; a grocery clerk offers me (but not my date) change for the bus; the guy working out next to me breaks training to flirt. After they've noticed me, people usually want to get to know me, and that's helped to open some doors. My looks hold people's attention long enough for me to strut my stuff—to show them I can produce. If my looks intrigue someone, I don't mind using them. That doesn't mean I'd wear a bustier and miniskirt to a job interview, but I don't try to hide my looks either. It's highly unlikely that someone will hire me on appearance alone, but at least I'll get the interview. 14

I haven't quite figured out why my looks intrigue. It seems to boil down to simple curiosity; maybe people wonder if I have as much luck in other areas as I've had with my looks. But people do seem attracted to attractiveness, pleased by it, happy to be in the company of it. 15

I know I am. Sometimes just being with someone I think is good-looking makes me feel special by association. I don't choose my friends because they're beautiful, but still, looks *are* alluring. People tend to assign positive traits to those 16 they find attractive. That's why new acquaintances often seem to have decided that they like me almost as soon as we've met. My appearance can speed up the process that makes people choose to be my friends.

It's my first day on the job at a publishing house. I'm making the rounds, introducing myself to co-workers. One woman is so absorbed in her work, and so uninterested in meeting the new kid on the block, that she doesn't even look up when she says hello. A few days later, she suddenly becomes cordial, even palsy. I realize that I've passed her test; she's sized me up and I look right. She's intrigued, I can tell, not by who I am—she's barely spoken to me before this burst of chumminess—but rather by how I look. 17

The effect of my looks is even more apparent in my romantic involvements. I'm not the first to have noticed that people pair up with their equals—10s with 10s, 7s with 7s, and so on. Studies have proven it. It's certainly true for my boyfriend, Josh, and me. I think he's at least as good-looking as my friends tell me I am. But there's one big difference: my looks matter more to him than his do to me. I'm not sure why, but it doesn't bother me. In fact, I'm happy Josh is proud of the way I look. If I thought he loved me only for my looks, that would be different. 18

But then there are those middle-of-the-night doubts. What if he wakes up one day and sees me looking lousy? I don't mean being caught without makeup, since I rarely use cosmetics anyway. What I'm talking about is getting older. I worry about it. So I work out—a lot, sometimes two hours a day. Makeup can disguise the effects of aging, but exercise can actually delay them. I won't hand over my looks to age without a fight. I worry that if time robs me of my beauty, I'll also lose my magic, the power my looks give me. I've felt a twinge of this already. At my ten-year high-school reunion last year I panicked that my former classmates would think I'd gone downhill, and I'm not sure that some of them didn't. But before I started yearning for my old Best-Looking banner, I told myself that nobody looks as good as they did when they were seventeen. 19

I guess admitting that losing my looks worries me is a giveaway that I care about them a great deal. But while I have them, I might as well capitalize on them. If they can make me feel better when I'm blue, why not? 20

It's a Sunday, a couple of years ago. I'm out running errands when I bump into Craig—a man I've just started dating. He's friendly but not exactly passionate in his hello—not like last Friday night, anyway. I ask him if he'd like to catch a movie tonight, but he hedges. He then tells me that he's started seeing his old girlfriend again. The next moment, he hops in a cab and is gone. I feel like I've been socked in the stomach, but I catch a glimpse of myself in a store window and automatically think, "Well, at least I look good." It doesn't bring Craig back, but I do feel better. 21

When I feel good about my looks, others pick up on it. The day I met my current boyfriend, I was feeling fabulous about my work, my friends, and the way I looked. I was waiting in the tiny backseat of a Triumph for a ride home from a party when there he was—a gorgeous man scrunching his six-foot-one frame in beside me. He was first attracted to me, he says, mostly by my looks, but also my attitude—enough to fold himself in two to sit next to me. 22

This doesn't happen every day, though. Let me dispel the myth that pretty women have men knocking down doors or squeezing into sports cars just to be near them. I've gone through several long and lonely stretches without a single eligible man in sight, stretches made worse by the loaded question, "How come a pretty girl like you doesn't have a boyfriend?" 23

True, being pretty may help me catch a man's eye across a room or spark his interest during a brief encounter in an elevator, but more often I end up getting propositioned by overly aggressive guys who aren't my type at all. During my dating dry spells, I used to rationalize that men must have assumed that I had a boyfriend, and were afraid to ask me out. Although there's no way to prove it, I don't really think this was often the case. Instead, the reasons I found it hard to meet the right men were the same reasons all women have trouble meeting men—but that's another story. 24

There can be a kind of beauty backlash in other social situations, too. I've noticed some women giving me nasty looks for no apparent reason; I've also felt them act strangely aloof. Rather than instantly *liking* me because of how I look, they seemed to take an instant *dislike* to me. That they may have been jealous doesn't make me feel any better about their reactions. 25

My exercise class is small: only two other women and our instructor. It's hard to ignore the fact that my classmates won't talk to me. I am shy, but at least I try to be friendly. I try small talk in the locker room, but I get no response. I ask our instructor, Todd, why he thinks they're so aloof. "Two reasons—you're tall and lean. Period," he says. That's ridiculous. Judy has a great job and Beth's got a husband worth bragging about. Two things I envy them for. How can they be jealous of me? I'm hurt, but I'm also angry. How can they judge me on such trivial grounds? But then I think: how can I be annoyed if they judge me negatively on looks alone, when I love it if people assume I'm great just because I'm attractive? 26

Still, all things considered, if you ask me how I'd like to be known, I'd say I'd rather be considered intelligent. Why then, I wonder, was I so disappointed after I met my boyfriend's brother for the first time? He told Josh later he thought I was really bright. Didn't he think I was sort of, well . . . beautiful? 27

Essay Topics: Writing in Response to "Born Beautiful"

1. Paige's thesis is that "looks count." Drawing on the points made in the essay and your own experience, agree or disagree with that thesis. Your audience consists of your classmates, and your purpose is to convince your readers of the truth of your view.
2. Paige says, "In high school there were no secrets. Our reputation as freshmen followed us to senior year." Review your own high school years, and write an essay that tells whether your own experience and that of your classmates is reflected in Paige's statement. Your audience is your instructor, and your purpose is to share your experience and inform your reader.
3. Write an essay explaining how some aspect of your physical makeup (such as your height, your athletic ability, your overall appearance, your

gender, or your skin color) has affected your life. Be sure to provide examples to illustrate your points. Your audience is your classmates, and your purpose is to share and inform.

4. Paige worries about getting older, afraid she will "lose [her] magic, the power [her] looks give [her]." Write an essay predicting what Paige's life will be like when she is 60 and her beauty has faded. Also, recommend what Paige should do when "time robs [her] of [her] beauty." Your audience is Paige herself, and your purpose is to inform.
5. Are Paige's essay and the point of view it reflects sexist? What impact does the author's point of view have on women's drive for equality? Argue your point of view for a local chapter of the National Organization of Women, a politically active feminist group.
6. Is what Paige says about physical beauty also true for males? Answer this question in an essay meant to inform readers of *Psychology Today*.
7. Degree of physical attractiveness is only one of several accidents of birth that affect who we are. Birth order, gender, number of siblings, age of parents, location in an urban or rural area, living in a large or small town—all these influence our personality. In the library, research the effects of one of these accidents of birth on scholastic achievement, and write a report to inform members of the National Education Association.

Democracy

Amy Tan

Best-selling author of The Joy Luck Club, *Amy Tan ponders the meaning of* democracy *for her family in China.*

How much we Americans take our freedoms for granted. We already have the rights: freedom of expression, contracts and legal departments to protect them, the right to put differences of opinion to a vote. We put those rights in writing, carry them in our back pockets all over the world, pull them out as proof. We may be aliens in another country, but we still maintain that our rights are inalienable. 1

I try to imagine what democracy means to people in China who dream of it. I don't think they are envisioning electoral colleges, First Amendment rights or civil lawsuits. I imagine that their dreams of democracy begin with a feeling in the chest, one that has been restrained for so long it grows larger and more insistent, until it bursts forth with a shout. Democracy is the right to shout, "Listen to us." 2

That is what I imagine because I was in China in 1987. I saw glimpses of another way of life, a life that could have been mine. And along with many wonderful things I experienced in my heart, I also felt something uncomfortable in my chest. 3

In Shanghai in 1987, I attended the wedding of my niece. After the ceremony, she and her husband went home to the three-room apartment shared with 4 her mother, father and brother. "Now that you're married," I said with good humor, "you can't live at home anymore."

"The waiting list for government-assigned housing is sixteen years," replied 5
my niece's husband. "We will both be forty-eight years old when we are assigned our own place."

My mouth dropped. He shrugged. 6

While on a boat trip down the Huangpu River, I asked a tour guide how she 7
had chosen her career. She told me matter-of-factly that people in China did not choose careers. They had jobs assigned to them.

She saw my surprised expression. "Oh, but I'm lucky. So many people can't 8
get any kind of good job. If your family came from a bad background—the bourgeoisie—then, no college. Maybe only a job sweeping the streets." At a family dinner in Beijing, I learned that my sister's husband could not attend our get-together. He was away at his job, said my sister.

"When will he return?" I asked. My mother explained that his job was in a 9
city thousands of miles away. He had been living apart from my sister for the past ten years. "That's terrible," I said to my sister. "Tell him to ask for a transfer. Tell him you miss him."

"Miss, not miss!" my mother sniffed. "They can't even ask." 10

One of my sisters did ask. Several years ago, she asked for a visa to leave 11
China. Now she lives in Wisconsin. A former nurse, she now works six days a week, managing a take-out Chinese restaurant. Her husband, trained as a surgeon, works in the kitchen. And recently I've met others who also asked, a waiter who was once a doctor in China, a taxi driver who was formerly a professor of entomology, a housekeeper who was an engineer. Why did they ask to leave? I found it hard to understand how people could leave behind family, friends, their motherland and jobs of growing prestige.

My sister in Wisconsin helped me understand. After my novel was pub- 12
lished, she wrote me a letter. "I was once like you," she said. "I wanted to write stories as a young girl. But when I was growing up, they told me I could not do so many things. And now my imagination is rusted and no stories can move out of my brain."

My sister and I had the same dream. But my brain did not become rusted. I 13
became a writer. And later, we shared another dream, that China and our family were on the verge of a better, more open life. We did not imagine that the blood that is thicker than water would be running through the streets of Beijing. We did not believe that one Chinese would kill another. We did not foresee that an invisible great wall would rise up, that we would be cut off from our family, that letters would stop, that the silence would become unbearable.

These days I can only imagine what has happened to my family in China. 14
And I think about the word democracy. It rolls so easily off my English-speaking tongue. But in Beijing it is a foreign-sounding word, so many syllables, so many clashing sounds. In China, democracy is still not an easy word to say. Many cannot say it.

Hope then. 15

Essay Topics: Writing in Response to "Democracy"

1. In paragraph 1, Tan states that "Americans take our freedoms for granted." Look up the Bill of Rights in an encyclopedia. Select one of the rights guaranteed by the Bill and explain what life would be like without it. Your audience is your classmates, and your purpose is to help them come to a greater appreciation of one of their freedoms.
2. In paragraph 11, Tan tells of the Chinese who left everything behind to come to the United States. If you had to leave everything behind and emigrate to a new country, what do you think you would miss the most? Why? Write your essay for your classroom instructor to help that person learn more about what is important to you.
3. Tan's niece and new husband were forced to live with her mother, father, and brother in a three-room apartment. Explain what effects this kind of living arrangement is likely to have on the family members. Your audience is your sociology professor, and your purpose is to show that you understand how people are affected by their living conditions.
4. Write your own definition of *democracy* and explain how that definition might compare and contrast with the meaning of the word for people who live in dictatorships. Your audience will be non-United States citizens, and your purpose is to inform them of what democracy means to one citizen of the United States.
5. In your campus library, research the Chinese democratic movement over the last 10 years or so, and then write an account of that movement. Your audience is the students in a history class, and your purpose is to inform.

Nazi Hate Movies Continue to Ignite Fierce Passions

Rebecca Lieb

Rebecca Lieb, who lives in Germany, looks at a thorny issue: should we ban the viewing of Nazi propaganda films, which inflame hatreds and promote violence?

Do the propaganda films made by the Nazis to inspire anti-Semitic prejudice still have the power to stir up hate? Are they dangerous or should they be shown? If they are to be shown, who will show them and under what circumstances? Is there anything to be learned from them or are they too horrifying even to contemplate? 1

Some 1,400 films were made under the supervision of Joseph Goebbels, Hitler's minister of propaganda. At least three ("Jud Süss," "The Rothschilds" and "The Eternal Jew") were rabidly anti-Semitic. Widely shown, they were used to turn Germans against their Jewish neighbors and to inure them to the march of the Holocaust. 2

The most vitriolic of the films is the pseudo-documentary "The Eternal 3

Jew," shot in the Warsaw ghetto in 1940. Jews are portrayed as a lice-infested, lazy and avaricious people, who disguise themselves in European garb to infiltrate and usurp Western civilization. Jewish migration is compared visually to a plague of rats. Prominent individuals are attacked, including the "deadly enemy" Charlie Chaplin and "the relatively Jew" Albert Einstein. Graphic scenes of kosher butchering, showing Jews as bloodthirsty and sadistic, climax the diatribe.

Whether "The Eternal Jew" and the other Nazi films should now be seen is stirring debate in the United States and Germany. In the United States, a major archive for films about Jewish life is restricting access to the movies. In Germany, the state-appointed custodian of the films has launched a campaign against an American who has distributed videocassettes of the films. Those believing they are dangerous, including the German Government and some Jewish groups in the United States, demand that the films be kept in vaults, inaccessible to all but a scholarly few. Arguments over morals, censorship, freedom of speech and copyright are raging over whether the films should be seen by the public, historians or film scholars. 4

The major archive, the National Center for Jewish Film at Brandeis University, obtained prints of "The Eternal Jew" and other anti-Semitic films from the German Government in 1988. Sharon Rivo, the executive director of the center, is opposed to allowing the films to be shown to the public and will only permit scholars to see them after a panel has reviewed their applications. 5

"This is not a First Amendment issue," says Ms. Rivo. "We are protecting the rights of the dead." She likens the portrayal in "The Eternal Jew" of the Warsaw ghetto, whose detainees were later deported to concentration camps, to the videos of Iraqi-held American hostages televised during the gulf war. 6

Jeffrey Abramson, a professor of politics at Brandeis who was chairman of a recent forum on the validity of showing "The Eternal Jew," disagrees. "If this film isn't a test case for the First Amendment, then I don't know what is." But he calls the film "the ultimate snuff movie" because it was made to inspire Nazis to kill Jews, and the Jews who appeared in it were killed. 7

While Mr. Abramson cautiously asserts that there may be social benefits to allowing "The Eternal Jew" to be shown, Ms. Rivo says that without a study to measure the impact of the film on audiences, the center will continue to severely restrict access. The National Center for Jewish Film has twice applied for and been denied a Federal grant for the study, and now its plans for the film are in limbo. Ms. Rivo recently denied a request from Bill Moyers to use clips from the film in a PBS special on hate. The move fanned allegations of censorship. 8

The center's efforts to control "The Eternal Jew" are also frustrated by legalities. Ms. Rivo asserts that her archive is the only legally authorized distributor of the films in the United States. The center struck an agreement with the German Government to disallow transfer of the films to video to hinder piracy and dissemination. But videos of the films have been in the United States for a long time, and despite the center's claim on exclusive rights, most legal experts agree that the films are in the public domain. Anyone can purchase or rent video and film copies from four or five mail-order sources. 9

Both Ms. Rivo and Karl Wörner, president of Transit Film, a German Gov- 10 ernment–owned distributor that claims to control world rights to the films, allege that any distribution in the United States other than by the Jewish film center or German Government is illegal. (In Germany, showing any Nazi propaganda film is prohibited, including Leni Riefenstahl's 1935 documentary of the rise of Nazism, "Triumph of the Will," which is widely available in the United States.) Mr. Wörner has launched a campaign in the German press against Americans who sell the films or videos. Peter Bernotas, president of International Historic Films, a Chicago-based company that has distributed Nazi videos since the early 1980's, has been the target of criticism. His activities have led Mr. Wörner to publicly call him a Nazi sympathizer who supplies hate groups with propaganda material.

Mr. Bernotas makes no reply to the contention. He declines to address the moral issues that others raise about his business affairs. He says that it is company policy never to sell Nazi films to hate organizations, and that his cassettes carry disclaimers warning viewers that the films are "extremely prejudicial in nature." Mr. Bernotas says his market for the films is Jewish groups and Holocaust study centers, adding that hate groups already have the films. 11

Mr. Bernotas's activities were called into question when it was discovered that his company advertised Nazi films in *The Spotlight,* a magazine published by the Liberty Lobby, described by the Anti-Defamation League of B'nai B'rith as "the wealthiest and most active anti-Semitic organization in the United States." Mr. Bernotas says the ads were placed by an advertising agency, which described the paper to him only as "conservative and anti-Communist." Although the ads stopped, the revelation was damning. Lawrence Grossman, an advocate of free access to Nazi films, which he obtained from Mr. Bernotas for his company, the Jewish Video Library, severed business contacts with Mr. Bernotas after the disclosure. 12

The Anti-Defamation League does not support blocking Nazi films. The league's research director, Alan Schwartz, said the group is "opposed to censorship and keeping films under lock and key." Mr. Schwartz calls for responsible handling of the material. 13

Others, like the documentarian Frederick Wiseman, call for a ban on any restrictions. "I can't believe anyone with an ounce of intelligence could take that film seriously," he said of "The Eternal Jew." But a viewer who considers himself a free-speech absolutist, seeing "The Eternal Jew" for the first time, found the film's fierce racism extreme to a degree of near absurdity. "The real danger," said Andrew Horn, a director, "is that this could become a cult film." 14

Essay Topics: Writing in Response to "Nazi Hate Movies Continue to Ignite Fierce Passions"

1. Assume your history professor is contemplating showing one or more of the Nazi propaganda films in your classroom. Write an essay that argues that the films should or should not be shown. Your audience is your history professor, and your purpose is to convince that person to adopt your view.

2. Anti-Semitism and other forms of bigotry still exist. Consider how our schools can address the problem of bigotry, and then write a proposal for your state board of education. Your proposal should consider whether there is a place in the schools for films like the *The Eternal Jew, Roots, Schindler's List,* and so forth. Your purpose is to convince the board to adopt your plan.
3. In paragraph 8, Lieb explains that the National Center for Jewish Film has been denied a Federal grant to study the effects of *The Eternal Jew* on audiences. If you disagree with that decision, write an essay to convince the government to change its mind.
4. Lieb's essay raises the issue of censorship. Write an essay that explains your position on censorship. Are you for it under certain circumstances or against it under any circumstances? Explain and defend your view for an audience of your classmates.
5. In paragraph 6, Sharon Rivo is quoted as saying that refusal to show the films " 'is not a First Amendment issue.' " In the library, research the complexities of the First Amendment and then write a paper that agrees or disagrees with Rivo's view. Your audience will be film historians, and your purpose will be to convince them to share your view.

Animal Rights versus Human Health

Albert Rosenfeld

Albert Rosenfeld presents his side of the controversy surrounding animal experimentation. As you read, consider how fairly he presents his view and the opposition perspective.

Stray dogs and cats by the hundreds of thousands roam the streets of our cities. Usually they wind up in animal shelters, where hard-pressed staffs must find ways to dispose of them. One legitimate disposal route has been the research laboratory. But in southern California—with its impressive collection of research centers—antivivisectionists and animal rights groups recently have been leaning hard on animal shelters, effectively cutting off much of the supply. *1*

About 30 years ago Los Angeles voters soundly defeated a proposal to prohibit the release of animals for laboratory use. But today, with new proposals being submitted to city councils and county boards, the results could well be different. And the new proposals are much more sweeping. They would, for instance, create review boards for all animal experimentation, requiring researchers to justify in advance any experiment they were planning and to submit a detailed research protocol before even applying for a grant. Alarmed, a group of southern California investigators have organized a committee for animal research in medicine. *2*

"Most scientists don't realize the danger," says Caltech neurobiologist John M. Allman, who uses monkeys to study the organization of the brain. "Such movements in the past—in this country, at least—have largely been the efforts of *3* small, fragmented, and relatively ineffective groups. But this new movement is carefully orchestrated, well organized, and well financed. Moreover, this is not just a local issue. It is going on intensively at the national and even at the international level. We'd be foolish to underestimate these people. They have clout. And if they attain their goals, it will effectively kill a lot of important research."

To doubly ensure the protection of human experimental subjects, a number of restrictions and regulations that admittedly are burdensome have been adopted over recent years. They take a great deal of time and energy. They generate a considerable amount of extra paper work. They often slow research (indeed, make some projects impossible) and render it much more difficult and costly at a time when budgets are shrinking and inflation is making further inroads. While these procedures are accepted as the price of seeing that human subjects volunteer freely and with fully informed consent, are we willing to pay a similar price on behalf of animal subjects who can in no way either give or withhold consent? 4

It is easy to look at the history of animal experimentation and compile a catalog of horrors. Or, for that matter, to look around today and find research projects that might be hard to justify. But the day is long past when a researcher can take any animal and do anything he pleases to it with a total disregard for its welfare and comfort. "People don't realize," says Allman, "that we are already extensively reviewed. In my work I must follow the ethical codes laid down by the National Institutes of Health and the American Physiological Society, among others. And we might have a surprise visit at any time from the U.S. Department of Agriculture's inspectors. It's the USDA field veterinarians who do the enforcing. Believe me, these inspections are anything but routine, and these fellows have a great deal of power. Because their reports can adversely affect federal funding, their recommendations are, in reality, orders. 5

"More than that, we are all required to keep detailed reports on all our animal experiments. And if pain or surgery is involved, we must tell them what anesthetics we used and in what dosages, what postoperative pain relievers and care were given, and so on. These reports are filed annually with the USDA, and they keep tabs on what goes on all over the country." 6

For all these precautions, however, it is fair to say that millions of animals—probably more rats and mice than any other species—are subjected to experiments that cause them pain, discomfort, and distress, sometimes lots of it over long periods of time. If you want to study the course of a disease with a view to figuring out its causes and possible therapies, there is no way that the animal to whom you give the disease is going to be happy about it. All new forms of medication or surgery are tried out on animals first. Every new substance that is released into the environment, or put on the market, is tested on animals. 7

In fact, some of the tests most objected to by animal advocates are those required by the government. For instance, there is a figure called the LD-50 (short for "lethal dose for 50 percent") that manufacturers are required to determine for any new substance. In each such case, a great many animals are given a lot of the stuff to find out how much it takes to kill half of them—and the survivors aren't exactly in the pink. 8

The animal rights advocates, except for the more extreme and uncompro- 9 mising types, are not kooks or crackpots. They tend to be intelligent, compassionate individuals raising valid ethical questions, and they probably serve well as consciousness raisers. It is certainly their prerogative—or anyone's—to ask of a specific project: Is this research really necessary? (What's "really necessary" is of course not always obvious.)

But it's important that they not impose their solutions on society. It would be tragic indeed—when medical science is on the verge of learning so much more that is essential to our health and welfare—if already regulation-burdened and budget-crunched researchers were further hampered. 10

In 1975, Australian philosopher Peter Singer wrote his influential book called *Animal Liberation,* in which he accuses us all of "speciesism"—as reprehensible, to him, as racism or sexism. He freely describes the "pain and suffering" inflicted in the "tyranny of human over nonhuman animals" and sharply challenges our biblical license to exercise "dominion over the fish of the sea, and over the fowl of the air, and over every living thing that moveth upon the Earth." 11

Well, certainly we are guilty of speciesism. We do act as if we had dominion over other living creatures. But domination also entails some custodial responsibility. And the questions continue to be raised: Do we have the right to abuse animals? To eat them? To hunt them for sport? To keep them imprisoned in zoos—or, for that matter, in our households? Especially to do experiments on these creatures who can't fight back? To send them into orbit, spin them on centrifuges, run them through mazes, give them cancer, perform experimental surgery? 12

Hardly any advance in either human or veterinary medicine—cure, vaccine, operation, drug, therapy—has come about without experiments on animals. And it may be impossible to get the data we need to determine the hazards of, say, radiation exposure or environmental pollutants without animal testing. I certainly sympathize with the demand that we look for ways to get the information we want without using animals. Most investigators are delighted when they can get their data by means of tissue cultures or computer simulations. But as we look for alternative ways to get information, do we meanwhile just do without? 13

I wonder about those purists who seek to halt all animal experimentation on moral grounds: Do they also refuse, for themselves and others, to accept any remedy—or information—that was gained through animal experimentation? And do they ask themselves if they have the right to make such moral decisions on behalf of all the patients in cancer wards and intensive care units and on behalf of all the victims of the maladies that afflict our species? And what of the future generations that will be so afflicted—but who might not have been—had the animal rightists not intervened? 14

Essay Topics: Writing in Response to "Animal Rights versus Human Health"

1. If a cure for AIDS could be found at the expense of thousands of monkeys who would suffer and die during laboratory experiments, could the use of the animals be justified? Argue your point of view for an audience of animal rights activists.

2. Draft a law describing under what circumstances and in what ways research labs may use animals in experiments. Then go on to argue for the passage of this law by your state legislature.
3. Do we, as Rosenfeld asks, have the right to keep animals in zoos? Write an essay to convince your classmates of the correctness of your point of view.
4. We do not need to eat animal products, including meat, to survive. If you believe in the rights of animals, write an essay to persuade your classmates to become vegetarians.
5. Define *speciesism* and go on to explain whether you are guilty of speciesism. When you answer, consider what you eat, whether you hunt or fish, what you wear, and whether you have a pet. Your audience is your instructor, and your purpose is to share and inform.
6. In the library, research the use of animals in cosmetics manufacturing, and go on to argue in your essay for or against a law that would outlaw this use of animals.

CHAPTER 15

Research Writing

Because research is an important part of a college student's life, you must learn your way around your campus library and become comfortable with the conventions for handling research material. To help you achieve these goals, this chapter will explain procedures for locating and handling material for a research paper that explores an issue in some depth. In addition, you will learn how to use research material to supplement your own supporting details in more traditional essays like the ones you have been writing so far.

WRITING THE RESEARCH PAPER

The research paper allows you to explore a topic in depth, analyze and interpret the information you discover, and report your findings in a conventional format. Although the research paper summons up fear and dread in many students, the task can be a pleasant and satisfying one if you take the time to find a topic you are genuinely interested in and if you follow the procedures described in this chapter so that you are operating efficiently.

FAMILIARIZING YOURSELF WITH THE LIBRARY

To operate efficiently in your campus library, you must know what resources are available to you, where those resources are located, and how to use them. The most frequently used resources are described below. You should visit your library to locate and examine each of them. Even better, see if your library offers tours.

Books, the Card Catalog, and the Computerized Catalog

Obviously, libraries have books—lots of them. These books are on a variety of subjects so vast that listing them here would take considerable space. How, then, do users determine which of the library's many books are the ones of interest to them? The answer is the card catalog.

The card catalog is a file of every book in the library. Card catalogs usually have two parts. First is the catalog file of books alphabetized according to author and title. In this section of the catalog, every book will have a card filed under its title and another card filed under its author's last name (books with two or more authors will have two or more author cards). Second, the card catalog has a subject file that arranges books alphabetically according to the subjects they treat. Thus, the book *Cholesterol and Heart Disease* could be listed in the subject portion of the card catalog under the following headings: "Cholesterol," "Health," "Heart Disease," "Medicine," "Nutrition," and "Physiology."

Most often you do not know the specific titles you want. Instead, you know only that you want books on a certain subject. This means that you should go to the subject file of the card catalog, rather than to the author/title file.

If you do not know what heading to check, or if you look up a heading and find nothing, consult the book called *Library of Congress Subject Headings.* This book, located on or near the catalog, will give the official headings used in the catalog so that you can be sure you are checking the correct listing.

In the upper-left corner of every card in the catalog is an identification number known as the "call number." The call number (a Library of Congress or Dewey decimal number, depending on which system your library uses) will indicate where in the library a given book can be found.

Here is an example of a subject card that can be found in many card catalogs. The numbered features are explained on the next page.

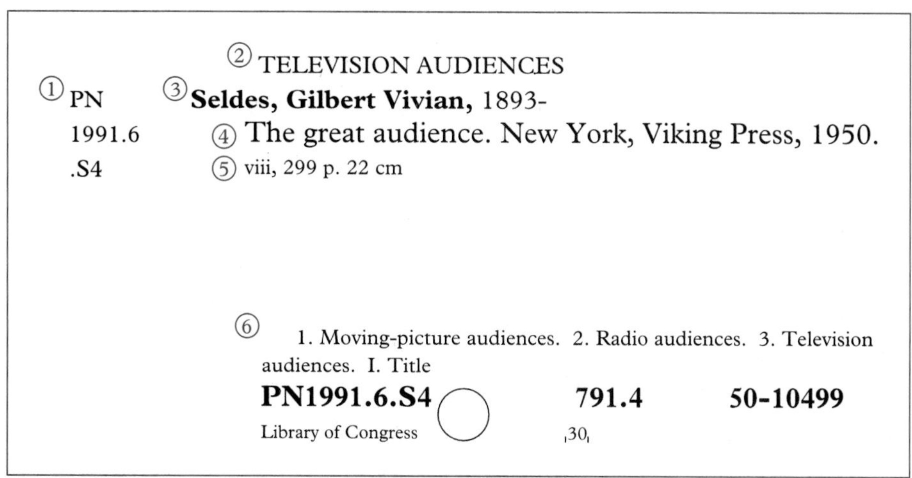

① call number
② subject heading that card is filed under
③ author and date of birth (date of death often given as well)
④ title of book and publication data
⑤ pages before the first Arabic-numbered page, number of pages, height of book
⑥ tracings noting other headings this book is filed under

Today, many campus libraries have computerized their card catalogs, so to discover books on your subject you will work at a computer terminal. You will be delighted by how easy it is to use the computer. Instructions, posted near the machines or available on the screen, require you to type in the desired subject heading. (If necessary, check *Library of Congress Subject Headings.*) The screen will then display the library's holdings on that subject. In addition to displaying all the information found on traditional cards, the display will often note how many copies of the book are in the library, whether the title has been checked out, and when it is due back.

Once you have identified a book you want, make note of the call number in the upper-left corner of the card or on the computer screen. A sign posted near the catalog will tell you where books with that range of numbers are shelved. Go to the appropriate place to get the book. (If your library does not allow access to the shelves, fill out a request form to get the book.) If the book is not shelved, check at the circulation desk to learn if it is on reserve, checked out, or lost. Ask to be notified when the book is returned.

Periodicals, Indexes, and Databases

A wealth of information exists in the form of periodicals. **Periodicals** are magazines, journals, and newspapers that come out at regular intervals (that is, "periodically"). Periodicals can be of particular use to the researcher because they contain the most current material available on a subject since, unlike books, they may be published as often as daily, weekly, monthly, or quarterly. Because periodicals contain the most up-to-date information, responsible researchers always investigate them.

Access to periodicals is provided by indexes, which give an alphabetical listing by subject of articles appearing in periodicals. Like the card or computerized catalog, indexes can be found in the library reference room.

To find periodical material, look up your subject in the appropriate index. Under the subject heading, you will find the titles of articles and the names and specific issues of the magazines, journals, or newspapers the articles appear in. For example, if you were researching marriage and religion, you could check the "marriage" heading in the *Humanities Index,* where you would find the entry reproduced on the next page.

To discover magazine articles, you can use the *Reader's Guide to Periodical Literature,* which is published once a month. The *Reader's Guide* indexes articles

1. subject
2. pertinent titles listed under headings below
3. title of article
4. author of article
5. abbreviated title of journal that article appears in
6. volume number of journal
7. pages article spans
8. date of journal
9. article is *about* William Marshall, rather than written *by* him
10. article contains a bibliography

(1) MARRIAGE

(2) *See also*

Endogamy and exogamy

Married people

Early feminist themes in French utopian socialism: the St-Simonians and Fourier. L. F. Goldstein. J. Hist Ideas 43:91–103 Ja/Mr '82

Protestant churches

(3) To preserve the marital state: the Basler Ehegericht, 1550–1592. T. M. Safley. bibl. J Fam Hist 7:162–79 Summ '82

(4) (10) (5) Ghana (6) (7) (8)

State and society, marriage and adultery: some considerations towards a social history of pre-colonial Asante. T.C. McCaskie. J Afric Hist 22 no 4:477-94 '81

MARRIAGE (canon law)

See also

Clandestinity (canon law)

MARRIAGE, Clandestine (canon law) See Clandestinity (canon law)

MARRIAGE and employment. See Married people-Employment

MARRIAGE in literature

See also

Courtship in literature

Of sex and the shrew, M.D. Perret. Ariel 13:3–20 Ja '82

Thel. Thelyphthora, and the daughters of Albion. E.B. Murray. Stud Romant 20:275–97 Fall '81

Third text of Sav me viit in be brom. O.S. Pickering. Eng Stud 63:20–2 F '82

MARRIAGE law

Great Britain

Thel. Thelyphthora, and the daughters of Albion. E.B. Murray. Stud Romant 20:275–97 Fall '81

Switzerland

To preserve the marital state: the Basler Ehegericht. 1550–1592. T.M. Safley, bibl J Fam Hist 7:162–79 Summ '82

MARRIED people

Employment

'Til newsrooms do us part. B. Buresh. Colum Journalism R 21:43–6 My/Je '82

MARRS, Suzanne

Eudora Welty's snowy heron. Am Lit 53:723–5 Ja '82

MARSHALL, John

Hypothetical imperatives. Am Philos Q 19:105–14 Ja '82

MARSHALL, Peter

Nicole Oresme on the nature, reflection, and speed of light. Isis 72:357–74 S '81

MARSHALL, William, fl 1630–1650

about

(9) Milton's Greek epigram. J.K. Hale. II Milton Q 16:8–9 Mr '82

MARSHALS

See also

Montgomery of Alamein, Bernard Law Montgomery, 1st viscount

Ypres, John Denton Pinkstone French, 1st earl of

by subject from over 100 popular magazines, such as *Time, Newsweek, Saturday Evening Post, Ladies' Home Journal,* and *Harper's Bazaar.* Popular magazines are general-interest publications like those available on most newsstands. Such magazines contain useful information, but it will not be of a scholarly nature.

For more detailed, more scholarly information, turn to journals. **Journals** are periodicals published by scholarly, professional organizations—groups like the American Psychological Association and the Modern Language Association. The treatment of subjects in journals is more detailed—aimed less at the general reader and more at the reader knowledgeable in the given field. However, this fact should not discourage you from using journal articles, because they can be understood by the college student. In fact, the more scholarly approach of the journal article often makes it a more satisfying choice than the magazine article.

To discover useful journal articles, check the indexes appropriate to your subject. In addition, check the abstracts. An **abstract** is a book listing articles by subject matter and providing a brief summary of each article's content in addition to information about where the article can be found. Following is a list of some of the most common indexes and abstracts. If these do not provide what you need, check with the librarian.

Agricultural Index
Applied Science and Technology Index
Art Index
Basic Books and Periodicals of Home Economics
Bibliography of Modern History
Bibliography on Women: With Special Emphasis on Their Roles in Science and Society
Biological Abstracts
Business Periodicals Index
Chemical Abstracts
Drama Bibliography
Education Index
Energy Index
Engineering Index
Film Index
Health and Development: An Annotated Indexed Bibliography
Historical Abstracts
Humanities Index
Index to Economic Journals
Index to Religious Periodical Literature
International Bibliography of Geography
International Bibliography of Political Science
International Computer Bibliography
International Nursing Index
MLA International Bibliography of Books & Articles on the Modern Languages & Literature

The Music Index
Nursing Literature Index
Psychology Abstracts
Social Sciences and Humanities Index
Social Sciences Index
Women: A Bibliography

Newspapers are often the best source of the most immediate information on subjects so current or so regional that books and other periodicals do not treat them. However, newspapers also cover a wide variety of subjects also treated in books and other periodicals. Articles related to the arts, health and medicine, history, politics, travel, fashion, ecology, nuclear energy, economics, and more are found in newspapers. Three of the most useful newspaper indexes are *The New York Times Index, The Wall Street Journal Index,* and *The Washington Post Index.*

Many libraries have large computerized databases that index periodical material. To use these databases, you sit at a terminal hooked up to a CD-ROM (compact disc, read-only memory) player. CD-ROM indexes in your library may include one or more of the following: *Humanities Index, Social Sciences Index, Readers' Guide to Periodical Literature, Business Periodicals Index, Education Index, Modern Language Association International Bibliography, and Health Index,* among others. In addition, your library may have *Info Trac General Periodicals Index,* which indexes over a thousand periodicals on a wide range of subjects.

If you need help using the computerized databases or learning which subject headings to type in to launch a search, ask the librarian. Computer searches are efficient, but keep in mind that the database may cover only recent years. For older material, you must consult the paper indexes and abstracts.

Once you have identified the articles you want to consult, you are ready to locate the material in your library. The first step is to see if your library carries the magazines, journals, and newspapers you want. To find out, consult the catalog of periodicals, which will be a computer printout near the indexes or a catalog in drawers in the periodicals room. The catalog should also tell you which issues of the periodicals the library has. Recent issues will be in the current periodicals room and older issues will be bound and shelved according to the call number given in the catalog.

Government Documents

The United States government publishes more material than any other publisher, and it publishes on a wide variety of subjects, including business and economics, domestic and foreign affairs, social sciences, education, and ecology. For this reason, researchers often turn to government publications for some of their information. To find a U.S. document on a particular subject, you can check the subject-index section of the *Monthly Catalog of U.S. Government Publications,* .the *Congressional Information Service,* which indexes U.S. Congress publications, and *Public Affairs Information Service,* which indexes documents in the social sciences.

Reference Works

Reference works provide general information about a subject. They are helpful when you need an overview of a subject or when you want background information. For this reason, reference works are a good place to look for ideas for narrowing a topic. The most common reference works are usually shelved in the reference room. They are designated in the card or computerized catalog with "Ref." above the call number. Reference works cannot be checked out, so you must use them in the library.

Some of the most helpful reference works include the following.

Dictionary of Banking and Finance
Encyclopaedia of Judaica
Encyclopedia of American Ethnic Groups
Encyclopedia of American Political History
Encyclopedia of Education
Encyclopedia of Film and Television
Encyclopedia of Feminism
Encyclopedia of Psychology
Encyclopedia of World Art
Facts on File
International Encyclopedia of Social Sciences
McGraw-Hill Encyclopedia of Science and Technology
A Political Handbook of the World

UNDERSTANDING THE RESEARCH PROCESS

Without an understanding of the research process, you can waste a great deal of time, become frustrated and confused, and end up with an unsatisfactory paper. However, with the right procedures, you can work efficiently and produce a paper to be proud of. A sound research process requires you to:

Choose a subject
Narrow to a topic
Develop a preliminary thesis
Compile a working bibliography
Take notes
Reconsider your preliminary thesis
Outline
Draft
Revise and edit

The rest of this chapter will explain these stages of the research process.

Choosing a Subject

Above all, your research subject should interest you. If an interesting topic does not strike you right off, browse through newspapers and newsmagazines for ideas, think about subjects covered in your classwork, and consider your personal reading. If none of that helps, try leafing through a general knowledge encyclopedia like *World Book*.

Even if they interest you, some subjects are not suitable and should be avoided.

1. Avoid subjects that do not require research because one good book will say it all. These are subjects like "the circulatory system" and "the life of Abraham Lincoln."
2. Avoid subjects that are so current or so regional in scope that finding sources will be difficult.
3. Avoid subjects that have been researched so extensively that nothing new can be said. These are subjects like legalizing marijuana and abolishing capital punishment.
4. Avoid subjects that lack scientific foundation, subjects like UFOs, the Bermuda Triangle, reincarnation, and ESP.

Narrowing to a Topic

After choosing a subject, you must narrow that subject to a topic that meets the terms of the assignment and that can be completed in the appropriate length. Be particularly careful to avoid anything too broad. Broad topics (like "media violence") cover so much territory that you cannot take it all in, but more narrow topics (like "the effects of televised violence on preschoolers") allow for an in-depth discussion in a manageable length.

A good way to move from general subject to narrow topic is to frame a question about your subject. For example, if your subject is *televised violence*, you can ask these questions to come up with a narrow topic.

General Subject: Televised Violence

Questions	*Narrow Topic*
1. How does televised violence affect preschoolers?	1. The Effects of Televised Violence on Preschoolers
2. Why do teenagers enjoy televised violence?	2. Why Teenagers Enjoy Televised Violence
3. Should the government regulate the amount of violence on television?	3. The Benefits (or Drawbacks) of Government Regulation of Violence on Television

Before finalizing your narrow topic, be sure that your campus library has enough material on it. If you cannot get the books and periodicals required for your research, your topic is unworkable.

To move from general subject to a workable narrow topic, you should do some preliminary reading, which involves the following steps.

1. Survey the titles on your subject in the card or computerized catalog for topic ideas.
2. Survey the titles in the appropriate indexes for topic ideas.
3. Skim one or two encyclopedia articles on your subject to learn how it can be broken down into topics.
4. Skim a few book chapters and periodical articles for topic ideas.

Developing a Preliminary Thesis

After identifying your narrow topic, you should shape a **preliminary thesis,** which includes your subject and narrowing. Here are some examples.

1. `Magnet schools offer a positive alternative to traditional public schools.`
2. `Television violence contributes to the violence in our society.`
3. `Paying women to be stay-at-home mothers would reduce the number of people on welfare.`

NOTE: For a review of the qualities of an effective thesis, see page 34.

The purpose of a preliminary thesis is to help guide your research. You can make decisions about how useful individual sources are and what to take notes on based on how related the material is to your thesis. At the same time, this thesis is subject to change in light of the information your research brings forth.

Compiling a Working Bibliography

A **working bibliography** is a list of potentially useful sources—sources you should look at closely later, when you take notes. To compile a working bibliography, follow these steps.

1. Look up your subject in the card or computer catalog and make a bibliography card for any book that looks promising. Although some people place their working bibliography on notebook paper, index cards are a better choice. The wise researcher writes up the cards to follow the appropriate works-cited forms, which are given beginning on page 384. Here is an example of a bibliography card.

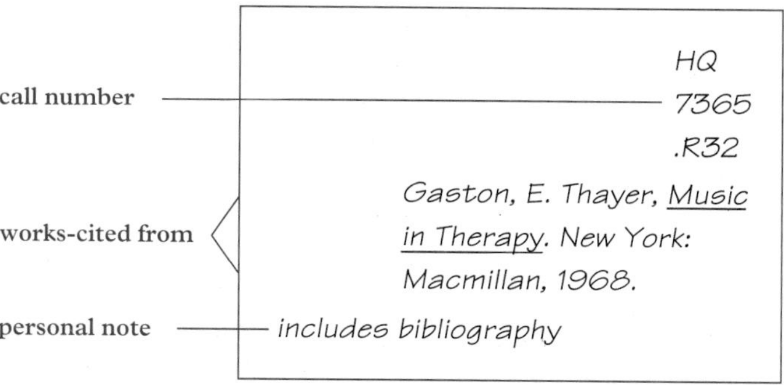

2. Look up your topic in the appropriate indexes and make bibliography cards for promising sources, following the form for periodicals given beginning on page 38.
3. Check the *Essay and General Literature Index,* which references chapters and essays in books. This index is helpful because sometimes a book's title may not indicate that the work contains material on your topic.

NOTE: To save space, indexes are heavily abbreviated. To understand these abbreviations, refer to the key at front of the index.

When deciding whether to make a bibliography card—that is, when determining whether a source holds promise—you must make a decision based on the title of the work. This is a judgment call, but not a difficult one. If there is even an outside chance that a work might be useful, make a card.

Whether you are dealing with a book or periodical, any source you encounter will be one of two kinds: primary or secondary. A **primary source** is one that forms the subject of your essay. For example, if you were writing about the symbolism in *Moby Dick,* then *Moby Dick* would be a primary source. Similarly, if you were writing about the lives of pioneer women, a diary written by a pioneer woman would be a primary source. A **secondary source** is an author's commentary on your subject. A journal article about the symbolism in *Moby Dick* is a secondary source, as is a book written in 1990 that describes the lives of pioneer women. Both primary and secondary sources are important to a researcher, and whenever possible you should check both.

Taking Notes

After compiling a working bibliography, you are ready to examine your promising sources and take notes. To make note taking as efficient as possible, keep the following points in mind.

1. Evaluate the source to determine its usefulness. When was the material written? An old source is not suitable for some topics (like recent experimental drug treatments for cancer). Is the material written at the right

level? If the material is too technical to understand, pass it by. Similarly, if it is so general that it lacks substance, it may offer little. Does the author have a bias? An article by the National Rifle Association on gun control may not present an objective viewpoint. Does the material present facts, opinions, statistics, case studies, points of view, or background information to support your preliminary thesis? If so, you will probably want to take notes on it.

2. If the source is acceptable, take notes on index cards, but avoid the temptation to fill each card. Instead, write one piece of information on each card. This way, you can shuffle your note cards into a suitable order later when you organize your paper. Your notes will be in the form of quotations, paraphrases or a combination of these, all of which are discussed later in this chapter.
3. Be sure to indicate on each card the source and page number the note is taken from so that you can document the material in your paper. If you forget to do this, you will have to run around at the last minute trying to locate sources of information. You can also label your card as a reminder of its content. Here is an example of an acceptable note card.

Why some children like to watch violence.	Atkin, p. 6
Children will choose to watch television shows that correspond to their own tendencies toward aggression.	

4. As you take notes, ideas of your own may occur to you. You may think of a way to handle your introduction, or you may have an idea in response to what you have read, or you may think of a piece of information you should look up. When these ideas strike you, write them on note cards too, so you do not forget them—just be sure to label these ideas as your own, so you do not confuse them with borrowed information.

Paraphrasing

To **paraphrase**, you restate an author's ideas in your own words and style. Most of your notes should be paraphrases so that your paper has your own distinctive style. When you paraphrase, remember the following points:

1. You must alter the style and wording of the original material.
2. You may not add any ideas.
3. You may not alter the meaning of the original material in any way.

A good procedure for paraphrasing is to read over the original material several times until you are sure you understand its meaning. Then pretend you must explain what you just read to a friend and write the paraphrase the way you would make the explanation. Check the note to be sure you have altered style and wording without altering or adding meaning. If you are paraphrasing a long passage, break it down into parts and write the paraphrase part by part.

To appreciate the difference between an acceptable and unacceptable paraphrase, study the following examples.

source: When advertising executives are called upon to defend the advertisements they create for television, they do so by noting that such ads make consumers aware of the best products in a given field. However, this is far from the truth, for rather than informing us about the *best* products, TV ads are more likely to create in us the desire for products we don't really need.

unacceptable paraphrase: When people in advertising have to defend television ads, they do so by saying that the ads tell consumers what the best products in a particular area are. Yet this is not the truth because these ads really make us desire products we do not really need and that is really immoral.

explanation: The above paraphrase is unacceptable for two reasons. First, the style is too close to that of the original. Second, the last sentence of the paraphrase includes an idea that does not appear in the original.

acceptable paraphrase: Television commercials have been defended on the grounds that these ads let people know which of the available products are the best ones. Actually this is not really the case. Instead, these ads cause people to want unnecessary products.

explanation: The above paraphrase has a style different from that of the original, but the meaning of the original has not been changed, nor has any meaning been added.

When you paraphrase, you may find it necessary or desirable to retain a key word or phrase from the original. If the word or phrase is part of the author's distinctive style, place it in quotation marks, as this example illustrates.

Television commercials have been defended on the grounds that these ads let people know about "the best products in a given field." Actually this is not really the case. Instead, these ads cause people to want unnecessary products.

Quoting

To make sure your paper retains your distinctive style, most of your notes should be paraphrases. However, when you encounter material expressed in a particularly effective way, or when you encounter material very difficult to paraphrase, you can use quotation. When you quote, remember these guidelines.

1. With very few exceptions (these will be noted below) you may not alter the spelling, capitalization, punctuation, or wording of anything you quote.

2. Short quotations (those fewer than five lines in your paper) are worked into your sentence, but long quotations (those five or more lines in your paper) are set off by triple-spacing before and after the quote, and by indenting the quote 10 spaces on the left. Indent the first word 15 spaces if the quotation marks the beginning of a paragraph in the source. No quotation marks are used unless they appeared in the source, in which case double quotation marks are used. The introduction to a long quote is followed by a colon. (See p. 397 for an example of a long quotation.)

3. To omit some portion from the middle of a quotation use ellipses (three spaced dots). Be sure when you omit words that you do not distort the original meaning.

source: Professional sport is in fact no more violent than it used to be.

quotation with ellipses: "Professional sport is . . . no more violent than it used to be."

NOTE: The word *no* cannot be omitted, for the meaning would be altered. If the omission comes at the end of a sentence, use a period and then the ellipses.

source: It's a poorly kept NFL secret that hooliganism increases during Monday-night games, which, when played in the east, start at the relatively late hour of 9 p.m. to accommodate west coast TV viewers.

quotation with ellipses: "It's a poorly kept NFL secret that hooliganism increases during Monday-night games, which, when played in the east, start at the relatively late hour of 9 p.m. . . ."

4. When you must add a word or phrase to a quotation to clarify something or work the quotation into your sentence, place the addition inside brackets.

source: The OTA awarded a contract to the UCLA School of Public Health for a study of adverse effects of Agent Orange on American ground troops in Vietnam.

quotation with addition: "The OTA [Office of Technology Assessment] awarded a contract to the UCLA School of Public Health for a study of adverse effects of Agent Orange on American ground troops in Vietnam."

5. When part of the material you are quoting appears in italics, underline the part in italics.

source: Acupuncture relieves pain *even after the needles are withdrawn.*

quotation with underlining: "Acupuncture relieves pain <u>even after the needles are withdrawn.</u>"

6. Sometimes all or part of what you are quoting is itself a quotation. In this case, use single quotation marks wherever double quotation marks appear in the original. Continue to use double quotation marks to mark the place where the quoted material begins and ends.

source: "Crowd behavior is the most sensitive issue in sports today," says a Pinkerton's, Inc., official, who coordinates security at several racetracks and arenas.

quotation with single quotation marks: "'Crowd behavior is the most sensitive issue in sports today,' says a Pinkerton's, Inc., official, who coordinates security at several racetracks and arenas."

7. When you work the quotation into your paper with an introduction containing the word *that,* the first word of the quotation is not capitalized and no comma is used after the introduction. However, if the introduction in your text does not have the word *that,* then a comma is used and the first word of the quotation is capitalized.

example with "that": Smith says that "few adolescents feel secure."

example without "that": Smith says, "Few adolescents feel secure."

Combining Paraphrase and Quotation

Many passages lend themselves to a combination of paraphrase and quotation, as the following example shows:

source: The commission of crimes by using a computer is a growing phenomenon. One only has to pick up a newspaper or watch TV news to get frequent updates on one of the newest forms of white-collar crime. The most frequently reported stories involve sophisticated computer technology; these can readily be sensationalized. Most Americans, for example, know the term "hackers" and have heard of their high-tech intrusions into some of the nation's largest, most sensitive computer systems.

paraphrase and quotation: `The number of computer-assisted crimes is increasing, as anyone who watches TV or reads the newspaper knows. Most well known are the cases involving "sophisticated computer technology," including "high-tech intrusions into some of the nation's largest, most sensitive computer systems."`

Reconsidering Your Preliminary Thesis

When your notetaking is complete, you will know much more about your topic than you did when you wrote your preliminary thesis. As a result of this increased knowledge, you may want to rewrite your thesis to refine it or to take it in a new direction. First, review your note cards to refresh your memory about the information you collected. Then shape your thesis to reflect what you discovered in the library. Remember, however, that this version of your thesis is still not final. You may continue to rework it during drafting and revising.

Outlining

Because writing up research findings is a complex process, you should write a formal outline, even if you do not customarily favor outlining. In fact, you may need to outline more than once before you are satisfied with the organization. The following guidelines can help.

1. Make a list of ideas to reflect your own thinking on your topic. If necessary, do some idea generation to discover what you think.
2. Review your list of ideas and cross out the ones you do not want to include. Place the remaining ideas on index cards, one idea per card.
3. Sort your note cards and the cards with your ideas into piles so all the related cards are stacked together.
4. Label each card "main idea" or "supporting detail." (You may not use all your cards—that's fine. You cannot know during note taking exactly what will prove to be useful and what will not.)
5. Using your cards as a guide, write a formal outline with the format explained on page 67.

6. In the course of writing your outline, you may discover that you need additional information to support a point or explain an issue. If so, return to the library for additional research.
7. After completing your outline, you may want your instructor to look it over and make suggestions.

Writing the First Draft

Using your outline as a guide, write out your first draft the best way you can without worrying over anything, particularly grammar, spelling, punctuation, capitalization, or usage. (See page 74 for more on handling the first draft.) Although your outline is a guide, feel free to depart from it if a better idea occurs to you.

When you get to the point where you will write out a paraphrase or a quotation, you can tape the appropriate note card to the draft, if you like.

As you draft, avoid stringing quotations and paraphrases together one after another. Instead, comment on borrowings by analyzing them, showing their significance, indicating their relationships to something else, and so forth. Here is an example of commenting on a borrowing, taken from "How Parents Can Lessen the Effects of Television Violence" on page 396. Notice that the author comments on the borrowing by showing its application.

> Professor Charles Atkin explains another reason children should not be completely restricted from viewing violence. He suggests that children will choose to watch television shows that correspond to their own tendencies toward aggression (6). Thus by observing the types of programs their children prefer, parents can gain a better understanding of their personalities. A child who continually elects to watch violence may have aggressive tendencies. Parents need to know whether their children are too aggressive so they can intervene, and one way they can discover this is to observe their children's viewing preferences.

In this example, the first two sentences are the paraphrase, and the rest of the paragraph shows how the idea in the paraphrase can be applied.

Finally, when you draft, you must document all borrowed material by introducing paraphrases and quotations, writing parenthetical text citations, and including a works cited page. These issues will be taken up next.

Introducing Borrowings

Because your paper will include your own ideas along with those you have discovered in the library, you must distinguish what is yours from what is borrowed.

This is done by introducing each borrowing with a phrase that indicates its source. Consider, for example, the following passage taken from a student paper. The introductions are underlined as a study aid.

> Businesses in the United States and the world over lose great sums of money because of the alcoholic employee. Estimates of the Department of Health, Education, and Welfare and a study done by Roman and Trice show that the number of alcoholics ranges from as high as ten out of every one hundred workers to a low of three to four out of one hundred (Williams and Moffat 7). Alcoholism, as Joseph Follman states, is "a problem so far reaching and so costly [it] must have an effect upon the business community of the nation." Follman goes on to say, "The result is impaired production, labor turnover, and increased costs of operation" (78). In terms of impaired productivity, the cost in the United States alone is said to be $12.5 billion a year, as the National Council on Alcoholism estimates (Follman 81-82). Obviously, someone must pay these costs, and no doubt it is the consumer who pays higher prices for goods and services. Yet reduced productivity because of alcoholic employees and the resulting higher prices could be held in check by the sound implementation of company programs to rehabilitate the alcoholic employee.

The paragraph includes both borrowed material and the writer's own ideas. Each borrowing has an introduction to identify it as someone else's words or ideas. A close look reveals the following points about introducing borrowed material.

1. Regardless of when the source material was written, the introduction is in the present tense. This **present-tense convention** is followed because printed words live on, even if their author died long ago.
2. Introductions usually appear before the borrowing, but they can also be placed in the middle or at the end.
3. The verbs used in your introductions should be varied to avoid monotony. Instead of repeatedly writing "Smith says," you can also use "Smith explains" (notes, estimates, reveals, demonstrates, believes, contends, feels, and so on).
4. An introduction can refer to the author of the borrowing ("Smith finds"), or to the credentials of the author ("one researcher believes" or "a prominent sociologist contends"), or to the title of the source ("according to *Advertising Age*").

Writing Parenthetical Text Citations

In addition to introducing your borrowings, you must cite your source of information within parentheses immediately after the borrowing. This is true whether your borrowing is a paraphrase or a quotation. You must document this way so your reader knows exactly where the borrowing comes from. Furthermore, it is only fair to acknowledge when you use the words and ideas of others.

1. When your borrowing has been introduced with the author's name, your parenthetical note includes the page number or numbers the borrowing appeared on in the source:

    Ruth Caldersen agrees that corporal punishment is not a legitimate form of discipline in schools (104).

2. When the introduction does not include the author's name, your parenthetical citation should note this name along with the appropriate page number or numbers:

    One high school principal remarks, "I've never known corporal punishment to improve the behavior of unruly students" (Hayes 16).

3. When more than one source by the same author is cited in your paper, include the author's name in the introduction and use a short form of the title in the parenthetical citation:

    Rodriguez feels that a teacher who resorts to corporal punishment is acting out of frustration (Discipline 86).

    The above title is a short form of Discipline in the Public Schools. It distinguishes the source from another of Rodriguez's works cited, Education in an Enlightened Age.

NOTE: A citation for a long quote that is set off appears after the period (see page 397 for an example).

Writing the "Works Cited" Page

In addition to introducing borrowings and providing parenthetical text citations, proper documentation requires you to provide a "works cited" page or pages at the end of your paper. This is an alphabetical listing of all the sources from which you paraphrased and quoted—it is *not* a listing of all the sources you consulted during your research. For an example of a "works cited" page, see page 394. Notice that you list the entries alphabetically by the author's last name. If the source has no known author, then alphabetize the work according the first important word in the title (excluding *a, an* or *the*). Double-space each entry and double-space between each entry.

Below are the forms you should model for papers written according to the Modern Language Association (MLA) style sheet. Most humanities papers are written in accordance with MLA guidelines. Instructors in the social sciences may want you to use the American Psychological Association (APA) style sheet (see page 386), while science instructors may favor the American Chemical Society (ACS) format. When in doubt, check with your instructor to secure a copy of the appropriate style sheet.

Forms to Use for Books

BOOK WITH ONE AUTHOR

Gaston, E. Thayer. Music in Therapy. New York: Macmillan, 1968.

BOOK WITH TWO AUTHORS

Fisher, Seymour, and Rhoda L. Fisher. What We Really Know about Child Rearing. New York: Basic, 1976.

BOOK WITH THREE AUTHORS

Richardson, Charles E., Fred V. Hein, and Dana L. Farnsworth. Living: Health, Behavior, and Environment. 6th ed. Glenview, Ill.: Scott, 1975.

BOOK WITH MORE THAN THREE AUTHORS

Shafer, Raymond P., et al. Marijuana: A Signal of Misunderstanding. New York: NAL, 1972.

BOOK WITH AN EDITOR

Arnold, Matthew. Culture and Anarchy. Ed. J. Dover Wilson. Cambridge: Cambridge UP, 1961.

EDITION OTHER THAN THE FIRST

Langacker, Ronald W. Language and Its Structure: Some Fundamental Linguistic Concepts. 2nd ed. New York: Harcourt, 1973.

SELECTION IN AN ANTHOLOGY

Kafka, Franz. "The Metamorphosis." Introduction to Literature. Ed. Roger Greene. 4th ed. Boston: Appleby, 1990. 215-86.

ENCYCLOPEDIA ARTICLE

"Lombard." The World Book Encyclopedia. 1973 ed.

BOOK WITH A TRANSLATOR

Medvedev, Zhores A. Nuclear Disaster in the Urals. Trans. George Sanders. New York: Norton, 1979.

MORE THAN ONE WORK BY THE SAME AUTHOR

Tannen, Deborah. That's Not What I Meant! New York: Ballantine, 1986.

———. You Just Don't Understand: Women and Men in Conversation. New York: Ballantine, 1990.

Forms to Use for Periodicals

AUTHOR UNKNOWN

"Night of Horror." Sports Illustrated, 13 Oct. 1980: 29.

ARTICLE FROM A SCHOLARLY JOURNAL (CONTINUOUS PAGINATION)

Crumley, E. Frank. "The Adolescent Suicide Attempt: A Cardinal Symptom of a Serious Psychiatric Disorder." American Journal of Psychotherapy 26 (1982): 158-65.

ARTICLE FROM A SCHOLARLY JOURNAL (SEPARATE PAGINATION)

Tong, T. K. "Temporary Absolutisms Versus Hereditary Autocracy." Chinese Studies in History 21.3 (1988): 3-22.

MAGAZINE PUBLISHED MONTHLY

"TV and Movies May Contribute to Crime." Ebony Aug. 1979: 88.

MAGAZINE PUBLISHED WEEKLY

Kanfer, Stefan. "Doing Violence to Sport." Time 31 May 1976: 64-65.

NEWSPAPER ARTICLE

Farrell, William E. "Ex-Soviet Scientist, Now in Israel, Tells of Nuclear Disaster." New York Times 9 Dec. 1976: 8.

EDITORIAL

"Patience on Panama." Editorial. Philadelphia Inquirer 12 May 1989, sec. A: 22.

Other Forms

RADIO OR TELEVISION SHOW

Moyers, Bill, and Robert Bly. A Gathering of Men. Public Broadcasting System. WNET TV New York. 8 Jan. 1990.

PERSONAL INTERVIEW

Humphrey, Neil. President, Youngstown State University. Personal interview. Youngstown, OH. 1 March 1988.

GOVERNMENT PUBLICATION

United States. Department of Labor. Bureau of Labor Statistics. BIS Measures of Compensation. Washington: GPO, 1986.

Using APA Documentation

The methods for documenting borrowed material explained so far have been those of the Modern Language Association (MLA). They are appropriate for papers written in the humanities (including writing courses). For papers written in the social sciences, your instructor may want you to follow the American Psychological Association (APA) format. The APA format for handling parenthetical citations and the final list of sources is different from the MLA format.

Parenthetical Citations

In the APA format, parenthetical citations include the publication date, but page numbers are given for quotations only—not for paraphrases—and *p.* or *pp.* is used before the page number(s). There is another difference as well: a comma appears between the name of the author and year, and between the year and the page number. Here are some examples:

quotation: For mutual gains bargaining to work, "all parties must undergo rigorous training in nonconfrontational dispute resolution" (Haines, 1991, p. 40).

paraphrase: For mutual gains bargaining to work, everyone involved must have extensive training in how to resolve conflict without confrontation (Haines, 1991).

when borrowing is introduced: For mutual gains bargaining to work, Haines (1991) says that "all parties must undergo rigorous training in nonconfrontational dispute resolution" (p. 40). For mutual gains bargaining to work, Haines (1991) says that everyone involved must have extensive training in how to resolve conflict without confrontation.

List of References

Rather than a "Works Cited" page, APA format calls for a list of sources with the heading "References." The "References" page includes the same information as the "Works Cited" page, but it is presented in a different format, as the following representative examples illustrate.

BOOK WITH ONE AUTHOR

Dretske, F. (1988). Explaining behavior: reasons in a world of causes. Cambridge, MA: MIT.

BOOK WITH TWO OR MORE AUTHORS

Bosworth, J., & Toller, T.N. (1898). An Anglo-Saxon dictionary. Oxford: Oxford University Press.

MAGAZINE ARTICLE

McIntyre, R. S. (1988, April 2). The populist tax act of 1989. The Nation, pp. 445, 462-464.

JOURNAL ARTICLE WITH CONTINUOUS PAGINATION

Sudrann, J. (1970). Daniel Deronda and the landscape of exile. ELH, 37, 433-455.

NOTE: If you write a paper with the APA format, be sure to get a copy of the complete style sheet, so you have models of all the possible forms.

Revising and Editing

Revising and editing research writing is complex because, in addition to all the usual revising and editing concerns, you must consider the special conventions of research. Thus, you should increase the time you spend revising and editing, and you should revise and edit in stages so you stay alert. In addition to the checklist on page 80, the following checklist can help you revise and edit.

1. Have you commented on each of your paraphrases and quotations so that you do not string borrowings together?
2. Have you introduced each paraphrase and quotation?
3. Have you provided a parenthetical citation for each paraphrase and quotation?

4. Are your quotations accurate?
5. For quotations, have you
   a. Used ellipses for omissions?
   b. Used brackets for additions?
   c. Underlined where italics appeared in the source?
   d. Used single quotation marks for quotations within quotations?
   e. Set off quotations of more than four lines?
   f. Omitted the capital letter and comma when *that* is part of the introduction?
6. For paraphrases, have you
   a. Used your own style and wording?
   b. Avoided adding meaning?
   c. Avoided altering meaning?
7. Are your "Works Cited" entries in alphabetical order and in the correct form?

TRYOUT

1. Assume that you are writing a paper on the ways magazine advertisements influence people to buy, and you are seeking explanations of specific persuasive techniques used. With this in mind, do the following:
   a. Check the subject file of the card or computerized catalog and write two bibliography cards for two different, promising books.
   b. Check the appropriate indexes and write one bibliography card for a promising journal article, one for a promising magazine article, and one (if possible) for a promising newspaper article.
   c. Check *Essay and General Literature Index;* if possible, make a bibliography card for one promising source.
2. Paraphrase the second paragraph of "The Egalitarian Error" on page 278. Be sure to alter style but not meaning.
3. Quote directly the first sentence of paragraph 6 of "The Egalitarian Error." Introduce the quotation with the authors' names and *that*. Remember to use single quotation marks and underlining where necessary.
4. Quote directly the last two sentences of "The Egalitarian Error," omitting everything from the dash on. Remember to use ellipses. Also introduce the quotation with the authors' names but omit *that*.
5. Quote the first sentence of paragraph 3 of "The Egalitarian Error." In brackets add a definition of "behavior of this kind." (The definition can be found in the previous paragraph.) Follow the quotation with a parenthetical text citation.

SAMPLE RESEARCH PAPER

The following research paper, written by a student, illustrates many of the points discussed so far. The marginal notes call your attention to some of the key features.

William Wasser
Professor Gabriel
English 103,
May 17 1992

Human Impact on the Freshwater Mussel Fauna of the Eastern United States

Intro provides background

Quotations and paraphrases help establish the problem and lead into thesis.

Thesis

1 In recent years, scientists and naturalists have expressed great concern about the alarming rate at which biological diversity is being lost. Many of our species have suffered significant population reductions, while others are extinct or in danger of becoming extinct. As a result, much of the genetic variability characteristic of earlier periods is being lost. The diversity problem has not gone unrecognized by the United States government; in a 1987 report by the Office of Technology Assessment, the authors note that "the rate of diversity loss is now far greater than the rate at which diversity is created" (U.S. Congress, Office of Technology Assessment 82). Kyu Chin Kim attributes the loss to "human activity" which fragments and pollutes many natural habitats (128). Evidence for such destruction caused by humans has been clearly documented for the rivers of the eastern United States, where there has been a dramatic depletion of the freshwater mussel fauna.

2 Dr. David H. Stansbery, a leading authority on freshwater mussels, estimates that seventy-eight species of mussels inhabited Ohio's rivers

Wasser 2

Author's name in parenthetical citation because Stansbery is referred to in Laycock article.

Transitions link borrowings.

Introduction to paraphrase is in present tense.

Key word in quotation marks.

approximately two hundred years ago; he adds that only fifty-nine of these species exist there today (qtd. in Laycock 26). This is a 24 percent reduction in mussel species for the state. Similar results have been reported for single-river studies. For example, Reginald W. Taylor reports that six of the twenty-one species of mussels recorded in earlier investigations were not found during his survey of Elk River in West Virginia (25). Likewise, Charles R. Bursey reports an apparent 28 percent reduction in freshwater mussel species for the Shenango River, in Mercer County, Pennsylvania (43). Several factors have contributed to the decline in mussel populations, most of which are related to human activity. Kenneth W. Cummins notes that a significant reduction in the dissolved oxygen content, a dramatic increase in fine sediments, heavy metal ions, and pesticides directly eliminate the majority of macroinvertebrate species from our rivers by producing conditions that underlie or exceed their limits of tolerance (187). Interestingly, various human activities have been responsible for creating such conditions in our rivers. With respect to these detrimental factors, the freshwater mussel is not exempt. As Samuel Fuller points out, there can be no doubt that man-made substances and activities have seriously harmed our mussel fauna (246).

3 The construction of dams has caused serious, adverse effects on mussel populations. The damming of a river changes its character dramatically. Stansbery reports that dams convert the shallow "riffles" of the river into slow-flowing pools that are prone to collect silt and precipitated organics on their substrates; he adds that the accumulation of organics reduces the

No capital letter or comma preceding quotation because of "that."

Student author comments on borrowing.

No need to document scientific fact.

Author's name is in introduction to quotation, so only page number is given in parenthetical citation.

Wasser 3

dissolved oxygen content, elevates the carbon-dioxide level, and as a consequence lowers the pH (<u>Rare and Endangered</u> 6). Fuller stresses that "these conditions are inimical to the great majority of mussels" (252). Obviously, such changes in the oxygen/carbon dioxide content would pose a serious threat to these animals since they depend upon the gradient for respiration. Silt presents yet another problem for bivalves. Stansbery reports that forest clearing and agricultural tilling allow large amounts of topsoil (<u>Rare and Endangered</u> 9), silt, and clay to be carried into the streams (<u>Eastern</u> 10). He adds that the silt and clay could, in effect, suffocate some species by "clogging the gills or stimulating excess mucus secretion" (<u>Eastern</u> 10). In either case, gas exchange would be dramatically hindered.

4 Organic waste discharged from sewage plants creates a similarly intolerable situation for mussels. With the release of organic materials into a stream, bacteria already present in the water begin to breakdown these organics through oxidative processes. As the bacterial count increases, more and more oxygen is utilized and the result is an environment with an extremely low, dissolved oxygen content. A study of mussels in the Big Vermilion River, Illinois, found the river to be completely devoid of mussels for 22 km downstream of a domestic sewage input (Wilhm 383). In reference to domestic pollution, Robert Pennak states that "the zone of recovery may begin anywhere between one-quarter mile and 100 miles downstream from the source of pollution" (11). Thus it is evident that the construction of dams which restrict the flow of water, forest clearing, agricultural tilling, and organic

Wasser 4

wastes all has the effect of depriving the mussel of essential oxygen, and if the condition persists, metabolic processes cease.

5 Pesticide runoff has also been considered a factor in the decline of mussels. While Stansbery points out that there is no scientific data concerning the specific effects of pesticides on freshwater mollusks (Eastern 10), it is probable that they at least indirectly contribute to mussel mortality. A study has shown that mussels exposed to toxic substances will close their shells and cease the filtration process for extended periods of time (Bedford, Roelofs, and Zabik 123). With regard to this effect, J.W. Bedford, E.W. Roelofs, and M.J. Zabik consider the presence of pesticides in the water or starvation to be the probable cause of mussel mortality in their experiment (123). This again reminds us of the importance of the filtration process in obtaining food and oxygen.

Abbreviated title of work in citation because two sources by Stansbury are used.

Student author draws a conclusion.

6 The industrial discharge of heavy metals has also been responsible for eliminating mussels from our streams. While most aquatic organisms are affected by exposure to high levels of heavy metal toxins, Tackett holds that "mollusks [the phylum to which mussels belong] are the least resistant . . ." (qtd. in Wilhm 383). Wurtz proposes a hierarchy of the most toxic heavy metals; he holds that zinc is the most toxic, and copper, mercury, and silver decrease in toxicity respectively (Fuller 246). Wurtz further stesses that "mollusks would be the first animals eradicated when the heavy metal content of a stream started to rise" (qtd. in Whitton and Say 293).

Brackets mark addition to quotation.

Ellipses mark deletion from quotation.

Parenthetical citation for work by two authors.

7 Human activity continues day after day with little or no regard for the fragile river ecosystem and its

Wasser 5

community. The decimation of freshwater mussel populations throughout the eastern United States attests to that fact. Vast segments of our rivers have been rendered completely uninhabitable for many species. Efforts to preserve these natural resources have been hindered by a lack of funds. Stansbery points out that neither industry, the U.S. Army Corps of Engineers, nor the U.S. Environmental Protection Agency has been willing to fund his inexpensive mussel research (Laycock 27). Additionally, the authors of a U.S. document concerning biological diversity urge that additional public and private funds are needed to support conservation efforts (U.S. Congress, Office of Technology Assessment 83). Undoubtedly, little can be done to preserve our freshwater mussels without a cooperative effort on the part of industry, government, and the private sector. Until such an effort is made, the river will continue to be a graveyard of countless empty shells.

The conclusion restates the thesis and draws a conclusion from the research.

Wasser 6

Works Cited

Journal article with continuous pagination

Bedford, J. W., E. W. Roelofs, and M. J. Zabik. "The Freshwater Mussel as a Biological Monitor of Pesticide Concentrations in a Lotic Environment." Limnolology and Oceanography 13 (1968): 118-26.

Bursey, Charles R. "The Unionid (Mollusca: Bivalvia) Fauna of the Shenango River in Mercer County, Pennsylvania." Proceedings of the Pennsylvania Academy of Science 61 (1987): 41-43.

Selection in an anthology

Cummins, Kenneth W. "Macroinvertebrates." River Ecology. Ed. Brian A. Whitton. Los Angeles: U California, 1975. 170-98.

Fuller, Samuel L. H. "Clams and Mussels (Mollusca: Bivalvia)." Pollution Ecology of Freshwater Invertebrates. Ed. Samuel L. H. Fuller and C. W. Hart, Jr. New York: Academic, 1974. 215-73.

Kim, Kyu Chin. "Assessing and Monitoring Our Biological Diversity: A National Biological Survey." Proceedings of the Pennsylvania Academy of Science 61 (1987): 127-32.

Monthly magazine

Laycock, George. "Vanishing Naiads." Audubon Jan. 1983: 26-28.

Pennak, Robert W. Fresh-water Invertebrates of the United States. 2nd ed. New York: Wiley, 1978.

Two sources by same author

Stansbery, David H. "Eastern Freshwater Mollusks: The Mississippi and St. Lawrence River Systems." Malacologia 10.1 (1970): 9-22.

——. "Rare and Endangered Freshwater Mollusks in the Eastern United States." Proceedings of a Symposium of Rare and Endangered Mollusks (Naiads) of the U.S. Ed. Sven Jorgensen. United States Department Interior, Fish and Wildlife Service, Sport Fisheries and Wildlife, Region 3, 1971. 5-18.

Wasser 7

Journal article with separate pagination

Government document

Taylor, Reginald. "The Freshwater Naiads of Elk River, West Virginia with a Comparison of Earlier Collections." The Nautilus 95.1 (1981): 21-25.

United States. Cong. Office of Technology Assessment. Technologies to Maintain Biological Diversity. OTA-F-330. Washington: GPO, 1987.

Whitton, Brian A., and P. J. Say. "Heavy Metals." River Ecology. Ed. Brian A. Whitton. Los Angeles: U California, 1975. 286-11.

Wilhm, J. L. "Biological Indicators of Pollution." River Ecology. Ed. Brian A. Whitton. Los Angeles: U California, 1975. 375-402.

USING RESEARCH TO DEVELOP ESSAYS

Research writing is not limited to the traditional research paper discussed so far in this chapter. You can also use researched material to supplement your own supporting details to develop essays.

Say that you want to argue against the elimination of the foreign language requirement for business majors at your school. If you are a management student who has taken 6 years of Spanish, you could make many points as a result of your own experience, but consider how much more convincing you could be with statements testifying to the importance of a second language for those in middle- and upper-management positions—statements made by respected authorities in the business world.

Now say you want to show the differences between public and private high school educations in order to explain why private school students score higher on college entrance exams. If you have attended both kinds of schools, your own experience offers much for supporting detail. As you develop your essay, however, you begin to wonder whether private school students score higher because they are advised of test-taking strategies, while their public school counterparts are not. To learn whether this is the case, you go to the library and research the point. If you discover that private school students are told of certain strategies but public school students are not, you would have an important point to add to your essay.

The possibilities for using research to supplement your own ideas are limitless. To understand some of these possibilities, study the following example written by a student.

How Parents Can Lessen the Effects of Television Violence

"Mommy, I'm bored." 1

"Don't bother me now, Junior; I have a headache. *Why don't you go watch TV?*" 2

Conversations like this often take place between parent and child because no parent, no matter how conscientious, can spend every minute with his or her child. And let's face it, television *is* a way to keep a bored child quiet and occupied. And yes, television *can* be a good form of entertainment and even a valuable learning tool. 3

Almost everyone agrees that television can have a great influence on how children view the world and how they act within it. As a result, almost everyone agrees that it is important for parents to supervise what television their children watch. Usually, this means that parents are advised to restrict the amount of violence viewed. 4

Introduction of borrowing is in the present tense.

Anne Somers, for example, cites the National Commission on the Causes and Prevention of Violence, which published a report, *To Establish Justice, to Insure Domestic Tranquility,* in 1969. A portion of the report dis- 5 closes that many of the experiments done with children show that aggressive behavior is learned by viewing violence on television. The report states that while television is a serious influence on our society's level of violence, it is not necessarily the main cause. However, it goes on to say that the influence of television on children is stronger now, when the authority of the "traditional institutions" of religion, education, and family is questionable. The concern expressed in the report is that since so much of television broadcasting expresses antisocial, aggressive behavior, and since television is such a strong influence on children, children will be learning to behave aggressively (210–11).

Parenthetical text citation to document paraphrase.

Certainly the literature expressing the dangers of television violence for children is abundant; one can find it published in everything from *TV Guide* to the most scholarly journals. Yet does it all mean that parents must be sure their children never view violence on the small screen? I think not, for there is evidence that not all children who view televised violence become overly aggressive. The child's interpretation of what is viewed is a crucial factor in how he or she will behave afterward. Sociology professor Hope Lunin Klapper believes the following: 6

Quotation of more than 4 lines is set off. Ellipses signal omission.

Text citation for a long quotation is after the period.

> The child itself plays an active role in the socialization process. The consequences of television *for* a child are thus in part a consequence *of* the child. . . . It is the child's perception which defines the stimulus. . . . The consequences of television involve . . . two major steps: first, the child's perception or translation of the content, and second, his or her response or lack of response to that perception. (427)

Thus, whether televised violence will adversely affect a child will depend on that child. The conclusion to be drawn from Klapper is that some children will not become violent just because they have viewed violence on television. Klapper says that whether a child behaves aggressively will be, in part, a result of his or her perception of the viewed violence, and this says a lot about what the parental role should be. Parents could counteract any negative effects that television violence could have on a child's behavior by taking advantage of the opportunity presented to teach the child some of the values that they feel are important. As a child watches a violent program, the parents could explain that the behaviors displayed do not coincide with their values. In this way, a child could be taught that even though such behaviors exist, they are not desirable. After all, violence does exist in the world. If parents constantly shield their children from this fact, then the children will be unable to cope with this reality of life. On the other hand, exposure to violence, through television and parental explanation about what is viewed, can be a healthy education in the reality of violence and how to avoid it. 7

Professor Charles Atkin explains another reason children should not be completely restricted from viewing violence. He suggests that children will choose to watch television shows that correspond to their own tendencies toward aggression (6). Thus by observing the types of programs their 8 children prefer, parents can gain a better understanding of their personalities. A child who continually elects to watch violence may have aggressive tendencies. Parents need to know whether their children are too aggressive so they can intervene, and one way they can discover this is to observe their children's viewing preferences. If the child is consistently choosing violent shows, the parents can, as Atkin explains, "effectively mediate their children's predispositions" (12) and make their child understand that although violence does exist in reality, there are other aspects of life as well.

Exact words appear in quotation marks, and parenthetical citation is used.

Thus, parents can help their children's personalities develop in a positive manner by observing how they respond to television violence and by influencing accordingly how they interpret what they see. Parents can use televised violence to assess their children's tendency toward violence, and they can use it to voice their disapproval to show violence is wrong. Of course, this means parents must watch violent shows *with* their children, even when they have a headache. 9

Your Works Cited section begins a new page.

Works Cited

Atkin, Charles, et al. "Selective Exposure to Televised Violence." *Journal of Broadcasting* 23 (Winter 1979): 5–13.

Klapper, Hope Lunin. "Childhood Socialization and Television." *Public Opinion Quarterly* 42 (1978): 426–30.

Somers, Anne R. "Television and Children: Issues Involved in Corrective Action." *American Journal of Orthopsychiatry* 48 (1978): 205–13.

Topic Suggestions

1. Several topics can come from the subject area of advertising. Consider one impact that advertising has on our lives or whether advertisers play fair or how advertisers persuade or to what extent advertisers shape taste and to what extent they reflect it. To shape a narrow topic, consider selecting ads for a particular class of products (say, cosmetics or liquor) and a particular medium (such as television or magazines).
2. Several interesting topics can be shaped about the women's movement. For example, you might compare or contrast some aspect of our culture (family life, education, advertising, etc.) before and after the movement became a strong influence. You could explain why the Equal Rights Amendment failed. You could describe the effects of working mothers on the American family or American business. You could define the contemporary woman or man in light of sexual equality. You could also discuss the effect changing roles have had on child rearing or marriage or dating.
3. Many topics can come from the subject area, education. Should teachers be accountable? Should high school seniors have to pass a competency exam to graduate? Is a return to the basics a good idea? Should disabled children be included in standard classrooms? Should prayer be permitted

in schools? Answering these questions can lead to excellent topics. In addition, you could describe the impact of preschool education on the education system, or you could explain why there has been a decline in SAT scores, or you could define the ideal education. You could also compare or contrast the advantages of homogeneous and heterogeneous groupings of students.

4. The general subject of television can yield suitable topics. You might compare or contrast the portrayal of some group (police officers, mothers, teachers, doctors, etc.) with the way this group functions in reality. You might describe how television shapes our perception of something (marriage, sex roles, war, etc.). You could examine whether TV news provides responsible coverage of world events. You could argue that programs aimed at children should be free of commercials, or you could argue for or against network censorship (or argue that this censorship is or is not adequate). Answering the following questions can also lead to topics: What do you think of children's programming? Is programming too violent? Is there too much sex on TV? Should the number of hours children watch television be restricted? Does television reflect public taste or shape it?
5. You can shape many topics about health and nutrition. For example, you might argue that places of business and industry should provide exercise facilities for their employees. If you are a runner or a walker, you might describe the benefits of the activity. You might explain the pros or cons of a vegetarian diet or argue for or against banning a particular food additive. You could explore whether medical schools should admit the brightest students or the most compassionate, or you could use illustrations to show whether or not the aged get adequate health care in this country. Should cigarettes be classified as drugs? Are hospices for the terminally ill and their families effective? Do school lunch programs provide balanced meals? Are birth control pills safe enough? Answering these questions can lead to interesting topics.
6. Government and politics is a general subject that many topics can come from. You could look at the advantages (or disadvantages) of the electoral college system for electing the president. You might explore whether the most able candidate is elected or the one with the largest campaign fund. You might describe how congressional lobbyists operate, or you could describe how a candidate's media image affects his or her popularity. You could compare or contrast the way your local schools are currently funded with an alternative method. You could criticize the current defense budget. You could also select some current political issue on the local, state, or national level and argue for or against some aspect of it.

PART 3

An Editing Guide to Frequently Occurring Errors

CHAPTER 16

Editing for Word Choice

TROUBLESOME WORDS AND PHRASES

Below are some tips for eliminating words and phrases likely to annoy an experienced reader.

1. Eliminate phrases like *"as this paragraph will explain," "my paper will prove," "as I have shown,"* and *"the following paragraphs will tell."* These formal announcements of intent are common conventions in certain business, scientific, and technical writing, but in informal essays they are considered poor style because they are intrusive.

2. Eliminate the phrase, "In conclusion." Over the years, it has been so overworked that it seems trite.

3. Do not refer to people with the relative pronoun, *which.* Instead, use *who, whom, or that.*

avoid: Donna is the woman <u>which</u> won the essay contest.

use: Donna is the woman <u>who</u> won the essay contest.

use: Donna is the woman <u>that</u> won the essay contest.

4. Do not use *plus* as a synonym for *and.*

avoid: My car needs new tie rods <u>plus</u> shock absorbers.

use: My car needs new tie rods <u>and</u> shock absorbers.

5. Avoid using *etc., and more, and so forth,* and *and such.* These expressions suggest that you could say more but do not want to. At times, these expressions are appropriate, but usually you should say whatever you *could* say.

avoid: For his camping trip, Kevin bought a tent, a sleeping bag, a lantern, etc.

use: For his camping trip, Kevin bought a tent, a sleeping bag, a lantern, a stove, and a first aid kit.

6. Do not use *etc.* with *such as*. *Such as* suggests you are listing only representative items in a group, so there is no need to use *etc.* to indicate other things are included.

avoid: For his camping trip, Kevin bought several items, such as a tent, a sleeping bag, a lantern, etc.

use: For his camping trip, Kevin bought several items, such as a tent, a sleeping bag, and a lantern.

7. Do not use *and etc. Etc.* means *and so forth;* therefore, *and etc.* means *and and so forth.*

8. Avoid phrases such as *I believe, in my opinion, it seems to me,* and *I think.* Because you are writing the essay, the ideas expressed are clearly your beliefs, opinions, and thoughts. Reserve these expressions for distinguishing your ideas from another person's.

avoid: In my opinion, the mayor's refusal to endorse the safety forces' pay raise is shortsighted.

use: The mayor's refusal to endorse the safety forces' pay raise is shortsighted.

use: The city council president believes that the mayor is right to criticize the pay raise for the safety forces, but I believe the mayor's refusal to endorse the raise is shortsighted.

9. Do not use *irregardless.* Use *regardless* or *irrespective of.*

10. Replace *a lot* and *a lot of* with *many, much,* or *a great deal of*

avoid: Juan earned a lot of respect when he told Peter he would not cheat for him.

use: Juan earned a great deal of respect when he told Peter he would not cheat for him.

If you do find it appropriate to use *a lot* (in quoting conversation, for example), remember that it is two words.

11. Eliminate *at this point in time* and *in today's world.* These phrases annoy the experienced reader; use now or currently instead.

avoid: At this point in time, our public schools need more financial support.

avoid: In today's world, our public schools need more financial support.

use: Our public schools currently need more financial support.

12. Eliminate *the reason is because.* Use *the reason is that* or *because* instead.

avoid: The reason fewer people are becoming teachers is because teachers' salaries are not competitive.

use: The reason fewer people are becoming teachers is that teachers' salaries are not competitive.

use: Fewer people are becoming teachers because teachers' salaries are not competitive.

13. Do not use *very* to intensify things that cannot be intensified. The temperature can be *hot* or it can be *very hot,* but some words are as strong as they can get. Words like *dead, gorgeous, incredible, outstanding, unique,* and *perfect* cannot be made stronger by adding *very.*

14. Avoid using *so* as an intensifier unless it will be followed by a clause beginning with *that.*

avoid: After studying for midterm exams, I was so tired.

use: After studying for midterm exams, I was very tired.

use: After studying for midterm exams, I was so tired that I slept for 12 hours.

15. Eliminate *vice versa.* If you want to indicate that the opposite is also true, write out exactly what that opposite is.

avoid: My mother is always criticizing me and vice versa.

use: My mother is always criticizing me, and I am always criticizing her.

16. Avoid *being as* or *being that* as synonyms for *since* or *because.*

avoid: Being that final exams begin next week, I must take a leave of absence from my job to study.

use: Because final exams begin next week, I must take a leave of absence from my job to study.

use: Since final exams begin next week, I must take a leave of absence from my job to study.

17. Avoid using *expect* as a synonym for *suppose.*

avoid: I expect dinner will be ready in an hour.

use: I suppose dinner will be ready in an hour.

18. Do not use *of* to mean *have.*

avoid: He could of (should of, would of) gone if he had the time.

use: He could have (should have, would have) gone if he had the time.

19. Avoid using *real* to mean *very.*

avoid: The weather was real hot in Arizona.

use: The weather was very hot in Arizona.

20. Use *try to* rather than *try and.*

avoid: Try and understand my position.

use: Try to understand my position.

21. Avoid modifying nouns and adjectives with the suffix *-type.* Find the accurate word for what you mean.

avoid: She likes a desert-type climate.

use: She likes a dry climate.

22. Avoid unnecessary qualifications with words such as *really, different,* and *particular.* They add no meaning to your sentences, but make them wordy.

avoid: In this particular case, I agree.

use: In this case, I agree.

avoid: She served three different kinds of sandwiches.

use: She served three kinds of sandwiches.

EXERCISE

Troublesome Words and Phrases

Edit the following paragraph to eliminate the troublesome words and phrases.

Irregardless of how busy you are, you can become more organized and efficient if you get in the habit of making a to-do list. To keep the list from doing more harm than good, however, decide what you need to do plus establish a reasonable amount of time to allocate to each task. A lot of people become frustrated because they make up lists with goals very impossible to achieve in a reasonable amount of time, such as cleaning the entire house, grocery shopping, studying, etc. in one day. Being that a list that is too ambitious can add to your stress, your goals must be attainable. In my opinion, you should identify reasonable goals, set priorities, allow flexibility, and cross items out as they are completed. Most important, you should try and avoid annoyance if all your goals are not met, for another list can be made tomorrow. The most productive people which I know are list-type people, but they content themselves with what they *do* accomplish and do not not worry about what they do *not* accomplish.

DOUBLE NEGATIVES

The following words are **negatives** because they communicate the sense of *no.*

no	none	nothing	hardly
not	nowhere	no one	scarcely
never	nobody		

Be sure to use only *one* negative to express a single negative idea.

no (two negatives): `No one` can do `nothing` to help.

yes (one negative): `No one` can do anything to help.

no (two negatives): I `cannot` go `nowhere` with you.

yes (one negative): I `cannot` go anywhere with you.

yes (one negative): I can go `nowhere` with you.

Contractions often include a form of *not,* which is a negative.

no (two negatives): She `can't hardly` wait for Leonard to arrive.

yes (one negative): `She can't wait for Leonard to arrive.`

yes (one negative): `She can hardly wait for Leonard to arrive.`

no (two negatives): `Henry wouldn't be nothing without you.`

yes (one negative): `Henry would be nothing without you.`

yes (one negative): `Henry wouldn't be anything without you.`

EXERCISE **Double Negatives**

Rewrite the following sentences to eliminate the double negatives.

1. The school board will not never agree to abolish the dress code.
2. In the back row, we can't hardly hear what the actors are saying.
3. I don't know nothing about cars, but I will try to help you change your spark plugs.
4. We baked so many cookies that the dozen we ate won't hardly be missed.
5. That stupid dog won't never learn to fetch my slippers.

FREQUENTLY CONFUSED WORDS

accept, except

Accept is a verb that means "to receive" or "to agree to."

```
Mary was pleased to accept the scholarship.
I accept the conditions of employment you explained.
```

Except is a preposition that means "excluding."

```
Except for the color, Joe liked the car.
```

advice, advise

Advice is a noun that means "a recommendation."

```
Harriet always values Jan's advice.
```

Advise is a verb that means "to recommend."

```
I advise you to quit while you are ahead.
```

affect, effect

Affect is a verb meaning "to influence."

> `The trade deficit affects the strength of our economy.`

Effect is a noun meaning "result."

> `The effects of the drug are not fully known.`

Effect is a verb meaning "to bring about."

> `The new company president plans to effect several changes in corporate policy.`

all right, alright

A knowledgeable reader is likely to prefer *all right.*

allusion, illusion

Allusion is a noun meaning "indirect reference."

> `I resent your allusion to my past.`

Illusion is a noun meaning "something false or misleading."

> `Having money can create the illusion of happiness.`

already, all ready

Already means "by this time."

> `I would stay for dinner, but I have already eaten.`

All ready means "prepared."

> `Now that I have packed, I am all ready to leave.`

altogether, all together

Altogether means "thoroughly."

> `The teacher was altogether convinced that Sam could read better if he had glasses.`

All together means "everyone or everything in one place."

> `Clear the table and put the dishes all together on the counter.`

among, between

Between is usually used to show the relationship of two things.

> `The animosity between Charles and Carlotta has existed for years.`

Between can be used for more than two things when it means "within."

> `The floor between the stove, refrigerator, and table is hopelessly stained from years of wear.`

Among is used to show the relationship of more than two things.

> `The friendship among Kelly, Joe, and Stavros began in third grade and has continued for 15 years.`

amount, number

Amount is used for a unit without parts that can be counted individually.

> The amount of suffering in the war-torn nation cannot be measured.

Number is used for items that can be counted.

> The number of entries in the contest will determine the odds of winning the grand prize.

anxious, eager

Anxious means "fearful."

> Jeffrey becomes anxious whenever he goes to the dentist.

Eager shows strong interest.

> We are all eager for the first signs of spring.

are, our, hour

Are is a plural form of the verb to be.

> The teachers are certain to get a raise in September.

Our is a plural possessive pronoun.

> Our efforts will not go unrewarded.

Hour refers to 60 minutes.

> In one hour the plane will land in Denver.

beside, besides

Beside means "next to."

> Dad put his book down beside his glasses.

Besides means "in addition to" or "except for."

> Besides a crib, the expectant parents bought a changing table and a dresser.
> I have nothing to tell you besides watch your step.

breath, breathe

Breath is a noun.

> The skaters held their breath as the judges announced the scores.

Breathe is a verb.

> At high altitudes it is more difficult to breathe.

choose, chose

Choose means "to pick."

> Choose the one you want so we can leave.

Chose is the past tense of *choose.*

```
I chose the one I wanted, and then we left.
```

clothes, cloths

Clothes means "garments."

```
The vagrant's clothes were torn and filthy.
```

Cloths are pieces of fabric.

```
Clean diapers make the best cleaning cloths.
```

coarse, course

Coarse means "rough."

```
Because wool is coarse, I do not like to wear it.
```

Course means "path," "route," or "procedure."

```
To speed your progress toward your degree, summer school is
your best course.
```

complement, compliment

Complement means something that completes.

```
Red shoes will complement the outfit nicely.
```

Compliment is "praise" or "flattery."

```
Your compliment comes at the right time because I was
beginning to doubt myself.
```

conscience, conscious

Conscience is an awareness of right and wrong.

```
When in doubt, follow your conscience.
```

Conscious means "aware."

```
Eleni is always conscious of the feelings of others.
```

dessert, desert

Dessert is the sweet at the end of a meal.

```
Ice cream is everyone's favorite dessert.
```

Desert means "abandon."

```
Kim is a good friend because he never deserts me in my time
of need.
```

Desert is dry, sandy land.

```
When driving across the desert, a person should have a
survival kit in the car.
```

different than, different from

Experienced readers are likely to prefer *different from.*

disinterested, uninterested

Disinterested means "impartial."

In labor disputes, a federal mediator acts as a disinterested third party.

Uninterested means "lacking interest" or "bored."

Giselle is uninterested in my problem because she has troubles of her own.

farther, further

Farther refers to distance.

It is not much farther to the restaurant I told you about.

Further means "in addition" or "additional."

The senator believed further that the tax bill was favoring the rich.
Any further discussion is a waste of time.

fewer, less

Fewer is used for things that can be counted individually.

There were fewer A's on the test than I expected.

Less is used for one unit without individual members that can be counted.

The less you know about what happened, the happier you will be.

hear, here

Hear refers to sensing sound with the ear.

I hear the distant ringing of church bells.

Here means "in this place."

Here is the picnic spot we have always enjoyed.

hole, whole

Hole is an opening.

The street department dug a hole in my yard to repair the gas line.

Whole means "entire."

The whole class agreed that the test was fair.

human, humane

Human refers to men and women and the qualities men and women possess.

If we did not make mistakes, we would not be human.

Humane means "compassionate."

Our society is not known for humane treatment of the elderly.

imply, infer

Imply means "to suggest something without stating it."

> Your attitude implies that you do not care.

Infer means "to draw a conclusion from evidence."

> I can infer from your sarcasm that you do not agree with me.

it's, its

It's is the contraction form of *it is* or *it has.*

> It's unfair to accuse Lee of lying without proof.
> It's been 3 years since I saw George.

Its is a possessive pronoun.

> The dog buried its bone at the base of the oak tree.

know, no

Know means to understand or be aware of.

> I know it is only October, but I am starting my Christmas shopping.

No is a negative.

> There is no way I can finish the report by Friday.

loose, lose

Loose means "unfastened" or "not tight."

> Joey's loose tooth made it impossible for him to eat corn on the cob.

Lose means "misplace."

> Every time I buy an expensive pen, I lose it.

maybe, may be

Maybe means "perhaps."

> Maybe I can help you if you explain the problem more clearly.

May be means "might be."

> If her plane lands on time, Zahava may be here for dinner.

passed, past

Passed means "went by."

> Summer passed far too quickly.

Past refers to a previous time.

> The past week was hectic because I had to work overtime at the store and study for final exams.

precede, proceed

Precede means "to come before."

> A preface precedes the main part of a book.

Proceed means "continue."

> I am sorry I interrupted you; proceed with what you were saying.

principal, principle

Principal is a school administrator (as a noun); as an adjective *principal* means "first in importance."

> The principal suspended the students for fighting on the playground.
> The principal issue here is whether we can afford to spend the extra money.

Principle is a truth or a moral conviction.

> My principles will not allow me to lie for you.

quiet, quite

Quiet means "with little noise" or "calm."

> Jake needs a quiet place to study.
> The sea is quiet despite the earlier storm.

Quite means "very."

> I am quite happy with my new job.

set, sit

Set is a verb that takes a direct object.

> For daylight saving time, set your clock ahead one hour.

Sit is a verb that does not take a direct object.

> Sit near the door, and I will find you when I arrive.

stationary, stationery

Stationary means "unmoving" or "unchanging."

> This fan is stationary; it does not rotate.

Stationery is writing paper.

> More men are using pink stationery for personal correspondence.

than, then

Than is used for comparisons.

> The car I bought is more fuel efficient than the one I traded in.

Then is a time reference; it also means "next."

> I went to college in the 1970s; students were politically active then.
> Spade the ground thoroughly; then you can plant the seeds.

there, their, they're

There indicates place. It is also a sentence opener when *their* or *they're* does not apply.

> I thought my car was parked there.
> There are 12 people going on the ski trip.

Their is a possessive pronoun.

> Children rarely appreciate what their parents do for them.

They're is the contraction form of *they are.*

> Lyla and Jim said they're coming, but I will believe it when I see them.

threw, through, thorough

Threw is the past tense of *throw.*

> The pitcher threw the ball to third base.

Through means "finished" or "into and out of."

> We should be through by noon.
> When I drove through the Lincoln Tunnel, I forgot to put my headlights on.

Thorough means "complete."

> In the spring, many people give their houses a thorough cleaning.

to, too, two

To means "toward." It is also used with a verb to form the infinitive.

> After 5 years, Kathleen finally saved enough money to go to Florida.

Too means "also" or "excessively."

> The child whined because she did not get to go ice skating too.
> When the curtain went up, Carlos was too frightened to say his lines.

Two is the number.

> Lenny gets along well with his two roommates.

weather, whether

Weather refers to climate conditions.

> The weather this March has been unseasonably warm and dry.

Whether means "if."

```
Whether I go depends on my health.
```

were, where

Were is a past tense form of *to be.*

```
Our trips to London and Rome were exciting.
```

Where means "in which place."

```
Where are my car keys?
```

whose, who's

Whose is the possessive form of *who.*

```
Whose books are on the kitchen table?
```

Who's is the contraction form of *who is* and *who has.*

```
Who's going with you?
Who's been in the cookie jar?
```

your, you're

Your is the possessive form of *you.*

```
Your car is parked in a tow-away zone.
```

You're is the contraction form of *you are.*

```
Let me know if you're coming with us.
```

EXERCISE **Frequently Confused Words**

Select five sets of frequently confused words that you are not completely comfortable using. Use each word in a sentence that you compose.

CHAPTER 17

Editing for Sentence Fragments

A **sentence fragment** results when you punctuate and capitalize a phrase or subordinate clause as if it were a sentence.

phrase fragment: The bus driver and his wife spent over $500 on toys for their children. Most of it on the two girls.

Although the period and capital letter give the underlined phrase the appearance of a sentence, the words do not have enough completeness for sentence status. Hence, they are a fragment. Here is another example.

subordinate clause fragment: Since she was graceful as well as daring. She was an excellent dancer.

The underlined subordinate clause forms a fragment. Despite the period and capital letter, the word group lacks enough completeness to function as a sentence.

NOTE: For a more complete discussion of subordinate clauses, see page 98.

A fragment also results when an incomplete or incorrect form of a verb is used, as the following examples illustrate.

incomplete verb fragment: The game been delayed because of rain.

incorrect verb fragment: The band being too loud.

CORRECTING SENTENCE FRAGMENTS

1. To correct a fragment that results when a phrase is punctuated and capitalized like a sentence, you can connect the fragment to the appropriate sentence before or after it, or you can rewrite the fragment so that it forms a sentence. These correction methods are illustrated below.

fragment: `The bus driver and his wife spent over $500 on toys for their children. Most of it on the two girls.`

correction: `The bus driver and his wife spent $500 on toys for their children, most of it on the two girls.`

correction: `The bus driver and his wife spent over $500 on toys for their children. Most of the money was spent on the two girls.`

2. To correct a fragment that results when a subordinate clause is punctuated and capitalized like a sentence, connect the fragment to the appropriate sentence before or after it, as the following example illustrates.

fragment: `Since she was graceful as well as daring. She was an excellent dancer.`

correction: `Since she was graceful as well as daring, she was an excellent dancer.`

3. To correct a fragment that results from an incomplete verb, add the missing verb part, like this.

fragment: `The game been delayed because of rain.`

correction: `The game has been delayed because of rain.`

4. To correct a fragment that results from an incorrect verb, correct the verb form, like this.

fragment: `The band being too loud.`

correction: `The band is too loud.`

FINDING SENTENCE FRAGMENTS

If you have a tendency to write sentence fragments, you should edit a separate time, looking just for fragments. Study each group of words you are calling a "sentence." Read each group aloud and ask yourself if it sounds complete enough to be a sentence. Do not move on to the next group until you are sure the one you are leaving behind is a sentence. For this method to be effective, you must move slowly, listening to each word group independent of what comes before and after it. Otherwise, you may fail to hear a fragment because you complete its meaning with a sentence coming before or after. Of course, each time you find a fragment, correct it before going on.

Composing at the Computer

If you compose at the computer or word processor, the following two tips may help you edit for sentence fragments.

1. These words often begin sentence fragments.

after	because	such as
although	especially	unless
as	even though	until
as if	for example	when
as long as	if	whenever
as though	since	while

Use your computer's search function to locate these words in your draft. Each time you locate a word group beginning with one of them, check to be sure you have a sentence rather than a fragment.

2. Isolate every word group you are calling a sentence by inserting eight spaces before each capital letter that marks a sentence opening. Then read each word group separately to check for completeness. With word groups visually isolated this way, you are less likely to overlook a fragment by mentally connecting it to a sentence before or after it. After checking everything, reformat the text.

EXERCISE

Sentence Fragments

Where necessary, edit the following to eliminate the fragments. Some are correct as they are.

1. After returning from the beach. The children were exhausted.
2. The rain showed no signs of letting up, so flash flood warnings were issued.
3. After Howie had attended drama class several times and bought a subscription to *Variety*. He was sure he would become a big star.
4. Although Marie missed several training sessions. She learned to use the new computer.
5. By midnight the party was over.
6. John neglecting his assigned duties and spending time on independent research.
7. The reigning dictator, being an excellent administrator and former army officer.

8. Being the most indispensable of the Channel 27 news team. Antonio got a raise.
9. Karen dropped calculus. Which she had dropped several times before.
10. Sean went to his karate class and when he came home. He had been burglarized.
11. After awhile, the fog cleared.
12. How can you expect that of me?
13. Carlotta skipped breakfast. Although she needed the nourishment.
14. Working together to save our environment. We can leave the world a better place than we found it.
15. Dad cleaning the hull of the boat, helping to set the lobster traps and still finding time to teach his younger daughter how to bait her own hook.

Edit the paragraphs below to eliminate the fragments.

1. My sister, who waited two years to become a high school cheerleader. Frequently complained that the student body had no school spirit. What did she expect? Our school, Fairmont High, had the football team with the state record. For losing the most consecutive games in a row. The only people who even attended the football games being the members of the marching band and some of the players' parents. The only contest on the field was the one at halftime. When the two marching bands competed to see who was the best. Things were so bad that our team felt a sense of accomplishment when they scored 6 points. No wonder the student body was spiritless.
2. Much literature written for adolescents is of the highest quality. For example, *IOU'S,* by Ouida Sebestyen, being a well-written story of adolescent conflict that both teens and adults would enjoy. The main character is 13-year-old Stowe. A boy who lives with his divorced mother. The novel chronicles Stowe's efforts as he wrestles with an important decision, struggles with friendships, and makes peace with his family. Like most adolescents, Stowe longs for the independence of adulthood at the same time he fears it. Briskly paced, tightly narrated, and thought-provoking, *IOU'S* is a novel teens will see themselves in. And a novel that will remind adults of the struggles inherent in adolescence. It is poignant, funny, and subtle. And above all realistic.

CHAPTER 18

Editing for Run-On Sentences and Comma Splices

A **run-on sentence** occurs when two or more main clauses are written without any separation. (Main clauses, discussed on page 98, are word groups that can stand as sentences.)

main clause: `the power was out for two days`

main clause: `most of the food in my refrigerator spoiled`

run-on sentence: `The power was out for two days most of the food in my refrigerator spoiled.`

A **comma splice** occurs when two or more main clauses are separated by nothing more than a comma.

main clause: `Rocco studied hard for his final exams`

main clause: `he passed them all with high marks`

comma splice: `Rocco studied hard for his final exams, he passed them all with high marks.`

CORRECTING RUN-ON SENTENCES AND COMMA SPLICES

Run-ons and comma splices can be corrected in four ways.

1. You can separate the main clauses with a period and capital letter to form two sentences.

run-on: `The power was out for two days most of the food in my refrigerator spoiled.`

correction: `The power was out for two days. Most of the food in my refrigerator spoiled.`

comma splice: `Rocco studied hard for his final exams, he passed them all with high marks.`

correction: `Rocco studied hard for his final exams. He passed them all with high marks.`

2. You can separate the main clause with a semicolon.

run-on: `The personnel department was praised for its efficiency all the workers received a bonus.`

correction: `The personnel department was praised for its efficiency; all the workers received a bonus.`

comma splice: `I never like to wear wool, its coarseness irritates my skin.`

correction: `I never like to wear wool; its coarseness irritates my skin.`

3. You can separate the main clauses with a comma and coordinating conjunction *(and, but, or, nor, for, so, yet).*

run-on: `The new computer's manual is very clear Enrico learned to use the machine in an hour.`

correction: `The new computer's manual is very clear, so Enrico learned to use the machine in an hour.`

comma splice: `The hospital layed off 100 workers, most of them will be called back in three months.`

correction: `The hospital layed off 100 workers, but most of them will be called back in three months.`

NOTE: A frequent cause of run-ons and comma splices is confusing the following conjunctive adverbs for coordinating conjunctions:

therefore	moreover	thus
however	hence	for example
also	consequently	furthermore
indeed	nevertheless	nonetheless

Conjunctive adverbs cannot be used to join main clauses with a comma; only the coordinating conjunctions *(and, but, or, nor, for, so, yet)* can do this.

run-on: I was certain my interview went well therefore I was surprised when I was not among the finalists for the job.

correction: I was certain my interview went well; therefore, I was surprised when I was not among the finalists for the job.

comma splice: The Christmas party was dull, consequently I left early.

correction: The Christmas party was dull; consequently, I left early.

4. You can change one of the main clauses to a subordinate clause.

run-on: My car stalls when I accelerate quickly the carburetor needs to be adjusted.

correction: Because the carburetor needs to be adjusted, my car stalls when I accelerate quickly.

comma splice: Spring is supposed to be a happy time, many people get depressed.

correction: Although spring is supposed to be a happy time, many people get depressed.

FINDING RUN-ON SENTENCES AND COMMA SPLICES

If you have a tendency to write run-ons and comma splices, edit a separate time, checking just for these errors. Study each group of words you are calling a "sentence," and ask yourself how many main clauses there are. If there is more than one, be sure the proper separation exists. When you find a run-on or a comma splice, make the correction according to the following guidelines.

run-on: The door slammed shut the dog awoke with a start.

comma splice: The door slammed shut, the dog awoke with a start.

correction with semicolon: The door slammed shut; the dog awoke with a start.

correction with comma and coordinating conjunction: `The door slammed shut, and the dog awoke with a start.`

correction with period and capital letter: `The door slammed shut. The dog awoke with a start.`

correction with subordinate clause: `When the door slammed shut, the dog awoke with a start.`

Composing at the Computer

If you compose at the computer or word processor, the following two tips may help you edit for run-on sentences and comma splices.

1. Use your computer's search function to locate these conjunctive adverbs in your draft.

therefore	moreover	thus
however	hence	for example
also	consequently	furthermore
indeed	nevertheless	nonetheless

Each time you locate one of these conjunctive adverbs, check for main clauses on both sides. Wherever you have main clauses on both sides, be sure you have used a semicolon before the word.

2. Isolate every word group you are calling a sentence by inserting eight spaces before each capital letter marking the beginning of a sentence. The visual separation will allow you to check the number of main clauses more easily. After finding and eliminating run-ons and comma splices, reformat your text.

EXERCISE

Run-on Sentences and Comma Splices

Correct the following run-ons and comma splices using any of the methods discussed.

1. My first bike will always be special to me it was a yellow dirt bike named Thunderball.
2. Sophia loves to gossip about others she becomes angry if she even thinks someone is gossiping about her.
3. Yesterday the fire trucks raced up our street three times it must be the summer brushfire season.

4. The large black ants marched upside down across the kitchen ceiling, I wonder where they came from.
5. The package of chicken fryer parts was obviously spoiled he returned it to the manager of the market demanding a refund.
6. My daughter's baseball pants are impossible to get clean, why does the league insist on purchasing white pants?
7. Randy is a terrible soccer coach, he cares more about winning than he does about the children he manages.
8. Stevie is so warm and open that it is hard to resist his charm, he seems to smile all the time.
9. Cotton material is all that they claim it is—lightweight, soft, and comfortable be careful when laundering it often shrinks.
10. My mother has often been my best friend, she is caring, supportive, and nonjudgmental.

Rewrite the paragraphs below to eliminate the run-on sentences and comma splices.

1. My day off made me wish I was back at my job everything went wrong. First I overslept and neglected to get my son to day camp on time. Then there was no milk for breakfast my son ate pizza. The dog had raided the wastebasket during the night half-chewed paper and bits of garbage littered the living room carpeting. I plugged in the sweeper, one of the prongs broke off in the outlet. I drove to the local hardware store to purchase new plugs. I returned home to discover the plug was the wrong size for the sweeper cord I drove back to the store to exchange the plug for the proper size. Then I cut my finger when the screwdriver slipped while I was trying to attach the new plug. In the middle of all this chaos, the phone rang, the neighbor was calling to tell me that my German shepherd had chased the letter carrier away from her house. By the time I was finished listening to her, I started to itch I looked down to see the unmistakable red blotches of poison ivy rising on my arms and calves.
2. I had been on my own for 18 years by the time I was 36, but I never really thought of myself as an adult. I left for college at 18 and was earning my own living by 22. I was married by the time I was 23, I was raising a family of three by age 30. But not until I was 36 did I see myself as an honest-to-goodness grownup. It was then that my parents announced they were selling the house I grew up in. Then it hit me, then I really understood. I was out on my own my old room would be inhabited by some stranger. I could not go "home" to Mother and Dad anymore my "home" would not be there. How strange it seemed that I would never again enter that familiar haven and savor the warmth of the living room or the comfort of the kitchen. I would never again return to "my" bedroom where "my" furniture remained just as I left it when I went to college. When my folks called to announce they were moving to an apartment, I realized I was indeed an adult on my own. I must confess that the awareness came as a painful jolt. I wanted to go home, however, I was already in my home.

C H A P T E R 1 9

Editing for Subject-Verb Agreement and Tense Shifts

SUBJECT-VERB AGREEMENT

The rule for **subject-verb agreement** is straightforward: a verb should always agree with its subject *in number.* That is, a singular subject requires a singular verb, and a plural subject requires a plural verb.

singular subject,
singular verb: `Green ink is often difficult to read.`

plural subject,
plural verb: `The desks are highly polished.`

Most of the time subject-verb agreement is easily achieved. However, some instances present special agreement problems, and these are discussed below.

Compound Subjects

A **compound subject** occurs when two or more words, phrases, or clauses are joined by *and, or, nor, either . . . or,* or *neither . . . nor.*

1. If the parts of a compound subject are linked by *and,* the verb is plural.

`The lioness and her cub share a close bond.`

2. If subjects are preceded by *each* or *every,* then a singular verb is used.

`Each lioness and each cub faces starvation on the drought-stricken plain.`

3. Singular subjects linked by *or* or *nor* (or by *either . . . or* or *neither . . . nor*) take a singular verb.

> Drought or famine threatens all wildlife.

4. Plural subjects linked by *or* or *nor* (or *either . . . or* or *neither . . . nor*) take a plural verb.

> Neither the children nor their parents are enjoying the play.

5. When a plural subject and a singular subject are joined, the verb agrees with the nearer subject.

> Disease or predators are also a danger to newborn cubs.
>
> Neither the scouts nor their leader is willing to camp out on such a cold night.

(NOTE: For a more pleasant-sounding sentence, place the plural form last: *Neither the leader nor the scouts are* willing to camp out on such a cold night.)

Subject and Verb Separated

Words, phrases, or clauses that come between the subject and verb do not affect the subject-verb agreement rule.

> The chipmunks, burrowing under my flower bed, also raid my garden.

The subject *chipmunks* is plural, so the plural verb *raid* must be used. The phrase *burrowing under my flower bed* does not affect that. Here is another example:

> One of the demonstrators was fined $100.

Although the phrase between the subject and verb contains the plural word *demonstrators,* the singular subject *one* still requires the singular verb *was.*

Inverted Order

1. When the verb appears before the subject, the word order is *inverted.* Be sure the verb agrees with the subject and not some other word close to the verb.

> Flowing through the steep canyons was the Colorado River.

2. Sentences which begin with *there* or *here* often have inverted order, as do sentences that ask a question.

There are many causes of cancer.

Here is the box of records.

Why are your questions so hard to answer?

Indefinite Pronouns

1. *Indefinite pronouns* refer to some part of a group of people, things, or ideas without specifying the particular members of the group referred to. The following indefinite pronouns are singular and require singular verbs.

anyone	everybody	something
anybody	everything	none
anything	someone	no one
each	either	nobody
one	neither	nothing
everyone	somebody	

Nobody ignores an insult all the time.

Everybody retaliates once in a while.

No one likes to be the butt of a joke.

NOTE: Although *everyone* and *everybody* clearly refer to more than one, they are still singular in a grammatical sense and take a singular verb.

Everyone is invited to the party after the show.

2. It is tempting to use a plural verb with a singular indefinite pronoun followed by a phrase with a plural word. However, in this case too the singular verb is used in formal usage.

Each of the boys *is* willing to help rake the leaves.

Everyone of us plans to contribute a week's salary to the Christmas fund.

3. The following indefinite pronouns may be singular or plural, depending on the meaning of the sentence.

all	some	most
any	more	

```
Most of the players are injured.
Most of the pie is gone already.
All of the bills are paid.
All of the hem is torn.
```

Collective Nouns

Collective nouns have a singular form and refer to a group of people or things. The following are examples of collective nouns.

audience	class	majority
committee	family	faculty
crew	team	jury

1. Collective nouns take a singular verb when the noun refers to the group as a single unit.

```
The number of people attending the concert was staggering.

The women's basketball team is still in contention for the
state championship.
```

2. Collective nouns take a plural verb when the members of the group are functioning individually.

```
A number of those in attendance were over 30 years old.

The faculty have agreed among themselves to promote tougher
admissions standards.
```

EXERCISE

Subject-Verb Agreement

Choose the correct verb form in the following sentences.

1. Three wolves and a grizzly bear (stalk/stalks) the grazing caribou herd.
2. The hunter, not natural enemies, (is/are) responsible for the decline in the bald eagle population.
3. Only recently (has/have) we seen the rebirth of violent protest.
4. There (is/are) few American holidays more popular than Thanksgiving.
5. None of us really (know/knows) anyone else.
6. All of us often (disguise/disguises) our real feelings.
7. Neither of the cubs born to the huge female grizzly (appear/appears) undernourished.

8. The chief reasons for the country's high unemployment rate (has/have) been the attempts to bring inflation under control.
9. Each of the campers (is/are) responsible for bringing cooking utensils.
10. A majority of people (feel/feels) insecure about something.
11. There (is/are) few presidents more admired than Lincoln.
12. Neither time nor progress (has/have) diminished the affection most Americans feel for our sixteenth president.
13. One of my favorite poems (is/are) "The Rime of the Ancient Mariner."
14. Most of the beetles (is/are) trapped.
15. Either Whitney Houston or Billy Joel (deserve/deserves) the Grammy for record of the year.
16. Your family often (demand/demands) to know your innermost secrets.
17. Each of us (decide/decides) who we will trust.
18. Everyone (need/needs) someone to talk to.
19. Fifteen adult white-tailed deer and a single fawn (was/were) observed by the backpackers.
20. All the elements of nature (act/acts) to maintain the balance of the animal population.

Rewrite the following paragraph to eliminate problems with subject-verb agreement.

One of the islands in the Caribbean Sea is called Bonaire. A number of tourists are attracted to Bonaire because it is a nesting sight for pink flamingoes. However, the clear waters of the sea makes the area a perfect spot for diving. There is numerous underwater attractions for either the experienced diver or the amateur who requires a guide. On the coral reef is groupies and moray eels. Also, there are small "cleaner fish," called hogfish, who eat the harmful parasites off the larger fish. The colorful reef itself is a spectacular sight where one can observe a variety of coral. Throughout the reef is sea anemones, shrimp, and crabs for the diver to observe. Although the underwater attractions of Bonaire is not commonly known, time and word of mouth will bring more vacationers to this island off the coast of northern South America.

TENSE SHIFTS

Verbs have **tense** to indicate past, present, and future time. Once you begin with a particular verb tense, maintain that tense as long as you are referring to the same period of time. Switching tense without a valid reason creates a problem called **tense shift**. The following paragraph contains unwarranted tense shifts (the verbs are underlined to help you recognize the shifts).

> Hockey player Bill Mosienko dreamed of making his way into the record books, and on March 23, 1952, his dream comes true. His team, the Black Hawks, was playing the New York Rangers. Black Hawk Gus Bodnar gets the puck and passes it to Mosienko, who scores. At the following face-off, Bodnar gains possession, passes to Mosienko, who scored again. Bodnar won the face-off again and passed to Gee. Gee passed to Mosienko, who scores again--for three goals in twenty-one seconds.

The verbs in this paragraph shift back and forth from present to past, interfering with an accurate representation of the action of the game. To prevent confusion about time sequence, once you use a verb tense, maintain that tense consistently and shift time only when the shift is justified.

A corrected version of the example paragraph reads like this.

> Hockey player Bill Mosienko dreamed of making his way into the record books, and on March 23, 1952, his dream came true. His team, the Black Hawks, was playing the New York Rangers. Black Hawk Gus Bodnar got the puck and passed it to Mosienko, who scored. At the following face-off, Bodnar gained possession and passed to Mosienko, who scored again. Bodnar won the face-off again and passed to Gee. Gee passed to Mosienko, who scored again--for three goals in twenty-one seconds.

A shift from one tense to another is appropriate when the time frame at issue has changed.

> When I first began working as a waiter, I hated my work. Now I am enjoying my job more than I thought possible.

In the above example, each shift (from past to present to past) is justified because each verb accurately reflects the time period referred to.

EXERCISE

Tense Shifts

Revise the following sentences to eliminate inappropriate tense shifts. One sentence is correct.

1. While you were turned around, a miracle happened. The line drive hits the base runner, so no runs were scored.
2. Just when Katya thought her homework was finished, she remembers she has history questions to answer.

3. Grandma Rodriguez seemed totally bored with the baseball game when suddenly she jumps up and screams, "Park it, Jimmy!"
4. Many educators in the United States believe in the principle of grouping students according to ability because as long as bright students were competing against other bright students, they performed better.
5. By the end of her essay exam, Jeanine had her facts all confused; she is positive, though, that she passes the multiple-choice section of the test.
6. The governor announced a new tax proposal and explained that he is confident it will solve the state's budget problems.
7. Young people in the sixties demanded a religion that calls for a simple, clean, and serene life.
8. Marty asked Lynn if she wants to go out with him, but she brushed him off and left with Jerome.
9. As Sue collected her clubs and new golf balls, she thinks how difficult this tournament will be.
10. Consequently, we can see that the human race has progressed or at least seemed to have progressed.

Rewrite the following paragraph to eliminate unwarranted tense shifts.

When Ian bought his compact disc player, he shopped with caution. First, he goes to a store that had the same amplifier and speaker he owned so he could listen through brands he was accustomed to. Then he listens to CD music he is already familiar with so he could better judge the quality. He was also careful to listen to drums so he could check the quality of the bass and to brass so he could check the quality of the upper registers. While the CD player is operating, Ian taps on it to be sure it is not affected by slight movements such as those created when someone walks through a room. Finally, he checks to be sure the disc is easy to put in and take out. Only after such careful checking did Ian make his purchase.

CHAPTER 20

Editing for Problems with Pronouns

A **pronoun** substitutes for a noun to help writers and speakers avoid unpleasant repetition, as the following example shows.

unpleasant repetition: `The kitten licked the kitten's paw.`

pronoun used: `The kitten licked her paw.`

PRONOUN CASE

Pronouns that can function as the subject of a sentence are in the **nominative case**. Pronouns that can function as the direct object, indirect object, or object of a preposition are in the **objective case**. Here is a chart of nominative and objective pronouns.

Nominative Case	*Objective Case*
I	me
we	us
you	you
he	him
she	her
it	it
they	them
who	whom
whoever	whomever

Choose pronouns on the basis of their function in the sentence, not on the basis of how the pronoun sounds.

subject pronoun in nominative case: `She gave a pint of blood at Red Cross headquarters.` (She underlined)

object pronoun in objective case: `Mark cooked dinner for her.` (her underlined)

Most of the time, choosing the correct pronoun is not a problem. However, in a few special circumstances, pronoun choice can be tricky. These circumstances are described below.

Choosing Pronouns in Compounds

1. Use nominative case for subjects and objective case for objects:

subject: He and I prefer to drive to Nashville.

object: Police authorities gave them and us citations for bravery. [indirect object]

object: Professor Whan asked her and me to help out after class. [direct object]

object: Joyce sat down near him and her. [object of preposition]

2. When a pronoun is paired with a noun, you can often tell which pronoun is correct if you mentally cross out everything except the pronoun.

For example, which is it?

Ricardo asked Dale and me to leave.

or

Ricardo asked Dale and I to leave.

Cross out everything except the pronoun to find out.

Ricardo asked ~~Dale and~~ me to leave.
Ricardo asked ~~Dale and~~ I to leave.

Now you can tell that the correct form is:

Ricardo asked Dale and me to leave.

Choosing Pronouns after Forms of *To Be*

In strict formal usage, the nominative case is used after forms of *to be (am, is, are, was, were).*

> It is I.
>
> The stars of the play are Carlotta and she.

Choosing Pronouns in Comparisons

1. When *than* or *as* is used to compare, some words may go unstated. You can choose the correct pronoun by mentally adding the unstated words.

For example, which is it?

> Jackson works longer hours than I.
>
> Jackson works longer hours than me.

Add the unstated words to decide.

> Jackson works longer hours than I do.
>
> Jackson works longer hours than me do.

With the unstated words added, the correct choice is clear.

> Jackson works longer hours than I.

2. Sometimes the pronoun chosen affects the meaning of the sentence.

> I enjoy Ivan as much as she. [This sentence means that I enjoy Ivan as much as she does.]
>
> I enjoy Ivan as much as her. [This sentence means that I enjoy Ivan as much as I enjoy her.]

Choosing Pronouns in Appositives

Appositives are words that rename. When a pronoun is followed by an appositive, you can choose the correct form by mentally crossing out the appositive.

For example, which is it?

> We students resent the tuition increase.

or

> Us students resent the tuition increase.

Cross out the appositive.

We ~~students~~ resent the tuition increase.
Us ~~students~~ resent the tuition increase.

Now the choice is clear:

We students resent the tuition increase.

Choosing *Who, Whoever, Whom,* and *Whomever*

1. *Who* and *whoever* are the nominative forms and are used as subjects.

Henry is the one who understands Phyllis. [*Who* is the subject of the verb *understands*.]

2. Recast questions into statements and use the nominative *who* after forms of *to be (am, is, are, was, were).*

For example, which is it?

Who was the top point scorer in the game?
Whom was the top point scorer in the game?

Recast the question as a statement.

The top point scorer in the game was who.

Now it's clear that the correct form is:

Who was the top point scorer in the game?

3. *Whom* and *whomever* are the objective forms and are used for direct objects, indirect objects, and objects of prepositions.

direct object: Whom did you take with you? [You did take whom with you.]

indirect object: Give the job to whomever you want.

object of preposition: Seat yourself near whomever you wish.

EXERCISE

Pronoun Case

Fill in the blank with the correct form given in parentheses.

1. (She and I/Her and me/She and me) ____________________ expect to graduate a year early because we attended summer school.
2. (I/me) Gloria is a much better math student than ____________________.
3. (we/us) The union plans to strike to win a 10 percent pay raise for ____________________ dock workers.
4. (who/whom) Ask Lionel ____________________ he plans to train as his replacement.
5. (We/Us) ____________________ adult learners add an important dimension to the classroom.
6. (he/him) It is ____________________ who can tell you what you need to know.
7. (who/whom) Mario is the young man ____________________ I was telling you about.
8. (they/them) Give that box of records to Alice and ____________________ to store in the basement.
9. (he/him) If I were as good at science as ____________________, I would major in chemistry or physics.
10. (I/me) Because of our vision problems, all colors look similar to Lisa and ____________________.

PRONOUN-ANTECEDENT AGREEMENT

Pronouns must agree with the nouns they refer to (**antecedents**) in **gender** (masculine, feminine, or neuter) and **number** (singular or plural). Many times this agreement is easily achieved, as is the case in the following example:

Kurt lost his tennis racket, but he eventually found it.

The pronouns *he* and *his* are singular and masculine to agree with the number and gender of the antecedent *Kurt,* and the pronoun *it* is singular and neuter to agree with *racket.*

At times, pronoun-antecedent agreement is not as obvious as in the above sentence, and these instances are discussed in the rest of this chapter.

Compound Subjects

A **compound subject** is formed by two or more words, phrases, or clauses joined by *and, or, nor, either . . . or,* or *neither . . . nor.*

1. If the parts of the antecedent are joined by *and,* a plural pronoun is used.

The shoes and baseball cap were left in their usual places.

Linda, Michelle, and Audrey finished their group project early.

2. If a part of the antecedent is preceded by *each* or *every,* the pronoun is singular.

Every citizen and each group must do its part to elect responsible officials.

Each school and athletic department must submit its budget to the superintendent.

3. Singular antecedents joined by *either . . . or* or *neither . . . nor* require singular pronouns.

Has either Sean or Frank taken his batting practice today?

Neither Melissa nor Jennifer has finished packing for her trip.

4. Plural antecedents joined by *either . . . or* or *neither . . . nor* require plural pronouns.

Neither the teachers nor the students are eating their lunches.

5. If one singular and one plural antecedent are joined by *or, either . . . or,* or *neither . . . nor,* the pronoun should agree with the antecedent closer to it.

Either Clint Black or the Oak Ridge Boys will release *their* new album soon.

NOTE: Placing the plural antecedent second makes a smoother sentence.

Collective Nouns

Collective nouns have a singular form and refer to a *group* of people or things. Words like these are collective nouns.

group	committee	jury
class	society	audience
team	panel	band

1. If the collective noun is functioning as a single unit, the pronoun that refers to it is singular.

A civilized society must protect its citizens from violence.

2. If the members of the group are functioning individually, a plural pronoun is used.

`Yesterday the team signed their contracts for next season.`

Indefinite Pronouns

Indefinite pronouns refer to some part of a group of people, things, or ideas without specifying the particular members of the group referred to. Indefinite pronouns can be antecedents.

1. The following indefinite pronouns are singular, and in formal usage the pronouns referring to them should also be singular.

each	somebody	one
everybody	someone	either
everyone	anybody	neither
nobody	anyone	none
no one		

`Anyone who has finished his or her essay may leave.`

`Nobody on the football team should assume that his position is safe.`

`Neither of the young mothers forgot her exercise class.`

NOTE: See the discussion on nonsexist pronouns that follows.

2. In formal usage, a pronoun referring to a singular indefinite pronoun is singular, even when a phrase with a plural word follows the indefinite pronoun.

`Each of the boys selected his favorite bat.`

3. *Few* and *many* are plural, and so pronouns referring to them must also be plural.

`Many of my friends have already bought their tickets.`

4. The following indefinite pronouns may be singular or plural, depending on the meaning of the sentence.

all	some	most
any	more	

`Some of the book is still attached to its binding.`

`Some of the band forgot their sheet music.`

Nonsexist Pronouns

When a singular noun or indefinite pronoun designates a person who can be either male or female (*lawyer, student, director, pianist, anybody,* and so on), agreement can be achieved in one of three ways.

1. The masculine pronoun can be used.

`Each contestant must bring his birth certificate.`

This method is grammatically correct, but it does not acknowledge the presence of females and hence is considered sexist by many. For this reason, many people prefer methods 2 and 3 below, which are nonsexist.

2. A masculine and feminine pronoun can be used.

`Each contestant must bring his or her birth certificate.`

3. The sentence can be recast into the plural.

`All contestants must bring their birth certificates.`

EXERCISE Pronoun-Antecedent Agreement

Choose the correct pronoun.

1. Neither Angelo nor Doug volunteered (his, their) services for the Downtown Cleanup Crusade.
2. Each teacher and principal agreed that (he or she, they) would contribute to the United Way.
3. The secretary of the Scuba Club urged everybody to pay (his or her, their) dues by the end of the month.
4. Anyone wanting a successful college experience must spend much of (his or her, their) time studying.
5. A dog and two cats could take care of (itself, themselves) very nicely with just our family's table scraps.
6. The hostess asked that either Cara Smith or the Dennisons move (her, their) car.
7. Both Matt and Joey lost (his, their) lunch money.
8. Few of these candlesticks are in (its, their) original boxes.
9. That tribe holds (its, their) sacred initiation rites each autumn.

10. When asked to make statements, the sheriff and his deputy insisted on (his, their) right to remain silent.
11. The company fired (its, their) inefficient workers.
12. The herd moves ever westward as (it, they) grazes.
13. The Ski Club held (its, their) first meeting immediately following the holiday season.
14. The squad of police antiterrorists took (its, their) positions around the abandoned warehouse.
15. The city council debated whether (it, they) should pass the new antismoking ordinance.
16. No one should force (his or her, their) vacation choice on other members of the family.
17. Questioned by the precinct worker, neither Annette nor DeShawn would reveal (her, their) party affiliation.
18. To prepare for hurricanes, each coastal town has (its, their) own special warning system.
19. Most of the Pep Club had (its, their) pictures taken for the yearbook.
20. Both Jeff and Greg took (his, their) lunch to work.

Rewrite the following paragraph to eliminate problems with pronoun-antecedent agreement.

With five children to feed and get off to school, I find mornings the worst part of the day. I begin waking the kids, whose ages range from 6 to 17, at 7:00. Each child pulls the covers over their heads and refuses to get up, so I turn all their radios on full blast until every one of them is up and functioning. Then there is the complaining: Jill or Janet cannot get their hair the way they want it; Marla's favorite sweater is not washed and she *has* to wear it; Jeff refuses to change out of Peter's sweat pants. Tony cannot find his books. Of course at least one of them forgot to do their homework, so there is the last minute panic and chaos. They never agree on what they will have for breakfast, so I always prepare five different things. If they all catch his or her buses on time, its a miracle. I almost always end up driving one of them to school. Any mother who survives mornings with five school-age kids deserves a Congressional medal.

PRONOUN REFERENCE

If you fail to provide a clear, stated antecedent for a pronoun, you create a problem with **pronoun reference.** The most common kinds of pronoun reference problems are described below.

Ambiguous Reference

Ambiguous reference occurs when your reader cannot tell which of two possible antecedents a pronoun refers to.

ambiguous reference: When I placed the heavy vase on the shelf, it broke. [What broke, the vase or the shelf? Because of the ambiguous reference, the reader cannot tell.]

To eliminate the ambiguous reference, replace the pronoun with a noun.

correction: When I placed the heavy vase on the shelf, the shelf broke.

Unstated Reference

Unstated reference occurs when you fail to supply an antecedent for a pronoun to refer to. Unstated reference occurs in the following situations.

1. Unstated reference occurs when a pronoun refers to an unstated form of a stated word.

unstated reference: Carla is very ambitious. It causes her to work sixty hours a week. [*It* is meant to refer to *ambition,* but that word does not appear; *ambitious* does.]

To correct a problem with unstated reference, substitute a noun for the pronoun.

correction: Carla is very ambitious. Her ambition causes her to work sixty hours a week.

2. Unstated reference occurs when *this, that, which, it,* or *they* has no stated antecedent. To eliminate the problem, supply the missing word or words.

unstated reference: When I arrived at the office, they said my appointment was cancelled. [*They* has no antecedent to refer to.]

correction: When I arrived at the office, the receptionist said my appointment was cancelled.

unstated reference: During my last appointment with my advisor, I decided to major in marketing. This has made me feel better about school. [*This* has no word to refer to.]

correction: `During my last appointment with my advisor, I decided to major in marketing. This decision has made me feel better about school.`

3. Unstated reference occurs when *you* appears with no antecedent. To solve the problem, replace the pronoun with a noun.

unstated reference: `A teacher becomes frustrated when` <u>`you`</u> `do not ask questions.` [*You* has no antecedent to refer to.]

correction: `A teacher becomes frustrated when` <u>`students`</u> `do not ask questions.`

4. Unstated reference occurs when a pronoun refers to a possessive form. To solve the problem, eliminate the possessive form.

unstated reference: `In Barbara Kingsolver's novels,` <u>`she`</u> `writes about strong women.`

correction: `In her novels, Barbara Kingsolver writes about strong women.`

EXERCISE

Pronoun Reference

Rewrite the sentences to eliminate problems with pronoun reference.

1. The song lyrics were particularly offensive to women. This caused many radio stations to refuse to play it.
2. Doris explained to Philomena that she had to help clean the apartment.
3. I left the spaghetti sauce and the milk on the counter, and when I answered the phone, my cat knocked it over.
4. I was nervous about today's midterm examination. It made sleep impossible last night.
5. Rodney's car is double-parked. He is certain to get a ticket.
6. Dale is a very insecure person. It is his most unattractive trait.
7. The personnel director explained that I am entitled to 12 vacation days a year, which is guaranteed by the union contract.
8. By the time I arrived at the Dean's office, they had left for lunch.
9. Julius was on the phone with Roberto when he realized that he forgot to go to the bank and cash a check.
10. Dr. Wang is known to be a patient math instructor. It is the reason so many students sign up for his course.

PERSON SHIFTS

When you refer to yourself, you use **first-person pronouns.** When you speak to other people directly, you use **second-person pronouns.** When you refer to other people and things, you use **third-person pronouns.**

first-person pronouns: I, we, me, us, my, mine, our, ours

second-person pronouns: you, your, yours

third-person pronouns: he, she, it, they, his, her, hers, its, their, theirs, him, them

When using the above pronouns, be consistent in person because shifts can be confusing and annoying.

shift from third to second person: If a football player works hard, he has many chances for financial aid, and you might even be eligible for a full scholarship.

shift eliminated: If a football player works hard, he has many chances for financial aid, and he might even be eligible for a full scholarship.

shift from second to first person: An empathetic friend is one you can tell your most private thoughts to. This kind of friend also knows when I want to be alone and respects my wish.

shift eliminated: An empathetic friend is one you can tell your most private thoughts to. This kind of friend also knows when you want to be alone and respects your wish.

EXERCISE

Person Shifts

Revise the following sentences to eliminate person shifts.

1. In high school, I liked geometry because it came easily to me, and you could progress at your own rate.
2. I enjoy riding to the top of the city's tallest building where you can see for miles in all directions.
3. After we received our boots and uniforms, you were shown how to polish and fold them according to army regulations.

4. We are all painfully aware that you can't depend on the boss for help.
5. While taking part in a marathon, a runner should never think about what you're doing.
6. When I ask Sybil to help with some typing, she never turns you down.
7. When a person drinks to excess, you should never attempt to drive a car.
8. In July, people welcome a cool evening, but you know that it is probably only a temporary relief from the heat.
9. By the end of a person's first term as committee secretary, you feel that you are finally beginning to understand the job.
10. I liked my research course better than any other this year. You were on your own searching the library for references.

Eliminate the unwarranted person shifts from the following paragraph.

As soon as we entered the room, you could sense the tension in the atmosphere. This was the day for the first exam to take place. Students were quietly taking his and her places. Pencils were being sharpened; papers were being prepared. Once the class was under way, the quiet tension spread. The only sounds were of paper shuffling and pens scratching. We all hoped that your first efforts would be successful. Finally, the instructor announced, "Anybody who is finished can turn in your papers and leave." Exhausted and relieved, the tired students filed from the room leaving their papers on the teacher's desk.

CHAPTER 21

Editing for Problems with Modifiers

A **modifier** is a word or word group that describes. Modifiers make sentences more vivid and interesting. However, you must be careful to avoid two problems: dangling modifiers and misplaced modifiers.

DANGLING MODIFIERS

A modifier with no stated word to describe is a **dangling modifier.** Dangling modifiers impair meaning and often create silly sentences. Consider the following sentence with a dangling modifier.

While basting the turkey, the sweet potatoes burned.

While basting the turkey is a modifier, but there is no word for the modifier to refer to or describe. As a result, it seems that the sweet potatoes basted the turkey.

There are two ways to correct a dangling modifier. You can leave the modifier as it is and supply a word for the modifier to refer to. *This word should appear immediately after the modifier.*

dangling modifier: `Listening for the telephone, the doorbell rang.` (Listening for the telephone underlined)

explanation: Because there is no word for *listening for the telephone* to refer to, the phrase is a dangling modifier. The sentence indicates that the doorbell listened for the telephone.

correction: `Listening for the telephone, I heard the doorbell ring.`

explanation: The word *I* is placed immediately after the modifier as a word the modifier can logically refer to.

A second way to eliminate a dangling modifier is to rewrite the modifier as a subordinate clause (see page 98).

dangling modifier: <u>Jogging along the side of the road</u>, a car splashed me with mud.

explanation: Because there is no word for *jogging along the side of the road* to refer to, the phrase is a dangling modifier. The sense of the sentence is that the car did the jogging.

correction: While I was jogging along the side of the road, a car splashed me with mud.

explanation: The modifier is rewritten as a subordinate clause to eliminate the dangling modifier.

As the above examples illustrate, dangling modifiers often occur when sentences begin with an *-ing* verb form (present participle). However, a dangling modifier can also occur when a sentence begins with an *-ed, -en, -n,* or *-t* verb form (past participle) or when it begins with the present-tense verb form used with *to* (infinitive).

dangling modifier (present participle): <u>While rocking the baby</u>, the cat purred contentedly.

correction: While rocking the baby, I heard the cat purr contentedly.

correction: While I was rocking the baby the cat purred contentedly.

dangling modifier (past participle): <u>Tired from the day's work</u>, weariness overcame me.

correction: Tired from the day's work, I was overcome with weariness.

correction: Because I was tired from the day's work, weariness overcame me.

dangling modifier (infinitive): <u>To excel in sports</u>, much practice is needed.

correction: To excel in sports, a person needs much practice.

correction: If a person wants to excel in sports, much practice is needed.

EXERCISE

Dangling Modifiers

Rewrite the following sentences to eliminate the dangling modifiers.

1. Feeling it was too late to apologize, the disagreement was never resolved.
2. While sitting at the drive-in movie, shooting stars could be seen in the clear night sky.
3. Climbing across the pasture fence, Peter's pants were torn in two places.
4. To understand the latest computer technology, these courses should be taken.
5. Faced with the possibility of suspension, studying became more attractive to me.
6. When listening to the stereo, cleaning the apartment does not seem so hard.
7. To get to class on time, my alarm is set for 6:00 A.M.
8. Struggling to earn enough money to pay next term's tuition, the job came along just in time.
9. To study in quiet surroundings, the library is the best place to go.
10. After ending the relationship with Carl, loneliness was Anita's biggest problem.

MISPLACED MODIFIERS

A **misplaced modifier** is positioned too far away from the word it describes. The result is an unclear, silly, or illogical sentence.

misplaced modifier: The strolling musicians played while we were eating dinner softly.

explanation: The modifier *softly* is intended to describe *played.* However, the modifier is too far removed from that word, so *softly* seems to describe *were eating.*

To correct a sentence with a misplaced modifier, move the modifier as close as possible to the word it describes.

The strolling musicians played softly while we were eating dinner.

A misplaced modifier can be a word, a phrase, or a clause:

misplaced modifier (word): There must be something wrong with this cookie recipe, for it <u>only</u> requires a half-cup of sugar. [Placement of *only* indicates no other ingredients are needed.]

correction: There must be something wrong with this cookie recipe, for it requires <u>only</u> a half-cup of sugar.

misplaced modifier (phrase): Across the street, <u>playing far too wildly</u>, we saw the young children. [The phrase seems to describe *we*.]

correction: Across the street we saw the young children <u>playing far too wildly.</u>

misplaced modifier (clause): We brought the rubber tree into the house <u>which was at least 8 feet tall</u>. [The clause seems to describe the house.]

correction: We brought the rubber tree, which was at least 8 feet tall, into the house.

EXERCISE

Misplaced Modifiers

Rewrite the following sentences to eliminate the misplaced modifiers.

1. The mattress was built for people with bad backs with extra firmness.
2. Most viewers have misinterpreted the significance of the president's State of the Union address completely.
3. The Chevrolet's muffler fell off after we turned the corner with a loud bang.
4. Kathleen sold her bike to a neighbor with stripped gears for $25.
5. The little girl wore a flower in her hair that had pink petals.
6. We were fortunate to get a cabin by the lake with three bedrooms.
7. The child ran after the ball pulling the rusty wagon down the street.
8. The old car raced down the street with its muffler dragging.
9. The missing wallet was finally found by my aunt Norma under the couch.
10. Turning to go, Lee waved to the gang in the van listening to the stereo.

CHAPTER 22

Editing for Punctuation

Punctuation marks aid communication because they signal where ideas end, how ideas relate to one another, which ideas are emphasized, which ideas are downplayed, and which ideas are expressed in someone's spoken words. Most of the time, specific rules govern the placement of punctuation, and experienced readers will expect you to follow those rules.

THE COMMA (,)

Writers who do not know the comma rules tend to place commas wherever they pause in speech. However, listening for pauses is not always a reliable way to place commas, so if you have not yet learned the rules, study the next pages carefully.

Commas with Items in a Series

A **series** is three or more words, phrases, or clauses. Use commas to separate each item in the series.

words in a series: The gardener sprayed the <u>grass, trees</u>, and <u>shrubs</u> with pesticide.

phrases in a series: George Washington was <u>first in war, first in peace</u>, and <u>first in the hearts of his countrymen</u>.

clauses in a series: Before his first day of school, <u>Shonda took her kindergartner on a tour of the school, she introduced him to the principal, and she bought him school supplies.</u>

If the items in the series are separated by *and* or *or*, do not use a comma.

```
The only vegetables Harry will eat are carrots or broccoli or
corn.
```

Some writers omit the comma after the last item in the series, but you should get in the habit of using the comma to avoid misreading.

EXERCISE

Commas with Items in a Series

Place commas where they are needed in the following sentences. One sentence is already correct.

1. The vacation brochure promised us fun relaxation and excitement.
2. The trouble with the mayor is that she does not delegate responsibility she does not manage city finances well and she does not work well with city council members.
3. Before you leave, clean your room and sweep the downstairs and take out the trash.
4. The instructor explained that the class could write a paper on a childhood memory on a decision recently made or on a favorite teacher.
5. When you edit, be sure to check spelling punctuation and capitalization.

Commas with Introductory Elements

Elements placed before the subject are usually followed by a comma.

1. An introductory subordinate clause is followed by a comma (see also p. 101).

```
Although she promised to meet me for lunch, Caroline never
arrived at the restaurant.
```

2. Introductory phrases are followed by a comma.

```
By the end of the first half of the tournament, our team had
won nine games.
```

3. Introductory adverbs are followed by a comma. (See also page 120.)

```
Reluctantly, Mr. Simpson told his oldest employee that he was
selling his business.

Quickly yet cautiously, the store detective moved in on the
suspected shoplifter.
```

4. You may omit the comma after a very brief opener.

```
Unfortunately, the midterm exam grades were lower than
expected.
```

or

```
Unfortunately the midterm exam grades were lower than
expected.
```

EXERCISE

Commas with Introductory Elements

Insert commas in the following sentences where they are needed.

1. When Sherry arrived at the resort she was disappointed to find that there were no rooms available.
2. When he was 20 he believed that everything would always work out for the best.
3. Very slowly and silently the deer moved toward the water hole.
4. As a result of the devastating heat wave the death toll rose to 108.
5. Frequently we accuse others of the behavior we dislike most in ourselves.
6. After we checked to be sure all the doors were locked we left the beach house until next summer.
7. During the long, bleak evenings of winter a cozy fire in the fireplace is especially welcome.
8. At the time of the space shuttle's arrival the heavy crosswinds had finally died down.
9. Lovingly the young mother stroked her new daughter's chubby cheek.
10. Hastily the 6-year-old wiped the telltale signs of strawberry jam from the corners of his mouth.

Commas to Set Off Nouns of Direct Address

The names of those directly addressed are set off with commas.

```
Dorrie, you must get ready for school now.
Get away from that hamburger, you mangy dog.
If you ask me, Juan, we should turn left.
```

EXERCISE

Commas to Set Off Nouns of Direct Address

Supply commas to set off the nouns of address.

1. Ben help me carry the groceries into the house.
2. You know Son it's too cold to be outside without a jacket.
3. Friends may I have your attention please?
4. Heidi make sure you give fresh seed and water to the bird.
5. Can you help me with my math tonight Alice?

Commas with Nonessential Elements

Nonessential elements are words, phrases, and clauses that do not limit or restrict the meaning of the words they refer to. In other words, nonessential elements are not necessary for clear identification of what they refer to.

nonessential element: `Uncle Ralph, who has been on the police force 20 years, believes handgun legislation is the key to reducing violent crime.`

explanation: *Who has been on the police force 20 years* is nonessential because the person it refers to (Uncle Ralph) is already clearly identified.

essential element: `The student who wins the state finals in speech will get $1000.`

explanation: *Who wins the state finals in speech* is necessary for identifying which student will win $1000; therefore, it is an essential element.

1. Use commas to set off nonessential clauses.

`Sara Summers, who is a senior, was voted president of senior council.`

`My roommate collects beer cans, which she stacks against the wall.`

but

`Dr. Kingsley is a person whose opinion I respect. (Clause is essential.)`

2. Use commas to set off nonessential phrases.

The sparrows, hunting for food in the snow, sensed the cat's approach and took off suddenly.

but

The child playing in the sandbox is my nephew. (Phrase is essential.)

3. Use commas to set off nonessential appositives. An **appositive** is a word or word group that renames the noun it follows.

nonessential appositive: My brother, an investment banker, makes $200,000 a year. (*An investment banker* renames *my brother,* so it is an appositive. However, since it is not necessary for identification, commas are used.)

essential appositive: My son the doctor is not as happy as my son the actor. (*The doctor* is an appositive renaming *my son,* and *the actor* is an appositive renaming the second *my son.* In both cases the appositives are essential for identifying which son is referred to, so no commas are used.)

EXERCISE

Commas with Nonessential Elements

Place commas where they are needed in the following sentences.

1. My father who worked for the Bell System for over 30 years has made many sacrifices for me.
2. A Democratic city councilperson who supports his party will try to support the policies of a Democratic mayor.
3. The Luray Caverns which I visited this year are a breathtaking sight.
4. A blue wool suit sporting brass buttons and a classic, traditional cut is always in style.
5. The Empire State Building once the tallest building in the world still dominates the New York City skyline.
6. Dale Norris a brilliant teacher will retire next month.

Commas with Interrupters

Interrupters are words and phrases that "interrupt" the flow of a sentence; they function more as side remarks than as integral parts of sentences. Sometimes transitions interrupt flow and are considered interrupters, which is why the following partial list of interrupters includes some transitions.

`in a manner of speaking`	`after all`
`as a matter of fact`	`in fact`
`to tell the truth`	`in the first place`
`it seems to me`	`to say the least`
`for example`	`consequently`
`by all means`	`of course`

Interrupters are usually set off with commas. However, commas may be omitted after short interrupters coming at the beginning of sentences.

commas used: `The students' behavior at the concert,` <u>`it seems to me`</u>`, was exemplary.`

comma omitted for short introductory interrupter: <u>`Of course`</u> `not everyone shares my concern about this issue.`

comma for short interrupter: <u>`Of course`</u>`, not everyone shares my concern for this issue.`

EXERCISE

Commas with Interrupters

Where appropriate, set off the interrupters with commas in the following sentences.

1. The children it seems will always find something to complain about.
2. As a matter of fact the lamp needs a larger-watt bulb.
3. This report I feel is inadequately prepared.
4. The customer insists for example that the ten-speed bike was never properly assembled.
5. However I am not convinced this is the right time to begin our fundraising project.

Commas with Main Clauses

1. When two main clauses are connected with a coordinating conjunction *(and, but, or, nor, for, so, yet),* place a comma before the conjunction (see also page 100).

The match was over, <u>but</u> the spectators refused to leave.

The garden was heavily fertilized, <u>so</u> the yield of vegetables was even higher than expected.

2. Do not use a comma before a coordinating conjunction linking two elements that are not main clauses.

no: Michael asked for my forgiveness, and promised to try harder.

yes: Michael asked for my forgiveness and promised to try harder.

EXERCISE

Commas with Main Clauses

Place commas where needed in the following sentences.

1. Janice had been rejected many times yet she retained her sense of humor and her cheerful disposition.
2. The water department explained that the pipe to the house was broken and we would have to assume the cost of fixing it.
3. Jacob wanted to fly to Montana but Betty Jo had always wanted to drive across country.
4. The students were lazy and insolent so the instructor assigned them extra pages to study.
5. Karen fastened red bows to the lampposts for the holiday season was fast approaching.

Commas between Coordinate Modifiers, Commas for Clarity, and Commas to Separate Contrasting Elements

1. **Coordinate modifiers** are two or more modifiers referring equally to the same word. Commas separate such modifiers when they are not already separated by *and* or *but*. (If the order of the modifiers can be reversed or if *and* can be used to join the modifiers, they are coordinate and should be separated with a comma.)

An <u>expensive, well-tailored</u> suit is a necessary investment for a young executive. [Order of modifiers can be reversed: a well-tailored, expensive suit.]

They ate their picnic lunch under the <u>blossoming apple</u> tree. (<u>And</u> cannot be used between the modifiers, nor can the order be reversed.)

She is certainly a happy and carefree person. [No comma because and is used.]

2. Sometimes a comma is necessary for clarity, to prevent misreading of a sentence.

For Easter, lilies are the most popular flower. (Without the comma, a reader might read the first three words as a single phrase.)

3. Commas set off an element that contrasts sharply with what comes before it.

Lee is only lazy, not stupid.

EXERCISE **Commas with Coordinate Modifiers, Commas for Clarity, and Commas with Contrasting Elements**

Place commas where needed in the following sentences.

1. The muddy rough course was made even worse by the two-day downpour.
2. Ohio State's noisy enthusiastic Pep Club congregated in the middle section of the bleachers.
3. The twins were young not inexperienced.
4. Many new songwriters use concrete visual images to set a mood.
5. The rough manuscript is promising although rambling.
6. Of all spectator sports fans seem to enjoy football most.

When Not to Use the Comma

Below are some cautions about when *not* to use commas.

1. Do not use a comma to separate a subject and verb.

no: The governor-elect, promised to work to change the way public education is funded in our state.

yes: The governor-elect promised to work to change the way public education is funded in our state.

2. Do not use a comma between a preposition and its object.

no: The United States has a government of, the people.

yes: The United States has a government of the people.

3. Do not use a comma between a verb and its object.

no: Carl smacked, the ball out of the park.

yes: Carl smacked the ball out of the park.

4. Do not use a comma between a verb and its complement.

no: Louise will become, a concert pianist if she continues to study.

yes: Louise will become a concert pianist if she continues to study.

5. Do not use a comma after a coordinating conjunction linking main clauses.

no: I have tried to understand Juan but, his behavior continues to puzzle me.

yes: I have tried to understand Juan, but his behavior continues to puzzle me.

6. Do not use a comma before the first item or after the last item in a series.

no: The math test covered, improper fractions, common denominators, and, mixed fractions.

yes: The math test covered improper fractions, common denominators, and mixed fractions.

6. Do not use a comma between a modifier and the word it modifies.

no: The frayed, curtains must be replaced.

yes: The frayed curtains must be replaced.

7. Do not use a comma after *such as* or *like.*

no: Kurt believes in some unusual ideas such as, reincarnation, transmigration, and mental telepathy.

yes: Kurt believes in some unusual ideas, such as reincarnation, transmigration, and mental telepathy.

no: `Medical technology students must take difficult courses like, physiology, biochemistry, and pharmacology.`

yes: `Medical technology students must take difficult courses like physiology, biochemistry, and pharmacology.`

8. Do not use a comma between *that* and a direct quotation.

no: `The school board president said that, "we are considering a ten-month school year."`

yes: `The school board president said that "we are considering a ten-month school year."`

EXERCISE

Using Commas

Place commas where needed in the following sentences. You will need to draw on all the comma rules discussed in this chapter. (Not all sentences require commas.)

1. Jimmy the janitor said to pick up the paper in the halls.
2. Carlotta go get the newspaper from the front porch roof.
3. I will take a small perfect carnation and a snapdragon for my mom's birthday bouquet.
4. Angelo wanted to play kickball but Harry wanted to play baseball.
5. Joey and Matt by the way are excellent baseball players.
6. Although the season has just begun Matt has hit four home runs this year.
7. Joey as a matter of fact pitched his first no-hitter this season.
8. On the other hand Jeremy had made more errors than anybody in the whole league.
9. It seems to me that we worry about problems before they even occur.
10. My dad takes care of the yard, cleans the pool, coaches a Pony League baseball team and still he works at a full-time job.
11. In order to stay in good condition the wide redwood deck requires a preservative stain every year.
12. The old leather chair with the matching footstool is soft and comfortable.
13. Before the heat wave we all longed for some sunshine but now we badly need rain.
14. Your novel which will be published in the fall shows promise.
15. My instructor an expert in urban affairs is an adviser to our state senator.
16. Before every race, Carla eats a light meal takes a nap and meditates.

THE SEMICOLON (;)

1. A **semicolon** separates two main clauses when they are not linked by a coordinating conjunction.

The canvas raft floated near the edge of the pool; it was pushed by a gentle summer breeze.

The old uniforms were worn by the A team; the B team wore new ones.

2. Use a semicolon before a conjunctive adverb that joins two main clauses. Here is a list of conjunctive adverbs:

also	however	thus
besides	instead	meanwhile
nonetheless	therefore	certainly
likewise	then	nevertheless
next	furthermore	similarly
subsequently	still	consequently
moreover	indeed	finally

When you join two main clauses with a semicolon and conjunctive adverb, place a comma after the conjunctive adverb.

The car I want to buy is a real bargain; <u>furthermore</u>, the bank is offering me an excellent financing rate.

The test grades were low; <u>consequently</u>, Dr. Barnes agreed to let us retake the exam.

3. For clarity, a semicolon separates items in a series that already contains commas.

The following sun-belt cities have experienced phenomenal growth in the past five years: Las Vegas, Nevada; Phoenix, Arizona; and Orlando, Florida.

EXERCISE

Semicolons

Place semicolons where they are appropriate in the following sentences.

1. The ideal football player is dedicated, for he must work long, hard hours intelligent, for the game is very much one of strategy and physically tough, for he must endure a great deal of punishment.

2. The hand-tied rope hammock was made to hold the weight of two people it was the hook that broke sending Christie and Jim crashing to the ground.
3. The quarterback hesitated for an instant then he passed the ball to the wide receiver, who waited in the end zone.
4. College can create anxiety because of the pressure for grades, which is unceasing the concern for future job opportunity, which is always present and the uncertainties that come from life away from home, which are most unnerving of all.
5. We tried for two hours to start the car finally we gave up and started the long trek back to town.
6. The trip was canceled because of the snow storm however, it has been rescheduled for next weekend.

THE COLON (:)

Use a colon after a main clause to introduce a word, phrase, or clause that explains or particularizes.

Colon to introduce a phrase that particularizes: Five occupations were represented in the union membership: secretaries, data processors, maintenance workers, cafeteria workers, and bookkeepers.

Colon to introduce a word that explains: Rick writes soap opera scripts for one reason: money.

Colon to introduce a clause that explains: All Terry's efforts were directed toward one goal: she wanted to learn how to skydive.

Do not use a colon between a verb and its object or complement or between a preposition and its object.

colon: The following students will compete in the debate: David Haynes, Lorenzo Ruiz, and Clara Jakes.

no colon: The students who will compete in the debate are David Haynes, Lorenzo Ruiz, and Clara Jakes.

colon: I am afraid of these: heights, small rooms, and water.

no colon: I am afraid of heights, small rooms, and water.

EXERCISE **Colons**

Place colons where appropriate in the following sentences. (Not all sentences require a colon.)

1. My courses for next semester are these political science, algebra, biology, and Advanced Composition I.
2. The basket overflowed with fresh fruit peaches, grapes, apples, and bananas.
3. Mr. Grantley seems to have one mission in life making everyone around him miserable.
4. There are complicated reasons for our company's poor safety record we do not supply incentives for employees to exercise more care on the job, our safety equipment is obsolete and ineffective, and we don't require enough proper training for new employees.
5. I knew that success in my journalism class would require curiosity, energy, and writing skill.
6. Of all the distance runners, only one seems to run effortlessly Mark.

THE DASH (—)

A **dash,** formed on the typewriter or word processor with two hyphens, indicates a pause for emphasis or dramatic effect. It should be used sparingly and thoughtfully so that its emphatic or dramatic quality is not weakened by overuse. Often dashes can be used in place of commas, semicolons, colons, or parentheses; the mark used depends on the effect you want to create.

`Jake told me--I can't believe it--that he would rather stay at home than go to Las Vegas.` (Parentheses may also be used.)

`I know why Tony's bike disappeared--it was stolen from the backyard.` (Semicolon or colon may also be used.)

`Vinnie is 35--although he won't admit it.` (A comma may also be used.)

EXERCISE **The Dash**

Place dashes where appropriate in the following sentences.

1. The new Corvette red, shiny, and powerful was just the thing to make her friends drool.
2. Certain members of this family I won't mention any names are going to lose their allowances if they don't start doing their chores.

3. My history professor at least he calls himself a professor is the most boring teacher on campus.
4. I have only one comment to make about your room yuk!
5. There is a very obvious solution to your school problems study.

PARENTHESES ( )

1. Parentheses enclose elements you want to downplay. Often parentheses signal a side comment or incidental remark.

```
Louise Rodriguez (you remember her) has been elected president
of the Women's Action Council.

When I was in college (over 20 years ago), composition was
taught very differently.
```

Commas or dashes often set off material that could also be enclosed in parentheses. However, commas and dashes will emphasize the material, whereas parentheses will deemphasize it.

parentheses deemphasize: `This week's lottery prize (an incredible $12 million) will be split between two winners.`

dashes emphasize: `This week's lottery prize--an incredible $12 million--will be split between two winners.`

commas give more emphasis than parentheses but less than dashes: `This week's lottery prize, an incredible $12 million, will be split between two winners.`

2. Do not place a comma before the element enclosed in parentheses.

no: `Most of the class, (easily 30 of us) felt the test was too long to complete in an hour.`

yes: `Most of the class (easily 30 of us) felt the test was too long to complete in an hour.`

3. A comma or end mark of punctuation is placed *outside* the closing parenthesis.

```
The new parking deck is an imposing structure (it has 15
levels), but it has a serious drawback (people have trouble
finding their cars in it).
```

4. Use a period and capital letter with a complete sentence enclosed in parentheses if the sentence is not interrupting another sentence.

no: `After three days (Most of us wondered what took so long.) the winners were announced.`

yes: `After three days the winners were announced. (Most of us wondered what took so long.)`

yes: `After three days (most of us wondered what took so long) the winners were announced.`

5. Parentheses can enclose numbers and letters in a list of items.

```
The Citizens' Coalition has three reservations about endorsing
Smith for mayor: (1) she is inexperienced, (2) she opposes
increasing city taxes, and (3) she has no clear position on
minority hiring practices.
```

Because numbers in a list can distract a reader, writers generally try to avoid them.

```
The Citizens' Coalition has three reservations about endorsing
Smith for mayor: she is inexperienced, she opposes increasing
city taxes, and she has no clear position on minority hiring
practices.
```

EXERCISE

Parentheses

Place parentheses where they are appropriate in the following sentences.

1. The police officer gave David a ticket he was traveling 50 miles per hour in a school zone.
2. Recent reports indicate that fewer workers are smoking probably because of increased awareness of the health hazards.
3. Sales of computers particularly those with extensive word processing capabilities are at an all-time high.
4. At Debby and Antonio's wedding what a fiasco Antonio forgot the ring, Debby tripped on the hem of her dress, the best man was late, the caterer served undercooked chicken, and the band played so loudly that everyone got a headache.
5. Lee's favorite meal scrambled eggs, spaghetti, and corn disgusts most people.

THE APOSTROPHE (')

The apostrophe is used most frequently to show possession. It is also used to form contractions and certain kinds of plurals.

The Apostrophe to Show Possession

The apostrophe is used with nouns and certain indefinite pronouns (see page 428 for an explanation of indefinite pronouns) to signal possession.

1. To form the possessive of a noun or indefinite pronoun that does not end in *s*, add an apostrophe and an *s*.

apartment + 's

The apartment's bedroom is much too small.

anybody + 's

Anybody's help would be appreciated.

women + 's

The university has agreed to fund a library for women's studies.

2. To form the possessive of a singular noun that ends in *s*, add an apostrophe and an *s*.

Charles + 's

Charles's stolen car was found across town.

business + 's

The business's stock climbed three points.

3. To form the possessive of a plural noun that ends in *s*, add just the apostrophe.

governors + '

The five governors' council on aging will examine the issue of adequate health care.

4. To show joint possession of one thing, use an apostrophe only with the last noun. To show individual ownership, use an apostrophe with every noun.

Manuel and Louise's committee report was thorough and clear. (One report belonging to both Manuel and Louise.)

Jason's and Helen's financial problems can be solved with better money management. (Jason and Helen have separate financial problems.)

5. To show possession with a hyphenated word, use the apostrophe only with the last element of the word.

The editor-in-chief's salary was cut in half after the magazine's circulation decreased dramatically.

I have planned a surprise party to celebrate my mother-in-law's sixtieth birthday.

6. Do not use apostrophes with possessive pronouns *(its, whose, hers, his, ours, yours, theirs).*

incorrect: The expensive vase fell from it's shelf and shattered.

correct: The expensive vase fell from its shelf and shattered.

incorrect: The book that is missing is her's.

correct: The book that is missing is hers.

The Apostrophe to Indicate Missing Letters or Numbers and for Some Plurals

1. A **contraction** is formed when two words are joined and one or more letters are omitted. In a contraction the apostrophe stands for the missing letter or letters. Here are some common contractions; notice that the apostrophe appears where the letter or letters are omitted.

isn't (is not)	we'll (we will)
hasn't (has not)	who's (who is or who has)
they're (they are)	that's (that is, or that has)
we're (we are)	she'll (she will)
haven't (have not)	it's (it is or it has)
I'll (I will)	shouldn't (should not)

2. When you reproduce dialect or casual speech, use the apostrophe for missing letters in words that are not contractions.

`add 'em up` (add them up)

`sugar 'n' spice` (sugar and spice)

`ma'am` (madam)

3. The apostrophe stands for missing numbers.

`The class of '67 will hold its annual reunion the day after Thanksgiving.` (The apostrophe stands for the missing *19*.)

4. The apostrophe and an *s* form the plural of letters, numbers, and words meant to be taken as words themselves.

`If I get any more` <u>`D's`</u>`, I will lose my scholarship.`

`How many` <u>`t's`</u> `are in omit?`

`Mark makes his` <u>`3's`</u> `backwards.`

`Janice is too polite; I am tired of all her` <u>`yes sir's`</u> `and` <u>`no ma'am's`</u>`.`

NOTE: Underline letters, numbers, and words used as terms. In printed copy, these words may be set in italics.

EXERCISE

Apostrophes

Use apostrophes where they are needed in the following sentences. In some sentences, you will need to add an apostrophe and an <u>s</u>.

1. The panel awarding the scholarships spoke to several instructors about the three finalists grades and motivation.
2. In 85, my sister-in-laws German shepherd saved the life of a 5-year-old by dragging the sleeping child from her burning bedroom.
3. I can never read Harrys writing because his *os* look like *as*.
4. No one thought that Al and Janets business would do so well in its first 3 months of operation.
5. Todays women still dont earn equal pay for equal work, but in some ways womens lot has improved.
6. Charles older sister is encouraging him to major in computer science, but he isn't sure he wants to.
7. The hot dog vendor bellowed, "Get em while theyre hot."
8. Recent studies confirm that televisions effects on childrens attention spans should be a source of concern.

9. When I graduated in 70, students social consciousness was at an all-time high.
10. Lois new car must be a lemon, because its engine is not running well, and its been in the shop three times in a month.

QUOTATION MARKS (“ ”)

1. Quotation marks are most frequently used to enclose the exact words somebody spoke or wrote. For information on this use of quotation marks see page 157 and page 378.

2. Use quotation marks to enclose the titles of short published works (poems, short stories, essays, and articles from periodicals). Titles of longer, full-length works (books, magazines, and newspapers) are underlined in type and italicized in print.

> "To His Coy Mistress" is my favorite poem, and The Sun Also Rises is my favorite novel.

Do not use quotation marks or underlining for unpublished titles, including the titles of your own writings.

3. Use quotation marks around words used in a special sense.

> Your "humor" is not funny.

EXERCISE **Quotation Marks**

Add quotation marks where needed in the following sentences.

1. Be sure to read The Rime of the Ancient Mariner on page 99 of your poetry anthology.
2. Tell me the whole story, I said to Linda.
3. I always worry when my mother tries to fix me up with a date who has a nice personality.
4. Chapter 1, Idea Generation, is the most important chapter in the writing book.
5. Your frugal ways are costing me money.

THE HYPHEN (-)

1. If a word is too long to fit at the end of a line, use a hyphen to divide the word between syllables. If you are unsure of the correct syllable break, check your dictionary. (Never divide a one-syllable word.)

```
Duane hired a clown, a magician, and an acro-
bat to perform at his daughter's birthday party.
```

2. Use a hyphen between two or more words used to form an adjective or noun.

```
high-interest loan    state-of-the-art computer
low-cost mortgage     sister-in-law
```

The exception to this rule is: Do not use a hyphen with an *ly* adverb.

```
lowly freshman    badly reviewed play
```

3. Use a hyphen with the prefixes *all-*, *ex-*, and *self-*.

```
all-inclusive    ex-husband    self-starter
```

CHAPTER 23

Editing for Mechanics

CAPITALIZATION

Below are rules governing the most frequent uses of capital letters. In addition, if you are unsure whether to capitalize a word, you can consult a dictionary.

Capitalize proper nouns and adjectives derived from them.

1. Capitalize proper names of people and animals.

Harry	Rover
Joe Popovich	Einstein

2. Capitalize names of nationalities, languages, and races.

American	Asian	Chinese art
Spanish	Italian architecture	French cooking

3. Capitalize names of specific countries, states, regions, places, bodies of water, and so on.

Minnesota	Crandall Park	North Pole
Zimbabwe	Trumbull County	Fourth Avenue
Lake Huron	Europe	Brooklyn

Do not capitalize: the park, the beach, a large city, the town hall

4. Capitalize proper names and titles that precede them but not general terms.

Judge Walters	Uncle Don
Prime Minister Gandhi	Grandpa Johnson
Professor Kline	President Bush

Do not capitalize: the judge, a president, the chairman

5. Capitalize words designating family relationships only when these are not preceded by a possessive pronoun or article.

Grandma Moses	Mom (as in I asked Mom to come along.)
Aunt Donna	Cousin Ralph

Do not capitalize: my uncle, his aunt, her mom

6. Capitalize specific brand names but not the type of product.

Coca-Cola	Colgate
Crisco	Nike

Do not capitalize: soda pop, toothpaste, oil, tennis shoes

7. Capitalize directions when they refer to specific geographic regions.

the Midwest	the Middle East	the South
the East Coast	the Pacific Northwest	the North

Do not capitalize: east on I-680, 3 miles south, the northern part of the state

8. Capitalize specific courses titles and all language courses.

History 101	Intermediate Calculus
French	English

Do not capitalize studies which do not name specific courses: math class, chemistry, drama

9. Capitalize the names of ships, planes, and spacecraft.

the Enterprise	the Challenger
the Queen Elizabeth	the Titanic

10. Capitalize the names of specific buildings, institutions, and businesses.

the Empire State Building	South Bend Water Department
Chrysler Corporation	Harvard University

11. Capitalize names of religions, sacred books, and words that refer to God.

the Almighty	Jewish	the Koran
Moslem	the Holy Bible	Buddha
Jesus Christ	Catholic	Jehovah
the Old Testament	the Scriptures	Mohammed
Christianity	Protestantism	the Trinity

12. Capitalize modifiers derived from proper nouns.

French accent	Renaissance art
Georgian hospitality	Shakespearean comedy

13. Capitalize the first and last word of a title; in between capitalize everything except articles, short prepositions, and short conjunctions.

Star Wars	Of Mice and Men
The Grapes of Wrath	The Last of the Mohicans
The Sun Also Rises	The Sound and the Fury

NOTE: For discussions of capitalization rules for direct quotation, see page 157 and page 378.

EXERCISE

Capitalization

Capitalize where necessary in the following sentences.

1. Jessica lived in the south all her life.
2. When Mrs. Torres read *Gone with the wind,* she became fascinated with the old south.
3. One of our most unpopular presidents was president Nixon.
4. After my mother died, my aunt raised my sister and me.
5. When professor Blake entered the room, his sociology 505 class became quiet.
6. The Monongahela and Allegheny rivers flow into the Ohio river.
7. The Republican party's presidential nominee will be the incumbent president.
8. Most people believe that the first day of spring is march 21st.
9. Davy Crockett, a confirmed westerner, spent several years as a congressman living in washington.

10. Learning french was very difficult for harry.
11. Of all the fast-food restaurants, burger king is aunt Mandy's favorite.
12. The national centers for disease control, at its Atlanta headquarters, announced its findings on Legionnaire's disease.
13. Lovers of jazz acknowledge that miles davis was the world's finest jazz trumpeter.
14. Designed by frank lloyd wright, falling water has been acclaimed for its unique structure and its harmonious coexistence with the natural beauty that surrounds it.
15. The Golden Gate bridge is a modern architectural wonder.

UNDERLINING AND ITALICS

Material that is machine-printed in **italics** (slanted type) is underlined in handwriting and typewriter type.

1. Underline or italicize the titles of full-length works (books, magazines, newspapers, plays, television series, and movies). However, do not underline or italicize unpublished titles, including the titles of your own works.

```
Animal Dreams is the last novel I read, and
Phantom of the Opera is the last play I saw.
```

Shorter works, such as poems, and parts of longer works, such as magazine articles, appear in quotation marks. (See page 468.)

2. Underline or italicize foreign words and phrases.

```
Enrico graduated magna cum laude.
```

3. Underline or italicize words, letters, and numbers used as words.

```
Your 3's look like B's to me.
```

4. Underline or italicize words or phrases that you want to emphasize.

```
What do you mean, we have a problem?
```

EXERCISE **Underlining and Italics**

Add underlining where necessary in the following sentences.

1. The company president wants to build an esprit de corps among white collar and blue collar workers.

2. As both a book and movie, Schindler's List is powerful.
3. You forgot to cross the t's in tattoo.
4. What does politically correct mean to you?
5. I Love Lucy and The Dick Van Dyke Show are classic television comedies.

ABBREVIATIONS AND NUMBERS

1. Use A.M. (a.m.) and P.M. (p.m.) for exact times of day. Either uppercase or lowercase is acceptable; just be consistent.

```
We left home at 6:30 A.M. and arrived at 7:00 P.M.
```

2. Use A.D. before the year and B.C. after the year.

```
The artifact is dated 50 B.C., but it is similar to items
dated A.D. 500.
```

3. Do not use periods with abbreviations of common terms.

```
FBI     CIA     NATO
AT&T    UFO     MTV
```

4. Some titles come before a person's name, and some come after.

```
Ms. Jenkins              Mr. Hank DuBos
Dr. Louise Garcia        Louise Garcia, MD
Vincent Minelli, CPA     Mrs. Atwood
```

Ordinarily, do not use titles both before *and* after a person's name.

no: Professor Lee Morrison, Ph.D.

yes: Professor Lee Morrison

yes: Lee Morrison, Ph.D.

5. Use *U.S.* as a modifier and *United States* all other times.

```
The U.S. ski team did well in the olympics.
The United States has a huge national debt.
```

6. Do not abbreviate place names, except in addresses.

no: `The Metropolitan Museum of Art in N.Y. has over a million exhibits.`

yes: `The Metropolitan Museum of Art in New York has over a million exhibits.`

7. Avoid *etc.* in humanities writing. Use *and so on, and so forth, and the like* instead. Never use *and etc.*

8. Although publishers often fail to do so, you should use words rather than numbers for anything that can be written in one or two words. Two-word numbers between 21 and 99 are hyphenated. Numbers that require three or more words are written with numerals (a hyphenated number is one word). Finally, any number that opens a sentence should be written with words.

```
eighteen    fourth    twenty-five    1,503    one-third
```

9. Use numerals for measurements, time, addresses, page numbers, decimals, and percentages.

```
5 A.M.            2 feet 3 inches    page 3
100 Oak Street    15 percent         1.5 ounces
```

EXERCISE

Abbreviations and Numbers

Correct any problems with abbreviations and numbers.

1. 3 of my best friends have job interviews with I.B.M.
2. At 8:00 pm, we left for Cooks Forest with Dr. Joshua Schwartz, MD.
3. The Centers for Disease Control in Atlanta, GA is aggressively researching the origin of a new strain of virus.
4. Here in the U.S., 1/4 of all women are victims of abuse.
5. People between 30 and 45 now make up one-third of the student body of this campus.

APPENDIX 1

Solving Writing Problems

Some of the most frequently occurring writing problems are listed for you below, along with strategies for solving these problems. If you get stuck, consult this list for a solution to your problem. However, since no one can guarantee that any technique will provide results, what appears below is a selection of strategies that *may* help.

1. *If you have trouble coming up with ideas:*
   a. Try a prewriting technique you have never used before (see Chapter 1).
   b. Leave your writing and think about your topic while you are doing other things. Keep a notebook with you so that you can jot down ideas as they occur to you.
   c. Think about what people who disagree with you might say. Use the counters to these opinions as your departure point.
   d. Have someone ask you questions about your topic (or draft, if you have one). Your answers can supply supporting detail.
   e. If you have a draft but need additional detail, go through the draft and check-mark every generalization that is inadequately supported. Then go back and develop these generalizations with one or more examples.
2. *If you have trouble identifying an audience:*
   a. Ask yourself who would benefit from reading an essay on your topic.
   b. Use someone who would disagree with you as your audience.
   c. Write to someone in authority with the power to act in accordance with the ideas in your essay.
   d. Write to the "average, general reader"—someone who knows something about your topic, but less than you do.
   e. Ask yourself who would be interested in an essay about your topic.
3. *If you have trouble establishing your purpose:*
   a. Ask yourself, "What can I accomplish with this writing?"
   b. Ask yourself, "What would I like to accomplish with this writing?"

   c. Decide whether you want to share something with your reader, inform your reader about something, or persuade your reader to act or think a certain way.
4. *If you have trouble organizing your ideas:*
   a. Try one of the outlining techniques you have not used yet (see Chapter 3).
   b. Ask yourself whether your ideas seem to follow a chronological, spatial, cause-and-effect, or progressive order.
   c. Write your draft without an outline and see what happens. When the draft is complete, check for logical ordering, and if there is a problem, number your ideas in the way you think they should appear.
   d. Check to see if instead of an organization problem, you really only lack transitional devices that signal how your ideas relate to one another and flow one to the next (see Chapter 4).
5. *If you have trouble getting your first draft down:*
   a. Skip your introduction and begin with your first body paragraph. You can write your introduction later.
   b. Select one idea—one you know the most about or feel most comfortable with—and write up that point in its own body paragraph.
   c. Write your draft as you would speak your ideas to a close friend, or write the draft as a letter to a friend.
   d. Go back to the prewriting stage and generate more ideas; you may not have enough material yet to begin a draft.
   e. Write your draft as a form of freewriting, going from start to finish without stopping and without evaluating your work. Feel free to ramble, write silly notions, and even write the alphabet when you are stuck—you can refine later; for now just get something down to work with.
   f. Consider reshaping your topic to something easier to write about.
   g. Leave your work for a while. Your ideas may need an incubation period before you come to your draft. However, think about your draft while you are doing other things.
6. *If you have trouble writing your introduction:*
   a. Skip it and come back to it after drafting the rest of your essay, but jot down a tentative thesis to guide and focus the remainder of your draft.
   b. Keep your introduction short and simple, perhaps writing just one or two sentences to create interest and then a thesis.
   c. Supply background information or explain why your topic is important.
   d. Try the eight steps on pages 39–40.
7. *If you decide you don't like your draft:*
   a. Don't make any final decisions on the worth of your draft until after leaving your work to restore your objectivity.
   b. Have realistic expectations for your draft. Remember, it is supposed to be rough. You still have to revise, after all.

c. Do not reject your draft without trying to identify portions that can be salvaged and improved with revision.
d. Do not reject your draft without asking a reliable reader to react to it; this reader may see merit where you do not, or the reader may be able to suggest changes that make the draft salvageable.
e. If you must begin again, take a hard look at your topic to determine if it is the source of your difficulty, and consider reshaping it. Starting over is not a tragedy; sometimes writers must discover what does not work before they discover what does work.
f. If necessary because of time constraints, do the best you can with what you have.

8. *If you have trouble deciding what revisions to make:*
   a. Leave your work for a while to clear your head.
   b. Type your draft; weaknesses are more apparent in type than in your own handwriting.
   c. Read the draft aloud to listen for problems.
   d. Ask yourself if you are considering too many aspects of your draft at the same time. Consider evaluating your draft in stages.
   e. Ask a reliable reader to review your draft and make suggestions.
   f. Trust your instincts. If they suggest that something needs to be reworked, they are probably right.
9. *If you are having trouble making your revisions:*
   a. Leave your draft for a day to clear your head and to allow time for ideas to form.
   b. Revise in stages, taking a break after each stage or two. Avoid attempting too much at one time.
   c. If you cannot solve a problem, try to get around it by expressing an idea in another way, using a different example, generating another idea to replace the one you are having trouble writing, and so forth.
   d. Work your easiest revisions first to build your momentum and confidence.
   e. Settle for less than ideal. Once you have done your best, no more can be expected, even if your best is not as good as you want it to be this time.
10. *If you discover you have a relevance problem:*
    a. Try to reshape the detail or slant it so that it becomes relevant.
    b. Alter your thesis or topic sentence to accommodate the detail—but be careful that the change does not create a relevance problem elsewhere.
    c. Eliminate the detail—but be sure this does not create a problem with adequate detail. If it does, add what is necessary.
11. *If your detail is not adequate:*
    a. Check-mark each generalization in your draft, and then look at how much support each generalization gets. For each sketchily supported or unsupported generalization, add several sentences of explanation. Make sure these sentences are specific rather than general.

   b. To show rather than just tell, use examples.
   c. Ask a reliable reader what additional information he or she needs.
   d. Write each underdeveloped generalization on a separate sheet of paper. Below each generalization, list every point that could be made about it. Next, review your list of points for ones you can add to your essay.
   e. If you are unable to generate adequate detail, consider the possibility that your thesis is too narrow and should be broadened to be less restrictive.

12. *If you have trouble finding the "right" words:*
   a. Read through your draft and underline the words you want to change because they are vague or inaccurate.
   b. If after studying what you have underlined, you are unable to find the words you want, consult a dictionary or thesaurus for synonyms. Be careful, however, that you understand the meaning of words from these sources.
   c. You may not be able to take out one word and substitute another. Instead, you may have to substitute phrases and sentences for individual words to get the meaning you are after.
   d. Remember, effective word choice is specific, yet simple.
   e. If you cannot express your ideas effectively one way, write a different sentence expressing your ideas in another way.

13. *If your essay does not flow well:*
   a. To help identify where the flow needs to be improved, read your draft out loud.
   b. Look at the structure of your sentences. If too many in a row are the same length, shorten or lengthen where necessary. If too many begin with the same structure, alter the beginning of some sentences (see page 119).
   c. Use coordination and subordination to join ideas (see page 98).
   d. Use transitions to ease flow (see page 102).

14. *If you have trouble with your conclusion:*
   a. Try an approach other than the one in your draft (see page 49).
   b. Summarize your main points if this will be helpful to the reader.
   c. Give your thesis or main points a larger application by showing their significance beyond the scope of your essay.
   d. Keep your conclusion brief—perhaps even a single sentence.
   e. Try the three steps on page 51.

APPENDIX 2

A Student Essay in Progress

The following pages reproduce a student essay as it progressed from idea generation to finished piece. The student's idea generation material is followed by her first draft. The second draft appears next, followed by the finished essay. Studying this work through some of its stages (the idea-generation material and comments on the drafts have been simplified and the number of drafts reduced to two for ease of study) will help you appreciate how a writer works through a series of refinements to reach a satisfying finished product.

Idea Generation List

Effects of growing up in a large family

√ food—Milk dry & canned, Beans, Soups, Oats & Mush

Audience—General

Purpose—Share

° trips—none
√ money—little
√ eating out
°√ Christmas
° Birthdays
√ Clothing—hand me downs
√ Shoes—1 pr—worn a longtime
√ Haircuts
√ teeth
√ Nothing new

} Points to bring out

~~treats once every 2 wks payday~~

° Car—old-wouldn't go real far
Helen's Hungry Brood—Title
Commercial—50's—intro?
Mom—pregnancy—easy deliv.

Dad—Bakery Checker
Dad—Budgeted finances
° *farthest went was to town 3 mi away*
Ending
8th Grade—Father died

FIRST DRAFT WITH REVISIONS

In the '50s or '60s there was a commercial on T.V. that made reference to a big family. It showed the husband and wife looking out their window at a car pulling up to their house with kids in it packed like sardines in a can. The wife screams, "Here come Helen and her hungry brood, what are we gonna do for food?" I really thought at the time that they were referring to my family. Someone in the neighborhood had to have told them about us. My mother's name was Helen. She had seven children. To get us all in the car to go anywhere was a real fiasco. The doctor told her she was built to have *babies* ~~kids~~.

add family joke about only sleeping together on Saturday

I guess the most devastating fact about being in this large family was not enough money. My dad had a steady job at the bakery as a checker, but the pay was *not very good* ~~pretty crummy~~. My dad never took a vacation. We needed the money too badly. He had to do some pretty tight budgeting to pay the bills. This lack of money led to many other hardships.

Food was a problem. We never went hungry but the foods we ate were those you could make a large amount of at one time, that stretched a long way and weren't too expensive, like beans, soup, and mush. Since only *9* ~~nine~~ quarts of mil~~d~~*k* were delivered to our house, we had to substitute canned milk and water or powdered milk on our cereal quite a few times. We rarely got store bought candy or sweets. We never experienced the privilege of going to a restaurant. ~~Again the culprit is lack of money.~~

We were never choosy about the clothes we wore. We couldn't afford to be choosy. Since we girls had two older brothers, we ended up wearing old faded jeans/^ I can never remember getting any new clothing. It was always my brothers' or sisters' or someone else's. The one thing I do remember

never dreaming that one day they would be the in thing and girls would actually <u>want</u> to wear them.

getting new are shoes. We had one pair each. We wore them a long time ~~till~~ *until* they couldn't be patched and on payday we got a new pair. That was ~~a great~~ *special* feeling.

Professional haircuts were not to be had. We didn't have the money for such frivilous things. My uncle cut everyone's hair. Regular dental work was also out of the question. We only went to the dentist when we had a toothache or when we might loose a tooth through decay.

tell about Uncle Charlie

We never owned a real nice car. My dad would keep the thing running but you couldn't depend on it to go too far. The grocery store ^ was about the extent of our travel.

3 miles away in town, & that was

As a member of a large family you took a few things for granted: you never took long trips, Christmas was never thought of for its material gain, and birthday parties were unheard of. 〈These are a few of the disadvantages experienced.〉?

When I was in 8th grade, I was sitting in English class and the teacher was lecturing. Our princi~~ple~~*pal* appeared in the doorway and calmly said to the teacher that I was supposed to go with him. I wondered what all the mystery was about. I knew I hadn't done anything wrong. What could he want with me? When we reached the corridor I saw my older brother standing there waiting for me. I knew something was wrong. "Dad died," he managed to get out. I couldn't believe it. We hugged and cried.

tell about heart attack from stress.

Living within a large family structure had meant many hardships, but the hardship of living without a dad was one that would never be overcome. *We seven kids went without a lot, but all we really missed was Dad.*

SECOND DRAFT WITH REVISIONS

In the '50s or '60's there was a commercial on T.V. that made reference to a big family. It showed the husband and wife looking out their window at a car pulling up to their house with kids in it packed ~~like sardines in a can~~. The wife screams, "Here comes Helen and her hungry brood, what are we gonna do for food?" I really thought at the time that they were referring to my family. Someone in the neighborhood had to have told them about us. My mother's name was Helen. She

as tightly as olives in a jar.

had seven children. To get us all in the car to go anywhere was a real fiasco. The doctor told her she was built to have babies, and she tried to prove him right by having two in one year. The weird thing about our large family was that my mom and dad only slept together one night a week. My dad was a checker in a bakery and worked all night. He only had Saturday evenings off. The relatives would always kid my parents about this. Nevertheless, seven kids were the end result, and I don't mean lucky number seven.

I guess the most devastating fact about being in this large family was not enough money. My dad had a steady job ~~at the bakery as a checker,~~ but the pay was not very good. ~~My dad never took a vacation. We needed the money too badly.~~ He had to do some pretty tight budgeting to pay the bills. This lack of money led to many ~~other~~ hardships.

Soups like potato, bean and vegetable, poor man's stew, hamburgers, oatmeal, and mush were usually on the menu.

We would make chocolate oatmeal fudge or ice cream from the snow in the winter.

Food was a problem. We never went hungry but the foods we ate were those you could make a large amount of at one time, and that stretched a long way and weren't too expensive. ~~like beans, soup, and mush.~~ Since only 9 quarts of milk were delivered to our house, we had to substitute canned milk and water or powdered milk on our cereal quite a few times. We rarely got store-bought candy or sweets. We never experienced the privilege of going to a restaurant.

We were never choosy about the clothes we wore. We couldn't afford to be choosy. Since we girls had two older brothers, we ended up wearing old faded jeans, never dreaming that one day they would be the in thing and girls would <u>want</u> to wear them. I can never remember getting any new clothing. It was always my brothers' or sisters' or someone else's. The one thing I do remember getting new are shoes. We had one pair each. We wore them a long time until the holes ~~they~~ couldn't be patched with cardboard, and then on payday we got a new pair. That was a special feeling.

Professional haircuts were not to be had. We didn't have the money for such fr<u>ivi</u>lous (sp?) things. My uncle cut everyone's hair. I can remember my Uncle Charlie coming over with his barber shears and electric razor. He'd start with my dad and go on down the line. "Who's next for a trimming?" he'd ask ~~say~~. Only the brave would step forward. His haircuts left something to be desired. Regular dental work was also out of the question. We only went to the dentist when we had a toothache or when we might lose a tooth through decay.

We never owned a real nice car. My dad would keep the thing running, but you couldn't depend on it to go too far. The grocery store was 3 miles away in town, and that was about the extent of our travel.

As ~~a~~ members of a large family ~~you~~ we took a few things for granted; ~~you~~ we never took long trips, Christmas was never thought of for its material gain, and birthday parties were unheard of.

When I was in 8th grade, I was sitting in English class and the teacher was lecturing. Our principal appeared in the doorway and calmly said to the teacher that I was supposed to go with him./ Fill this gap I wondered what all the mystery was about. I knew I hadn't done anything wrong. What could he want with me? When we reached the corridor I saw my older brother standing there waiting for me. I knew something was wrong. "Dad died," he managed to get out. I couldn't believe it. We hugged and cried. Later I found out my dad had a heart attack. The stress of raising a large family with never enough money had taken its final toll.

Living ~~within~~ in a large family ~~structure~~ had meant many hardships, but the hardship of living without a dad was one that would never be overcome. We seven kids went without ~~a lot~~ a great deal, but all we really missed was our dad.

HELEN'S HUNGRY BROOD (FINAL VERSION)

In the 1950's or 1960's there was a commercial on television that made reference to a big family. It showed the husband and wife looking out their window at a car pulling up to their house with kids in it packed as tightly as olives in a jar. The wife screams, "Here comes Helen and her hungry brood, what are we gonna do for food?" I really thought at the time that they were referring to my family. Someone in the neighborhood had to have told them about us. My mother's name was Helen. She had seven children. To get us all in the car to go anywhere was a real fiasco. The doctor told her she was built to have babies, and she tried to prove him right by having two in one year. The weird thing about our large family was that my mom and dad only slept together one night a week. My dad was a checker in a bakery and worked all night. He only had Saturday evenings off. The relatives would always kid my parents about this. Nevertheless, seven kids were the end result, and I don't mean lucky number seven.

I guess the most devastating fact about being in this large family was not enough money. My dad had a steady job, but the pay was not very good. He had to do some pretty tight budgeting to pay the bills. This lack of money led to other hardships.

Food was a problem. We never went hungry, but the foods we ate were those that you could make a large amount of at one time, that stretched a long way, and that weren't too expensive. Soups like potato, bean, and vegetable; poor man's stew; hamburgers; oatmeal; and mush were usually on the menu. Since only 9 quarts of milk were delivered to our house, we had to substitute canned milk and water or powdered milk on our cereal quite a few times. We rarely got store-bought candy or sweets. We would make chocolate oatmeal fudge or ice cream from the snow in the winter. We never experienced the privilege of going to a restaurant.

We were never choosy about the clothes we wore. We couldn't afford to be choosy. Since we girls had two older brothers, we ended up wearing old faded jeans, never dreaming that one day they would be the in thing and girls would *want* to wear them. I can never remember getting any new clothing. It was always my brothers' or sisters' or someone else's. The one thing I do remember getting new are shoes. We had one pair each. We wore them until the holes couldn't be patched with cardboard, and then on payday we got a new pair. That was a special feeling.

Professional haircuts were not to be had. We didn't have the money for such frivolous things. My uncle cut everyone's hair. I can remember my Uncle Charlie coming over with his barber shears and electric razor. He'd start with my dad and go on down the line. "Who's next for a trimming?" he'd ask. Only the brave would step forward. His haircuts left something to be desired. Regular dental work was also out of the question. We only went to the dentist when we had a toothache or when we might lose a tooth through decay.

We never owned a real nice car. My dad would keep the thing running, but you couldn't depend on it to go too far. The grocery store was 3 miles away in town, and that was about the extent of our travel.

As members of a large family we took a few things for granted; we never took long trips, Christmas was never thought of for its material gain, and birthday parties were unheard of.

When I was in eighth grade, I was sitting in English class and the teacher was lecturing. Our principal appeared in the doorway and calmly said to the teacher that I was supposed to go with him. I rose from my seat with my books in hand and followed him into the empty hallway. "Take your books to your locker, Emma," he said. I did as I was told, not saying a word. The slamming of my locker door sounded like a small bomb exploding in the quietness. "Please come with me to the office," he instructed. I wondered what all the mystery was about. I knew I hadn't done anything wrong. What could he want with me? When we reached the corridor I saw my older brother standing there waiting for me. I knew something was wrong. "Dad died," he managed to get out. I couldn't believe it. We hugged and cried. Later I found out my dad had a heart attack. The stress of raising a large family with never enough money had taken its final toll.

Living in a large family had meant many hardships, but the hardship of living without a dad was one that would never be overcome. We seven kids went without a great deal, but all we really missed was our dad.

Acknowledgments

Baker, Russell. "The Plot Against People" from *The New York Times.* Copyright © 1968 by The New York Times Company. Reprinted by permission.

Bredemeier, Brenda J. and David L. Shields. "Values and Violence in Sports Today" from *Psychology Today,* October 1985. Reprinted with permission from *Psychology Today* Magazine. Copyright © 1985 (Sussex Publishers, Inc.).

Britt, Suzanne. "Neat People vs. Sloppy People" from *Show and Tell,* 1982. Reprinted by permission of the author.

Carson, Rachel. "A Fable for Tomorrow" from *Silent Spring* by Rachel Carson. Copyright © 1962 by Rachel L. Carson, renewed 1990 by Roger Christie. Reprinted by permission of Houghton Mifflin Co. All rights reserved.

Castro, Janice. "Spanglish Spoken Here" from *Time* July 11, 1988. © 1988 Time, Inc. Reprinted by permission.

From *Humanitites Index,* Vol. 9, page 1110. Copyright © 1943 by The H. W. Wilson Company. Material reproduced with permission of the publisher.

Galarza, Ernesto. "A Mexican House" from *Barrio Boy* by Ernesto Galarza. © 1971 by University of Notre Dame Press. Reprinted by permission of the publisher.

Godwin, Gail. "The Watcher at the Gates" from *The New York Times,* January 9, 1977. Copyright © 1977 by The New York Times Company. Reprinted by permission.

Gregory, Dick. From *Nigger: An Autobiography* by Dick Gregory. Copyright © 1964 by Dick Gregory Enterprises, Inc. Used by permission of Dutton Signet, a division of Penguin Books USA Inc.

Gunnerson, Ronnie. "Parents Also Have Rights" from *Newsweek,* 1987.

Hemphill, Paul. "The Girl in Gift Wrap," from *Too Old to Cry* by Paul Hemphill. Copyright © 1970, 1971, 1972, 1973, 1974, 1975, 1978, 1979, 1981 by Paul Hemphill. Used by permission of Viking Penguin, a division of Penguin Books USA Inc.

Hirschfelder, Arlene. "It's Time to Stop Playing Indians" from *The Los Angeles Times,* November 25, 1987. Reprinted by permission of the author.

Holt, John. "School Is Bad for Children" from *The Saturday Evening Post.* Reprinted by permission from The Saturday Evening Post © 1969.

Jacoby, Susan. "When Bright Girls Decide That Math Is 'A Waste of Time.' " Copyright © 1983 by Susan Jacoby. Reprinted by permission of Georges Borchardt, Inc. for the author.

Kazin, Alfred. Excerpt from *A Walker in the City,* copyright 1951 and renewed 1979 by Alfred Kazin, reprinted by permission of Harcourt Brace & Company.

King, Martin Luther, Jr. "The Ways of Meeting Oppression" from *Stride Toward Freedom* by Martin Luther King, Jr. Reprinted by arrangement with The Heirs to the Estate of Martin Luther King, Jr., c/o Joan Daves Agency as agent for the proprietor. Copyright 1958 by Martin Luther King, Jr., copyright renewed 1986 by Coretta Scott King.

Krentz, Harold. "Darkness at Noon" from *The New York Times,* May 24, 1976. Copyright © 1976 by The New York Times Company. Reprinted by permission.

Lee, Laurie. "Appetite" from *I Can't Stay Long* by Laurie Lee. (Penguin Books 1977, first published by André Deutsch). Copyright © Laurie Lee, 1975. Reproduced by permission of Penguin Books Ltd.

Leggett, John. "Ross and Tom" from *Ross and Tom* by John Leggett. Reprinted by permission of Sterling Lord Literistic, Inc. Copyright © 1974 by John Leggett.

Lieb, Rebecca. "Film: Nazi Hate Movies Continue to Ignite Fierce Passions" from *The New York Times,* August 4, 1991. Copyright © 1991 by The New York Times Company. Reprinted by permission.

Mead, Margaret and Rhoda Metraux. "The Egalitarian Error" from *A Way of Seeing,* by Margaret Mead and Rhoda Metraux, pp. 73–76. Copyright © 1961 . . . 1970 by Margaret Mead and Rhoda Metraux. Reprinted by permission of William Morrow & Company, Inc.

Negri, Sam. "Loafing Made Easy" from *The New York Times,* July 12, 1980. Copyright © 1980 by The New York Times Company. Reprinted by permission.

Otten, Alan. "This Is Progress?" from *The Wall Street Journal.* Reprinted with permission of The Wall Street Journal © 1978 Dow Jones & Company, Inc. All rights reserved.

Paige, Ellen. "Born Beautiful: Confessions of a Naturally Gorgeous Girl" from *Mademoiselle,* February 1988. Reprinted by permission of the author.

Pride, William M. and O.C. Ferrell. From *Marketing: Concepts and Strategies,* Ninth Edition. Copyright © 1995 by Houghton Mifflin Company. Reprinted by permission.

Purdy, Ken. "The Honest Repairman—A Vanishing American." Reprinted by permission of the author and the author's agent, Scott Meredith Literary Agency, L.P., 845 Third Avenue, New York, NY 10022.

Roiphe, Anne. "Why Marriages Fail" from *Family Weekly,* February 27, 1983. Reprinted by permission of International Creative Management, Inc. Copyright © 1983 by Annie Roiphe.

Rosenfeld, Albert. "Animal Rights versus Human Health" from *Science* 1981. Reprinted by permission of the author.

Rowan, Carl T. "Unforgettable Miss Bessie." Reprinted with permission from the March 1985 *Reader's Digest.* Copyright © 1985 by The Reader's Digest Assn., Inc.

Selby, Roy. "A Delicate Operation." Copyright © 1975 by *Harper's Magazine*. All rights reserved. Reproduced from the December issue by special permission.

Soto, Gary. "Looking for Work" by Gary Soto © 1985. Used by permission of the author.

Spotted Elk, Clara. "Indian Bones" originally titled "Skeletons in the Attic" from *The New York Times,* March 8, 1989. Copyright © 1989 by The New York Times Company. Reprinted by permission.

Stanat, Kirby. "How to Take A Job Interview" from *Job Hunting Secrets and Tactics* by Kirby Stanat and Patrick Reardon. Reprinted by permission.

Tan, Amy. "Democracy." Copyright © 1989 by Amy Tan. Originally published in *Glamour,* September 1989. Reprinted by permission of the author and the Sandra Dijkstra Literary Agency.

Tuite, James. "The Sounds of the City" from *The New York Times*. Copyright © 1966 by The New York Times Company. Reprinted by permission.

Viorst, Judith. "What, Me? Showing Off?" Copyright © 1982 by Judith Viorst. Originally appeared in *Redbook*. Reprinted by permission.

"Why Drug Testing Is Needed." From *Security Management,* August 1987. © 1987 American Society for Industrial Security, 1655 N. Fort Myer Drive, Suite 1200, Arlington, VA 22209. Reprinted with permission from the August 1987 issue of *Security Management.*

Wolfe, Tom. "Columbus and the Moon" from *The New York Times,* July 20, 1979. Copyright © 1979 by The New York Times Company. Reprinted by permission.

Wright, Barbara. "How I Wrote 'Fat Chance' " from *College English,* March 1982. Copyright 1982 by the National Council of Teachers of English. Reprinted with permission.

Index